Cajun Country
GUIDE

Cajun
Country
GUIDE

SECOND EDITION

Macon Fry and Julie Posner

PELICAN PUBLISHING COMPANY
Gretna 1999

First edition, October 1992
Second printing, August 1993
Third printing, April 1996
Second edition, February 1999

Library of Congress Cataloging-in-Publication Data

Fry, Macon.
    Cajun country guide / Macon Fry and Julie Posner.—2nd ed.
      p.   cm.
    Includes bibliographical references (p.) and index.
    ISBN 1-56554-337-8 (pbk. : alk. paper)
    1. Louisiana—Guidebooks. 2. Cajuns—Louisiana. I. Posner,
Julie. II. Title.
F367.3.F79 1998
917.6304'63—dc21   97-37430
                                              CIP

Information in this guidebook is based on authoritative data available at the time of printing. Prices and hours of operations of businesses listed are subject to change without notice. Readers are asked to take this into account when consulting this guide.

Maps and charts by Julie Posner unless otherwise indicated

Cover photo by Greg Guirard

Printed in Canada

Published by Pelican Publishing Company, Inc.
1000 Burmaster Street, Gretna, Louisiana 70053

Contents

	Preface	7
	Acknowledgments	9
	How to Use This Book	11
Chapter 1	The Land	13
Chapter 2	The People	21
Chapter 3	The Climate	31
Chapter 4	Flora and Fauna	33
Chapter 5	The Economy: Major Industrial and Agricultural Products	45
Chapter 6	Food	51
Chapter 7	Music	63
Chapter 8	Recreation	73
Chapter 9	Transportation	81
Chapter 10	Mississippi River Region	85
Chapter 11	Bayou Country	121
Chapter 12	Teche Country	179
Chapter 13	Central Cajun Country	271
Chapter 14	Cajun Heartland	337
Chapter 15	Western Cajun Country	395
Appendix A	Special Events in Cajun Country	449
Appendix B	Recommended Books	452
Appendix C	Recommended Recordings	454
Appendix D	Sources for Recorded and Printed Material on Cajun Country	456
	Bibliography	459
	Index	461

Preface

Less than forty-eight hours after arriving in New Orleans, I found myself a bleary-eyed passenger in a packed car speeding across the Atchafalaya Throughway at 8 A.M. As the sun smoldered along the tops of the black willow and cypress, I looked down from the interstate at the blackness of the nation's largest freshwater swamp and pondered how different and beautiful South Louisiana was.

Our destination was the town of Mamou and the tiny bar, Fred's Lounge, that hosts a live radio broadcast every Saturday morning beginning at 9 o'clock. We stopped in Eunice and everyone piled out of the car and into a small grocery, where about a dozen people were lined up to purchase steaming links of Cajun boudin sausage for breakfast. Back in the car, clutching cold drinks and incendiary sausages, we screamed out across the prairie for the final 20 miles, our anticipation fired by the first strains of live Cajun accordion wheezing on the radio.

Had I not already been thrown into shock by waking before sunrise and spending an hour driving over water, or by consuming a boudin sausage and cold beer before 8:30 A.M., the surprise when we entered Fred's might have been lethal! In a room with about as much floor space as twenty phone booths, at least fifty country folks, men and women, were drinking and dancing about a postage-stamp-size band area. Through the smoke I could read a few signs on the wall—"No standing on the jukebox" and "No substitute musicians." The man in western wear by the bar was chatting in French with proprietor Fred Tate, and the singer was singing in Cajun French, but I had no trouble understanding the message here: *Laissez les bon temps roulez!* (Let the good times roll!) Despite the attempts of historians to deromanticize Cajun history, despite the efforts of folklorists to analyze the culture and the efforts of Cajuns throughout South Louisiana to destroy the stereotypes surrounding themselves, Cajun Country of South Louisiana remains one of the most intoxicatingly different and exotic places in America.

MACON FRY

7

Hot boudin and cold beer sign. (Photo by Julie Posner)

Acknowledgments

This book is dedicated with love to my grandparents, Dr. Wesley Fry and Virginia Tapscott, and parents, Ann and William Fry.

No one contributed more to this book than Anna Graham Hunter, who not only proofread but put up with me during the rewrite.

Joe Sasfy remained a writer's best friend and, as always, had plenty of advice.

Countless folks in Cajun Country provided encouragement and assistance on this guide and I was fortunate to come away with several new pals. Thanks to Mary Tutwiler for the good tips and good company and to Sigrid Bonner for the swell digs in Lafayette.

Also thanks to Todd Mouton, Todd Ortego, Lee Lavergne, Floyd Soileau, Judy and Tony Zaunbrecher, Greg Guirard, and the many folks who showed me what Cajun hospitality is all about.

The personnel at the regional visitors' centers were tremendously helpful and special thanks are due to Gerald Breaux and Kay Broussard in Lafayette and Jane Breaux in New Iberia.

Mike Lach put out computer fires and Dale Ladner and Woody Walk helped with the hardest part of writing (contracts and finances).

The great Louisiana sounds of KBON radio 101.1 in Eunice made each mile a joy to drive.

MACON FRY

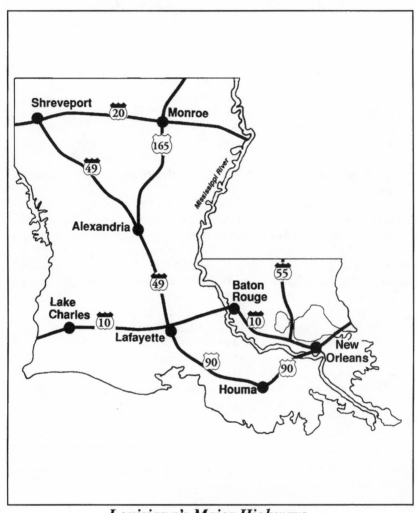

Louisiana's Major Highways

How to Use This Book

In the introductory chapters you will find general information on the land, people, climate, flora, and fauna found in Cajun Country. There are also background chapters about the economy, food, music, recreation, and transportation. In the second part of the book, Cajun Country is broken into six regional chapters, which describe the major towns and attractions in each area, with critical reviews of restaurants, dance halls, and accommodations.

Because Cajun Country is a small area (easily traversed in a day or two), it is important to consider the area as a whole when planning activities. For instance, if you are staying in Lafayette (Central Cajun Country), you may want to make a morning trip to Jefferson Island (Teche Country), go to the live Roundez Vous Des Cajuns dance in Eunice (Cajun Heartland) in the afternoon, and eat dinner at Hawk's Crawfish Restaurant (Western Cajun Country) in the evening. To facilitate planning across regions, consult the introductory chapters on food, music, and recreation, which have maps and lists of many recommended destinations.

SYMBOLS USED IN THE TEXT

★ A star denotes restaurants, attractions, and accommodations that we highly recommend.

$ A dollar sign denotes restaurant prices. One dollar sign indicates that a meal may be purchased for under $10, two dollar signs indicate a price of $10-$20, and so on. All prices are exclusive of alchoholic beverage.

Swamp. (Photo by Julie Posner)

1

The Land

WHAT IS CAJUN COUNTRY?

Cajun Country is a land of black coffee and bayous, steaming crawfish and swamps; it is a place where the wheezing push-pull of an accordion hangs in the air over the upland prairie like a blanket of humidity. Cajun Country is set apart from the rest of Louisiana and the country as a whole by a landscape that continues to confound road builders and a regional culture so distinct that until recently people of Anglo descent were often referred to as *les Américains*. On the state map the area has been dubbed Acadiana, in honor of the Acadian people who settled there in the mid-eighteenth century.

The "official" state boundaries of Acadiana roughly form a triangle-shaped region in South Louisiana, with a base extending along 300 miles (as the crow flies) of jigsawed Gulf coast. The east side of the triangle follows the Mississippi River north from just above New Orleans, while the west side slants in from the Louisiana and Texas border to an apex about 200 miles northwest of New Orleans in Avoyelles Parish. The entire triangle composes less than half the state, or twenty-two mainly rural parishes (as counties are known in Louisiana), and contains none of the state's three largest cities. In fact, Lafayette, its biggest city, has a population of about 105,000 residents, a distant fourth behind New Orleans, Baton Rouge, and Shreveport. This guide focuses on areas where the food, music, language, and other expressions of the Cajun and Creole cultures are strongest.

The unique and enduring cultures of Cajun Country owe their survival in the twentieth century in no small way to geographic isolation. For years after most of the rest of the country was linked by super-highways, the jungle of the Atchafalaya Basin defied engineers and left Cajun Country unreachable by high-speed interstate traffic. Interstate 10, the main east-west route linking New Orleans and Baton Rouge with Lafayette, Lake Charles, and Houston, was not completed until 1973. It took the most expensive stretch of interstate ever constructed to span the yawning Atchafalaya Basin Swamp and connect

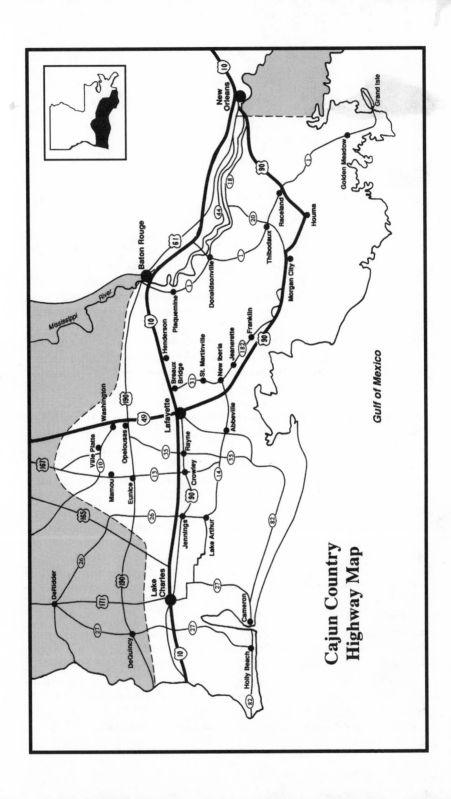

Cajun Country
Highway Map

the state capital of Baton Rouge with the hub city of Cajun Country, Lafayette. Deeper into Cajun Country, difficulties in travel were even more marked. Until well into the twentieth century some towns were inaccessible by road and children traveled to school by schoolboat. When the oil industry began exploring the coastal wetlands south of Houma in the forties, they discovered Houma Indian communities whose residents spoke archaic French thriving in watery isolation.

GEOGRAPHY

When you talk about the geography of South Louisiana, two adjectives come to mind: "flat" and "wet." Driving down the moss-draped byways of Cajun Country, a glance out the window generally reveals a more liquid than solid landscape. Land in South Louisiana is a relatively recent occurrence, emerging from the receding waters of the last ice age about six thousand years ago. When the first humans came to the continent via the land bridge, all of Cajun Country was under water. Today the region has nearly three thousand square miles of water surface. Some places that appear to be solid are actually a barely congealed goo that will suck a leg in as far as the thigh and steal a sneaker on the way out.

Cajun Country is located entirely within the Gulf Coastal Plain. Along the southern edge of the region the Gulf Coast Marsh forms a roughly thirty-mile-wide band bordering the Gulf of Mexico. To the east are the fertile fields and swamps of the Mississippi Alluvial Plain, while the west is characterized by the vast flat lands of the "Cajun" Prairie. Even on the high and dry Cajun Prairie, however, water is visible everywhere, as mechanically flooded rice fields stretch to the horizon.

Gulf Coast

One calculation estimates that Louisiana's 400-mile-long coast measures 6,952 miles of actual shoreline if you trace the myriad indentations, bays, and sounds that etch its boundary with the Gulf of Mexico. Along this tattered coastline, the Gulf Coast Marsh contains over 30 percent of the coastal wetlands in the contiguous forty-eight states. In the eastern section of Cajun Country, the marsh is a drainage field for the Mississippi and Atchafalaya rivers and is laced with bayous and channels. In the west, the coast is more stable and less marked by the meanderings of these rivers. The only significant high ground in the western Gulf Coast Marsh is a series of ridges called *cheniers* (French for oaks) or "islands." Even at times of low water, these tree-covered mounds appear as "islands" in the sea of surrounding marsh grass.

Coastal marsh. (Photo by Julie Posner)

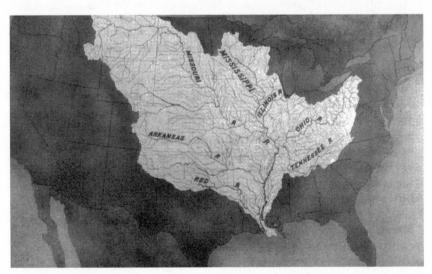

Drainage in the Mississippi Valley. (Courtesy of U.S. Army Corps of Engineers)

Like fire ants clinging to the unsubmerged portion of a floating log, the *cheniers* form a string of tiny communities across southern Cameron and Vermilion parishes that are inhabited by oil workers, fishermen, trappers, and ranchers, and frequented by bird watchers and recreational fishermen.

Mississippi River and Alluvial Plain

The Mississippi Alluvial Plain stretches from just east of the Mississippi to the western edge of Lafayette Parish. This wedge of land and water forms a gigantic funnel or basin that drains the runoff water from over half the continent through its two mighty rivers, the Mississippi and Atchafalaya. The rivers ride high above surrounding plains for miles, confined between man-made embankments called levees (French for "raised up"). These levees prevent the rivers from covering a third of the state with water at flood stage.

For over three thousand years the Mississippi River, or Meche Sebe, as the Indians called it, has been the primary tool building and shaping South Louisiana. Its vagaries have etched themselves into the present map of the state in a tangle of old distributaries and former channels like Bayou Teche and Bayou Lafourche. The high land along these streams is hugged by roads, sugarcane plantations, and farming and fishing communities. In many cases, waterways, with their parallel roads, drop south into impenetrable marsh, leaving travelers to retrace their steps. From the levees on either side of bayous and rivers, the land drops away into a viscous muck the consistency of barely cooled Jell-O.

Cajun Prairie

Most of western Cajun Country is occupied by the expansive Cajun Prairie. The Prairie, about twice the size of Delaware, stretches from the Vermilion River west of Lafayette to the Texas border above Lake Charles. From an elevation of about seventy feet above sea level in Mamou, the Coastal Plain tilts down at a gentle slope of a foot a mile to the lakes and permanently wet prairie marsh along the coast of Cameron and Vermilion parishes. It is covered with rice, crawfish, and soybean farms and dotted with cattle and rail towns. The Prairie is not a part of the state that folks hear about much, as Hollywood prefers images of gators and trappers to fields of rice and Cajun or Zydeco dances. Little is left of the towering grasses and abundant wild flowers that greeted the first visitors, but the Prairie is one of the most romantic and culturally unspoiled areas of the state.

Fisherman in Atchafalaya Basin. (Courtesy of U.S. Army Corps of Engineers)

Atchafalaya River and Basin

The Atchafalaya River (pronounced uh-chaf-uh-lie-uh), a primary distributary of the Mississippi and Red rivers, courses through the heart of the Mississippi Alluvial plain between New Orleans and Lafayette. Surrounding the Atchafalaya, at an average width of 20 miles and a rough length of 150 miles, is America's largest freshwater swamp, the Atchafalaya Basin. This vast jungle within levees is an area of natural beauty on the scale of the Grand Canyon. Unlike the canyon, however, the Basin (as it is referred to locally) is teeming with wildlife that has supported generations of Cajun trappers, hunters, moss pickers, lumbermen, fishermen, and most recently a burgeoning oil and gas industry. Today the Basin, which flows south between Lafayette and Baton Rouge before pouring into the Gulf below Morgan City, is mainly inaccessible by road. Most folks seldom see more of the Atchafalaya Basin than the tops of black willow trees as they speed across the elevated Atchafalaya Throughway. They miss a place where nature labors overtime producing fantastic blooms, lush foliage, and forage for a host of exotic animals.

The Basin in Balance

The tranquillity of the Basin teeters in a delicate balance. If it were not for controls established upstream at the intersection of the Atchafalaya and False rivers, the Mississippi River would have long ago jumped from its present course and roared through the Basin. The mighty Mississippi has made at least three such moves in the last 7,000 years. Were this to happen today, miles of Basin land would be inundated, including hundreds of gas and oil wells and Morgan City, which lies behind huge walls in the middle of the floodplain. Factories and deepwater ports that cling to the Mississippi below Baton Rouge would be left on the banks of a sluggish stream, and New Orleans' drinking water would be contaminated with salty Gulf water.

Both to prevent this catastrophe and in immediate response to the

Tent city, for refugees of 1927 flood. (Courtesy of Lafayette Courthouse Archives)

mind-boggling sweep of waters in 1927 that is referred to pic-
turesquely (and hopefully) as the "hundred-year flood," the United
States Corps of Engineers set about building new levees along the
Basin. Entire regions that were once within the floodplain were
lopped off, residents were moved outside of the levees, and a plan
was developed for the "final" control of the flow of water between the
Mississippi River and the Atchafalaya. The floodgates were only a
decade old and the Corps had not finished touting their invincibility
when the flood of 1973 came along and undermined a large portion
of the structure. Were it not for emergency measures, the final switch
of the Mississippi's course would have been accomplished!

The Threatened Basin

In creating levees and controlling the flow of water into the area,
the Corps of Engineers is also controlling the flow of alluvial sediment,
channeling it into the now artificially walled area and filling in old
waterways at an alarming rate.

Some areas of the Basin are laced with a spider web of abandoned
oil and natural-gas pipes and wellheads. Many pipelines hang rusting
in the swamps, deserted by companies that have been out of business
for decades. Of course, this type of "cut and burn" mentality is not new
to the Basin. The destructive power of the lumber industry that
thrived in the Basin around the turn of the century is plainly visible
in vast cemeteries of tombstone-like tree stumps.

2

The People

From its language to its food and music, Cajun Country is a land defined by its people. High-speed interstates and bridges may have spanned the geographic barriers isolating the region, but the people of South Louisiana still possess an indomitable spirit of independence and self-sufficiency. Many still live life close to the land, not untouched, but unmarred by the opening of the countryside in the last half a century.

The most quantifiable difference between the folks in Cajun Country and their upstate neighbors is the predominance of the Catholic Church in the south and Protestant faith in the north. The northern

(Photo by Julie Posner)

boundary of Acadiana neatly divides the twenty-two predominantly Catholic parishes of the south from the forty predominantly Protestant upstate parishes. The people of North Louisiana are mainly hardworking folks who are not too different from other rural Southerners, scrubbing sustenance from hardscrabble farms and from the gas and lumber industries in the piney hills. The denizens of Cajun Country, however, are best known for their leisure skills. Whether they are cooking, making music, recounting a good story over a drink, or making a friendly wager, there is a marked value placed on the simple pursuit of "passing a good time." It is not indolence, but a zest for life or "joie de vivre" that separates South Louisiana from the rest of the state (and country) and makes it a paradise for anyone seeking to get away from the headlong pursuit of work and money for soul-satisfying indulgence in great food and music.

The largest, best known, and culturally predominant group in South Louisiana are the Cajuns, but the area is actually inhabited by many people of diverse ancestry. There are three surviving Indian tribes, a large black Creole population, many Anglos, and significant numbers of people who trace their roots back to several different European countries. Some of the earliest immigrants to the area were Germans who settled on the banks of the Mississippi River at a place about thirty miles north of New Orleans that is now known as the German Coast. Other European nationalities include Italians, who arrived in the early twentieth century, and people of Spanish and French descent. Among those of French descent are three distinct groups—Cajuns, French nationals, and refugees from Saint-Domingue. All of these people have mixed with the Acadians and contributed to the unique food, music, philosophy, and way of life in Cajun Country.

INDIAN TRIBES OF CAJUN COUNTRY

Most of the Indian people of South Louisiana suffered fates common to tribes around the country. Although the first European visitors were initially welcomed by most Louisiana tribes, the Indian populace was soon treated to disease, enslavement, and decimation by war.

Chitimacha

The Chitimacha are the only tribe in South Louisiana still living on some of the same traditional lands they occupied in 1700. Originally the Chitimacha inhabited a wide area surrounding the Atchafalaya Basin from the Mississippi River at Bayou Plaquemine down Bayou

Lafourche. During the early 1700s these otherwise peaceful people became engaged in armed conflict with the French that led to the enslavement and slaughter of the majority of the tribe. Most of the surviving members hid in the swampland between Bayou Teche and Grand Lake, near the present-day towns of Jeanerette and Charenton. By 1925, when the federal government officially recognized the tribe and established a reservation at the site, there were only about fifty members surviving. Today the tribe numbers about 970 members, with 300 living on the reservation. Their language and most of the customs and lore have been lost. A half-dozen artisans are preserving

Chitimacha basketmaker. (Photo by Macon Fry)

the craft of split cane basketry. A selection of baskets and other artifacts are on display in a museum and tribal center operated by the
park service at the Charenton reservation.

Coushatta

The Coushatta, also known as Koasati, moved to South Louisiana in
the early 1800s and represent the most ethnically pure (nearly full
blooded) tribe in the state. Seven hundred or so tribal members now
live on or near the reservation in Elton, where the northwest Prairie
joins the pine hills of central Louisiana. While the Coushatta have
been fortunate in preserving their language (the Coushatta language
is still the first language of those living on the reservation) and many
customs, their insularity has had a high price. Deprived of a good public education until the sixties, 90 percent of the population had
incomes under three thousand dollars in the 1970s and only half the
heads of families were literate (Fred B. Kniffen, Hiram F. Gregory, and
George A. Stokes. *The Historic Indian Tribes of Louisiana.* Baton Rouge:
LSU Press, 1987). With the introduction of casino gambling on reservation land in the late nineties, employment and earnings have begun
to rise. A visitor and tribal center is open to the public with a small
display of local crafts.

Houma

From a nadir of sixty countable members in 1803, the Houma now
represent the largest Indian group in Louisiana, with a tribal roll of
about seventeen thousand. Like the Coushatta, the Houma were
relatively late arrivals in South Louisiana. They were forced from
prime agricultural lands along the Mississippi River and upper reaches
of Bayous Lafourche and Terrebonne to the soggy southern reaches of
Bayou Country, where they still extract their living from the fur, fish,
and mineral wealth of the wetlands. The largest concentration still live
in the wetlands south of the present-day city of Houma, where nearly
a thousand members of the tribe are within walking distance of the village of Dulac on Bayou Grand Caillou.

It is ironic that Louisiana's most populous Indian tribe has yet to be
recognized by the federal government. Recognition has been
impeded by the adoption of the French language by most of the
Houma people and by their extreme watery isolation. Several communities of Houma existed on marsh islands for a century, virtually
untouched by life in mainland Acadiana, until the oil industry began
making inroads in the marsh during the late forties.

CAJUNS

The Acadians in Nova Scotia

The ancestors of today's Cajuns were French pioneers who settled in Nova Scotia mainly in 1604 and 1632. The character and strength of the Cajun people today has its roots in their experience as colonists in the Acadia province of Nova Scotia, where they arrived at the beginning of a conflict between the British and French that was to stretch into nearly a hundred years of war. This conflict between superpowers effectively isolated the colonists from support by either country and left them to fend for themselves against alternate Indian and British aggression.

The Acadians were a mainly poor and illiterate people. They led an agrarian life, gathering solidarity from a strong attachment to the land, a strong faith in the Catholic Church, and an esprit de corps born of family affiliation and political isolation. In 1713, when Acadia was formally ceded to England in the Treaty of Utrecht, the British answered the colonists' pleas for neutrality with a demand for allegiance to the British Crown. The demand became an ultimatum in 1753; the French Acadians would either take an unconditional oath of allegiance or face confiscation of property and deportation to the British colonies. In what has been called the Grand Derangement of 1755, 16,000 French Acadians who had built a life in Nova Scotia for over a century were divested of their property and deported. Families and friends were separated and scattered throughout the British colonies, where some were pressed into servitude.

Acadians in Louisiana

When the British and French settled their differences in 1763, the Acadians who had spent the last ten years in scattered exile looked to reestablish their families, communities, and lives in freedom. The greatest numbers eventually found their way to South Louisiana, where they again became pioneers in new and unsettled lands. Ironically, when the Acadians began to arrive in Louisiana, the colony had just come under Spanish rule and they were again the subjects of a non-French crown. The Spanish government in New Orleans saw an opportunity to settle the area west of the Mississippi and offered Acadian and other immigrants of French descent a choice of lands on the frontier. The first settlers made homes on high lands along the "German Coast" of the Mississippi River, and then along bayous in the Lafourche, Teche, and Opelousas districts.

While New Orleans was a bustling cosmopolitan center, most of South Louisiana was still a rough-hewn territory occupied by Indians, trappers (known as *courir du bois*), and a few wealthy French plantation owners who relied on the protection of Spanish military outposts. The new immigrants adapted and thrived in South Louisiana, where most began raising cattle and subsistence crops. The ties of family and church were already in place, and the travail of displacement fostered a sense of solidarity and a desire for independence among the new settlers. By the end of the century the Acadian tradition of large families and the subdivision of early land grants had begun to stretch the seams of original settlements. Some of the settlers moved towards less fertile backlands, where they learned how to harvest the natural bounty of the swamps and marsh. Others sold their waterfront land to the growing Anglo and French planter class and headed for the prairie frontier west of the Atchafalaya Basin.

These movements began the pattern of Cajun communities that exist today. Large Acadian settlements were established on the banks of the Vermilion River at the present-day site of Lafayette and near the Spanish military Poste de Opelousas. During the nineteenth century the Acadians managed to continue as a group basically unenfranchised by the rest of the state or country. Although they had their statesmen, Civil War heroes, and an upwardly mobile urban class, for the most part the Acadians sought independence from larger political affairs and enjoyed an agrarian life of relative isolation.

Cajuns in the Twentieth Century

When the isolation of Southwest Louisiana began to crack at the turn of the century, the descendants of the Acadians were well established. The 1860 census counted over eighteen thousand Acadian-French surnames. The predominance of the Acadian way of life was such that they were actually absorbing many other ethnic groups in the region, forming a distinctive "Cajun" culture.

The frontier in Louisiana was opened by many of the same vehicles that opened other parts of the nation—the railroad, the radio, and the automobile. Perhaps the biggest harbinger of change was the discovery of oil at Jennings, Louisiana, in 1901. Along with the oil boom, the event that most impacted the Cajun culture was the implementation of a highly ethnocentric mandatory public education policy in 1916. When Cajun children began attending school, they were confronted with a policy that forbade speaking French on school grounds. This policy effectively deprived a generation of their native tongue and nearly eradicated the Cajun French language in South

Louisiana. By the time the offshore oil boom brought thousands of newcomers to Acadiana in the fifties, "Cajun" was a deprecatory term and many had learned to be ashamed of their heritage and culture.

Cajun Renaissance

There are nearly a million French-speaking descendants of the Acadians living in South Louisiana today. Nowhere else in the nation has a single ethnic group been as successful in assimilating others while resisting total mainstream assimilation itself. It is not uncommon to find "Cajuns" with non-French surnames like Schexnieder, Robert, Allemand, and Fernandez. Today's Cajuns, from urban professionals to rice and crawfish farmers, fishermen, and oilmen, have found a new pride in their distinctive culture. Beginning with the interest of folklorists in the early sixties and continuing with the efforts of the Council on Development of French in Louisiana (CODOFIL) and the Cajun French Music Association, Cajuns have once again begun to appreciate and cultivate their rich heritage. Their success can be measured in the vibrant music scene on the Cajun Prairie, the great restaurants of Lafayette, and the reintroduction of French in many of the public schools. It would seem that the unique food, music, and language of the region will thrive for at least one more generation among the descendants of the Acadian people, providing visitors to the region an opportunity to enjoy a nearly lost way of life.

CREOLES

Few words are open to as many interpretations as "Creole." From the Spanish word *criollo,* or "child of the colonies" (John Chase. *Frenchmen, Desire, Good Children,* 2nd Edition. New Orleans: Robert L. Crager and Company, 1960), it has been used to describe almost anything unique to South Louisiana, from tomatoes to horses to yams. In New Orleans and the old European settlements of St. Martinville and New Iberia, the term "Creole" was used to describe people of French or Spanish parentage who were born in Louisiana. When the slave trade in Louisiana grew in the late eighteenth century, the term was used to differentiate slaves born in the colonies (*esclavos Criollos*) from those brought from Africa (*esclavos Africanos*).

The term "Creole" generally fell out of frequent use as a descriptor for those of European descent in the years prior to the War Between the States, but in regards to the black population it developed deeper connotations. Many Creole slaves became free men before the war. Some of these people had children by their owners or were of partial Caribbean descent and were thus lighter skinned. They became known as Creoles of Color. Some went on to become prosperous businessmen and landowners, even plantation and slave owners, prior to the war, establishing a rich and largely undocumented culture of their own.

Today the term "Creole" in South Louisiana is usually used to describe Creoles of Color, or those brought up in the black French-speaking community. This group is sometimes incorrectly referred to as "black Cajuns," but the Creole people have a culture very much their own, including the distinctive Zydeco music. The French language has been best preserved among Creole people, as they were often isolated from the educational "opportunities" afforded the white populace after the War Between the States. Some of the biggest Creole communities today are in the St. Martinville and Opelousas areas, where Zydeco dance halls throw open their doors on weekends.

THE LANGUAGE AND EXPRESSIONS OF CAJUN COUNTRY

Despite the efforts of the Anglo state bureaucracy to eradicate the French language from public schools and courthouses since 1916, it is estimated that over a million Louisianians still speak French as a primary or secondary language. Although it is unlikely that non-French-speaking visitors will encounter a language barrier in Cajun Country (as they might have in the sixties), there are still fifth- and sixth-generation residents of the region who do not speak fluent English. In homes, bars, restaurants, and other places of relaxation (especially in the countryside), one can count on hearing Cajun French spoken, and a number of radio stations have introduced all French broadcasts. Those who speak standard French will find Cajun French understandable, but in many ways a very different language. The variation from standard is not nearly so surprising as the fact that the language is spoken at all, when you consider that it has existed exclusively as an orally transmitted tradition.

There are actually three distinct types of French spoken in South Louisiana: Acadian French, Creole French, and Standard Louisiana French (Hosea Phillips. "The Spoken French of Louisiana." In *The Cajuns: Essays on Their History and Culture,* edited by Glenn Conrad. Baton Rouge: USL Press, 1983). The most common French used in Louisiana is Acadian French. This is strictly a spoken language, which has maintained many archaic seventeenth-century forms while borrowing words from a number of other tongues. Although speakers from throughout South Louisiana have no trouble understanding each other, Acadian French varies widely from region to region. The distinct variant spoken along Bayou Lafourche has even been given the name "Lafourchaise." A second type of Louisiana French is Creole French, which is spoken mainly by the black population and was once referred to as Gumbo or Negro French. Like Acadian French, Creole French has been wildly altered during its transmission as a strictly spoken language. Creole French can vary widely between neighboring towns within the same region. The least-heard variant of the French language in Cajun Country is Standard Louisiana French, spoken primarily by an older, wealthier class who received an education at private French institutions. It is occasionally written and is used by few younger family members.

Although the impending loss of the distinctive forms of Cajun French is being justifiably lamented, it will be a long time before the language patterns, accents, and expressions of English-speaking Cajuns disappear. Cajun English will be as striking to many visitors as the often-heard Cajun French. Emphasis in Cajun English is often expressed by repetition. A fire can be merely "hot" or "hot hot!"; a strong cup of coffee may be dark or "black black!" In the casual way of the Cajun French that suggests that the good life comes without being tirelessly pursued, folks "pass a good time" rather than "have" one. A flirtatious gentleman would not be so bold as to "take" a look at a lady, but might "pass a look." As an expression of astonishment you will often hear the cry "Poo Yi!" Many lyrical expressions are drawn from the enchanting South Louisiana environment. The blustery weather of early March is often referred to as "the winds of Lent."

There is no capturing the poetry of Cajun French or Cajun English in writing, perhaps because they have never been written languages. The best way to appreciate these forms is to visit the region and pass a good time with the people of Cajun Country.

Hurricane floodwaters. (Courtesy of Louisiana Wild Life & Fisheries Commission; photo by Robert N. Dennie)

3

The Climate

Cajun Country enjoys a semitropical latitude. Lafayette, its biggest city, is about 30 degrees north of the equator, about the same latitude as Shanghai and Cairo. The climate is moist, warm, and luxuriant through most of the year, moderated by the warm waters of the neighboring Gulf of Mexico. People down here talk about the humidity as if it were an entity, much the way Chicagoans decry the wind-chill factor. The correct response when you step into an air-conditioned restaurant in mid-July and the waitress asks, "Hot out there?" is to wipe your brow and assert, "It's not so much the heat but the humidity."

Summers can be drippingly hot and humid, with daytime temperatures ranging from 85 to 95 degrees and the mercury seldom dropping below 65 at night. Rainfall averages about sixty inches a year, with nearly a third of that coming in June through August. In these months silver clouds float in from the Gulf and turn into afternoon thunderheads.

Fall and spring are probably the most pleasant times to visit Cajun Country. Autumn is the dry season, with cool evenings and warm days. Rice mills send clouds of chaff from their driers and the air is filled with the sweet smell of the sugarcane harvest and smoke from marsh fires. Occasionally disturbing the serenity of late summer and harvest time are huge tropical storms that play intermittent target practice with Louisiana's Gulf coast.

Winters are short and characterized by rain squalls and cloudy but mild weather followed by clear, cold weather. Daytime temperatures range from 55 to 65 degrees, with nighttime lows seldom dipping below 40. Only a few days are likely to go below freezing, so snowfall is rare. Because the weather in these parts is "supposed to be" so mild, visitors are often surprised at the grousing that accompanies a 40-degree "cold snap."

Spring begins early in Cajun Country. It is not unusual to find azaleas blooming in January. By late February the squalls and chills of winter give way to more generalized wind and showers and warm weather. Many people like to visit in the late winter and early spring for the

Cajun Mardi Gras celebration. The best advice is to pack for both warm and cold weather. I have been to Mardi Gras in January when people were sweltering so badly that they were discarding masks before noon; in 1988, when Mardi Gras fell on March 3, I had to wear gloves to keep beer cans from freezing to my hand.

HURRICANES

Hurricanes are the most feared climatic event in Cajun Country. While they are not unique to the area, South Louisiana's location on the northern rim of the Gulf of Mexico makes it a target for some of the most violent tropical storms to threaten the continent. The hurricane season runs June through November. During these months a common South Louisiana pastime is "tracking" the storms on special maps given out as promotional items at fast-food outlets.

While the majority of hurricanes striking the Louisiana coast make landfall around the mouth of the Mississippi River, some of the fiercest, such as Audrey (June 28, 1957), Carmen (September 8, 1974), and Danny (August 15, 1985) have struck to the west in Cajun Country. Here the low elevation and huge expanses of marsh allow storms to surge forward unimpeded. The already sodden ground often floods from severe rainfall even before punishing winds push the tidal surge ashore. Waves twenty feet high can roar in from the Gulf at speeds up to forty miles an hour, leaving cows in trees and trees in telephone lines as much as twenty miles inland from the coast. Lake Charles, Cameron, and Creole are left with grim reminders, in the form of mass graves, of the destructive powers of Hurricane Audrey, which slammed Cameron in 1957, claimed over five hundred victims, and did in excess of 150 million dollars of damage.

4

Flora and Fauna

A temperate climate and long growing season (230-300 days) cloaks much of South Louisiana in luxuriant vegetation year round. Something is always blooming and (notable if you are an allergy sufferer) going to seed. Although there is little variation in climate within the region, there is wide variation in the wild flora corresponding to differences in elevation and proximity to the coast. Swamps and freshwater areas are naturally more verdant than the salt marshes and prairie.

FLORA OF THE COASTAL MARSHES

Perhaps the harshest environment in South Louisiana is the coastal marsh, where life is battered by storms and shriveled by salt. With the

Louisiana alligator. (Courtesy of Louisiana Wild Life & Fisheries Commission)

completion of the Hug the Coast Highway and Creole Nature Trail in Cameron Parish, some of this isolated domain of seabirds and cordgrass has become accessible to auto touring. Only the hardiest plants, such as **coarse wire** and **three-corner grasses**, prevail here. On sand and shell ridges that striate the marsh are natural growths of live oaks. These ridges have been dubbed *cheniers* (French for oaks) for their twisted sylvan canopy that rises above the windblown miles of marsh and beach.

Of the fifteen species of oak found in Louisiana, none is more grand than the **live oak**, which grows wild in coastal Louisiana and in plantings throughout the state. The stately tree lends its dignity to hundreds of plantation grounds and an arbor of shade to countless backroads and highways in Cajun Country. Other oaks grow taller, but only the live oak has branches that sweep out up to two hundred feet in circumference. The trunks often measure over forty feet in girth, while each branch, large as an average tree trunk, supports its own small ecosystem of lichens, squirrels, birds, and strands of Spanish moss. The tree is so venerated that a Live Oak Society was created in 1934. To become a member, a tree must be at least a hundred years old. Among the most famous of the live oaks in Cajun Country is the Evangeline Oak, located in St. Martinville near the site where legend places the landing of Longfellow's heroine.

Live oaks on a coastal chenier. (Photo by Dr. E. L. Caze)

Spanish moss ranks with the bald cypress and live oak as a botanical symbol of Cajun Country. Its solemnly hanging strands are no doubt responsible for the haunted air believed to permeate so many plantation homes, the languid quality attributed to the atmosphere, and the mysterious allure ascribed to the swamps of the region. It grows in profusion on the outstretched arms of live oaks and festoons the borders of lakes, where the gray-green beards reach down to the soaring knees of the cypress.

This elegant plant has become the object of considerable legend. The Spanish dubbed it "Frenchman's wig," while the French supposedly called it *barbe espagnole,* or "Spanish beard." The current label is not botanically correct, as the plant is not a moss but a member of the pineapple family. It is not a parasite but an independent plant nourished by air that has no ill effect on the tree where it comes to rest. Indians and Acadian settlers used the "moss" as bedding and mixed it with mud for a construction material called *bousillage* by the French. Around the turn of the century, Spanish moss was harvested and dried for use as upholstery stuffing. The black inner fiber filled the seats of many a Model T.

FLORA OF THE
FRESH MARSHES AND SWAMPS

Whether you are entering Cajun Country from New Orleans in the east or the Texas border west of Lake Charles, the first vegetation you are likely to see is that of the saltwater marsh. Farther inland, in the brackish marsh and freshwater swamp, cattails, alligator grass, and marsh elder supplant the coarser salt vegetation. In the freshwater swamps and alluvial valleys between Lafayette and New Orleans lies Louisiana's richest plant growth. **Oak, pecan,** and **hickory** trees grow along ridges with an understory of **vines, wild muscadine grapes, blackberries, elderberries,** and **ferns. Tupelo** and **black gum, willow** and **bald cypress** thrive in the permanently moist areas. These shelter **palmetto, hibiscus, rosemallow,** and various wild flowers like the **giant purple and yellow iris.** Among the most striking and prevalent plants in the permanently flooded regions are water flowers like **American lotus,** which displays towering yellow blossoms over floating padlike foliage. **Duckweed** (the world's smallest flowering plant) forms a green carpet over slow-moving water, giving many of the bayous a "slimy" appearance.

The most ubiquitous of all water flowers is the **purple water hyacinth**. In warm-weather months water hyacinths, with their delicate lavender blossoms fading into purple, form a solid carpet over many

Water hyacinths choke a bayou. (Courtesy of Louisiana Wild Life & Fisheries Commission)

of the waterways in Cajun Country. This is one plant you will see in the summer wherever you go and regardless of how long you stay. From roadside ditches to bayous, rivers, and miles of swamp, the water hyacinth proliferates in mind-boggling numbers. The flowers can self-pollinate, with one plant generating up to sixty-five thousand others in a season. Dormant seeds may germinate twenty years later. Despite its beauty, the reproductive capabilities of the water hyacinth have made it a major nuisance and threat to aquatic life across South Louisiana. The plants form a blanket that shades waterways and robs their oxygen content, at times becoming so thick as to prohibit navigation. The lovely and troublesome flower is not a native to South Louisiana, but was introduced to the state during the Cotton Exposition of 1884 in New Orleans. The Japanese reportedly brought a large quantity of the flowers (native to South America) to give away as souvenirs. They were carried forth and distributed across the state. By 1897 they had already become a threat to waterborne commerce and the Corps of Engineers was called in to eradicate the plants. Thus began what has become the ongoing battle of the bloom, with man tossing arsenic, oil, flames, threshers, and a variety of chemical weapons at the happy and still hardy flowers.

Bald cypress, found in the moist, alluvial valleys and swamps of Cajun Country, is the state tree of Louisiana. It is distinguished by a wide, flared base that tapers upwards and a dark feathery green foliage that browns and falls in the colder months. One of the most unusual features of the cypress are the vertical outgrowths or "knees" that rise from the roots, piercing the surrounding water and soil surface; these are assumed to be a sort of breathing apparatus for the tree.

The state legislature may have considered the poetic beauty of the bald cypress bearded with Spanish moss when it appointed it state tree in 1964, but for years it was appreciated for its practical virtues as a building material. Cypress lumber became known as the "eternal wood." Unfortunately the lumber turned out to be a lot more eternal than most of the trees. In the late 1800s the lumber industry set about plundering the wetlands of South Louisiana. Some of the trees harvested in the nineteenth century were close to a thousand years old and big enough to provide enough lumber for a modest home. By the early twentieth century there were no longer enough harvestable trees left, and the mill owners packed it in.

Artisans continue to harvest cypress in the form of "sinker" logs. These are cut pieces of cypress that either sank or were lost in storms years ago. The most sought-after cypress is called "pecky." These logs have been eaten away inside by a mysterious fungal agent to create a lacy pattern when cut in cross-section. To see cypress more than two hundred years old today, one must look at the floors and moldings of plantation homes, gaze on the vistas of decapitated stumps rising from roadside wetlands, or take a swamp tour that reaches hidden corners of the Atchafalaya Basin.

FLORA OF THE CAJUN PRAIRIE

If you travel on Interstate 10 between Lafayette and the Texas border or spend any time in the Cajun Heartland of Evangeline and St. Landry parishes, you will find a flat and nearly treeless terrain that fails to comply with any of the swamp stereotypes of Cajun Country. A few feet beneath the level prairie surface lies a nearly impervious layer of clay that holds water on the surface and deters the growth of trees and other large plants. At one time this region was covered with towering grasses and wild flowers. Now most of the prairie has given way to the plow. Farmers have taken advantage of poor drainage and flooded fields to grow rice and crawfish. Where bayous and creeks cross the prairie, small groves of trees have sprung up in the stream beds. Towns that have grown by the shelter of these trees are often called coves or islands, as the patches of trees seem to float on the open prairie. Scraps of wild prairie growth still exist along roadsides, rail beds, and scattered in far-flung locations in the form of wild flowers such as **compass plant, blazing star, spiderwort, clover,** and **blue star** (*see* Eunice Prairie Wildflower Refuge).

NOTABLE FAUNA
Birds

Over 375 species of birds have been observed within the boundaries of Louisiana. (For information on bird watching *see* chapter 8.) A temperate climate makes Louisiana a comfortable permanent residence for nearly all avian species common in the Southeast, but the main factor contributing to the plethora of our winged friends is the state's location across the Great Mississippi Valley Flyway. Louisiana is a landing pad for birds from both eastern and western regions. Some stop and winter here while others grab a nap or some seafood and continue on their migration. In the Christmas bird count of 1953, 153 different species were counted in one day on a fifteen-mile-diameter chunk of marsh in Cameron Parish! Of special interest to hunters and bird watchers are the thousands of wild geese and ducks that visit the region each fall and winter.

South Louisiana is home to a variety of **egret.** These members of the heron family are tall, slender birds with long legs and necks. The graceful egret may be distinguished from other species in flight, as it holds its neck bent into an *S* shape. Perhaps the most beautiful is the **snowy egret,** whose lacy "nuptial feathers" are raised in a dazzling display during courtship. Once decimated by plume hunters, the population rebounded through the efforts of naturalist E. A. McIlhenny. They can now be seen anywhere in Cajun Country, silent sentinels searching for minnows or crawfish. Favored spots for viewing these birds are the rookeries in the Jungle Gardens, on Avery Island, and Lake Martin, near Breaux Bridge.

The **brown pelican** is the official state bird of Louisiana, which in turn is often called the "Pelican State." The pelican is one odd-looking bird. The adult is buff gray, stands about two feet tall, and has a large, scooplike bill. At one month old it uses this bill to harvest five pounds of fish a day. In the 1950s colonies of over five thousand were reported on coastal islands, but by the midsixties the bird had disappeared from

Egret foraging in swamp. (Courtesy of Louisiana Wild Life & Fisheries Commission)

the state, a victim of pesticide runoff. The state seal adopted in 1902 shows a distinctly white pelican, but this was presumably artistic license and not a prophecy of a time when the whites would outnumber the browns. Brown pelican colonies are now being reestablished on Rockefeller Wildlife Refuge and Grand Terre with birds imported from Florida.

Fur Bearers

The wetlands of Cajun Country support an enormous number of fur-bearing critters, from **otter** to **muskrat** and **nutria.** The Indians and the French trappers harvested large numbers of pelts. Although the fur-garment industry has taken it on the chin recently, there are still

Nutria. (Courtesy of Louisiana Wild Life & Fisheries Commission)

over ten thousand trappers who derive at least part of their livelihoods from the sale of animal skins. Louisiana remains the top wild-fur producer in the nation, harvesting more pelts during the 1980s than all of the Canadian provinces combined.

The nutria is the most unusual and plentiful of Louisiana's fur bearers, and one that will almost certainly be seen if you spend much time in the coastal marsh areas. They can even be seen sunning on the lakeside in front of the Governor's Mansion in Baton Rouge. The nutria is one in a long line of nuisance animals and plants that were introduced to Louisiana in the last hundred or so years. Brought to the state for experimental breeding by E. A. McIlhenny in the 1930s, it is actually an aquatic rodent that is native to South America, where it is called a *coypu*. It is a nine-pound cross between a beaver and a water rat, with huge, razor-sharp incisors and webbed hind feet for swimming.

From thirteen pairs, McIlhenny's experimental group grew to an estimated 300 individuals before a hurricane loosed the entire population into the marshes of South Louisiana in 1940. By 1957 the shaggy footballs were so numerous that they were devouring acres of marshland

and competing with the native muskrat. The legislature put out a twenty-five-cent reward for each nutria and scored a bountiful take of 510,000 animals in less than a year. The bounty was removed in the sixties and the pelts (politely referred to as "Hudson Bay Beaver" in New York markets) became popular among furriers in the seventies. Louisiana's fur market has fallen on hard times and the nutria is again considered a pest by all except the alligator population, which loves to snack on them.

Fish and Shellfish

Possessing America's largest freshwater swamp, the drainage basin of the nation's largest river (sopping the runoff from two-thirds of the country), and a thirty-mile-wide band of wetlands bordering on the Gulf of Mexico, it is not surprising that South Louisiana is home to an immense variety of aquatic and marine life. Although an aquarium was recently constructed in New Orleans, most people around Cajun Country still think about fish as something to either catch or eat (usually both). In fact, some assert that had the aquarium been constructed in Cajun Country, placards beside exhibits would have carried recipes rather than scientific names for each fish.

Louisiana produces a third of the nation's commercial fish catch and is home to nearly a quarter of the nation's marine recreational fishing activity (590,000 licensed recreational saltwater anglers). Among the most important commercial species are **shrimp, menhaden, crabs, oysters,** and **crawfish**—all categories in which Louisiana is a national leader. Favorites of recreational fishermen are **redfish, speckled trout, flounder, red snapper,** and **mackerel.** Freshwater anglers take their pick of **largemouth bass, bream, catfish,** and **crappie** (called *sac-a-lait* in Cajun Country).

If the alligator is the animal most closely associated with Cajun Country, it is closely followed by the **crawfish**. The crawfish, or "mudbug" as it is often called locally, was elevated to star status and a major industry at the same time that the Cajun people were rediscovering a pride in their unique culture in the late fifties. For this reason it has been adopted by Cajuns as a symbol or mascot in a way the gator never was. Once considered a lowly critter eaten mainly by denizens of the Atchafalaya Basin, the crustaceans that resemble miniature lobsters were first commercially "farmed" in stocked ponds in 1959. It was not long before the tasty creatures had moved from camp tables and Basin bars to restaurants across the region. In addition to the original Crawfish Festival in Breaux Bridge (the first weekend in April), Louisiana now celebrates the "mudbug" at an International Crawfish Tasting and

Trade Show, an annual World Championship Etouffée Cook-off Contest, and dozens of other fairs and festivals. For more on eating crawfish read chapter 6.

Crawfish is sometimes spelled, but never pronounced, *crayfish* in Cajun Country, where over twenty species exist in the wild. The two most popular food varieties are the Red Swamp and White River, which are harvested in profusion in the freshwater swamps of the Atchafalaya Basin. Crawfish are most active in the slow-moving freshwater swamps during warm weather. After breeding in April and May they generally leave the water and burrow in nearby mudflats, where they live two feet down until around October, when they seek water for their hatchlings. Thus, the crawfish season generally lasts from December until mid-June. During these months rice and soybean farmers flood their fields and harvest them with wire-mesh traps. In early summer, fields are drained for planting and the crawfish burrow again, leaving towering mud castles over their subterranean homes. The crawfish industry now touches virtually every citizen of the small towns around the Basin and surrounding parishes, where traps are made, bait is sold, boats are built and repaired, crawfish meat is processed, and the live ones are sold by the sack. Over 100 million pounds of crawfish are harvested in Louisiana each year, or almost 90 percent of the world's production!

Alligators

A private zoo operator in Bayou Country once told me, "You just don't have a tourist attraction in South Louisiana without alligators." No other animal is more consistently associated with Cajuns than *Alligator mississippiensas.* It is difficult to find a movie filmed in the region where one of the protagonists is not wrestling, trapping, eating, or being eaten by one of the huge reptiles. Although a good number of people in this part of the country eat alligator, and a growing number trap them, it is strictly a figment of the Hollywood imagination that many people wrestle or are eaten by them. They are voracious predators, but seldom attack humans unless provoked. The American alligator is found throughout Louisiana, with the greatest numbers living in coastal freshwater areas, where they seldom stray far from their nests (summer) or underground dens (winter). Alligators can grow to nearly twenty feet long. The largest ever recorded in Louisiana was a nineteen-foot-long gator observed in Vermilion Parish in January of 1890. In 1963, with alligator populations dwindling, the reptile was temporarily declared off limits for hunting and trapping. Populations recovered by 1975 to the point where carefully regulated

Alligator skin. (Courtesy of Louisiana Wild Life & Fisheries Commission)

trapping was permitted. Alligator trapping can be a very lucrative business for the short fall season. During the summer months the alligator is now ubiquitous in slow-moving-freshwater areas of Cajun Country.

The best way to see a gator in the wild is to take a swamp tour (*see* listing in chapter 8); however, there are many places where they can be observed close to the road. Try the nature trails at Lake Martin, Sabine Wildlife Refuge, Rockefeller Wildlife Refuge, Avery Island, or Chicot State Park. For more information on these spots consult the index.

Oil rig headed for the Gulf. (Courtesy of U.S. Corps of Engineers)

5

The Economy: Major Industrial and Agricultural Products

LOUISIANA OIL AND GAS INDUSTRY

Louisiana is the second leading producer of oil and natural gas in the nation. The industry is the backbone of the state's economy and has touched the lives of every individual in the predominantly agrarian Cajun Country. The first Louisiana oil well was "brought in" in 1901 shortly after oil was struck at the famous Spindletop gusher in Texas. In the year following that first strike at the Evangeline Field north of Jennings, seventy-six oil and gas companies began operating in the state. Unabated growth became a boom when the first offshore oil rig was brought in off the coast of Morgan City in 1947. Hundreds of companies moved their offshore offices to Lafayette.

In a state where antitaxation sentiment is a religion, the oil and gas industry has pumped billions of dollars of lease and royalty income into health care, education, and capital improvement programs (not to mention politicians' pockets). Following the first oil strikes, major oil companies built refineries in Louisiana and thousands of support industry jobs followed. Airplane and helicopter mechanics and pilots, roustabouts, seamen, steel fabricators, engineers, surveyors, and countless other workers turn their labors to the extraction of oil in the state. In Cajun Country the cultural impact of the oil rush was severe. Oil tycoons and roustabouts from around the nation came to seek a share of the mineral wealth. Advanced programs in engineering and computer sciences were instituted at the University of Southwest Louisiana, but the oil boom lured many Cajun youth away from school and traditional pursuits to high-paying, unskilled labor.

The stage was set for disaster in Louisiana when world oil prices collapsed in the eighties. In 1982 crude oil averaged nearly $40 a barrel. By 1986 the price had fallen to $12.50. Royalty and lease income to the

45

state withered from $624 million in 1982 to about $286 million in 1987. Funding for essential state programs disappeared and thousands of unskilled and uneducated laborers became unemployed. Lafayette and other industry hubs suffered bank closures whose numbers exceeded those of the Great Depression.

The nineties have seen a major reversal of fortunes in Louisiana's oil patch and related industries. This reawakening has begun to pour money into state coffers and local economies, but no one is daring to use the word "boom" again.

PETROCHEMICAL INDUSTRY

Louisiana's chemical industry is the fourth largest in the nation, and second to oil and gas in economic value to the state. In Cajun Country, where most plants are located, chemical manufacture provides almost 20 percent of industrial employment. The greatest concentrations of plants are on the Mississippi River above New Orleans and the Calcasieu River around Lake Charles, where there is plenty of fresh water for processing and deepwater ports for shipping.

The growth of the chemical industry has earned the lower Mississippi Valley a reputation as the "Chemical Corridor," the "American Ruhr," and, more to the point, "Cancer Alley" (*see* section on Environmental Issues later in this chapter). Most of the companies use the state's plentiful oil resources to produce petrochemicals like polyvinylchloride (that's PVC for short), acetone, polytetrahydrofuran, and a wide array of solvents, starter chemicals, fertilizers, and bases. These chemicals are not generally converted to consumer products here, but are sold in bulk and shipped to other locations for processing and packaging. Anyone interested in the chemical industry should drive the Mississippi River Road, where he or she can see massive Vulcan, Dupont, and Hooker facilities and actually tour the plant at DOW (*see* chapter 10 for details).

PLANT AND ANIMAL HARVEST
Seafood

Seafood, along with petroleum/natural gas and chemicals, is one of Louisiana's three major industries. The state produces a third of the nation's commercial fish catch, and leads the country in the harvest of shrimp, menhaden, crabs, oysters, and crawfish. Naturally the bulk of Louisiana's seafood is harvested from the estuaries and Gulf Coastal waters that fringe Cajun Country. Fishing has been a way of life for some Cajun communities for generations. It is perhaps the most

Shrimp boat in the Gulf of Mexico. (Courtesy of U.S. Corps of Engineers)

picturesque of the state's leading industries. Shrimp boats with towering booms line narrow bayous, traps are stacked neatly in front yards, and crawfishermen can be seen from afar, reaping a solitary harvest from open rice ponds. Prizing independence and self-sufficiency, many Cajuns build their own boats and construct their own nets and traps.

Sugarcane

Louisiana is the top sugarcane-producing state, with over half of the nation's crop. Historically, sugarcane is probably the most important crop in Cajun Country. Just as oil and gas have wrought huge economic and social change in the twentieth century, sugarcane held sway in the nineteenth century. Prior to the War Between the States, sugarcane created vast wealth for a few Anglo and French planters, who decorated the landscape with magnificent plantation homes. Cane production in Louisiana is concentrated along the main bayous and rivers between New Orleans and Lafayette. The biggest and wealthiest planters were located along the Mississippi River Road, while others moved west to Bayous Lafourche and Teche. As they moved westward, Anglo planters displaced many Cajun landholders and created a distinct sugar culture that thrived on cheap labor. They levelled endless fields and planted green rows of cane, six feet wide, on the fertile alluvial soils.

Since Etienne de Boré, a Mississippi River Road planter, perfected a technique for granulating sugar in 1796, the growing and milling of cane have become highly mechanized processes. One machine now does the work of dozens of laborers. Where there were once thousands of mills, processing is now managed at fewer than thirty locations. Despite this change, row upon row of verdant cane still dominates the landscape of eastern Cajun Country, where over 15,000 workers are employed in the industry. Life moves to the pace of the planting and harvesting cycle and the small shacks of field hands and former cane cutters stand alongside grand plantation homes. In the fall the smoke of burning fields (the useless husks are burned off before the cane is loaded) and steaming mills cloud the sky, as trucks rumble through normally quiet towns like Jeanerette and Franklin.

Rice

Louisiana ranks third in the nation in rice production, with the largest amount grown on the Cajun Prairie between Lafayette and the Texas border. Although rice can survive without large amounts of water, it is usually grown in flooded fields in order to control weeds and pests. The level prairie, with its impervious clay subsoil, proved perfect for mechanical flooding and, in recent years, crawfish have been alternated with rice crops. The growth of the rice industry coincided with the western expansion of the railroad following the War Between the States. The major growers in the rice industry were not Cajuns, but people of mixed European descent. Germans, Danes, and Anglos were recruited from the Midwest by railroad men and land speculators to settle the open prairie. Most of the rail towns that stretch west from Lafayette are still rice towns and are marked by giant silos and driers. Many of these towns have a distinctly non-Cajun set of family names and a Victorian ambiance, reflecting early settlement patterns.

Cattle

The cattle industry in Louisiana predates that of neighboring Texas. In fact, the famous Texas Longhorn originated in Louisiana. Early pioneers were allocated heads of beef to encourage settlement, and the first cattle drive in the United States is believed to have been along the Old Spanish Trail (roughly following the course of U.S. 90) in Southwest Louisiana. Folklorists have even traced some of the Western cattle songs (usually associated with Texas), with lines like "yippee-ki-yi," back to Cajun tunes with cries of "hipee-ti-yo." Among the unusual sights of Cajun Country are herds of hump-backed Brahmas (brought to the area for their resistance to insects) wandering unfenced on marshy pasture hemmed in by bayous. Along the coastal fringe, these unfenced herds are often tended by ranchers in small boats and brought to market by barge.

ENVIRONMENTAL ISSUES
Loss of Coastal Wetlands

The wetlands of Cajun Country are among the most recent and the most rapidly disappearing soils in the country. Louisiana's coastline is disappearing at a rate of forty-five to sixty square miles a year! In addition to that swept away in tropical storms, a large amount of marsh is simply subsiding, or sinking beneath the waters of the Gulf of Mexico. The areas of greatest loss are the coastal wetlands between the Mississippi River below New Orleans and the Vermilion River south of Lafayette. In these areas, roads that were once above water are now submerged at high tide and bayou-side homes stand isolated on stilts.

Until 1984 Louisiana had no State Department of Environmental Quality. Oil and lumber interests exploring in the wetlands drilled, cut timber, and dug canals with little or no oversight. As ground cover was removed and new channels were created, erosion increased dramatically in the swamps, carrying valuable soil into the Gulf. Places that were once narrow pipeline canals have become shallow ponds and lakes. The land loss has been rapid enough to confound the fishermen who rely on specific channels and landforms to navigate, as these landmarks often disappear from one season to the next. With the loss of land, saltwater encroaches further and destroys more natural land cover and habitat for animals like shrimp, crabs, and oysters that feed and breed in the marsh.

Toxic Waste

In addition to land loss, South Louisiana's oil and chemical industries have been pumping amazing amounts of toxic chemicals into the air, water, and land for most of a century. The state is the nation's second-leading toxic polluter (behind the vastly larger state of Texas). Damage through release of toxic chemicals is visible to the keen-eyed visitor in abandoned waste dumps, Superfund cleanup sites, and huge

Cypress killed by saltwater intrusion. (Photo by Julie Posner)

areas of swamp where cypress are devoid of foliage. Anyone taking a
swamp tour below Houma or in the oilfields around Henderson in the
Atchafalaya Basin will be struck by the miles of abandoned and rusting
pipeline.

The state is realizing a staggering environmental price tag for more
than half a century of virtually unregulated industrial activity. The
seafood industry is lamenting the loss of formerly productive fishing
grounds, recreational sportsmen are decrying diminished takes, and
even oil exploration companies are becoming involved in the fight to
save the nation's most extensive wetlands area.

6

Food

Every country had its own "Cajun cuisine," a cuisine that depended on the local environment. We just happen to be the luckiest of people; nature gave us, when I think of our area, the greatest natural pantry God has given anyone.

Chef John Folse

In the mid-eighties, "Cajun" and "New Orleans-style" restaurants began cropping up all over the country, spurred by the success of Cajun chef Paul Prudhomme. Words like "Jambalaya," "Crawfish Pie," and "Filé Gumbo" became known as more than just lyrics to a popular song. Like the region's music, the best South Louisiana cuisine is still simmering around the plains and wetlands of Cajun Country, where cooks have access to a wondrous variety of fresh seafoods and tasty fresh and smoked meats. Where else can one find pungent smoked tasso and andouille sausage, rabbit and quail, alligator, crawfish, and large Gulf shrimp alongside fresh, uncut beef and pork at the market?

The mere presence of fine and exotic ingredients cannot explain the variety or far-flung abundance of great eateries in an area so rural. In Cajun Country food and music are integral parts and expressions of the regional culture. Nowhere else, except perhaps in New Orleans, is eating an experience of such intense and often ritualistic proportions. Folks spend a week talking about and anticipating a big feed, but as soon as they are eating they begin discoursing on the last meal and the one to follow!

The best dishes in many Cajun Country restaurants reflect traditions carried out on home dining tables for centuries. Fresh seafood is served on Fridays, fried fish and crawfish etouffée abound during the Lenten season, and hot gumbo or "duck camp stew" warms up chilly winter days. Around Mardi Gras you may find boudin and hard-boiled eggs on the counter at cafes and bars out in the country, while Good Friday is celebrated with mounds of boiled crawfish. Throughout the

Making sweet-dough pies. (Photo by Julie Posner)

year stews, rice dishes, and fowl stuffed with dressing are served at the humblest and grandest restaurants alike. Many places have their own unique dishes, like *tarte à la bouillie* in Bayou Country, choupic burgers on Upper Lafourche, and barbecue basted in an oniony sauce in the Cajun Heartland. Try Steen's Cane Syrup (made in Abbeville) over morning biscuits with a dark cup of coffee or visit the Steamboat Restaurant and get traditional yams and gumbo. The variety is endless once you start to look and eat!

CAJUN OR CREOLE?

The food in Acadiana is often called "Cajun" or "Creole." With the growing popularity of Louisiana cuisine, these terms have often become confused. Although both are French Louisiana born, they describe quite different preparations. Traditional **Cajun food** combines simple French country cooking with the whole realm of locally available ingredients such as bay leaves, filé powder, and cayenne peppers. It is a cuisine born of life close to the land, prepared by people who frequently did not have anything except for the abundance of their own fields or gardens. It is highly seasoned, often flavored with onion, sweet green peppers, and celery. Frequently these savory ingredients are slow-cooked in one large pot. Cajun food is not necessarily hot, but if a menu lists an item as such, be forewarned that by anyone else's standards it is probably a three-alarm dish!

Unlike Cajun food, **Creole cuisine** has its roots in the urban environments of New Orleans and the French and Spanish settlements of St. Martinville, New Iberia, and Opelousas. In this sense Creole cuisine was the food of the wealthy, but it was often prepared by black cooks who introduced their own recipes and ideas. Creole dishes thus tend to be more complex and use a broader variety of spices, herbs, and sauces than traditional Cajun food.

RESTAURANT GUIDE

Many people will tell you they have not eaten at a bad restaurant in Cajun Country. I wouldn't go that far, but there are an improbable number of fine eateries for so small and sparsely populated an area. This chapter defines the food categories used in this book and the unique foods found in Cajun Country. It concludes with a list of my favorite restaurants and meat markets and a map to help locate them. After almost twenty years of traveling in Cajun Country, I still find interesting places or unusual dishes on almost every visit.

RESTAURANT CATEGORIES

Down Home

Down-home restaurants serve the kind of country cooking that Cajun people have enjoyed for centuries. Even Sonny Prudhomme, acclaimed chef at Prudhomme's Cajun Cafe, insists, "Give me a good round or sevin steak with potato salad or rice dressing, that's Cajun cooking. I got to have that blue plate!" From deli counters at grocery stores to fine restaurants like Prudhomme's you will find mouthwatering stews, gravies, and gumbos seasoned like no other simple food you have ever eaten.

Cajun/Creole

Those restaurants we describe as Cajun/Creole are not only among the finest in Cajun Country, but among the best anywhere. Their nationally and internationally recognized chefs marry regional ingredients with traditional Cajun, Creole, and classic French cooking to create simply incredible meals. You will find dishes such as crawfish fajitas, Cajun caviar (made with choupic roe), Kahlua-grilled shrimp, and seafood-stuffed eggplant pirogues. Some, like Joe's in Livonia and Prudhomme's Cajun Cafe in Carencro, are moderately priced and offer a selection of hearty Cajun cooking at lunch. Others, like Cafe Vermilionville, qualify as splurges.

Seafood

The restaurants in this category specialize in salt- and freshwater fish and shellfish (boiled seafood places are treated in a separate category). The most popular way to eat seafood in Cajun Country is fried, and for good reason—people down here really know how to fry! Not surprisingly, most of the restaurants recommended in this category are located along the coastal region. Shucks!, Black's, and Dupuy's in Abbeville deserve special mention, as they rank as three of the best oyster bars in the world!

Boiled Seafood

The biggest and best crawfish never leave Cajun Country but are served at rustic seafood patios or "boiling points," where they are piled on beer trays in steaming three- to four-pound mounds and carried

Eating boiled crawfish. (Courtesy of Louisiana Office of Tourism)

piping hot from the kitchen. These are places with cement or plank floors and tables covered with paper or plastic. A true mark of an old-fashioned boiling point is a sink in the dining area where you can wash your hands without, or before, entering the restrooms. Remember that many crawfish restaurants are seasonal, only open between January and mid-June.

Eating crawfish is easy once you get the knack, and there are plenty of folks willing to give you pointers. The process is similar to eating boiled shrimp. Remove the head and peel the shell to get to the succulent tail meat. Once you get the hang of it they are actually easier than shrimp, as the meat may be pulled out with your teeth without peeling the whole thing.

Local Faves

The places in this category don't necessarily serve Louisiana cuisine, but are local favorites you wouldn't find anywhere else. They range from old thirties roadhouses like Chester's, which specializes in prefast-food-outlet-style fried chicken and froglegs, to the glitzy Charly G's grill in Lafayette. Want a "Cajun pizza"? Try Dean-O's "Cajun Executioner"!

Meat Markets

It is hard to drive ten miles in Cajun Country without coming across a market, gas station, or grocery selling boudin and cracklins. Many small meat markets do their own slaughtering, cutting, smoking, and stuffing. They serve up a variety of goods found nowhere else: boudin, tasso, paunce, andouille, hog's head cheese, cracklins, garlic sausage, and beef jerky.

Surely the most popular meat item is a rice sausage known as boudin. The proper way to see Cajun Country is with a link of boudin in one hand and a cold beer in the other. Whenever I drive through, I take a cooler to pack with smoked meats and a glove compartment full of paper towels to clean up after hasty boudin and beef jerky stops.

The variety of meat preparations across Cajun Country is incredible. Folklorist Barry Ancelet advises, "The best boudin is always less than five miles from where you live!" Boudin varies from livery (heavy on the giblets) around the Lafayette area to spicy with plenty of lean pork in Opelousas and at Johnson's Meat Market in Eunice. South of Lafayette you can still find boudin rouge (blood sausage).

Regional differences in meats are not limited to boudin. The classic andouille sausage in LaPlace is made only with very lean and large chunks of pork, while in Opelousas it is made with chitterlings. The

(Photo by Julie Posner)

Prairie is the "smoke belt," whereas farther south fresh meats and sausages dominate market shelves.

FOOD GLOSSARY

Andouille (say *and-DO-we*) is a spicy (but not usually hot) smoked sausage that is usually stuffed with large pieces of lean pork. The Mississippi River Region between LaPlace (Andouille Capital of the World) and Gramercy is famous for andouille so lean you can slice it off and eat it as a snack, though most people use it for flavoring chicken or seafood gumbos. At several places around the Carencro and Opelousas area north of Lafayette you will find a "poor man's andouille" that is stuffed with spices and small bits of chitterlings.

Crawfish Bisque is a rich, roux-based crawfish soup filled with sweet crawfish tail meat, often served with a bowl of rice on the side that you may add to taste. The treasured morsel in crawfish bisque is a crawfish shell stuffed with chopped crawfish meat, herbs, and bread crumbs that rests at the bottom of the bowl and soaks up the flavor of the soup. Nowadays some places substitute a crawfish *boulette* for the stuffed shell.

A **boucherie** (pronounced *boo-share-REE*) is the traditional slaughtering and preparing of a hog, where the hard work offered by many neighbors is rewarded by generous samplings of cracklins, backbone stew, *cochon de lait* (suckling pig), and other products of the day's labor. Before refrigeration a *boucherie* was not only a social event but a means of distributing the meat to avoid spoilage. Each family with an animal for slaughter would take turns hosting the event. Refrigeration and modern slaughterhouses have removed the need for such gatherings, but they still continue as social events, accompanied by music and cold beer.

Boudin (*BOO-dan*) is a rich and well-seasoned rice and pork sausage that sometimes includes varying amounts of giblets. Boudin is sold precooked and still warm at thousands of places in Cajun Country. To eat boudin, cut the link in half and squeeze the stuffing out of its casing right into your mouth. These links are so popular that it has been said a seven-course Cajun meal is a six pack of beer and a pound of boudin. There is a wide variety of preparations, including newfangled "crawfish boudin" and "seafood boudin," which have no meat. For the brave there is traditional "boudin rouge" or blood sausage (made just as the name suggests). I have seen signs advertising "Rubber Boots, Hardware, Boudin" and others proclaiming "Fishing Tackle, Bait, Kerosene, Boudin," but the best places to get boudin are little meat markets, where it is made fresh every morning.

Boulette (*BOO-let*) is a ball-shaped fritter similar to a hush puppy, but usually seasoned with onion and pepper and often spiked with tender crawfish tails.

Chaudin (*SHOW-dan*) is basically the same as paunce, only made with pork stomach.

Cracklins, also known as Gratons, are fried strips of pork skin that often have thin strips of meat and fat attached. This is not exactly health food, but it is one heck of a great snack if properly seasoned and consumed with a cold beverage. Hey, George Bush likes the stuff. How can you go wrong?

Crawfish Etouffée (pronounced *eh-two-FAY*) is a dish in which the peeled crawfish tails are smothered in a stew of fresh chopped peppers, onions, and garlic that have been simmered in butter. There are hundreds of variations served in homes and restaurants around Cajun Country. Some have tomato in the stew. Some are thickened with butter, while others add a roux or corn starch to bind them. The best versions of this dish use the crawfish fat for extra richness and flavor.

The terms "**Dirty Rice**" or "**Rice Dressing**" refer to the same dish, which is made from a blend of rice cooked in broth, chopped chicken giblets, and sometimes bits of pork.

Filé (pronounced *FEE-lay*) is a seasoning and thickening agent made from ground sassafrass leaves and used in gumbos. The ingredient was introduced to the French by local Indian tribes. It is only added at the end of the cooking process and may be found on many restaurant tables. It is not used as often in seafood gumbos as in chicken, sausage, or wild game varieties. Just shake a bit into your bowl and stir it in.

Gumbo is a Cajun/Creole dish of epic stature. The term is so evocative it is used to describe music, art, people, and just about anything else that can have a rich blend of ethnic ingredients. From immigrants of African descent came the name and the use of okra (a popular thickening agent), the French gave the dish a roux and delicate seasonings, local Indians contributed the filé and hot peppers, and Acadians hunted the wild game or seafood that became the object of each soup. The end result is a soup that warms the whole body, starting with the palate and ending with the soul. There is an endless variety of gumbos served in Louisiana, the recipes guided more by what is "on hand" than any hard-and-fast rules. Among the most popular are Chicken and Andouille (or other smoked sausage), Shrimp and Crab, and basic Seafood Gumbo.

Jambalaya (pronounced *jum-buh-LIE-uh*) is a poor boy's dish of South Louisiana origin. In a traditional jambalaya, chicken, sausage, ham, and chopped vegetables are cooked and added with seasonings and liquid to an iron pot full of rice. Like gumbo, the ingredients to jambalaya depend only on what the chef has on his shelf. Some glamorous versions include shrimp or crab meat. Accomplished chefs sometimes add all the partially cooked ingredients to the pot before starting the rice, but most now cook them separately. At the last minute the rice and other ingredients are combined, stirred, and allowed to finish over a low flame.

Maque Choux (pronounced *mock shoo*) is a corn dish that varies in consistency from a stew to a chowder or soup. It always contains corn and frequently features tomato and bits of caramelized onion, tomato, and cayenne pepper.

Pain Perdu is called "lost bread" in New Orleans and French toast just about everywhere else. In Louisiana it is most often made with left over French bread, which gives the toast a firmer and richer flavor.

Paunce is stuffed calf stomach. It may be smoked or simply fresh and ready to cook in the oven.

A **Po' boy** is a New Orleans-style sandwich made on crusty French bread. The best Cajun Country varieties come stuffed with fresh fried seafood.

Roux (pronounced *roo*) is flour browned in butter or oil that may be used as a thickening, coloring, and flavoring agent in pot food like stews and gumbos.

Sauce Piquant (*pee-CAHNT*) can be made in many ways with any number of central ingredients from alligator to chicken or tasso. The common characteristic of these varieties is a fiery-hot, reddish gravy.

Tasso is a lean, smoked seasoning meat quite similar to beef jerky, only more highly spiced, more moist, and usually cut into thick ropes. It may be made from either pork or beef. Tasso is typically used to flavor pot food, but is sometimes sliced thin and cooked in a sauce to be served on rice or pasta.

Yam is the popular name for the bright orange and golden sweet potatoes grown mainly around Opelousas.

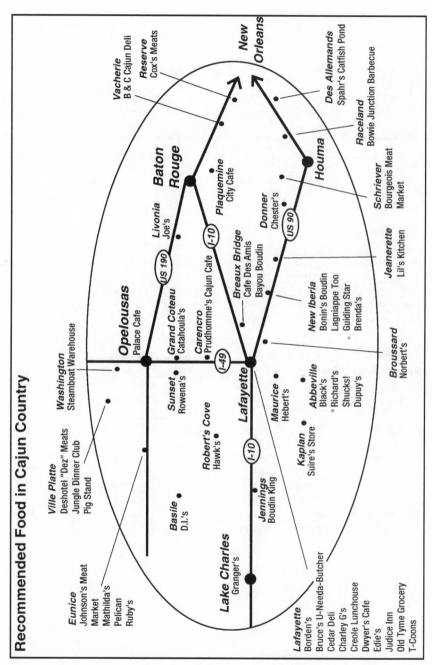

Restaurants map.

Recommended Food *$ = under $10, $$ = $10-$20, $$$ = $20-$30*

River Road

Restaurant	Type	Town	Price	Comments	Page
B&C Cajun Deli	Seafood	Vacherie	$	Fish, gumbo & gator	106
City Cafe	Local Fave	Plaquemine	$	Catfish, Italian	117
Cox's Meats	Meat Market	Reserve	$	Best andouille	90

Bayou Country

Restaurant	Type	Town	Price	Comments	Page
Bourgeois Market	Meat Market	Schriever	$	Cajun beef jerky	148
Bowie Junction	Local Fave	Chackbay	$	BBQ and jerky	125
Chester's	Local Fave	Donner	$–$$	Fried chicken, froglegs	175
Spahr's Catfish	Seafood	Des Allemands	$	Catfish capital	122

New Iberia

Restaurant	Type	Town	Price	Comments	Page
Bonin's Boudin	Meat Market	New Iberia	$	Awesome boudin!	220
Brenda's	Down Home	New Iberia	$	Soul food & cobbler	221
Guiding Star	Boiled Seafood	New Iberia	$–$$	Cool place for crawfish	222
Lagniappe Too	Local Fave	New Iberia	$–$$	Creative & simple fare	223
Lil's Kitchen	Local Fave	Jeanerette	$	Sweet potato bread Wed. & Fri.	212

Lafayette

Restaurant	Type	Town	Price	Comments	Page
Borden's	Local Fave	Lafayette	$	'50s soda fountain	295
Bruce's U–Need-A-Butcher	Meats	Lafayette	$	Best cracklins	306
Cedar Deli	Local Fave	Lafayette	$	Mideastern lunch	296
Charley G's	Local Fave	Lafayette	$$–$$$	Grilled seafood	301
Creole Lunch House	Down Home	Lafayette	$	Stuffed bread, soul food	301
Dwyer's Café	Down Home	Lafayette	$	Heaping plate lunches	297
Edie's	Down Home	Lafayette	$	Plate lunches/ potpies	303
Judice Inn	Local Fave	Lafayette	$	'40s burger stand	299
Old Tyme Grocery	Local Fave	Lafayette	$	Best po' boys in town	300
T–Coons	Down Home	Lafayette	$	Tasty plate lunches	297

Within 30 minutes of Lafayette

Restaurant	Type	Town	Price	Comments	Page
Bayou Boudin & Cracklin	Local Fave	Breaux Bridge	$	Sunday lunch	254
Black's	Seafood	Abbeville	$–$$	Great oysters & chowder	329
Café Des Amis	Cajun/Creole	Breaux Bridge	$–$$	Great food & ambiance	254
Catahoula's	Cajun/Creole	Grand Coteau	$$–$$$	Fine regional dining	320
Dupuy's	Seafood	Abbeville	$–$$	Great oysters since 1800s	329
Hebert's	Meat Market	Maurice	$	Stuffed/deboned chickens	323
Norbert's	Down Home	Broussard	$	Soulful lunch joint	303
Prudhomme's Cajun Café	Cajun/Creole	Carencro	$–$$	Classic Cajun, oyster loaf	304
Richard's	Boiled Seafood	Abbeville	$$	Rustic crawfish joint	331
Rowena's Market	Meat Market	Sunset	$	Rich & spicy boudin	321
Shucks!	Seafood	Abbeville	$–$$	Cold oysters & po' boys	330

Within 30 minutes of Opelousas and Eunice

Restaurant	Type	Town	Price	Comments	Page
Deshotel's ("Dez")	Meat Market	Ville Platte	$	Rich & spicy boudin	386
Joe's Restaurant	Cajun/Creole	Livonia	$–$$	Great food & value	338
Johnson's Grocery	Meat Market	Eunice	$	Best boudin!	373
Jungle Dinner Club	Boiled Seafood	Ville Platte	$$	Extra super hot crawfish	386
Mathilda's	Down Home	Eunice	$	BBQ, sweet-dough pies	375
The Palace Cafe	Local Fave	Opelousas	$–$$	'50s-style diner	349
Pelican	Down Home	Eunice	$	Sunday lunch spectacular	375
Pig Stand	Down Home	Ville Platte	$	BBQ, lunches & dinners	387
Ruby's Cafe	Down Home	Eunice	$	Hoppin' lunch joint	375
Steamboat Warehouse	Cajun/Creole	Washington	$$–$$$	On Bayou Courtableau	359

Western Cajun Country

Restaurant	Type	Town	Price	Comments	Page
Boudin King	Down Home	Jennings	$	Fast-food style Cajun	412
D.I.'s	Boiled Seafood	Basile	$$	Great crawfish, dancing	390
Granger's	Seafood	Lake Charles	$–$$	Wild place, good crawfish	426
Hawk's	Boiled Seafood	Roberts Cove	$$	Best crawfish	399
Miller's Café	Down Home	Lake Charles	$	Soul food	426
Suire's Store	Down Home	Kaplan	$	Lunch, turtle sauce piquante	401

Front-porch musicians in Opelousas. (Photo by Julie Posner)

7

Music

Be it Cajun, Zydeco, or Swamp Pop, the native music of Acadiana is the antithesis of the planned-out, self-conscious, commercial pap piped onto TV screens at urban discos and rock clubs. It is the music of working people, young and old, who love to dance and have a special knack for having fun.

The most astonishing thing about the traditional music of Cajun Country is how vibrant and how much a part of life it continues to be. Finding great regional music in Acadiana is almost as simple as rolling down the car window or spinning the dial on the radio. On weekends music pours from aging dance halls and bars in tiny Prairie towns like Lewisburg, Parks, and Mamou. It is played at festivals, Cajun restaurants, and church socials where the entire family can come and dance. It can even be heard in a smattering of country bars at nine o'clock in the morning on Saturdays! While a few Cajun and Zydeco artists have gained acclaim through Grammy nominations and club performances outside the state, the vast majority never leave the flat-pan Cajun Prairie where their records, recorded for tiny regional record labels, are played on radio and jukeboxes.

CAJUN MUSIC

Despite its current popularity, Cajun music has evolved through some lean years. Around the turn of the century Cajun was a predominantly fiddle based music played at house dances (*bals de maison*) and *fais-do-dos* (named for the separate room where children could be rocked to sleep). In the early 1900s, the diatonic accordion was adopted and by the thirties the music began to move out of homes and into dance halls and bars.

Traditional Cajun music suffered its first major blow at this time, when popular swing and country styles heard on the radio supplanted the older styles. The accordion was abandoned in favor of electric and steel guitars. In the late forties accordion-based music enjoyed a brief renaissance, spurred by Cajun hero Iry Lejeune. The boom was short-lived, however, as the banning of French in public schools, the oil boom, and improved roads and communication began to take a toll on traditional Cajun folkways. By the Eisenhower era "Cajun" had become a mainly deprecatory term and the music, like the Cajun-French language, was shunned by socially conscious Cajuns and non-Cajuns alike.

The flowering of Cajun music since the sixties can be attributed to many influences: folklorists who brought artists like Dewey Balfa before a national audience, stubbornly independent Cajun record men, the Council on Development of French in Louisiana, and the musicians who never gave up. Due to the efforts of these people, the music can now be heard in a wide variety of styles and venues. Whether it is a fiddle and squeeze-box waltz, pounding piano-accordion rock, or pedal-steel swing, Cajun music is still dance music made by working people who play as hard as they labor.

ZYDECO MUSIC

If you want to have fun you got to go way out in the country to the Zydeco.

Clarence ("Bon Ton") Garlow
from "Bon Ton Roule," 1950

You no longer need to go to Cajun Country at all to hear the highly rhythmic dance music of South Louisiana's black Creole population. Still, when you pull up behind the strip of cars and pickups lining a narrow blacktop and hear the grating of the rubboard or sound of an accordion drifting from an open door, you will know why Clarence Garlow directed everyone "way out in the country to the Zydeco." There is no place like the sprawling dance halls and ramshackle bars of South Louisiana to catch a big Zydeco dance.

Although several Creole musicians recorded in the 1920s and 1930s (in a style quite similar to Cajun musicians of the era), Zydeco music did not become a commercial entity until the years following World War II. Until that time Zydeco, like Cajun music, was played mainly at house parties and community social events across the countryside. The word "Zydeco" is believed to be phonetically derived from the French words *les haricots,* which were used in an old French blues song popularized by Clifton Chenier, "*Les Haricots Sont Pas Salés,*" translated as, "The snap beans have no salt." The song was about times so hard that there was no seasoning meat for the pot.

Like Cajun music, Zydeco has evolved since the early days, moving from house parties to dance halls and bars and adopting such

The late Cleveland and Clifton Chenier. (Courtesy of Ann Savoy)

nontraditional instruments as the saxophone, electric guitar, bass, and drums. If anything, the Zydeco scene today is even more vibrant than its Cajun counterpart. The success of Rockin' Sidney with his quasi-Zydeco national hit, "My Toot Toot," and the adulation heaped on the late Clifton Chenier have made the music attractive to a new generation of musicians. These youngsters have brought new ideas to Zydeco while maintaining its pounding Afro-Caribbean dance groove. Today the fiddle is seldom heard, as most songs are powered by a piano-style accordion and rasping *frottoir,* or rubboard. The rubboard is easily the most distinctive instrument in Zydeco music and a source of much of its energy. Fashioned after the old corrugated washboards, they are crafted in sheet-metal shops with curved metal shoulder straps. The rubboard hangs down over the chest and leaves both hands free to strike and scrape the surface with bottle openers.

SWAMP POP

Although Swamp Pop artists have sold millions of records (far surpassing their Cajun and Zydeco counterparts), Swamp Pop remains the least recognized and respected of South Louisiana's indigenous musics. Swamp Pop is a new term used to describe the distinctive South Louisiana rock-and-roll ballad style popularized in the late fifties and early sixties. The music is a blend of New Orleans R&B, Country, and Gulf Coast Blues sung with a Cajun French accent. Between 1959 and 1963 over fifteen of these distinctive records climbed onto the Billboard Top 100, while hundreds of others filled jukeboxes and radio playlists across the Gulf South. Although the name "Swamp Pop" may be unfamiliar to many, hits like "Mathilda," by Cookie and the Cupcakes; "This Should Go On Forever," by Rod Bernard; "Sea of Love," by Phil Phillips; "I'm Leaving It Up to You," by Dale and Grace; and "Sweet Dreams," by Tommy McLain remain some of the best-loved songs of the rock-and-roll era.

Incredibly, many of the great singers and musicians of Swamp Pop are still making music in the obscurity of the Lafayette and Lake Charles lounge scenes. In motel lounges and hideaway bars, artists like Warren Storm, Tommy McLain, T. K. Hulin, and Lil' Alfred are still performing their own songs and country hits in front of packed dance floors. These are the unsung heroes of South Louisiana music, plugging away five to six nights a week in smoky bars. Although songs like "Mathilda" have become veritable Cajun anthems, there is no new generation picking up the Swamp Pop torch. If you get the opportunity be sure to see one of these fine singers.

SOUTH LOUISIANA MUSIC MECCAS

Record Stores and Studios of Cajun Country

Remember the days when you could walk into a record store, pick out a forty-five, and listen to it before you bought it? How many people remember when records were sold from TV repair shops, instrument stores, and retail outlets tacked onto the front of recording studios? For those who do remember, South Louisiana will offer a step into the past.

Since the late forties a handful of stubbornly independent local "record men" (producers, distributors, and retailers) have catered to the musicians and music fans of Acadiana from little shops and studios. The continued operation of three of these homegrown enterprises (within a 150-square-mile area!) in an era dominated by huge record companies, MTV, and mass marketing speaks volumes about the special nature of the regional music scene. Although all of these tiny companies have had a glimmer of national success, it is the recording and sales of records never distributed outside of the region that has sustained them. South Louisiana is still an area where strictly local records get played on the radio and there is still such a thing as a "regional hit record" or a "jukebox hit."

Most South Louisiana record men do mail-order business, but a real treat awaits those who make the pilgrimage to visit the storefronts that invariably adjoin small studios or offices. Not only do these places offer a chance to find recordings unavailable anyplace else in the world, they often afford the opportunity to meet and chat with the enterprising men who have helped make decades of South Louisiana music. Like the pot-bellied stoves in country stores, the counters at these shops are often pulpits for bull sessions, but of a musical nature. There is usually a stereo available to play any of the obscure goodies you find, and you are likely to get a dose of gossip on how the record was made (and how drunk the musicians were at the time). Guys like Eddie Shuler, who operates Goldband Records out of his Quick Service TV Repair Shop, can tell you about legendary musicians like Iry Lejeune or Cleveland Crochet. Or you can go to Ville Platte and talk to Floyd Soileau about the year he had two records in the Billboard Top Twenty! A visit to one or all of these stores is essential for the fan of South Louisiana music.

Cajun and Zydeco Radio Shows

While DJs elsewhere in the nation are bound to rigid playlists, many

Live radio broadcast from Church Point. (Photo by Julie Posner)

shows in Cajun Country cater to local tastes. Regional hits are still made on the power of radio shows beaming locally produced records across the Prairie. Many shows are broadcast entirely in French, with only nonconforming words like "McDonald's," "Ford," and "rock and roll" popping out in English. Saturday and Sunday are the best days to find regional music and French-language broadcasts on the radio. Only KBON (101.1 FM) in Eunice is offering a format of all regional favorites (Cajun, Zydeco, Country, and Soul) throughout the week.

WHERE TO FIND CAJUN AND ZYDECO MUSIC
Old-Style Cajun Dance Halls

The old dance halls of Cajun Country are surely the most interesting places to listen and dance to Cajun and Zydeco music. Some of these, like Smiley's Bon Ami in Delcambre, have big dance floors and host Sunday-afternoon dances for an older clientele. Others, like Borque's in Lewisburg or Snook's in Ville Platte, are barrooms connected to small dance halls. It is free to sit in the bar (and watch through open windows), but usually costs $2 to enter and dance. Unlike the energetic dancing you see at urban dance halls, the movement of many of the old-timers here seems more like gliding across the floor. Most Cajun and Zydeco musicians and their audiences are working people, so old-time dances are usually held on weekends. See the list at the end of this chapter for recommended old-time dance halls.

Restaurant-Dance Halls, Music for the Family

During the thirties and forties bars and dance halls that barred minors began to supplant house parties and fais-do-dos. In recent years a new kind of venue, the restaurant-dance hall, has offered Cajun dance enthusiasts of all ages a chance to enjoy the music. Restaurants like Mulate's in Breaux Bridge, Randol's in Lafayette, and D.I.'s in Basile are now among the most popular dance halls, attracting locals, tourists, and serious dance fanatics. These halls offer a dependable schedule of music throughout the week, on days when the traditional dance halls are quiet. The chart at the end of this chapter lists recommended restaurant-dance halls.

Zydeco Dance Halls

Today's Zydeco dance halls maintain strong ties to the community;

when you first walk into one you are more likely to feel as though you have entered a house party than a nightclub. Halls like Hamilton's in Lafayette and Double D in Parks are operated by the same families that ran them thirty or more years ago. Often the proprietors live adjacent to the hall and maintain barbecue pits out back. I remember the first dance I went to at Papa Paul's; by the time Marcel Dugas had finished his set, the smoke from Papa's Barbecue was literally wafting into the dance hall. Admission is usually $4 or $5 and most places welcome "outsiders." The best way to show your appreciation is to get up and dance! Several recommended Zydeco dance halls are listed on the chart at the end of this chapter.

Cajun and Zydeco Special Events

Along with restaurant-dance halls there are many weekly and annual events and festivals that offer music and dancing for the whole family. The most popular of the weekly events are the Downtown Alive street dance in Lafayette and the Roundez Vous des Cajuns in Eunice. Thousands of regional-music fans kick up their heels at the annual Festival de Musique Acadien and Plaisance Zydeco Festival.

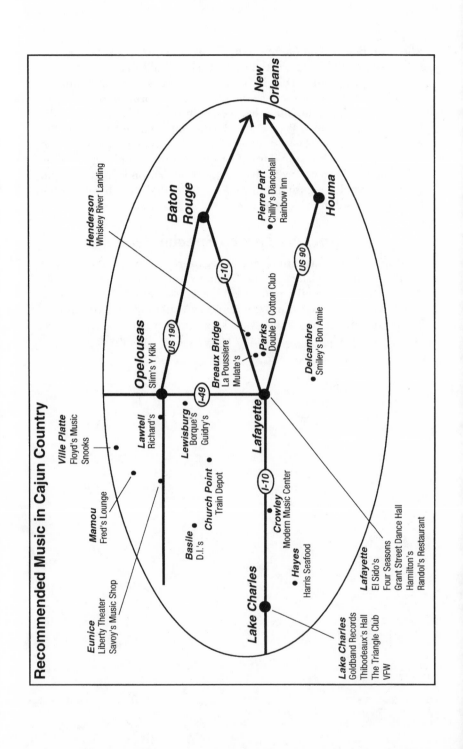

Recommended Music in Cajun Country

New Orleans

Henderson
Whiskey River Landing

Baton Rouge

Pierre Part
• Chilly's Dancehall
Rainbow Inn

Houma

US 90

I-10

Opelousas
Slim's Y Kiki

US 190

Parks
Double D Cotton Club

Breaux Bridge
La Poussiere
Mulate's

Delcambre
• Smiley's Bon Amie

Ville Platte
Floyd's Music
Snooks

Lawtell
Richard's

I-49

Lafayette

Eunice
Liberty Theater
Savoy's Music Shop

Mamou
Fred's Lounge

Lewisburg
• Borque's
Guidry's

Basile
• D.I.'s

Church Point
Train Depot

I-10

Crowley
• Modern Music Center

Lafayette
El Sido's
Four Seasons
Grant Street Dance Hall
Hamilton's
Randol's Restaurant

Hayes
• Harris Seafood

Lake Charles

Lake Charles
Goldband Records
Thibodeaux's Hall
The Triangle Club
VFW

Recommended Music

Central: Lafayette and Breaux Bridge Area

Place	Music	Town	Comments	Page
La Poussiere	Cajun	Breaux Bridge	Old dancehall, Sat.	258
Mulate's	Cajun	Breaux Bridge	Dine & dance nightly	258
Smiley's Bon Ami	Cajun	Erath	Cajun dancehall	335
Whiskey River Landing	Cajun	Henderson	Dance on Basin, Sun.	267
El Sido's	Zydeco	Lafayette	Urban dancehall	306
Four Seasons	Swamp Pop	Lafayette	Lounge, Wed.–Sun.	311
Grant Street Dancehall	Eclectic	Lafayette	Tipitina's–style	309
Hamilton's	Zydeco	Lafayette	Old dancehall	307
Randol's Restaurant	Cajun	Lafayette	Dine & dance nightly	308
Double D Cotton Club	Zydeco	Parks	Country dancehall	257

Morgan City Area

Place	Music	Town	Comments	Page
Chilly's Dancehall	Cajun, Swamp Pop	Pierre Part	On Lake Verret	195
Rainbow Inn	Swamp Pop	Pierre Part	'30s dancehall	195

Heartland: Opelousas, Eunice, Ville Platte

Place	Music	Town	Comments	Page
Train Depot	Cajun	Church Point	Jam session in depot	367
Liberty Theater	Cajun	Eunice	Broadcast Sat. 6 PM	369
Savoy's Music Center	Cajun	Eunice	Jam session, Sat. 10 AM	377
Richard's Club	Zydeco	Lawtell	Rustic dancehall	351
Borque's	Cajun	Lewisburg	Country dancehall/bar	366
Guidry's Lounge	Cajun	Lewisburg	Country dancehall/bar	366
Fred's Lounge	Cajun	Mamou	Broadcast Sat. 9 AM	381
Slim's Y–Ki–Ki	Zydeco	Opelousas	Old dancehall	350
Floyd's Record Store	Store	Ville Platte	Swallow Records	388
Snook's Bar	Swamp Pop	Ville Platte	Funky dancehall & bar	389

Western: Crowley to Lake Charles

Place	Music	Town	Comments	Page
Modern Music	Store	Crowley	Master Trak Records	403
Harris Seafood	Cajun	Hayes	Dine /Dance Wed.–Sat.	415
Goldband Records	Store/studio	Lake Charles	Home of Goldband	428
Thibodeaux's Hall	Zydeco	Lake Charles	'30s dancehall	430
Triangle Club	Swamp Pop	Lake Charles	'50s dancehall	420
VFW Post	Cajun	Lake Charles	Dance Sat. 8 PM	430

Roadside fishing. (Photo by Julie Posner)

8

Recreation

SWAMP TOURS

The most exotic of Cajun Country's sights are its freshwater swamps. To visit South Louisiana and not get a close-up view of its wetlands is like staying in a camp on the rim of the Grand Canyon and not looking out the window! Over a dozen tour companies now offer inexpensive excursions into places where you will find alligators, nutria, snakes, turtles, and all manner of creatures that are equally comfortable on land or water. In the deeper swamp, where palmetto and muscadine vines darken shadows beneath ancient cypress trees, one can hear the questioning call of horned owls and the cry of an eagle. Cypress knees touch tendrils of hanging moss. The turn of a bayou can display miles of bristling marsh or an open lake studded with cypress stumps and carpeted with American lotus blossoms.

Each tour offers something different depending on the guide, type of boat, and particular route. Many are aimed at families and tour buses. These tours glide through bayous and lakes on big, covered pontoon boats. Some of the best tours are on small boats or airboats (note, airboats can be very loud), which can get to places inaccessible to bigger craft. Many tours engage in the questionable practice of feeding alligators and these have been noted.

When to Go

What you see in the swamps depends largely on what time of day and what season you visit. A few tours offer flexible departure times. These are recommended, as they will allow you to leave in the especially serene morning and evening hours. If you are looking for alligators, any warm-weather month should do. Late fall and late spring are ideal times for viewing migratory birds. Something is always blooming except in the cold months of December through February. In March you will see wild iris, spider lilies, and dogwoods. By

73

early spring millions of hyacinth blossoms begin to choke off smaller waterways. In midsummer the towering stalks of American lotus produce gigantic yellow blossoms.

Remember, even if a tour operator offers regularly scheduled excursions, it is always recommended to *call first!* Tour availability may be affected by high water, weather conditions, or the sudden booking of a large group.

Recommended Swamp Tours

The following swamp tours are my favorites. Many other tours are offered; they are all listed in the index and reviewed in the text.

Airboats Tours, Inc.; 40 minutes from Lafayette. (318) 229-4457. Departs by appointment. Cost $10 for one-hour tour ($40 minimum). $20 for two-hour tour ($60 minimum). Airboat. French-speaking guide.

Atchafalaya Backwater Tours; 30 minutes from Houma. (504) 575-2371. Departs twice daily. Cost $20 for two-hour tour ($40 minimum). Small boat.

Atchafalaya Experience Swamp Tours; 20 minutes from Lafayette. (318) 233-7816. Departs by appointment. Cost $30. Small boat. French-speaking guide.

Cajun Man Swamp Tours; 15 minutes from Houma. (504) 868-4625. Cost $15 to $20 for two-hour tour. Covered pontoon boat. Feeds gators. French-speaking guide.

de la Houssaye's Swamp Tours; 20 minutes from Lafayette. (318) 228-2557. Departs twice daily except Sunday. Cost $20. Small boat.

Scully's; Morgan City. (504) 385-2388. Cost $15 to $20. Small boat or covered pontoon boat. Guide speaks some French.

FISHING

For the recreational fisherman Louisiana lives up to its motto, "The Sportsman's Paradise." Cajun Country has the widest variety of fresh- and saltwater fishing anywhere in the world. There are too many fishing places to list even the best ones! The city of Houma alone has over twenty-five boat launches and as many fishing charters. A good day or morning of fishing, crabbing, or castnetting can be as simple as pulling your car over, stepping out the door, and wetting a line.

Fishing Charters

There are three types of charters: freshwater (swamp), inside water (marsh), and offshore. Because most charters leave from remote locations there are no inexpensive and regularly scheduled hook-and-line expeditions. Offshore fishing usually means excursions to the oil rigs that dot coastal waters. These have legs reaching hundreds of feet down to the bottom that form man-made reefs that attract everything from red snapper to sharks. Offshore charters are generally the most expensive. Costs may range from $100 to $200 per person.

Inside-water (marsh) and freshwater expeditions are quicker and less expensive. Inside trips afford a chance to latch onto redfish and speckled trout while freshwater charters target bass, *sac-a-lait,* and bream. Costs for inside charters may range from $50 to $150 per person.

Finding a Charter

Most tourist bureaus in Cajun Country have complete lists and brochures of fishing charters in their area.

Louisiana Charter Boat Association: Private association of charter operators across South Louisiana (saltwater only). (318) 598-3268.

Louisiana Department of Recreation and Tourism: 1-800-33-GUMBO.

Southwest Louisiana Visitors Commission: Charters south of Lake Charles. 1-800-456-SWLA.

Lafourche Department of Recreation and Tourism: Charters leaving Leeville, Grand Isle, and elsewhere on Bayou Lafourche.

Houma-Terrebonne Visitors Commission: Charters south of Houma. 1-800-688-2732.

Iberia Parish Tourist Commission: Freshwater excursions into the Atchafalaya Basin Swamp. (318) 365-1540.

Shore-Fishing Spots

Grand Isle	*Rockefeller Refuge*
Point Aux Chenes	*Creole Nature Trail*
Cypremort Point	*Holly Beach*
Salt Point	*Cocodrie*

For more information see index.

Fishing Rules and Regulations

Size limits, creel limits, the cost of fishing licenses, and other regulations pertaining to recreational fishing are subject to frequent change and should be verified before you plan a trip by calling the State Department of Wildlife and Fisheries. Two-day and one-week fishing permits are available for $26 to $60. Fees are lower if you are going on a licensed charter; inquire from your charter captain.

Department of Wildlife and Fisheries: (504) 765-2496.

WAGERING SPORTS

It is not surprising that the Louisiana legislature finally approved a state lottery, video poker, and riverboat-casino gambling in the nineties (see gambling in the index for more on the casinos). The state has a history of tolerance for gambling that goes well with its reputation for political hijinks. Folks hardly noticed when former governor Edwin Edwards (the only Cajun governor in the twentieth century) organized a gambling junket to Monte Carlo to help pay his campaign debts. The most common wagering sports in Cajun Country are horse racing, cards, and cockfighting. All three of these are traditional pursuits in the region that date back to the colonial era.

Breeding fighting cocks. (Photo by Julie Posner)

Horse Racing

Kentucky is most famous for producing fine racehorses, but South Louisiana breeds championship jockeys. Eddie Delahoussaye (a two-time Kentucky Derby winner), Randy Romero, and Ray Sibille are just a few of the great Cajun jocks who have emerged on the national scene. Until Evangeline Downs opened in 1966, most horse-racing activity in Cajun Country took place on weekends at "bush tracks" behind country estates. These rude tracks were the proving grounds for the jockeys who have risen to national prominence and were vital community gathering spots for most of a century. Of the dozens of bush tracks that once proliferated in Cajun Country, the only track we found still operating regularly was Clem's in Abbeville, which has races on a very sporadic basis.

The bush tracks of Cajun Country disappeared mainly as a result of the opening of Evangeline Downs Thoroughbred Track and Delta Downs Quarterhorse and Thoroughbred Track, both of which have pari-mutuel betting and offtrack windows. Evangeline Downs is the premier track in Cajun Country, located just north of Lafayette in Carencro. The smaller Delta Downs, in extreme western Cajun Country, has the informal ambiance of a bush track. Some folks carry in lawn chairs. For more information on these tracks, consult the index.

Cockfighting

Louisiana is one of six states in the nation that still permit cock-fighting in some areas. Naturally there has been an outcry by animal rights activists against the activity, but state legislators (using the polit-ical savvy for which Louisiana politicians are famous) managed to declare that game fowl are not animals and therefore not subject to animal cruelty laws! Cockfighting is a particularly strong tradition in the rural parishes of Cajun Country, where the techniques of breed-ing, raising, conditioning, and fighting have been passed along within families from generation to generation.

Whether you visit a cockpit or not, you are likely to see game fowl being raised throughout the region. Because the birds are prone to attacking each other they are kept tethered to individual domiciles. A cock breeder can be identified by a yard covered with small teepees made of corrugated steel with cocks leashed to them.

A typical cockpit has a bar and lounge in the front. The pit itself can be as primitive as a barn but is usually a small arena with bleacher seating. Violence is generally confined to the birds in the fenced ring, and most pits attract a wide array of couples, families, and cockfight fanatics who come to make private wagers. These wagers are conveyed before and during the fight in indecipherable yells and hand gestures across the pit.

Fights are held in tournaments where trainers are required to enter a certain number of birds, which are paired by weight. The birds are equipped with razor-sharp spurs that are affixed to their natural heel spurs by leather thongs. The fights are presided over by a referee and follow clearly established written rules. A fight is over after one of the fowls attacks and the other refuses to fight for a specified number of consecutive pairings.

Due to the controversy over animal rights, cockers and pit owners are naturally a bit suspicious of outsiders, and forbid cameras in the pit area. There are, however, a couple of pits that are open to the public (usually for a $5 to $10 admission). For more information on these, refer to the index.

Cards

Nearly every town in Southwest Louisiana has a card bar. Many times I have entered a crowded club expecting to find a band playing and instead discovered a half-dozen tables of card sharps. By far the most popular game played at these bars, and in household gatherings around Cajun Country, is Bourré. There are a few popular variations on this game. Around Upper Lafourche country there are a half-dozen bars where a version called Pedro is the only game in the house.

BIKING

You don't have to be an Olympic athlete to take a bike tour in Cajun Country. The terrain is predominantly flat, so the main concern is climate. The best time to tour the region on bike or otherwise is in fall or spring, with fall being the drier of the two. The *Cajun Country Guide* should be equally useful to bicyclists and motorists. Many of the same areas and routes that are attractive for auto touring are also excellent on two wheels; bicyclists must use caution because most of the roads in Cajun Country are narrow, substandard, or have little shoulder. To avoid roads altogether you may ride atop the levees (packed dirt, gravel, and shell surface) that follow River Road and the Atchafalaya Basin. Campers may set up their tents on the green space at the foot of the levees.

Biking Tours

Pack and Paddle; 601 E. Pinhook Rd., Lafayette, La. 70501. (318) 232-5854. Joan Williams, the owner and manager of this outdoors store, is the number-one biking enthusiast in Cajun Country. She offers guided group tours to all the regions in this book. The tours include meals at restaurants, accommodations, and entrance fees at plantations.

A brochure detailing the Pack and Paddle tours is available free upon request. For the rider who wants a book with exact miles between each attraction and each turn, Joan Williams has published a bicycle guide to Cajun Country, *Backroad Tours of French Louisiana.*

HIKING

With the exception of the trails at Chicot State Park, none of the hiking paths in Cajun Country is over five miles long. The landscape is either too wet or given over to agricultural use. Most of the hiking referred to in this book is therefore of the casual day-trip variety. Some of the better paths are at Acadiana Park Nature Station in Lafayette, Lake Martin, Louisiana State Arboretum near Ville Platte, Magnolia Ridge Plantation in Washington, and Lake Fausse Pointe State Park near St. Martinville. Refer to these in the index for more detailed information.

BIRD WATCHING

Louisiana possesses several attributes that make it one of the best states in the nation for bird watching. It is located on the Mississippi Flyway, a busy thoroughfare for migrating birds, and it gets plenty of traffic from the Central Flyway. Cajun Country in particular encompasses a wild and wide variety of habitat types from beaches and open water to swamps, forests, and prairie.

Over 400 species of birds frequent the region, and it is not uncommon for birding parties to record a day's total of 100 to 150 species. Although South Louisiana is "birdable" throughout the year, spring is the most rewarding season. A cold front in April or early May often forces birds migrating north across the Gulf of Mexico to land in the first available trees. In this type of "fall out" the coastal woods and *cheniers* are boiling with warblers, vireos, tanagers, buntings, grosbeaks, and other perching birds, while the mudflats and marshes are carpeted by migrating shorebirds. (Above bird-watching text supplied by noted Louisiana expert Bill Vermilion. Used with permission.)

Prime Bird-Watching Areas and Contacts

Western Cajun Country: Cameron Parish is generally considered to be the best bird-watching area in Louisiana. It has the coastal woods needed for the spring "fall out" phenomenon plus lakes, marsh, beach, and mudflats. Cameron Parish includes such sites as Sabine, Cameron Prairie, Lacassine, and Rockefeller wildlife refuges, as well as the Proveto Woods Bird Sanctuary. Contact:

Gulf Coast Bird Club; Cameron/Lake Charles. Marianna Tanner. (318) 775-5347.

Southwest Louisiana Visitors Bureau; Lake Charles. 1-800-456-SWLA.

Central and Teche Regions: Many birding spots are located within 45 minutes of Lafayette; some of the best are Vincent Wildlife Refuge, Lake Martin Rookery, Avery and Jefferson Island, and Atchafalaya Basin levees. Contact:

Louisiana Birders Anonymous; Lafayette. Dave Patton. (318) 232-8410.

Acadiana Park Nature Station; Lafayette. Bill Fontenot. (318) 291-8448.

Bayou Country: Highways south of Houma, Fourchon Beach, and Jetties and Grand Isle provide good birding close to New Orleans. Contact:

Houma/Terrebonne Bird Club. Dave Coignet. (504) 594-2722.

Statewide Information:

Louisiana Ornithological Society. Dave Patton. (318) 232-8410.

Birders Hotline (rare-bird alert, news, field trips). (318) 988-9898.

Birders Hotline; Baton Rouge Audubon Society.

9

Transportation

AIR CONNECTIONS

Most visitors arrive in Cajun Country by way of New Orleans or Houston, cities with busy international airports. Flying into Lafayette has grown more economical since the mideighties, and rates into Lafayette Regional Airport are now competitive (sometimes better) than they are into Baton Rouge, Houston, or New Orleans. It may be worth comparing prices. None of the major airline subsidiaries (listed below) offers jet service into Lafayette at present.

American Eagle (800) 433-7300   Service to/from Dallas/
                                                                  Fort Worth

Continental Express (800) 525-0280   Service to/from Houston

Northwest Airlink (800) 225-2525   Service to/from Memphis

Atlantic Southeast (800) 282-3424   Service to/from Atlanta,
                                                                  Meridian

BY CAR

The best way to see Cajun Country is by car. Whether you are flying into Houston, New Orleans, Lafayette, or Baton Rouge you will want to rent a vehicle on arrival. Interstate 10 and Interstate 49, the two primary highways in South Louisiana, intersect in the hub city of Lafayette. Interstate 10, connecting New Orleans and Houston, is by far the busiest. The speed limit is 65 miles per hour on the interstates, except in developed areas, where it drops to 55, so driving time to Lafayette from Houston is about three and a half hours and from New Orleans about two and a half hours.

The best reason to travel I-10 between Lafayette and the state capital of Baton Rouge is to cross the spectacular twenty-mile Atchafalaya Swamp Throughway, the most costly stretch of interstate in the nation.

Of course the object is not to drive through, but to see Cajun

Country, so I recommend that east-west travelers consider taking U.S. 90, U.S. 190, or Rte. 14. The speed limit on these good two-lane routes is 55 miles per hour and traffic is light. If you have time to travel the Bayou Country between Lafayette and New Orleans, you will want to take Rte. 182 along Bayou Teche whenever possible (about two hours slower than I-10).

BY RAIL

Lafayette is served by Amtrak's Sunset Limited, which travels between Jacksonville, Florida and Los Angeles, California. Westbound trains arrive in Lafayette at 6:27 P.M. on Sunday, Wednesday, and Friday. Eastbound trains arrive on Sunday, Tuesday, and Thursday at 1:26 P.M. For specific information and rates, call Amtrak at (800) 872-7245.

BY BUS

Greyhound Bus Lines serves most of the larger towns in Cajun Country. There is frequent service daily between New Orleans and Houston, with connections in Houma, Lafayette, and Lake Charles. From Lafayette there is one bus a day to Eunice and a few to Opelousas. Call Greyhound for fare and schedule information, (800) 231-2222.

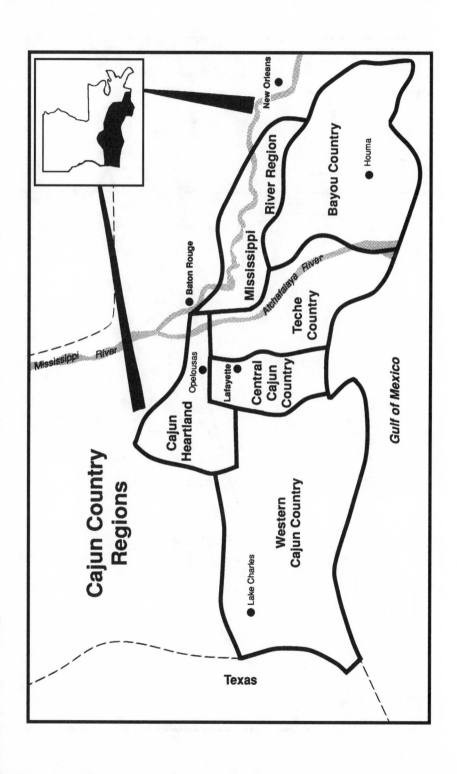

Cajun Country Regions

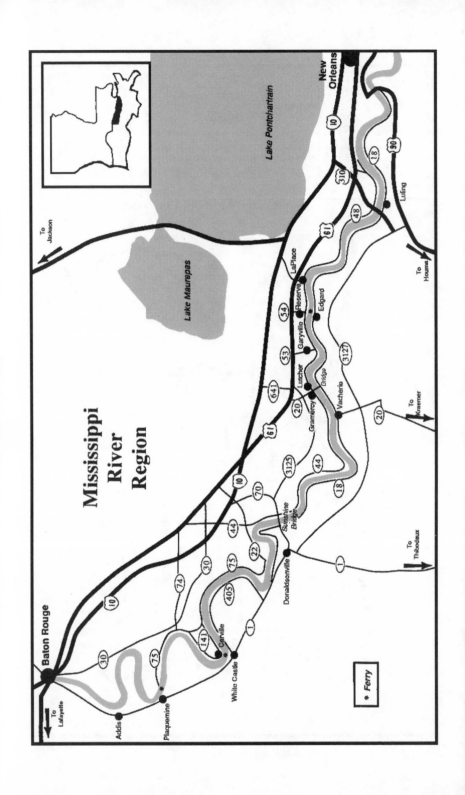

10

Mississippi River Region

The Great River Road offers an opportunity to go from a plantation tour to a plant tour, sample rich Creole and Cajun cuisine, and stay the night in some of the grandest domiciles ever constructed in America. There are many mythical stretches of highway in America, but none with the allure of this ancient road, clinging to the banks of America's mightiest stream. Indians, steamboat captains, and planters (who were at one time the nation's wealthiest class) have all coveted River Road addresses. Even today the narrow two-lane route is second in popularity only to New Orleans as a Louisiana tourist attraction. Because the river's main course is southward, its banks and the two adjacent River Roads are defined as "east" and "west." This makes sense, except in Cajun Country. Between New Orleans and Baton Rouge the river actually follows a mainly west-to-east course. Thus, attractions heading upriver from New Orleans are described as "west," despite the fact that the banks of the stream are still known as "east bank" and "west bank"!

The Mississippi, one of the three great rivers of the world, is the dominant force shaping life along the eastern border of Cajun Country. Since Indian times the river has been the focus of trade and industry and its natural levees have provided the high ground for successive waves of settlement. When the first white settlers arrived in New Orleans, they quickly moved upriver, establishing farms along the narrow swaths of raised earth on either side of the mighty stream. Among the early settlers were the first wave of Acadian immigrants, who arrived in 1765 and made their homes on the West Bank of St. James Parish along what became known as the Acadian Coast. The Acadians did not last long on this prized ground, and like the Indians were swept into the swamps to the west by the growth of the sugarcane and lumber industries and the influx of a wealthy European and Anglo planter class.

In the late eighteenth century, the river was the arterial highway of the western frontier and planters took advantage of busy riverboat traffic to ship raw goods to market in New Orleans. After the

War Between the States, the planter class, like the Acadians, was pushed aside by the arrival of lumber, petroleum, and the petrochemical industries. The remnants of these waves of settlement are everywhere, visible as you drive along the River Roads and Airline Highway (Rte. 61). There are old abandoned Acadian homes, stately plantation houses, and crumbling sharecroppers' shacks. The area is mainly rural and poor. Towns like Lutcher and Garyville, once lumber-mill communities, still sport company-built houses and networks of rail beds once used to pull cypress from the swamps. Dwarfing them are the stacks of huge chemical plants that have given the area its latest notoriety as "the cancer corridor of America."

TRAVEL TIPS

This chapter is organized in a linear fashion, tracing each river road from New Orleans to just south of Baton Rouge, with the few attractions on the adjacent Airline Highway (east bank) included in the continuum. At the end of the two sections you will find a list of restaurants and accommodations reviewed within. For those planning to take the River Roads all the way from New Orleans to Baton Rouge, it is important to remember that these are winding routes that can take over three hours to drive! To budget your time, plan no more than three plantation tours in one day with stops for lunch and leg stretching. For expediency and a varied view, it is recommended that travelers switch among the four main routes of the region: Interstate 10, Airline Highway (Rte. 61), and the east-bank and west-bank courses of River Road. The River Roads change route numbers along the way, but generally follow the fifteen- to twenty-foot-tall river levees. There is no view of the river from your car, so you may want to take advantage of the ferry service between the two banks or walk the levee for a glimpse of river traffic.

RIVER ROAD EAST BANK

This section is arranged in a linear east-to-west format traveling up River Road from New Orleans. At the end of the section you will find a list of restaurants and accommodations reviewed. The quickest way to reach the lower limits of the River Roads is to take I-10 west from the city and exit at I-310 south, just past the New Orleans Airport. You may get off I-310 on the East River Road at St. Rose or continue across the Hale Boggs Bridge to the West River Road. Alternately you may take Rte. 61 (Airline Highway) north from New Orleans. Three miles past the airport turn left on Rte. 50 (Almedia Road). Go one mile to reach River Road, which is labeled as Rte. 48 at this juncture.

★Destrehan Plantation River Road, St. Rose (I-10 exit #220).

Destrehan is two miles above St. Rose and a half-mile south of I-310. Built in 1787, it is the oldest plantation home in the lower Mississippi Valley. Twin wings were added to either side of the house in 1810 and a Greek Revival facade was built about ten years later, but otherwise the structure is in its original configuration. A forty-five-minute tour of the house begins with a short video depicting its history and appearance before renovations began. Upstairs living quarters are elegantly furnished with period antiques. One room has been left unfinished, its walls and ceilings opened to expose original construction techniques.

The history of Destrehan speaks of the changing character of the region. Following the War Between the States, the plantation was bought by Mexican Petroleum and was the site of an Amoco refinery through the midtwentieth century. When Amoco closed the refinery, the house fell apart. The petroleum giant has been instrumental in restoring the plantation. A Spring Plantation Festival with food and craft booths is held the first weekend in May. A Fall Festival occurs the second weekend in November. Tours are from 9 to 4 daily, except major holidays. Cost is $7 for adults, $4 for teens and seniors, and $2 for children. The last tour begins at 4. (504) 764-9315.

Ormond Plantation River Road just above St. Rose (I-10 exit #220).

Ormond Plantation (.5 mile above I-310) is a good example of how owners go about destroying the original character of a plantation home. Built in 1787, it lost all resemblance to its former appearance when the carriageways were enclosed and rear east and west wings added in 1942. In 1968, Ormond was purchased by developers who planned to turn it into the clubhouse of a golf course. They poured cement over the brick floors and destroyed much of the woodwork. Ormond is stuffed with a mind-boggling collection of miscellanea from the past two centuries. There is an antique-doll room, artifacts from the War Between the States, and a large cane collection on display. Tours are offered from 10 to 4:30. The tour costs $5 for adults, $4 for seniors, and $2.50 for children six to twelve.

Bed and Breakfast accommodations are available by reservation at $125 for double occupancy. A carafe of wine and a fresh fruit and cheese tray are served on the veranda in the evening. In the morning, hot coffee will be placed outside your bedroom, followed by a Continental-style breakfast. (504) 764-8544.

Building the Bonnet Carre Spillway. (Courtesy of U.S. Army Corps of Engineers)

★Bonnet Carre Spillway

Five miles north of I-310, River Road passes the industrial complex of Norco and one mile later crosses a levee and drops into the Bonnet Carre Spillway. The spillway is one of the huge and seemingly miraculous structures built by the United States Corps of Engineers to control the waters of the Mississippi at time of flood. The Bonnet Carre, constructed in 1935, is a floodgate and guide levee system built into the river levee wall. When the river threatens to flood areas to the south, the gates can be opened to allow water to escape through a mile-and-a-half-wide channel from the Mississippi into Lake Pontchartrain, seven miles to the north. This site was chosen for construction of the spillway based on the proximity of the lake and the demonstrated proclivity of the Mississippi to jump its banks at this point. In 1850 a crevasse occurred in the river levee here that remained open for six months, allowing water to spread across a 7,000-foot-wide area.

The folks at the Corps don't like to stir up the political muck that moves when large amounts of water are diverted, so it is unlikely you will find the gates open. Instead you will drive along the spillway bed below the surface of the river. A drive through the bottom of the 1.5-mile-wide floodbed provides a startling view of the placid pursuits that continue in the face of man's struggle against nature. At high water, there is always someone netting bait or fishing alongside the road. At extreme high water, the spillway road closes and traffic is diverted to Airline Highway. Most of the spillway is covered with bushes, trees, small streams, and ponds, fading to cypress swamp towards Lake Pontchartrain. Around March and April, the spillway is a popular spot for blackberry picking, picnicking, canoeing, fishing, and other recreational pursuits.

Bonnet Carre Spillway Recreation and Camping Area Airline Hwy.

Where Rte. 61 (Airline Highway) crosses the spillway there is a boat launch, picnic area, and free campground. A number of trails head out into the underbrush from this point. The camping is primitive. Porta-potties are provided for folks in tents (there is a maximum-stay limit of two weeks). To get to the recreation area, take Airline Highway west from New Orleans (9.2 miles from the airport). From River Road cut over to Airline at the town of Norco. The campground is beside the Spillway Bridge.

LaPlace

From the west side of the Bonnet Carre Spillway, River Road passes five and a half miles of industrial development and rubble before entering the town of LaPlace (10.5 miles from I-310 by way of River Road). Here the road veers away from the levee and becomes Rte. 44 (in town it is called Fifth Street). LaPlace is located near the site of the biggest slave revolt in American history. The revolt occurred in 1818 at Woodland Plantation and involved nearly six hundred slaves, who were defeated by the militia just west of New Orleans. Following their defeat, the slaves who were not dead were beheaded and their heads were placed on stakes along the River Road. Today LaPlace, the largest town on the river between Baton Rouge and New Orleans (population about twenty-five thousand), is a bedroom community for folks who work in the Crescent City. It is known as the Andouille Capital of the World. The history of this lean pork sausage has been clouded, but it apparently goes back to a settlement of Germans in the region in the eighteenth century. Andouille is different from other sausage varieties in Acadiana, having no filler, just big chunks of fatless pork seasoned with pepper and garlic, and smoked to an almost fully cooked state.

Wayne Jacob's Smokehouse Meat Market. 769A W. Fifth St. (River Road), LaPlace.

Jacob's is located 1.5 miles past the convergence of Rte. 44 and River Road in LaPlace. Although they have moved from the funky country store just down the road, the andouille is the same recipe that has been passed down in the Jacob family for generations. At least three branches of the family produce andouille at separate locations, but Wayne's is my pick of the litter. The country sausage and hog's head cheese are also excellent. Wayne Jacob's has a variety of dry goods, homemade jellies, and desserts for sale, too. The andouille sells for about $4.25 a pound. Jacob's is open Monday through Saturday, from 9 to 5. (504) 652-9990.

Airline Motors Restaurant Down Home, $-$$. 221 E. Airline Hwy. (I-10 exit #209).

Built in 1939, Airline Motors Restaurant is one of the few thriving landmarks of the days when Airline Highway was the only "fast" route between New Orleans and Baton Rouge. The restaurant is actually an oversized example of classic American diner decor. Festooned with curved corners, glass bricks, and plenty of neon, this place just sucks you in off the road. Inside there is a long counter, bar area, and large dining room. There are a dozen seafood and steak dinners for $10 to $15, but I recommend the gumbos, which are made with LaPlace's famous andouille. The fried food is well prepared and includes a variety of seafood po' boys and onion rings. Airline Motors Restaurant never closes. (504) 652-9181.

ABA (canoe) Rentals 1221 W. Airline Hwy., LaPlace.

If you want to explore the many streams and ponds around the Bonnet Carre Spillway, ABA Rentals in LaPlace is the closest place to rent a canoe. A canoe, two paddles, life jackets, roof pads, and tie downs cost $25 for 24 hours. You can rent a canoe (or flat-bottomed boat) here and within 15 minutes be paddling through the spillway (*see* Bonnet Carre Spillway Recreation Area above). ABA is open Monday through Saturday from 8:30 to 5:30. In the summer it also opens on some Sundays. (504) 652-7937.

Reserve

★Cox's Meat Market Andouille, $. River Road and Ninth Street, Reserve (I-10 exit #209).

Cox's is 17 miles from I-310, and 5 miles above LaPlace. This is the ultimate andouille palace. No one prepares a leaner or tastier sausage than Cox's. A tribute to their superlative meat came from the *Chef's Source Book,* which described it as "America's best andouille" in 1986.

Cox's andouille is the choice of dozens of New Orleans' finest restaurants. It is a bit less cooked than others and therefore holds together well in a gumbo. Unfortunately this means you won't be able to cut off a thin slice to nibble on in the car. From Airline Highway, go west (towards the river) on Rte. 53 just north of LaPlace. When you get to River Road head south ¼ mile. Cox's is open from 8 to 5, Monday through Saturday. (504) 536-2491.

Reserve to Edgard Ferry Rte. 53 (Central Ave.) and River Road.

If you are doing a short trip up River Road and want to get a look at the Waterford Three Nuclear Plant or Oak Alley (*see* West Bank of River Road section), you can cross the river here by way of the Ascension Ferry. This will also give you a fantastic view of the river and its heavy commerce. The ferry operates from 5 A.M. to 9 P.M., crossing approximately every 15 minutes. The last trip is at 8:45. There is a $1 fee for travel from the west to east banks.

Don's Country Store Meat Market/Andouille. 318 Central Ave., Reserve.

This unusual store sells meats, groceries, and a full line of hardware. If you are looking for a good, fully cooked andouille that you can carve a smokey taste off of, this is the spot. There is a recipe board by the butcher case with 24 free Cajun recipes to help you prepare the meat. From River Road, turn onto Rte. 53 (Central Avenue), go about 1.5 miles, and Don's is on the right. They are open Monday through Saturday, from 7 A.M. to 7 P.M., and Sunday, from 7 A.M. to noon. (504) 536-2275.

★San Francisco Plantation

Only 4 miles from Rte. 53 in Reserve (21 miles from I-310), San Francisco is the most perfectly restored of all the plantation homes in Acadiana. San Francisco was built at the height of River Road's grandeur in 1853. Builder Edmond Marmillion reportedly spent every cent he had making this home a jewel. From the paint to the furnishings, everything is either original or modeled after descriptions in Marmillion's inventories. Among the preserved details are seven deceptively painted faux marble mantels, a crushed-brick floor that resembles a rich, red carpet, and most spectacular, five ceiling frescoes. Outside, the home has the appearance of a steamboat with Gothic windows, galleries, and ornate woodwork. The roof has a small windowed room called a "widow's walk" from which residents could watch traffic on the river.

San Francisco has developed a symbiotic relationship with Marathon Oil Company. Marathon bought the place in 1974 and, though they desecrated the once immaculate grounds, they also sank two million

San Francisco Plantation. (Photo by Julie Posner)

dollars into restoring the house to the showpiece of River Road's eastern course. Tours are scheduled from 10 to 4 daily except holidays. Tours cost $7 for adults, $6 for seniors, $5 for military personnel, and are free for children under 5. (504) 535-2341.

Garyville

The best place for a glimpse of the River Region's once booming lumber industry is one mile north of San Francisco Plantation in the town of Garyville. The Chicago-based Stebbins Lumber Company mapped out, built, and populated Garyville. Between 1903 and the 1930s, the company harvested every twig of usable cypress from the nearby Blind River Swamp. Garyville is only three blocks wide and about eight blocks deep heading back from the river. East Street was built to accommodate black workers, Main Street housed the whites, and West Street was lined with homes for mainly Italian immigrants. Over sixty of the company homes are still standing and are listed on the historic register.

Little in these cottages suggests the vast sums that were earned when the mill was in business. Most of the money went to administrators in Chicago, not to the local laborers who slaved in the mill. The company office and mill yard were located a couple of miles back from the river. The office has been restored and turned into a museum (*see* review below). Across from the office is the Garyville State Bank, the only other commercial building to survive since the lumbering days.

Garyville Timbermill Museum Main Street and Railroad Avenue (I-10 exit #194).

The Timbermill Museum is housed in the former offices of the Stebbins Lumber Company. The company built and employed the entire town, so this museum contains documents and artifacts covering every phase of life in Garyville, from the birth to the death of a company town. The museum is struggling for funding and may have irregular hours. From River Road turn away from the river on Rte. 54 about 1 mile above San Francisco Plantation. About 1.5 miles from the river you will cross some railroad tracks; the museum is on the right. To find out when the museum is open, call the office at (504) 535-3202, call Garyville historian Carl Monica at (225) 642-4736, or inquire at the St. James Historical Society in Lutcher.

Cypress cut by Stebbins Lumber Company. (St. James Historical Society Museum)

Lutcher Moore lumber train in cut swamp. (St. James Historical Society Museum)

Gramercy and Lutcher/
Veterans Memorial Bridge

Between Garyville and Gramercy (27 miles north of I-310) there are 5 miles of hideous industrial scenery, courtesy of Nalco, DuPont, and LaRoche chemical companies. Just south of Gramercy, Hwy. 641 crosses the river at Veterans Memorial Bridge and links the River Roads with I-10 (exit #194). This is a good place to cross to the west bank to see Laura and Oak Alley plantations. Above the bridge Gramercy and Lutcher run together in an indecipherable grid of small streets. Like many other towns on River Road, they have narrow frontage on the river but stretch for several miles back towards Rte. 61 (Airline Highway).

Gramercy is an old sugar town, and home to the Colonial Sugar Mill. Many residents are now employed at the nearby Kaiser Aluminum and Chemical Plant, and other River Road industries. Rte. 20, the main route perpendicular to the river, forms a rough boundary with neighboring Lutcher and provides a 3.5-mile link between River Road and Airline Highway.

Lutcher, like Garyville downriver, is a former lumber-mill town. It was built and populated around the turn of the century by the Lutcher Moore Cypress Lumber Company. The mill and offices were located right on River Road, and the business district and residential areas were (and still are) located several blocks back from the river. This part of St. James Parish produces sugar, lumber, and chemicals and is noted as the only place in the country where Perique tobacco is grown. Perique is a strong, fermented tobacco that is usually blended with other milder leaves, but it is occasionally smoked unadulterated by locals.

Veron's Super Market Meat Market. Rte. 641, Lutcher.

Veron's is the only manufacturer I have found of "boudin blanc." Like the French sausage from which Cajun boudin developed, Veron's product is riceless. In consistency and flavor, the sausages more closely resemble hot dogs than your typical Cajun boudin. They are sold chilled in shrink-wrapped packages. Turn away from the river onto Rte. 20 and go 1.2 miles. Take a left onto Rte. 641. Veron's is .5 mile ahead on the left. It is open Monday through Saturday, from 6 A.M. to 7 P.M., and Sunday, until 1 P.M. (225) 869-3731.

Zapp's Potato Chip Factory 307 Airline Hwy. (Rte. 61), Gramercy.

Zapp's is located just south of Rte. 20 on Rte. 61. Since opening in the mideighties Zapp's has become a local snack-food favorite, producing fresh, spiced (and plain) chips at its tiny factory. Any potato-chip junkie knows that the fresh, local chip is always best, but Zapp's has a unique product. It slices its chips thick and cooks them in small, hand-stirred batches in vats of peanut oil. When removed from the fryer, the most popular variety is dusted with Ron Zappe's own "Cajun spice" mixture. The plant is now closed to tours but there is a concession for Zapp's T-shirts and caps where you might get a free sample of the latest flavor. Out-of-town chipaholics may mail order by calling 1-800-HOT-CHIP. Zapp's Potato Chips, 307 E. Airline Hwy, P.O. Box 1533, Gramercy, LA 70052.

★St. James Parish Historical Society Bonfire Museum (I-10 exit #194).

One mile north of Rte. 20 on the River Road you will find this fine one-room museum that is operated by the St. James Historical Society. The museum has vintage photographs, documents, and artifacts relating to Perique tobacco, the lumber and sugar industries, and the Christmas bonfire tradition (*see* review of Festival of the Bonfires below). There is a wall of photographs of plantation homes (many no longer standing), with captions explaining their fate. Many of the lumber artifacts here came from the office of the Lutcher Moore Mill, which is still standing on a lot behind the museum. One display contains Indian

St. James Parish Bonfire Museum. (Photo by Julie Posner)

artifacts removed from a mound a few miles away on Rte. 3125 (*see* Indian Mound below). Like the Timbermill Museum in Garyville, this collection provides a striking look at the changing industries and cultures along the River Road. Admission is free. The museum is open from 8 to 4 Monday through Friday. (225) 869-9752.

★**Festival of the Bonfires** Second weekend in December.

During the weeks before Christmas, civic groups from the communities along the river construct towering wooden structures on the crown of the levee. Spaced about 50 yards apart, the bonfire stacks resemble a two-mile row of log steeples. Cleaving to tradition, the bonfire festival is held on the weekend preceding winter solstice. One fire is lit each night of the festival and the flames shed a raging light on revelers and a brilliant reflection across the river. Bands perform under a big tent and festival food (funnel cakes, hot dogs, and beer) is consumed.

The bonfires have been a tradition in St. John, St. Charles, St. James, and Ascension parishes since the 1700s and historians point out that a similar tradition is still strong in the Alsace region of France and along the Rhine in Germany. Some trace the roots back to Druid celebrations of the summer and winter solstice. The tradition nearly died in the 1930s, when it was practiced mainly by blacks in the river parishes, but is now fully revived.

Stockpile Restaurant Down Home, $-$$. Rte. 3125, Grand Point.

The Stockpile Restaurant and Tavern is my favorite eatery on the east bank of the Mississippi above New Orleans (there are not many choices). It is a new place with a studied "rusticity," but owner Eric Larouque knows how to satisfy a working man's appetite. Plate lunches, like white beans and hamburger steak and crawfish bisque with potato salad, are served every day. On Thursday nights, workers from the nearby chemical plants flock in to feed on the Stockpile's "all you can eat" fried catfish. During crawfish season, there is often an "all you can eat" crawfish special, too. The Stockpile is a couple of minutes off River Road in the heart of the Perique tobacco-growing region above Lutcher. Two and a half miles above Rte. 20 on River Road, turn onto Rte. 642. The Stockpile is 1.4 miles north, at the intersection of Rte. 642 and Rte. 3125. They are open Saturday and Monday from 3 P.M. to 10 P.M. Tuesday through Friday and Sundays they are open from 10 A.M. to 10 P.M. (225) 869-9917 or 869-3529.

Indian Mound Rte. 3125, Grand Point.

Just over two miles west of the Stockpile Restaurant on the river side of Rte. 3125, a 30-foot-high Indian mound rises from the middle of a cultivated field. The mound was partially excavated (you can see artifacts in the Bonfire Museum) and found to be built before A.D. 400. Interestingly, the soil in the mound is not native to the region, but seems to have been brought from about 75 miles upriver in the Tunica Hills region.

★Manresa House of Retreats River Road, Convent (I-10 exit #194 or 182).

Just above Lutcher the river turns back on itself in a tight 14-mile kink. This bend holds the most beautiful stretch of the lower River Road. Industry thins out and oak trees crowd the blacktop. At the tip of the bend rests the idyllic grounds of Manresa House of Retreats.

Constructed in 1831 as Jefferson College, the Gothic Revival main building and 142-acre grounds have functioned as a Jesuit retreat for laymen since 1931. Retreatants spend three days at Manresa observing a code of silence that seems to lend an air of serenity to this entire stretch of River Road. Unscheduled visits to the grounds are not permitted as they might interfere with the solitude of retreatants. Manresa is about 10 miles above Lutcher and 12 miles below the Sunshine Bridge. For information about the retreat call (504) 529-3555 or (225) 562-3596.

★Lourdes Grotto/St. Michael's Church River Road, Convent (I-10 exit #182).

One of the unusual secrets of River Road, and a fine piece of religious folk art, is tucked behind the main altar of St. Michael the Archangel Church in Convent. Two of St. Michael's parishioners created a scale model of the grotto in France where the Virgin Mary appeared to Bernadette Soubirous in 1858. The work was donated to the church, where it was officially dedicated in 1876.

Florian Dicharry and Christophe Colombe manufactured the grotto from bagasse, the pressed pulp substance that remains after sugarcane is processed. The most remarkable aspect of the grotto is the small altar within, covered with hundreds of tiny clam shells, each tacked on with a single nail (obviously a work of devotion or divine patience!). A statue of the Virgin Mary looks down from a precipice, and the cliff is backed by a mural of the Lourdes countryside. The church is usually open during daylight hours. A short history of the grotto is available for a small donation.

Hymel's Seafood Restaurant Seafood, $-$$. River Road, Convent (I-10 exit #182).

Squeezed between Hymel's Tire Service and Hymel's Grocery, this restaurant has been serving no-frills fried and boiled seafood to families from up and down River Road since the 1950s. Enter through the lounge, roll up your sleeves, and order a beer. Make a little noise if you want. Hymel's is open for lunch from 11 to 2:30 daily. Dinner is served 5 to 9 Thursday and until 10 Friday and Saturday. Sunday hours are 11 A.M. to 8 P.M. (225) 562-9910.

Sunshine Bridge (Rte. 70) to Donaldsonville (I-10 exit #182).

About 18 miles north of Lutcher and 10 miles above Manresa/Convent, the loveliest bit of River Road ends in the glow and smoke of the industrial giant Agrico. Here the Sunshine Bridge connects the rural/industrial east bank with the town of Donaldsonville. Rte. 70 east provides a quick access to I-10.

Tezcuco Plantation/Village One mile north of Sunshine Bridge (I-10 exit #182).

Tezcuco is recommended less for the house, which was built in the Greek Revival style in the 1850s, than for the gardens and transplanted outbuildings. These outbuildings house the African American Museum (*see* review below), a flea-market antique shop, restaurant, and Bed and Breakfast accommodations. Tours are offered from 9:30 to 4:30 daily. Admission is $6 for adults and $3.25 for children. A fee of $4 is charged to see the grounds exclusive of the house. (225) 562-3929.

★African American Museum Tezcuco

Anyone touring the plantations of River Road should stop at this humble but growing museum and take a moment to consider the thousands of individuals—the suffering majority—who labored to sustain a life of wealth for a relative few. The work and achievements of the slaves who built the plantations of River Road, farmed them, and maintained the life-style of a handful of owners are seldom mentioned on plantation tours. In this tiny museum located behind the main house, local historian Kathe Hambrick has gathered and lovingly assembled the biggest known collection of information, artifacts, photographs, and genealogical data on the African-Americans who built the economy of River Road and their descendants. Hambrick's display makes it clear that African-Americans were not just the laborers of the region but were also designers, metallurgists, carpenters, and inventors (including Leonard Julien, who invented the sugarcane-planting machine). She hopes to move her museum to a new site where several buildings important to the development of African-American life in the River Region may also be relocated. The museum is now open from 1 to 5 Saturday and Sunday (by appointment other days). Call to confirm the location and hours. (225) 644-7955 or (225) 562-7703.

★Tezcuco Bed and Breakfast

Tezcuco has the best Bed and Breakfast accommodations on River Road, located in 19 separate wood-frame outbuildings within 100

Bed-and-breakfast cabin at Tezcuco. (Photo by Julie Posner)

yards of the main house. Most of these cabins have porches and work-ing fireplaces. Some have full kitchens, extra baths, and bedrooms. Furnishings range from lavish antiques to simple country-style appointments. Even the least expensive seem warm and homey. After a day of plantation hopping this is a great place to unwind with a bot-tle of wine and walk the grounds after the last tours leave. Double rates range from $60 to $160. (225) 562-3929, Fax (225) 562-3923.

TRAVEL TIP

In the 2.5 miles between Tezcuco and Houmas House, Rte. 44 turns north towards Burnside and River Road becomes Rte. 942.

The Cabin Restaurant Down Home, $-$$. Rte. 44, Burnside.

This is an area of few eateries and the simple fare here, like beans and rice, fried seafood, and po' boys, is merely serviceable. The big disappointments were the "World-Famous Gumbo" and "Legendary" buttermilk pie, which was mostly sugar. The main attraction is the quaint decorating and architecture, which seems to appeal to tour-bus guides. The restaurant is a conglomeration of slave cabins from the Monroe Plantation, which have been stuck together in ramshackle fashion. In one cabin, the walls are papered with old newspapers fixed in place with flour paste. My favorite room is the bathroom, fashioned from a huge cypress rainwater cistern and materials from the Old Crow Distillery in New Orleans. The Cabin is located at the corner of Rte. 22 and Rte. 44 (two miles east of River Road). It is open Monday through Wednesday from 11 A.M. to 3 P.M., Thursday and Friday until 9, and Sunday until 6. (225) 473-3007.

Houmas House 40136 River Rd. (I-10 exit #177).

Just short of four miles above the Sunshine Bridge on River Road is the oldest tourable plantation in the area. Alexandre Latil pur-chased the land from the Houma Indians and built a small, two-story structure in 1790. This original four-room house with outside stairways is now adjoined to the rear of a massive Greek Revival plantation built in 1840. In the years just before the War Between the States, Houmas House was the biggest sugar producer in the nation. Maybe we got the wrong guide, but I found the formal tour of the house a bit pedantic. Members of the huge group touring the house (which is very popu-lar with tour-bus operators) seemed to drift off, and one offered to pay the guide *not* to talk and just let him look! There is an excellent view of the river from the upstairs gallery. Daily tours are offered on every half-hour from 10 to 4 in winter and until 5 other months. The tour costs $8 for adults, $6 for teens, and $3 for kids. (225) 473-7841.

Private Plantation Houses

There are three notable antebellum homes (not open to the public) in the 15 miles above Houmas House. These are Bocage, Hermitage, and Ashland Belle Helene plantations.

TRAVEL TIP

Rte. 75 turns away from the river at Carville (7.5 miles above Ashland Belle Helene). In case you wondered, the Carvilles for whom this community was named are the same family that produced James Carville, the campaign wizard and advisor to President Clinton. To continue on River Road to the Carville-White Castle Ferry or Hansen's Disease Center (*see* review below) stay to the left on Rte. 141. Past the Hansen's Center the road passes through farmland and pecan groves owned by the state prison system and becomes gravel before intersecting Rte. 75 nine miles upriver.

Carville-White Castle Ferry (I-10 exit #177).

Two miles from the intersection of Rte. 141 and Rte. 75 is the Carville Ferry. The ferry runs from 4:30 A.M. to 8:30 A.M. and 3:30 P.M. to 7:30 P.M. and hits the west bank of River Road near Nottoway Plantation.

★National Hansen's Disease Center River Road, Carville (I-10 exit #177).

The National Hansen's Disease Center rests in a verdant oxbow bend of the Mississippi River, 85 miles north of New Orleans. Originally the site of Indian Camp Plantation, the land was purchased by the state of Louisiana in 1894 for the establishment of a "leper colony." The land was bought under the pretense of opening an ostrich farm, and the first seven residents were delivered from New Orleans in the dark of night on a coal barge. Our tour guide said bluntly, "This was a place where people came to stay, and to die." Believed to be highly contagious, the afflicted were forced into a life of isolation at the quiet, decaying plantation.

Because the 350-acre center was operated as an isolated "colony," it has all the trappings of a small village, including 100 buildings, two churches, a fire station, general store, 350-seat movie theater, golf course, tennis courts, and 20-acre fishing pond. The administrative offices are in the old plantation house. Today the center leads the world in research and treatment of Hansen's Disease (as leprosy is now known). Since the development of sulfone therapy at Carville in 1941, Hansen's can be rendered completely noncontagious. The 6,000 Hansen's Disease patients in the United States no longer need

National Hansen's Disease Center, Carville.

to be confined for long periods and the resident population at the Carville facility has dwindled from nearly 500 to less than 200.

It is very unlikely that the center will continue to treat Hansen's patients much longer. At present, tours are conducted daily by former residents or patients of the facility. The buildings on the tour, constructed mainly in the early 1900s, are connected by four miles of two-story-high masonry walkways with screened sides that afford a view of tranquil grounds and gardens. Many remaining patients glide quietly along the passageways on antique bicycles. The solitude is striking but inspires reflection on historically grim health-care practices.

Although it is unclear what use this facility will be put to, travelers on River Road can hope that the beautiful buildings and solemn walkways will remain open to visitors. Free tours are offered Monday through Friday at 1 P.M. (minimum age 16). From I-10, take exit #177 onto Rte. 30 west. Go 4 miles and turn left onto Rte. 73. Go 1.6 miles and you will hit River Road. Turn right on River Road for 4.8 miles. Given the unclear future of the center, I recommend that you call first. (225) 642-4755.

J.A. Barthel's Store

Four miles from the northern intersection of Rte. 75 and Rte. 141, on River Road in Sunshine, is Barthel's, a country store right out of a Norman Rockwell painting. In business since 1886, the store still sells the Sunshine community anything they could possibly want, from hardware to ham sandwiches. The tidy little crosscut sandwiches (available in double decker) on white bread make a nice picnic to carry to the top of the levee or to eat while you are waiting for the Plaquemine Ferry just five miles up the road.

Plaquemine Ferry

This ferry, 32.5 miles from the Sunshine Bridge and 78.5 miles from I-310, is the northern terminus of the East River Road tour. It is one of the oldest operating ferries on the lower Mississippi and the northernmost point on the Cajun Country tour of the eastern side of River Road. Cross the river here and you wind up in the old lumber and rail town of Plaquemine. The ferry operates daily from 5 A.M. until 9 P.M., departing on the half-hour. There is a $1 toll.

River Road East Bank Food and Lodging

For information on the restaurants and accommodations in this list, consult the text for the east bank of River Road.

LODGING

Best Western LaPlace Main St./Rte. 51 (I-10 exit #209). (800) 528-1234.

Ormond Plantation Bed and Breakfast River Road, St. Rose.

Holiday Inn 3900 Main St./Rte. 51 (I-10 exit #209), $60 to $75 double. (504) 652-5544, (800) 465-4329.

Millet Motel 1525 W. Airline Hwy. (I-10 exit #209), $40 to $50 double. (504) 652-4401.

★**Tezcuco Bed and Breakfast** River Road (I-10 exit #182), 1.2 miles above the Sunshine Bridge, $60 to $160. (225) 562-3929.

FOOD

Wayne Jacob's Smokehouse Meat Market/Andouille. 769A W. 5th St., LaPlace.

Airline Motors Restaurant Down Home, $-$$. 221 E. Airline Hwy., LaPlace.

★**Cox's Meat Market** Andouille, $. River Road and 9th St., Reserve.

Don's Country Store Meat Market/Andouille. 318 Central Ave., Reserve.

Veron's Super Market Meat Market/Boudin blanc. Rte. 641, Lutcher.

Stockpile Restaurant Down Home, $-$$. Rte. 3125, Grand Point.

Hymel's Seafood Restaurant Seafood, $-$$. River Road above Convent.

The Cabin Restaurant Down Home, $-$$. Rte. 44, Burnside.

WEST BANK OF RIVER ROAD

This section is organized in a linear fashion, moving upriver from New Orleans. There is a list of accommodations and restaurants at the end of the section. The west bank tour of River Road begins at the intersection of the I-310 (Hale Boggs) Bridge and River Road, about one mile north of Luling. From New Orleans, take I-310 south from I-10 (exit #220). You may also catch the Reserve ferry from the east bank to Edgard (17 miles north of I-310) or hit River Road at U.S. 90, just west of the Huey P. Long Bridge. The west bank features the same bizarre mixture of plants and plantations as the east side of the river. Attractions are fewer and farther between on the west bank, but it is home to Laura Plantation (the best of the River Road plantation tours).

Union Carbide-Taft Plant and Holy Rosary Cemetery

The juxtaposition of this sprawling industrial center six miles above I-310 and the tiny Holy Rosary Cemetery speaks volumes about

Holy Rosary Cemetery. (Photo by Julie Posner)

the history and future of the River Region. The cemetery was established in 1878 but is now surrounded by the erupting stacks of Union
Carbide, Agrico, and Louisiana Power and Light plants.

Waterford 3 Nuclear Plant and Visitors Center Rte. 3127, Taft.

Waterford 3, Louisiana's first nuclear power plant, is located seven
miles above I-310. A controlled nuclear reaction within an 882,000-
pound reactor vessel heats water, and the resulting steam is used to
power electricity-producing turbines. For safety and security reasons,
the reactor area is closed to the public. A visitors center houses a
model of the plant and a dozen or so "hands on" exhibits. You can test
your own ability to produce current on an exercise bicycle wired to a
display board. Pedal easy and a light bulb comes on. Pedal harder
and you can create enough juice to power an electric hair dryer.
Among the more sophisticated displays are a nuclear control room
simulator and a Geiger-counter test that measures the effectiveness
of various materials in shielding radioactivity. One mile north of the
Nuclear Unit on River Road, turn left on Rte. 3141. Go one mile and
turn left (east) onto Rte. 3127. Continue about a mile to the entrance.
The visitors center is open from 8 to 3, Monday through Thursday.
(504) 739-6072.

Edgard to Reserve Ferry

The Edgard Ferry is located 16.7 miles from I-310 and about 9 miles
upriver from the nuclear plant. This ferry connects the andouille
area of the east bank with a heavily industrialized portion of the west.
It provides a view of the river and its heavy commerce. The ferry is
located at the intersection of Rte. 53 and River Road. It operates from
5 A.M. to 9 P.M., crossing every 30 minutes. The last trip is at 8:30. A $1
fee is charged heading to the east bank only.

Veterans Memorial Bridge Gramercy to Vacherie (I-10 exit #194).

For nearly a decade this bridge hung unfinished over the river,
earning the nickname "Bridge to Nowhere." Now it is completed and
provides very fast access via Rte. 641 between Laura and Oak Alley
plantations on the west bank and the town of Gramercy and Interstate
10 on the east bank.

St. Phillip Bar and Lounge; Confectionery River Road, Vacherie.

This is the kind of place I can't stand to drive by without stop-
ping because I am afraid the next time I pass, it will be gone. The
Waguespack family (descendants of the Waguespacks who owned
Laura Plantation) have operated the place since the thirties, when
it was a busy grocery. Business flagged when the Lutcher/Vacherie
Ferry closed in the midnineties but nonagenarian Eva Waguespack

or her son Bubby can be found tending bar beneath the mounted antlers most weekends.

Rte. 20 to Kraemer Swamp Tours and Boudreaux's Restaurant

Rte. 20 intersects River Road about 30 miles above Veterans Memorial Bridge in the town of Vacherie (French for "ranch"). This is the best place to reach the swamps between the Mississippi and Bayou Lafourche. The narrow road drops quickly from River Road into the wetlands around Lake Des Allemands and Lake Boeuf. Within 5 miles you are no longer in the province of the wealthy sugar culture but in the domain of Cajun fishermen and trappers. To get to Boudreaux's Cajun Restaurant, head west 9 miles to the intersection of Rte. 307. Bear right on Rte. 307 and it is 3 miles to Chackbay. To get to Kraemer (site of two swamp tours), turn left on Rte. 307 and travel 10.5 miles (*see* Bayou Country chapter for more on Kraemer and Chackbay).

★**B&C Cajun Deli/Seafood** Seafood, $. River Road, Vacherie.

Nothing about the appearance of this seafood market and cafe indicates how really great its gumbos, stews, and fried seafood are! The place does a booming retail and wholesale business and the cutlery is plastic, but take my word, the tiny adjoining dining area is one of the best places on River Road to sit down for lunch. Geneva and Tommy Breaux went into business in the 1960s processing catfish from nearby Lake Des Allemands (the only catfish they will serve at B&C). Breaux touts the health benefits of the wild catfish as well as the flavor: "You can taste this fish, whereas pond-raised catfish taste like whatever you serve on it." I recommend the smoky chicken-andouille gumbo and rich crawfish stew. If you are in the mood for something unusual, try the ground choupic and garfish burgers or an alligator po' boy for under $5. The bread pudding with rum sauce is topnotch. B&C is only 45 minutes from New Orleans Airport, beside Laura Plantation (recommended). It packs seafood for travel and accepts credit cards. B&C is open Saturday and Monday through Thursday from 9 A.M. to 5:30 P.M. and until 6:30 P.M. on Friday. (225) 265-8356.

★**Laura Plantation** River Road, Vacherie (I-10 exit #194).

If you have limited time and can only tour one River Road plantation, see Laura! It is the only tour where guides present a direct and unvarnished account of plantation life. Unlike at other plantations, where slaves are referred to euphemistically as "servants" (or not mentioned at all), the guides at Laura know the names and tell the stories of the laborers who sustained the plantation life-style.

The passionate stories provided by Laura's tour guides are based on

Laura Plantation, home of Br'er Rabbit. (Photo by Ed Neham)

a wealth of rare documents and first-person accounts collected by the Locoul family, who built the house in 1805. Slave records and artifacts belonging to the original matron of the plantation were found in Paris, but the most exciting find was the memoirs of Laura, great-granddaughter of the builders. Laura kept a record of daily life on the plantation, family squabbles, and her own horror at the institution of slavery.

The house is one of the oldest on River Road but, because it was occupied by only two families (and vacant only a few years), remains in excellent condition. Laura is the only plantation on River Road that still has its original slave cabins. After the formal house tour, guests are invited to walk the grounds and inspect the humble structures where the majority of plantation residents lived.

It was here that Alcee Fortier recorded the West African folktales later published as Br'er Rabbit stories. (For more information on slave life, visit the African American Museum on River Road at Tezcuco.) A Bed and Breakfast is planned in two outbuildings. Tours are offered daily from 9 to 5 (French-language tours available upon request). They cost $6 for adults and $3.75 for students age 6 to 17. (225) 265-7690.

Oak Alley Plantation. (Photo by Ed Neham)

Oak Alley Plantation River Road, Vacherie (I-10 exit #194).

Oak Alley is one of the best-known houses on River Road, named for the quarter-mile oak-lined carriageway leading from the mansion to the river. The 28 trees on either side of the drive were planted by an unknown French settler in the early 1700s, before the big house was constructed. The mansion was built in 1837 by wealthy French sugar planter Jacques Telesphore Roman. In 1925, Andrew and Josephine Stewart rescued the place from decay and left it to the nonprofit group that operates tours today. The house contains many period antiques but is not the grandest of River Road manses. Its reputation, like its name, is owed to the beautiful ensemble of proud columns and the stately grounds. The plantation is visited regularly by the *American Queen* riverboat. It is a thrill to see the sternwheeler pull away from the levee with the steam calliope playing "Take Me Out to the Ball Game" and "In the Good Ol' Summertime." Bed and Breakfast accommodations are offered in the old cottages behind the plantation and a restaurant (not recommended) serves lunch from 11 to 3 daily. Tours are offered daily from 9 to 5:30 (until 5 from November to February). Tours cost $7 for adults, $5 for teens, and $3 for children. (225) 265-2151.

Oak Alley Plantation Bed and Breakfast

Overnight accommodations at Oak Alley are in small cottages behind the main house. These wooden tenant houses built around

1880 have been restored and are very sunny and bright, with new kitchens, baths, and central air and heat. The main attraction is the plantation grounds, which you may wander at will. A small creek runs through the yard. Walk out your door and see the sun set over miles of sugarcane. There are six cottages; two are shotgun doubles. Double occupancy rates are $95 to $125 a night. A small breakfast (included in the price of the room) is served at the restaurant from 9 to 11. Tours of the plantation cost an additional $7.

Bay Tree Plantation Bed and Breakfast 3718 Hwy. 18 (River Road), Vacherie.

Located adjacent to Oak Alley, Bay Tree is not a plantation but an 1850 Creole cottage occupied by owners Dinah and Rich Laurich. There are two guest bedrooms lavishly furnished with antiques. Actor Brad Pitt stayed here while filming *Interview with the Vampire*. There are also three bedrooms in a guest cottage out back, which are a bit less formal (each with its own motif). Dining-room tables are set with china and a full Southern breakfast is served. One fewer guest room in each house would make these accommodations seem a bit more private and less cramped. Double rate is $75 to $150 (the Brad Pitt suite). (225) 265-2109, (800) 895-2109.

Strategic Petroleum Reserve/First Acadian Settlement

Seven miles above Oak Alley you will find another of the strange contrasts that have become the rule on River Road. Across from a marker denoting the point where the Acadians established their first settlement on the Mississippi (known as the Acadian Coast) are the pipes and storage tanks of a National Strategic Petroleum Reserve facility. Over the next two miles you will pass two of the River Region's industrial giants, Chevron Chemical and Agrico Faustina.

Sunshine Bridge/Rte. 70 (I-10 exit #182).

Just below Donaldsonville, the Sunshine Bridge offers access to the east-bank River Road near Tezcuco Plantation. It also provides quick access to I-10 via Rte. 70 east. To visit Donaldsonville you may travel 4 miles west on Rte. 70. This cuts off a 7.5-mile oxbow in the river and allows you to bypass the belching stacks of the Triad Chemical plant.

Donaldsonville

Donaldsonville, with a population of about 8,000, is one of the four largest towns on either side of the river between New Orleans and Baton Rouge. In the mideighties it was a bustling if not quite vibrant old town. Recently old Donaldsonville has become a virtual ghost town. Whites have fled to the east bank of the river or to outlying developments, and unemployment has soared.

The town is located at a point where the Mississippi once turned and flowed south. When the river jumped to its present course in A.D. 1200, an Indian settlement grew at the juncture of the old channel. La Salle dubbed the Indian camp *Lafourche de Chetimachas* (fork of the Chetimachas). The former course of the Mississippi in turn became known as Bayou Lafourche. Following (strangely enough) the eviction of the Indians, the site became a major trading post and destination of a large number of Acadian immigrants in 1758. Sam Donaldson founded the city in 1806 on lands purchased from Acadian settlers. It became the seat of Ascension Parish and, for the year of 1830, functioned as the state capital.

Downtown Donaldsonville Walking Tour

In its uncontrolled wanderings the river spared Donaldsonville while it sliced off 4-6 blocks of other riverside towns. The 12-block historic district sandwiched between the railroad and the river has over 600 buildings constructed between 1865 and 1930. Unfortunately, most of the downtown is empty and posted for sale. The most interesting commercial buildings lie along Mississippi Street (River Road) and Railroad Street (Rte. 307). Mississippi Street was the business district when most goods were moved by steamer. Railroad Street intersects Mississippi Street and runs to the railroad depot about 10 blocks away. The city was burned by Union troops, so few of its buildings predate the war. In the 1870s, the railroad arrived and business began to grow towards the depot. Near the intersection of Railroad and Mississippi is a good place to bail out of the car for a short stroll. You can walk across the street, over the levee, and enjoy the view from a public observation platform overlooking the river, or check out a few of the downtown buildings and Italian eateries.

B. Lemann & Brothers, Inc. Mississippi and Railroad streets

The city brochure proclaims B. Lemann & Brothers, built in the thirties, to be the oldest department store in Louisiana. Unfortunately the old store closed in the midnineties.

Louisiana Square

When Sam Donaldson mapped out the city in 1806, this little park across from Lemann & Brothers was part of the plan. Along with the public observation platform on the river, the square is a prime spot to relax and enjoy a po' boy from nearby Railroad Cafe.

Ruggiero's Restaurant Local Fave, $-$$. 206 Railroad Ave.

After most of the original Acadian settlers left Donaldsonville in the early 1800s, the city remained a destination for many immigrants, and a large number of Italians settled in the area. Ruggiero's is one of two spaghetti houses along Railroad Avenue, and my favorite. Of course, they sell a lot more than spaghetti. This is Louisiana-Italian food. Try the garlic fries or hot shrimp salad. For a real splurge, attack a plate of Premier Garlic Shrimp and Spaghetti. There are a variety of po' boys, gumbos, seafoods, and steaks available, too. Carry-out orders are available. Ruggiero's is open for dinner Tuesday through Saturday from 5 to 9. Lunch hours are Tuesday through Friday from 11 to 1. (225) 473-8476.

Railroad Cafe Local Fave, $. 212 Railroad Ave.

This po' boy and plate-lunch place has a somewhat puzzling theme. One wall is covered with dry goods for sale, the other has an old bar (now an ice-cream counter), and in the back the cooks can be seen turning out nice sandwiches. Daily specials and plate lunches run about $6. You can eat inside or take your sandwich down to the river for a meal with a view. The cafe opens at 10 A.M. daily except Sunday. It closes at 2 P.M. Monday through Wednesday and at 8 P.M. Thursday through Saturday. (225) 473-8513.

TRAVEL TIP

In Donaldsonville, River Road (Rte. 18) briefly converges with Rte. 1. To the south Rte. 1 follows the banks of Bayou Lafourche for over 100 miles to the Gulf-coast town of Grand Isle (*see* the Bayou Country chapter for more on the Lafourche area). To the north Rte. 1 follows the river but cuts off a number of the oxbow bends. It is a four-lane highway with a 55-mph speed limit. It cuts the distance between Donaldsonville and Plaquemine in half (to 21 miles). There are numerous places to cut over from Rte. 1 to River Road as well as an entrance to Nottoway Plantation from either road.

White Castle-Carville Ferry

This ferry, 13 miles from the intersection of Rte. 405 and Rte. 1 in Donaldsonville, connects the two premier attractions of upper River Road, Nottoway Plantation on the west bank and the National Hansen's Disease Center on the east side in Carville. It departs every half-hour from 4:30 A.M. to 7:45 A.M. and 3:45 P.M. to 7:15 P.M. There is a $1 fee for traffic heading to the east bank.

White Castle

White Castle (population about 2,000) is located amongst acres of sugarcane, 15 miles above Donaldsonville by way of River Road. The town got its name from a sugar plantation, which was moved and finally disassembled when the U.S. Corps of Engineers chopped off part of the city to build new levees. The huge Cora-Texas sugar mill rises above the fields as you enter town from downriver. Founded in 1817, Cora is one of the oldest mills in the state. The few blocks of town along River Road are run-down, but as you cross Rte. 1 heading away from the river on Bowie Street, White Castle is revealed as a lovely though sleepy small town.

Old Dorseyville School Lacroix Road, above White Castle.

The Old Dorseyville School is one of the oldest African-American schools in the Delta. It is currently being restored as a museum. From Rte. 1 turn towards the river on Lacroix Road. The Old Dorseyville School is about a quarter-mile towards the river on the left.

★Nottoway Plantation (I-10 exit #182).

The most stunning and imposing of River Road plantations stands about 2 miles above the town of White Castle on Rte. 1 (17 miles from the Sunshine Bridge). Nottoway was built in 1859 at the height of opulence in the River Region, and its 50 rooms make it the largest antebellum plantation house in the South. The dimensions are startling. The home has 53,000 square feet of floor space and one curved wing has 22 square columns. No expense was spared in this jewel of the river. A bowling alley was built downstairs, two 5,000-gallon water cisterns in the attic provided ample running water, and a gas-producing plant was built in the back to light the house.

The planters of River Road engaged in a costly and proud game of one-upmanship. The builder of Nottoway was John Randolph of Virginia, who allegedly was determined to outdo another Virginia planter, John Andres, who had built Belle Grove Plantation nearby.

An exacting restoration was begun in 1980, and the house has been open for tours since that time. Nottoway is of the scale and proportions of a castle. Among the most impressive of its rooms is the downstairs ballroom. This parlor is in the semicircular west wing of the mansion and is painted glowing white, including the floors. The view from the upstairs gallery is equally amazing. At one time the house had acres between its front gate and the river. The levee has been moved to within throwing distance of the gallery and river traffic is plainly visible.

Many houses along the river boast ghost stories but, in character with its grandeur, Nottoway's most memorable claim to fame is how the house was saved by Southern hospitality. The manse had been selected for bombardment by Yankee gunboats until a commanding officer recognized the structure as a place where he had once been

Nottoway Plantation. (Courtesy of Louisiana Office of Tourism)

welcomed and entertained, and spared it from destruction. Nottoway has a large gift shop, a restaurant (not recommended), and regular tours daily. Tours are scheduled on the half-hour from 9 to 5 and cost $8 for adults and $3 for children. (225) 545-2730 or 545-2409.

Nottoway Plantation Bed and Breakfast

With its cheapest rooms priced at $135 (double), Nottoway is not for budget travelers. A bellhop handles your bags, a personal-size bottle of sherry appears in each room, and wakeup coffee and muffins arrive before breakfast. Despite this pampering, the best thing about a night at Nottoway is the opportunity to roam the house and its galleries alone at night. Moonlight sets the all-white downstairs ballroom aglow and you can relax on the upstairs balcony and watch ships passing on the river. There are 13 rooms available, with 9 in the main house and attached wings. All are furnished with period antiques and discreetly equipped with televisions. The four rooms in the 1839 overseer's cottage have a quiet view of the gardens. There is a small swimming pool for hot summer evenings.

Probably the biggest disappointment here was the food. From the wakeup muffins and coffee to breakfast and dinner at the restaurant (not included in the price of a room), the food quality was poor. Check-in time is 2:30 P.M. with check-out at 11 A.M. Rooms in the mansion and wings range from $190 to $125; accommodations in the overseer's cottage are $135; and three suites in the mansion cost $200 to $250 (all prices double occupancy). (225) 545-2730 or 545-2409.

Chapel of the Madonna River Road, Bayou Goula.

Have you ever noticed the plethora of privately constructed shrines and chapels around the country that claim to be "the smallest church in the world"? Cajun Country has at least three such edifices, but the Chapel of the Madonna is probably the most diminutive. If such arcane attractions interest you, look for this pine-sheltered place of prayer 4.5 miles north of Nottoway on River Road.

Plaquemine Ferry

The Plaquemine Ferry is located on River Road (Rte. 405) on the far east end of town. River Road turns away from the levee here and joins Rte. 75. To continue into Plaquemine turn west on Rte. 1. The ferry operates from 7 A.M. until 9 P.M. daily, departing on the half-hour. There is a $1 toll.

Plaquemine

River Road and Rte. 1 converge in the city of Plaquemine, 24 miles above the Sunshine Bridge. This formerly booming lumber, steamboat, and rail town is named for Bayou Plaquemine, which intersects the Mississippi here. New Orleans founder Iberville reportedly called the bayou "River Plaquemine" (from the Indian word for persimmon)

Plaquemine Lockhouse Visitors Center. (Courtesy of Louisiana Office of Tourism)

in 1699, after sampling the fruits of the trees along the stream. At its heyday around the turn of the century, steamers and trains converged at the Plaquemine locks, hauling lumber cut in the swamps of Iberville Parish onto river and rail. Five sugar mills operated near town, and 16 trains passed through Plaquemine daily. On Sundays, a horse track below town attracted several thousand spectators. By the 1940s, the lumber had been mostly depleted, and in 1961 the Plaquemine lock connecting the bayou to the river was permanently closed. Like the locks, many of the downtown buildings are now closed, and the railroad tracks through the heart of town seldom creak with cargo. New businesses have grown along Rte. 1 east of town, where you can find fast food, supermarkets, and discount stores.

★Plaquemine Locks State Commemorative Area Rte. 1 and Main Street.

The Plaquemine Lock complex, which includes a visitors center, museum, riverfront park, and observation tower, should be the first stop on any tour of Plaquemine. It is worth a detour if you are traveling the upper reaches of either side of River Road. A self-guided tour of the whole area should take about 45 minutes. Park your car here

Captain Joe in the Plaquemine locks. (Photo by Dr. E. L. Caze)

and you can walk to the major attractions and best restaurant in town. The lockhouse was built by a Dutch architect, using white ceramic brick and red roof tiles. Here you can get maps, brochures, directions, and see an eight-minute video history of the town and locks with some spectacular flood footage. The museum is filled with lockhouse artifacts and still photos of the steamer days, but most impressive is a small-scale working model of the locks and downtown area. Push a button and you can watch the entire process that allowed ships to drop from the higher Mississippi into the bayou. Push another button and the important buildings and landmarks of Plaquemine light up one at a time as a recorded voice gives their history.

After an information stop at the lockhouse you can walk outside and get a close-up view of the huge concrete-and-steel locks. The bayou had been widened and dredged since the first settlers arrived, but locks were not constructed until 1895. Built by Col. George W. Goethals (the main designer of the Panama Canal) and completed in 1909, the Plaquemine Locks had the highest freshwater lift in the world (51'). The locks operated on a unique gravity principle until hydraulic pumps were added. In 1961, when larger locks were installed upriver at Port Allen, the Plaquemine facility was permanently closed. In 1972, the lock was placed on the National Register of Historic Places. Across from the lock there is a small park on the river levee with a display of various types of boats used in the area, and an observation tower 40 feet above the river. From this tower you can see ships for miles in each direction. At the park area across from the lockhouse, there is a walkway leading down into the historic Turnerville residential district. The tower, locks, and other outdoor areas are open every day. The lockhouse is open Tuesday through Sunday from 10 to 4. (225) 687-7158 or 687-3560.

★**City Cafe** Local Fave, $. 53945 Main St. (near the Plaquemine Lock).

The City Cafe has been operated by the Miranda family since 1919 and remains the overwhelming lunch and dinner favorite of old-timers around Plaquemine. This is one of those places where everyone knows one another and conversation is exchanged freely between tables. Like family-run Italian restaurants in New Orleans, the City Cafe serves a variety of seafood, blue-plate specials, and spaghetti and meatballs in its two small dining rooms. The house special is catfish or chicken-fried steak with white gravy. Wednesday night you can order "all the catfish you can eat" with trimmings for $8. Other noteworthy fried dishes are fresh, thin-cut onion rings and fried dill pickle chips. Saturday night's spaghetti and meatballs with garlic bread draws a crowd. Tasty broiled catfish, red snapper, shrimp, and steaks are also available. If you are not very hungry, half-orders of all dishes are available upon request. Save room for the "three-in-one" dessert, the Cafe's own version of Mississippi Mud Pie. A crumb crust packed with pecans is layered with chocolate pie filling and covered with whipped topping. The City Cafe is open weekdays from 11 to 8:30 and until 9:30 on Saturdays. It is closed Sunday. (225) 687-7831.

★**DOW Chemicals Plant Tour** Rte. 1 and Rte. 1148, Plaquemine.

DOW Chemical Corporation's Plaquemine Plant is located 1.6 miles above the city on Rte. 1. After driving past dozens of plants along River Road, it is fascinating finally to get inside the gates for a close-up look at one. DOW began operating at the site in 1956. Today it is the largest petrochemical plant in Louisiana, with 18 separate production units on 1,400 acres of former cane fields. The DOW complex is like a small city, with its own fire department, 44 miles of railroad track, and a power-generating system. The coal gasification plant is the largest of its type in the world, generating enough power to supply Baton Rouge with electricity.

All of these resources are dedicated to the production of a number of base or "feeder" chemicals, which are shipped elsewhere for conversion to retail products. Among the substances routinely produced are chlorine, vinyl chloride, chlorinated polyethylene, and methocel, a wood pulp product "used to thicken McDonald's milkshakes" (yum yum).

Displays at the conference center diagram the chemicals manufactured here and their common uses (no appointment necessary). Call in advance to view a short video and get a tour through one of three nonhardhat areas: Environmental Operations, Polyethylene Plant, or Research Laboratories. Probably the most impressive part of the tour is simply traveling around the facilities, which bristle with power and hiss with steam. You will drive down avenues with such quaint names as Chlorine and Caustic roads, below pressurized storage tanks, and past blazing flares, which are constantly lit to burn off escaping wastes.

As you tour the plant, below you lies a pool of toxic chemical waste, more than 46,000 tons of it, that now covers over 30 underground acres. DOW dumped the chemicals, liquid, and sludge into 15-foot-deep unlined pits between 1958 and 1973 and is now investing huge sums of money to try to pump them back to the surface before they reach the drinking-water aquifer for the city of Plaquemine. The old dumping area and 224 pumps are not on the public tour.

To get to DOW from Rte. 1 in Plaquemine, turn right at the stoplight onto Woodland Road. Go about a half-mile and take a left towards the plant at the DOW sign. Before you pass the guard's gate, take a right to the visitors' parking lot and the conference center. Although the conference center display is open every weekday, to be sure of getting a tour it is suggested that you call a couple of days in advance. Tours are often conducted on Wednesdays, but the DOW staff is very accommodating. (225) 685-8000 or 685-6623.

Benoit's Meat Block Meat Market. Rte. 1, Addis.

This meat market 5 miles above Plaquemine and 15 miles south of I-10 is the last stop on the River Road west bank tour. Benoit's has a complete selection of Cajun meats, from fresh whole rabbits to homemade sausages and stuffed chickens. Everything is smoked or prepared on the premises. The specialties are tasso, andouille, and thick ropes of delicious Cajun beef jerky. I recommend visiting at lunchtime so you can try one of Benoit's heavy lunch plates (take-out service only) or well-stuffed po' boys. Lunch is sold Monday through Friday from 11 to 2. The market is open Monday through Friday from 8 A.M. to 6 P.M. and Saturday until 1 P.M. (225) 749-3869.

River Road West Bank Food and Lodging

LODGING

Oak Alley Plantation Bed and Breakfast River Road, Vacherie.

Bay Tree Plantation Bed and Breakfast River Road, Vacherie.

Nottoway Plantation Bed and Breakfast Rte. 1, 2 miles above White Castle.

FOOD

★B&C Cajun Deli/Seafood Seafood, $. River Road, Vacherie.

Ruggiero's Restaurant Local Fave, $-$$. 206 Railroad Ave., Donaldsonville.

Railroad Cafe Local Fave, $. 212 Railroad Ave., Donaldsonville.

★City Cafe Local Fave, $. 53945 Main St., Plaquemine.

Benoit's Meat Block Meat Market/Plate lunch. Rte. 1, Addis.

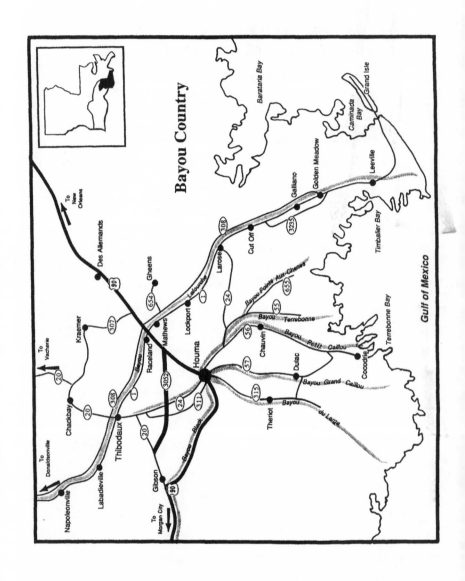

Bayou Country

11

Bayou Country

Bayou Country is a vast sodden expanse of land sandwiched between the Mississippi River and the Atchafalaya Basin just west of New Orleans, where the southeastern tip of Acadiana dips its frayed toe into the Gulf of Mexico. It is comprised of the coastal parishes of Lafourche, Terrebonne, and Assumption, which are connected to New Orleans and Teche Country by U.S. 90 in the south and reached from River Road by Rte. 1 in the north. Nearly three-quarters of the area is open water or wooded swamp, but its nickname arises from the dozens of bayous that meander southward towards the Gulf.

Bayou Country begins less than an hour west of the Crescent City. While it correctly bills itself as "the closest Cajun Country to New Orleans," many of its towns, which cling to narrow bayou levees and ridges, are among the most remote and unspoiled places in all of South Louisiana. Watery isolation has made the region a favorite destination among fishermen, bird watchers, and those interested in traditional Cajun language and folkways. Unfortunately, few places remain where one can hear Cajun music, and Zydeco is nonexistent in this predominantly white region.

Travel throughout Bayou Country is a truly unique experience, as roads cling to natural ridges. The coastal town of Grand Isle is 55 miles from New Orleans "as the crow flies" and about 100 miles by car. Port Fourchon on Bayou Lafourche is about 30 miles from Cocodrie on neighboring Bayou Terrebonne but is separated by 80 miles of road. Throughout much of the 19th century, the only way to get from Bayou Country (and other points farther west) to New Orleans was by boats traveling up Bayou Lafourche to the Mississippi, then back down the river to the city. Early ranchers developed trails for moving livestock from western ranges to market in New Orleans. These trails formed the basis for what is now the primary east-west route, U.S. 90 or the Old Spanish Trail. Even modern U.S. 90 has its surprises. Decades since construction commenced, engineers are still slogging through the swamp west of Houma. Just past Raceland the four-lane ends and motorists have the choice of following old U.S. 90 south through Houma (two lanes most of the way) or continuing west on two-lane Rte. 3052.

NEW ORLEANS TO LAFOURCHE
TRAVEL TIP

To reach the Bayou Country of Lafourche from the New Orleans Airport, travel west on I-10 about two miles and exit on I-310 South. I-310 connects with U.S. 90 at Boutte; from there it is only about 20 minutes to Bayou Lafourche. From New Orleans one may also connect with U.S. 90 at the Huey P. Long Bridge (Clearview Parkway South exit from I-10).

Des Allemands

The first Bayou Country town you will encounter driving west from New Orleans on U.S. 90 is Des Allemands. Named for the adjacent bayou and lake, this community, just 30 miles outside the Crescent City, is best known for catfish. According to LSU biologist Jerald Horst, "It is the most productive catfish fishery in the state, and Louisiana produces more catfish for its size than any other place." Several million pounds of catfish are caught here each year and the town rightfully calls itself the Catfish Capital of the Universe. It is home of the Catfish Festival (first weekend in July) and Spahr's Catfish Pond Restaurant.

Catfish Festival First weekend in July.

Thousands of pounds of the best catfish in the world, floured, fried, and for sale, make this a worthwhile event. When you get full, you can wander over and watch the catfish-eating contest. (504) 758-7542.

★Spahr's Catfish Pond Restaurant Seafood/Local Fave, $. U.S. 90 W., Des Allemands.

Spahr's has some of the best fried catfish anywhere! The regular lunch special of catfish filets and catfish sauce piquant is a steal. The dining room of this former service station has floor-to-ceiling windows that look south onto the Des Allemands marsh, where a family of goats wander unfenced on a small island of grass. Spahr's is located about a mile west of Bayou Des Allemands. It is open seven days a week from 10 A.M. to 9 P.M. (504) 758-1602.

Kraemer

About 9 miles past Des Allemands, a sign marks the turnoff for Rte. 307 to the swamp village of Kraemer. Even if you are not planning on taking one of the swamp tours from Kraemer, this is a great route for seeing the terrain and wildlife of Bayou Country. The drive north from U.S. 90 on Rte. 307 drops from cane fields to swamp in less than

10 miles. The present-day town of Kraemer (if you can call a place whose only two businesses are swamp tours and alligator processing a "town") was a cluster of homes called Bayou Boeuf (for the adjacent stream) until a few years ago when the postal service decided to move the Kraemer post office to this location. On the banks of cypress-shrouded Bayou Boeuf you will find Torres' and Zam's swamp tours. Also on the banks beside the bridge are the now-closed trading post and tiny wood-frame theater of old Bayou Boeuf. How did a community this size support a theater?

★Torres' Swamp Tours Rte. 307, at Bayou Boeuf Bridge.

Guide Roland Torres' family has lived on the banks of Bayou Boeuf for five generations of lumber men, trappers, and hunters. Like his ancestors, he enjoys a life close to the water, hunting alligator and deer and fishing on the miles of surrounding swamp. He remembers traveling by boat across Bayou Boeuf to go to school, but proudly asserts, "I got my Ph.D. in the swamp." Although this is not a deep-swamp tour (the cruise follows the shores of Bayou Boeuf), nobody can spot a snake on a tree branch or alligator in a thicket faster than Torres. Many tour guides talk a lot of "bull" for tourists. Torres just uses his life in the swamp, his 20 years as a Fish and Game Agent, and his honest warmth to make the trip come alive. He has a small zoo of alligators, nutria, turtles, and birds in his backyard and a sheltered picnic area with rest rooms. Torres usually operates one tour in the morning and two in the afternoon. The cost is $10 for adults and $5 for children (by reservation only). (504) 633-7739.

Zam's Swamp Tours Rte. 307, at Bayou Boeuf Bridge.

Zam's is operated by "Papa Gator" Tregle, who has an alligator hide and fur-processing business out back. The tour covers the same stretch of Bayou Boeuf as Torres', but the highlight is a stroll through his yard, where you will see dozens of hides, feet, heads, and other gator parts hung out to dry. The best time for this tour is in the late fall, when the alligator season is winding down and the processing business is gearing up. On one visit he let us hold a baby nutria and showed us its mother's freshly cleaned pelt! Even if the processing business is not in full swing, there are plenty of the reptiles to be seen in Tregle's own gator pond. You can purchase souvenir alligator parts (great for key chains and conversation pieces) from his eccentric gift shop for a fraction of what they cost in New Orleans. Tregle's daughter Diana acts as guide on the cruise (not deep swamp) up the banks of Bayou Boeuf. Tours are at 10 A.M. and 2 P.M. The tour costs $12.50 for adults and $6 for children. (504) 633-7881.

Tour guide "Papa Gator" Tregle. (Photo by Julie Posner)

Chackbay

There is not much to see in Chackbay, the hometown of U.S. Congressman Billy Tauzin, but the town, just 10 miles from River Road and Kraemer on Rte. 20, is a good food stop on a day trip from New Orleans. In early September Chackbay hosts a Gumbo Festival with Cajun bands.

★**Boudreaux's Restaurant** Down Home, $. 507 Rte. 20, Chackbay.

This working man's eatery occupies half of an old service station. It is a prime spot for sampling the bounty of the surrounding swamp. Whole fried alligator legs with all the trimmings are around $9, and a small serving of alligator or turtle sauce piquant is under $6. More delectable are the crawfish etouffée and stew. I recommend the homemade onion rings and (when it is available) *tarte à la bouillee* (boiled milk custard in a sweet-dough pie shell). It's delicious with a dark cup of blackeye coffee. From Kraemer take Rte. 307 10 miles to the intersection of Rte. 20. Turn onto Rte. 20 west and Boudreaux's is about 3 miles up on the right. Hours are Sunday and Tuesday through Thursday from 10 A.M. to 7:45 P.M. Friday and Saturday they close at 9:45. (504) 633-2382.

★Bowie Junction Barbecue Local Fave, $. U.S. 90, east of Raceland.

Get your ribs or Cajun beef jerky with a hefty side order of local history at the Junction. The dining room is decorated with photographs and artifacts from the phantom town of Bowie, which once thrived in the nearby swamp. You would never guess that the area had been a booming lumber town (bigger than Raceland) with a railroad depot and hotel. It is as if the swamp simply sucked it up. Actually, Bowie's complete disappearance may be credited to fire, flood, and the deforestation of valuable cypress shortly after the turn of the century. Bowie Junction proprietor Ronnie Cameron stumbled upon the town's dump while hunting in the swamp with a cousin and has since become the unofficial historian.

Fortunately you get more than history here. Ronnie's ribs, brisket, and baked beans are delicious. My top recommendation is the densely smoked and heavily seasoned beef jerky, the most pungent and truly tender I have ever eaten! It is apparently made from quarter-inch-thick strips of brisket that have been slathered with seasoning and smoked to perfection. It is not cheap, but a little goes a long way and is nice to have on a car tour or fishing trip down Bayou Lafourche. Bowie Junction is just west of the turnoff for Kraemer. Hours are 9 A.M. to 9 P.M. on weekdays and until 10 P.M. on weekends. (504) 537-3876.

INTRODUCTION TO LAFOURCHE

The grand stream of Bayou Country is Bayou Lafourche (French for fork). A former course of the Mississippi River, Lafourche snakes south for over a hundred miles from its severed junction with the Mississippi at Donaldsonville before reaching a terminus at the coastal fishing resort (and former pirate haven) of Grand Isle. Once the province of several Indian tribes, the bayou was settled by Germans and Acadians in the mid-18th century. On the upper reaches are dozens of plantations, which give way to small truck farms and fishing communities in the south.

The uninterrupted stretch of communities along the more densely settled west bank of the bayou has earned Lafourche the nickname "the longest Main Street in America." To drive the full length of Lafourche on the narrow roads (Rte. 308 and Rte. 1) that parallel each bank can take most of a day. There are bridges at each small town to permit access to either bank. Most travelers intersect Bayou Lafourche on U.S. 90 just below Raceland and head down Rte. 1 through the fishing villages of south Lafourche to spend time surf casting, beach combing, bird watching, or camping at Grand Isle State Park. Those interested in visiting the Acadian Cultural Center or Laurel Valley Village Plantation can head 20 minutes north to Thibodaux.

SOUTH BAYOU LAFOURCHE

South Lafourche is an easy day trip from New Orleans or side trip for travelers heading to Houma. Along the 65-mile stretch of bayou between U.S. 90 and the coastal village of Grand Isle, the Cajun language and culture are vibrant. Residents speak in a distinctive accent and employ their own variety of French known as Lafourchaise. The best drive follows Rte. 1 down the west side of the stream. A short drive south takes visitors to Adam's Market (and mounted-animal menagerie), Golden Ranch Plantation (on the east side), and the Louisiana Catalog Store. Land narrows to a thin strip on either side of the bayou, and cane fields give way to pasture. You may purchase handwoven garlands of fresh garlic, baskets of Creole tomatoes, or fresh Gulf shrimp. At Golden Meadow, the land plays out on the east side and traffic is funneled onto Rte. 1. Shrimp boats line the bayou and little bars accommodate offshore oil workers. From marinas and roadside vantage points, recreational fishermen ply some of the most productive waters in the state.

The history of settlement in southern Lafourche has been one of retreat. With the same disregard for brooding nature that sees men building condominiums on sea islands and mansions on seismic faults overlooking the Pacific, the earliest settlers of south Lafourche arrived in the early 19th century and established themselves directly on the Gulf. They bypassed higher land to nest on coastal *cheniers* (low-lying oak ridges) with access to prime fishing. Nature was kind until 1893, when a fierce hurricane drove 4 to 12 feet of water over most of Chenier Caminada. Two thousand lives were lost, the majority of homes were destroyed, and the *chenier* itself was wiped from the map. Most of the hardy survivors scavenged what remained of their homes, floated them northwest to Leeville on Bayou Lafourche, and rebuilt.

Shrimp boat on Bayou Lafourche. (Photo by Julie Posner)

In 1909 and 1915, two more catastrophic storms inundated the coast. The last of these erased Leeville and sent survivors fleeing northward again.

Lafourche Parish Tourist Commission Rte. 1, south of U.S. 90.

The Lafourche visitors center has information on all the attractions of the upper and lower bayou. French-speaking staff are always on duty and several brochures are available in French. It is right below the U.S. 90 bridge. The center is open Monday through Friday from 9 to 4 and Saturday from 10 to 3. (504) 537-5800.

Adam's Fruit Market 5013 Rte. 1 S., Mathews.

Adam's Fruit Market is a fine introduction to life on the southern bayou. Since 1939 this store has been serving Raceland and Lockport. You will find fresh local produce, cane syrup, honey, and an assortment of dry goods housed in a large room decorated with fishing pictures and mounted trophies. The owner does his own taxidermy work and has created a crazy exhibit of stuffed alligators, nutria, and snakes scattered among the shelves of food. Fishing licenses, supplies, and souvenirs are available along with advice on fishing spots, tides, and weather. Adam's is about 1.5 miles south of

U.S. 90. It is open seven days a week from 6:30 A.M. to 6:30 P.M. (504) 532-3165.

Golden Ranch Plantation Rte. 654, Gheens.

At Golden Ranch Plantation (on the east bank of Bayou Lafourche) you can see the ruins of an old sugar mill and the oldest brick slave cabin in South Louisiana (one of very few in the state still in existence). The only building open to the public is the original plantation store, with yards of empty shelves and a deserted post-office counter. Storekeeper Angeline Rogers grew up on the plantation. Her last regular customers were kids who stopped by for penny candies. You can still purchase snacks and work clothes.

The Golden Ranch rests amid one of the largest freshwater swamps south of U.S. 90. It was purchased in 1744 by Claude Dubreivl, who traded cattle to Indians for the property. John Gheens, for whom the community is now named, bought the ranch in 1879. As many as 100 families lived on the plantation, which had its own lumber and sugar mills, blacksmith, butcher, and boardinghouse. From U.S. 90 travel three miles down the bayou on Rte. 308 (east side). From the west bank cross the Mathews Bridge and turn right onto Rte. 308. One mile below the Mathews Bridge turn left on Rte. 654. The plantation is 6.5 miles east of the bayou. (504) 532-2524.

Lockport

Rte. 1 diverges from the bayou and crosses a former channel of the Intracoastal Waterway at this community of 3,000 about five miles south of U.S. 90. Lockport is one of three incorporated towns in Lafourche and the best place on the entire bayou to look for a lunch or supper. Most of its citizens find work in the oil, marine, or fishing industries. Some travel five miles south to the busy Bollinger Shipyard. For a break from the traffic on Rte. 1 turn towards the bayou on Vacherie Street (just below the Intracoastal Waterway) and drive until you reach Main Street, which parallels Bayou Lafourche. Here you will find the old downtown and the brick locks for which the town is named.

Bayou Lafourche Folklife Museum Main Street (Rte. 655), Lockport.

This little museum is located in the deco-style Louisiana Power and Light Building at the corner of Lafourche and Main streets, on the bayou. There is a small collection of artifacts, photos, and historical information. The best reason to visit the museum is to get off the bustle of Rte. 1 and see the old locks and small cluster of buildings that were downtown Lockport. The museum does not have regular hours, but is operated by Madonna Scurlock, who runs a Bed and Breakfast across the street. Turn towards the bayou on Vacherie Street. At the bayou turn left for one block on Main Street. (504) 532-3334.

FOOD

Blackie's Monorail Cafe Local Fave, $. Rte. 1, Lockport.

Blackie's is popular among local workers, serving hefty hot plate lunches and po' boys. It is also open for breakfast. The owner bought the old monorail depot from the New Orleans World Exposition, shipped the pieces to Lockport, and reassembled them in this simple eatery. Hours are 6 A.M. to 10 P.M. Monday through Saturday. (504) 532-5117.

Calais' Family Dining Local Fave, $. 5797 Rte. 1, Lockport.

This is one of my favorite places to eat on lower Bayou Lafourche. It beats expectations with overstuffed seafood po' boys and huge plate lunches in a pleasant environment. The most popular item is the lunch buffet, which draws crowds of workers on weekdays and families on Sundays (not available Saturdays). Although the food is simple (baked or fried chicken, beans, hamburger steaks, rice dressing), they use real potatoes, and cut and fry onion rings to order. Proprietor Bubba Townsend may lose more than a few customers if his food disappoints; he is also Lockport's mayor. Calais' is open Monday through Saturday from 10:30 A.M. until 9 P.M. and Sunday from 11 A.M. until 2 P.M. The buffet is available on weekdays and Sundays from 11 A.M. until 2 P.M. (504) 532-2925.

Joey's Seafood Boiled Seafood, $-$$. 5365 Rte. 1, North Lockport.

Joey's serves the best boiled seafood on lower Lafourche in a new dining room on the banks of the bayou. They also serve sandwiches, fried seafood, and gumbos, but the Spartan eating area and steaming tanks in the kitchen mark this as a boiling point. On weekend evenings folks queue up outside waiting for a table and platter of bright red boiled crawfish or crabs, so get there early. Hours are 10 A.M. to 9 P.M. Tuesday through Thursday and until 10 P.M. on weekends (closed Monday). (504) 532-5777.

LODGING

Gouaux House Inn 115 Lafourche St., Lockport.

Accommodations are in a large turn-of-the-century guesthouse (not in the owner's residence). Two groups of guests may occasionally be housed at one time. There are two rooms with full beds (each with private bath) and one room with two single beds. Gouaux House is walking distance to the bayou, locks, and museum. Owner Madonna Scurlock speaks some French. The double rate is $75 to $95. (504) 532-3334.

Bouverans Plantation Bed and Breakfast 7602 Rte. 1, Lockport.

Accommodations are in the owner's residence, an 1860 plantation house listed on the National Register of Historic Places. There is one guest room with a queen-size bed and private bath. A fold-out sofa is available. Owners Barbara and René Claudet speak some French. Doubles are $85-$95. Visa and Mastercard are accepted. (504) 532-6157.

Fort Romy Bed and Breakfast 102 Romy Dr. at Rte. 1, Lockport.

Hosts Mary Ann and Venice Esponge speak French fluently. In homestay style, guests share their sprawling modern house on Bayou Lafourche at the corner of Romy Drive. This B&B came to be known as Fort Romy for the imposing white wall the Esponges built around the house. Inside the compound are a large swimming pool and private outdoor sitting areas. Amenities include free laundry facilities, a billiards room, and a small chapel. Double rates are $75 and up. (504) 532-6177.

Larose

At this small community 16 miles south of U.S. 90, Rte. 1 shifts away from the bayou for a few blocks to cross the Intracoastal Waterway. Here you will find a modern supermarket, discount chain store, and several fast-food joints. At the north end of town Rte. 24 intersects Rte. 1, providing a scenic shortcut west through the swamp town of Grand Bois to the Pointe Aux Chenes Wildlife Area and Houma (*see* South of Houma section).

★**French Food Festival** Last weekend in October.

October is a great time to be out in Lafourche country and this wonderful little food festival is a great reason to make the trip. There is music and entertainment but the main attraction is Cajun cooking prepared by local residents. (504) 693-7355.

Gautreaux's Bed and Breakfast 507 W. 11th St., Larose.

Hosts Renella Chouest and Peggy Terrebonne speak fluent French. Their Bed and Breakfast is in a small Acadian-style cottage recently built by Ms. Terrebonne's father, who lives next door. The cottage, which has a bedroom, bath, kitchen, and fold-out sofa for extra guests, is in a quiet neighborhood just off the bayou. The double rate is $85. (504) 693-4316.

★Louisiana Catalog Store 1479 Rte. 1, Larose.

Author and film director Glen Pitre (best known for *Belizaire the Cajun*) founded the nation's biggest clearinghouse for printed and video material about Louisiana on the west bank of Bayou Lafourche. The store, now operated by Rochelle Gautreaux and Melanie Boulet, also carries a good selection of gifts and other quality materials relating to Cajun Country. Gautreaux is a native of Lafourche and you can get help finding local attractions by consulting her. Anyone interested enough in the area to drive down from U.S. 90 should make a point of stopping and browsing here; those with a special interest in the people and places of South Louisiana will want to make a special trip to visit this amazing store. The store has expanded to a 2,500-square-foot showroom at Rte. 1 and W. 70th Street. It is open Monday through Saturday from 10 to 6. To get a copy of the mail-order catalogue, write: P.O. Box 1610, Larose, La. 70373. 1-800-375-4100.

Cut Off

Is there another village with a more prosaic name than "Cut Off"? Like many of the "line villages" along Lafourche, Larose and Cut Off seem to just run together. It takes a local to distinguish which businesses are located in which town. The small shrimping community stretching along both sides of the bayou about 19 miles south of U.S. 90 earned some attention among sports fans who recognize it as the home of Bobby Hebert, former quarterback of the New Orleans Saints.

★Duet's Bakery 14410 W. Main St. (Rte. 1 at West 42nd), Cut Off.

One of the saddest experiences in researching this book was finding that Dufrene's Bakery had closed. One of the happiest moments was finding that Duet's (pronounced "doo-ways") was selling cookies, pies, and hardtack baked from the exact same recipes that Dufrene's used for over 50 years! The hardtack is the most unusual item, a brittle loaf sold by the bag to folks going out on boats. Better buys for hungry travelers are pecan tarts, custard pies, and fabulous pecan cookies. Everything here tastes homemade. There are no beverages and no seats available so get your cup of coffee at the McDonald's (upstream) and enjoy your treats by the bayou or while browsing at the Louisiana Catalog Store. Duet's is open Monday through Saturday from 6 A.M. to 5 P.M. (504) 693-6895.

Cut Off Net Shop Rte. 1 at Cote Blanche Bridge.

If you want to see nets being made and repaired, netmaker Troy

Terrebonne is at work every weekday and accommodates curious travelers who want to stop by for a snoop. Look for the bayou-side Cut Off Net Shop, just south of the Cote Blanche Bridge. (504) 632-3248.

Cajun Pecan House Rte. 1 and W. 67th St., Cut Off.

It seems as though the Cajun Pecan House is always closed when I pass by, but the King Cake (available between New Year's and Mardi Gras) and pecan pralines from this sweet shop have been highly recommended. They are only open from October to Easter. (504) 632-2337.

LODGING

Hassell House Bed and Breakfast 500 E. 74th St., Cut Off.

Hosts Tom and Rothie Hassell offer accommodations in a private two-room and two-bath cottage recently built behind their own new home in a subdivision on the east side of Bayou Lafourche. With a fold-out sofa, the cottage may hold up to six people. Guests will enjoy a screened porch, swing, and free laundry facilities. Doubles are $87. (504) 632-8088.

TRAVEL TIP/SHORTCUT

Rte. 3235 is a four-lane bypass around the towns of Galliano and Golden Meadow (notorious speedtraps). At the South Lafourche Bridge (120th Street), go right on Rte. 3162. Less than one mile west, turn onto Rte. 3235 (known locally as the "New Fourlane").

Andy's Meat Market Rte. 3235 (Rte. 1 bypass), Galliano.

This is your last stop heading south for hot boudin, cracklins, or beef jerky, all of which are nice to have in the car or cooler on fishing and camping trips. Andy's is open Monday through Saturday from 7 A.M. to 5 P.M. (504) 474-7575.

Golden Meadow

Talk about getting down! The fishing town of Golden Meadow, at two feet above sea level, might be more appropriately called Golden Marsh. It was reportedly named for the fields of goldenrod that early settlers found in the area. This village was not even on the map in 1915 when a great hurricane uprooted residents from homes farther south in Leeville. Many of the refugees packed their belongings and some actually moved their homes upstream to this scrap of "high" ground, and began the settlement of what is now Golden Meadow. Be aware

Shrine on lower Lafourche. (Photo by Julie Posner)

(and beware!)—Golden Meadow is serious about its speed limit!

★Duet's Bakery 18134 Rte. 1 (at W. 175th Street), Golden Meadow.
Duet's replaced Dufrene's Bakery, which had served Bayou Lafourche for nearly 70 years, and uses the same recipes! I recommend their pecan cookies and bars. You may want to call in advance to see if they have the local specialty, *tarte à la bouillee.* Duet's is open Monday through Saturday from 6 A.M. to 5 P.M.

★Randolph's Cajun/Creole/Seafood, $-$$. 806 Rte. 1, Golden Meadow.
Randolph's is the oldest restaurant on Bayou Lafourche and one of the best. At lunch, men linger over cups of black coffee and chat in French. The walls are decorated with fishing pictures and 1940s photos of the original dining room. Randolph's is an economical place to get tasty home-cooked-style food. A plate of catfish with white beans and gumbo costs about $7. Daily lunch specials vary, but there is always gumbo on Friday. Lunch specials are served on weekdays from 11 until they run out. Randolph's is open from 11 to 9 Wednesday through Sunday. (504) 475-5272.

Petit Corporal In the heart of Golden Meadow.

This small wooden boat on a platform beside the bayou (just south of Randolph's restaurant) is described as the "oldest boat in Southern Lafourche." Built in the mid-1800s, it remained in the Theriot family for a century, first powered by a sail and then a 3.5-horsepower engine. The boat was donated to Golden Meadow as a historical landmark and has been on display here since 1969. As I read the descriptive marker, a guy barreling past in a pickup hollered out his window, "That's my grandfather's boat!"

Leeville

When Leeville (about 57 miles south of U.S. 90) was settled by refugees from nearby Chenier Caminada around the turn of the century, it was an oak-covered "island." These people had barely reestablished themselves when storms erased Leeville Chenier from the map. There was so little ground left to build on that most of the twice-displaced residents moved north and established themselves at present-day Golden Meadow. Leeville remained largely unsettled until oil was discovered in the area in 1931. Today it is marked by a couple of shrimp docks, the oil field, and several bait stands. A large bridge spans Bayou Lafourche here, providing an expansive view of the mostly uninhabited coastal wetlands.

Smith Shrine Rte. 1, Leeville.

Another entry in the list of places claiming to be the World's Smallest Chapel was established just north of the Leeville Bridge in 1971. Noonie and Abraham Smith built the shrine commemorating their children's untimely death across the road from their gift shop "so we would remember to close it when it rains."

Port Fourchon

Just south of Leeville, Rte. 1 turns southeast to Grand Isle and Rte. 3090 heads west to the industrial superport of Fourchon. This is a primary jumping-off point for offshore oil industry workers, who head out for two-, three-, and four-week stints in the Gulf of Mexico. Three and a half miles from the turnoff there is a free boat launch, and four miles west of Rte. 1, Fourchon Road ends on a desolate stretch of sandbagged Gulf beach. You can drive your vehicle along the sandbag line, find a place to park and picnic, camp overnight for free, or cast a fishing line in the surf.

Kajun Sportsman Marina Rte. 1, Fourchon.

Kajun Sportsman is the newest full-service marina complex on Rte. 1. It has all the supplies you could want from bait to beer, a full-service restaurant, and a tavern. This is the last stop for folks heading out Rte. 3090 to the Fourchon Beach for fishing or camping. The marina store and gas station are open 24 hours, daily. The bait shop is open from about 7 A.M. to 3 P.M. (504) 386-2727.

Kajun Sportsman Cabins and R.V. Park Rte. 3090 at Rte. 1, Fourchon.

Located just around the corner from the marina, these raised cabins (three or four units in each) are some of the nicest accommodations on lower Lafourche. That is not saying much. Rooms are utilitarian, clean, modern, and quiet enough to provide comfort to someone other than a tired fisherman. The liveliest night life on lower Lafourche is around the corner at the marina bar and restaurant. Double rooms with queen beds, A/C, and cable TV are $50 to $65 (less in winter). (504) 396-2792.

Kajun Sportsman Restaurants Seafood, $ (lunch)-$$. Rte. 1, Fourchon.

Toupsie's Kajun Eatery serves fresh seafood, pasta, and steaks in a large dining room. The quality and price are okay for a place in the middle of nowhere. The **Bait House Restaurant** next door serves a hearty midday buffet. After dinner, visit the adjacent **Kajun Night Club** (featuring live music on weekends). Toupsie's is open Tuesday through Sunday from 11 to 9. (504) 396-2729.

Chenier Caminada

Just west of the bridge into Grand Isle, Rte. 1 crosses three small passes (excellent bridge-fishing spots). This watery area is the former site of Chenier Caminada. In the early 19th century, Caminada was a thriving community. Today there are a few camps on stilts beside a canal, but the community, like the land it was built on, was demolished by the hurricane of 1893.

Hurricane Centennial Marker/Mass Grave Rte. 1, Chenier Caminada.

All but 13 of the 300 homes in Caminada were destroyed in the hurricane of 1893 and over half of the 1,500 residents were killed. A mass grave and tiny cemetery beside Rte. 1 hold the remains of many of the victims. A hundred years after the tragic storm a historical marker and flag were raised at this site.

Elmer's Island Rte. 1, west of Caminada Bay Bridge.

This is a privately owned fishing and camping compound, open for an $8 fee. See description under Grand Isle Recreation. (504) 787-2509.

★Cigar's Store & Restaurant Rte. 1, west of Caminada Bay Bridge.

Launch, live bait, camping, tackle, and restaurant. See Grand Isle section.

Grand Isle

Since the late 1800s, Grand Isle has been the major attraction on Louisiana's Gulf coast. Too battered by storms to support an upscale resort, the island is instead a destination for fishermen, bird watchers, and anyone who likes the salt air and warm water of Gulf beaches. All of Grand Isle's beaches are public. Swimmers, sunbathers, and surf-casting fishermen find easy access to the sand by way of short paths and decks extending over dunes from Rte. 1. Elmer's Island and Grand Isle State Park provide an opportunity to camp, fish, and watch the thousands of migratory (winter) and tropical (summer) birds that nest on the island. There are motels and cottages (nothing upscale), which rent by the day, week, or season. It gets hot and humid on Grand Isle, and the Gulf water is warm, so the best time to visit is in the fall and spring. This is the off season for local vacationers, so

Grand Isle. (Courtesy of U.S. Army Corps of Engineers)

rates are lower and crowds thin. The off season is also prime time for bird watching and fishing!

Grand Isle is 74 miles south of U.S. 90, almost two hours' drive by way of Rte. 1. It is a barrier island about eight miles long and one mile wide. Stretching east to west along the Gulf coast, it protects Caminada and Barataria bays and their surrounding marsh. The northern or bay side is covered with oak and chinaberry trees and is home to most of the permanent residents of the island, while the coast side is lined with camps and commercial establishments. Grand Isle was connected to the mainland by the Caminada Bay Bridge in 1930. When the offshore oil industry took off in the 1950s, it became an important oil terminal. Rte. 1 leading to Grand Isle is now a veritable drag strip of oil workers heading home from weeks at sea and vacationers burning the pavement to get to their waterside retreats.

The island was first settled in the late 18th century. By the early 1800s it had a population of about 75. It was at this time that pirate activity in the area was at its most brazen. Jean Lafitte's buccaneers, known as Baratarians, developed a black-market trade with New Orleans' markets. They shipped goods through the shallow bays and bayous above Grand Isle to the swamps just west of the city.

Until shortly after the War Between the States, the island remained devoid of significant commercial development. Following the war, an unsuccessful sugar plantation was bought by banking interests in New Orleans, who began the development of a resort complex. Just one year after the grandest beachside hotel and recreation facility (the Ocean Club) was completed, the 160-room structure and other new resorts were smashed to smithereens in the hurricane of 1893.

RECREATION AND FISHING

Those looking for a refreshing swim may be disappointed by the lukewarm waters of the Gulf. They may also be put off by the spectre of dozens of oil rigs within sight of the beach and a plethora of flotsam. Most people come here to enjoy the sun, bird watch, and especially fish. There are plenty of opportunities to do all of these at surfside recreation areas on the island. Some of the best bird watching is at the far east end of the island near the Coast Guard Station, where Rte. 1 dead-ends into Barataria Pass.

The three primary areas to fish on Grand Isle are the surf, the roadside, and from bridges. The warm Gulf waters are perfect for surf casting. Late spring and summer are prime trout-fishing times. High-pressure systems hold the Gulf flat and the sun reveals dark forms of schooling fish 15 to 30 feet offshore. All you need is a medium-weight saltwater rod and reel and a couple of sparkle-beetle jigs from a local bait shop. Toss the jigs out and retrieve them in a jerky motion. Red-fish action heats up as the weather cools. The same fishing technique works for reds but a piece of fresh shrimp helps to sweeten the hook. The best beach fishing is in front of the Grand Isle Public Library on Rte. 1 and off of Elmer's Island (fee charged).

There are countless inland fishing places where you may catch red-fish, trout, drum, and croaker. The same technique may be used from these vantage points as in the surf, or try throwing shrimp beneath a weighted cork. Look for spots where current is flowing under the road and cast so that your bait is carried away from you. The most popular fishing structures are the three passes at Chenier Caminada, the west side of the wooden bridge leading onto Grand Isle (closed to vehicu-lar traffic), and the pier at Grand Isle State Park.

★Grand Isle State Park Rte. 1, east end of Grand Isle.

Whether you are visiting Grand Isle for the day or overnight, Grand Isle State Park is an essential stop. The park has a shaded pavilion with a descriptive display on the geology and history of the island. There is a three-story observation tower with a view of the entire island, a 400-foot fishing pier, and a number of bathhouses for swimmers. When the Gulf is rough, fishermen and crabbers can enjoy a small pier on the quiet bay side of the park. The wide beach is great for shelling, sunning, and picnicking.

Up to 100 overnight campers can pitch tents on the beach, but

Camping at Grand Isle State Park. (Photo by Julie Posner)

there are no hook-ups. On summer weekends and holidays, the park gets a lot of pressure and camping spaces fill up. Call in advance to check availability. The park is near the far east end of the island. Take Rte. 1 east about six miles from the bridge to the caution light. Stay to the right at the caution light and continue one block to the entrance. Admission is $2 a vehicle for up to four people. It costs $2 for adults and $1 for kids to fish from the pier. Camping is $10. The park is open from 6 A.M. to 10 P.M. in the summer and 8 A.M. to 7 P.M. in the winter (on Fridays and Saturdays during the winter it remains open until 10 P.M.). (504) 787-2559.

Elmer's Island Fishing/Camping. Rte. 1, west of Caminada Bay Bridge.

Elmer's Island is a privately owned fishing area and campground located on a spit of beach and marsh striated with canals. The island is totally undeveloped. A dirt road leads across several lagoons, which provide excellent trout and redfishing action on a high but falling tide. Find places where water is rushing under the road bed and throw your lures into the current. The road ends at a barren strip of beach, where you may fish for trout in the surf and camp out. Elmer's appeals to serious fishermen who are not troubled by a lack of electricity, running water, or sanitary facilities. It costs $8 a day to enter Elmer's whether you plan on fishing, camping, or both. (504) 787-2509.

SUPPLIES FOR FISHING AND CAMPING

Blue Water Sports Fishing and beach gear. Corner of Rte. 1 and Santiny.

This is one of a couple excellent supply stores on Rte. 1 in Grand Isle. You can purchase fishing licenses, rods and tackle, bait, camping gear, and anything you would want during a hot day on the beach. Blue Water is open from 8 A.M. to 6 P.M. daily during the summer and prime fishing months. (504) 787-2212.

★Cigar's Store Fishing gear, launch, camping, and seafood bar. Rte. 1 W.

Whatever you need pertaining to fishing you can get here, including live bait, tackle, rod and reel combos, and food. A boat launch provides access to Caminada and Barataria bays. The store opens around 5 A.M. and closes around midnight daily. (504) 787-3220.

UNUSUAL ATTRACTIONS

R&K's Oyster Place Oak Lane, one block off Rte. 1.

How do you list a place that is equally well known for its unusual collection of "oyster artifacts" and its fine fresh oysters? Raliegh and Kay Lasseigne run this oyster shop and shell museum in a tiny stand just off Rte. 1. Shells are displayed on every level surface and hung

Kay Lasseigne and her "po' boy oyster." (Photo by Macon Fry)

from the walls. There are massive and grotesque knots of shells, shells attached to all manner of objects, and shells of immense size. Kay calls the biggest specimen her "po' boy oyster" because it is big enough to fill a 12-inch loaf of French bread! Raliegh is a third-generation oysterman who spends his days harvesting and processing, while Kay tends the market. (504) 787-2444.

Grand Isle Tarpon Rodeo Last weekend in July.

In coastal Louisiana, fishing rodeos (tournaments) are more common than cowboy rodeos. This one is the craziest of all, with plenty of activities, food, music, and general carousing among the crowd that stays on shore. (504) 736-6400.

FOOD

There are not many places to eat in Grand Isle. Those spending a night might want to eat one meal at Cigar's and pick up (if you can't catch any) some fresh seafood or boiled crabs to take back to your camp. There is a large grocery store on Rte. 1.

Cigar's Cajun Cuisine Seafood, $-$$. Rte. 1 at the bridge.

This is the best eatery in Grand Isle, serving a variety of fresh seafood and Cajun fare. Cigar's is an informal place with nautical decor that caters to locals as well as the vacation crowd. A salad is delivered with even the most humble meal of soup and crackers. We got the oyster artichoke soup and gumbo and a couple of well-stuffed po' boys, but the fried seafood platters are most popular. For $6, you can purchase a lunch special of stew, salad, vegetable, bread, and dessert. Cigar's is located on the west end of the Caminada Bay Bridge. It is open from 10 A.M. to 10 P.M. daily. (504) 787-2188.

Cigar's Store Boiled Seafood. Rte. 1 by the bridge.

Cigar's Store sells the same boiled seafood as the restaurant, for a good bit less. In the evenings, fishermen and locals belly up to the counter for beers and dinner. You can get a tray of hard crabs ($1 each) or crawfish to eat at the bar or take back to your camp. They are open daily from about 5 A.M. to midnight. (504) 787-3220.

LODGING

Motels and Cottages: Grand Isle has hundreds of rooms, apartments, and cottages for rent. Most of these either cater to vacationers from Louisiana or attract overnight or weekend fishermen. Few of them are very modern. We have found the ones listed below to be clean and comfortable. Many are cute old cottages or rooms in older homes that have screened patios with cooking facilities so you can have an outdoor fish fry or crab boil. Off-season rates are usually offered October through April.

Sun and Sand Cabins 1 mile east of the bridge, $70 double.

Everything but towels is furnished. (504) 787-2456.

Tropical Motel, Inc. 3.5 miles east of the bridge, $89 cabins. (504) 787-3321 or 787-2898.

★Shady Rest Cottages Rte. 1 and Apple Street.

Individual cottages come with kitchens equipped with basic utensils. TV and A/C. There is a shady fish-cleaning and seafood-boiling area. Summer rates for one to four people are $60; larger cottages for five to six people are about $70 a night. (504) 787-3367.

★Bill's Shady Lawn Santiny Lane, one block off Rte. 1.

The proprietors of the Shady Lawn, Curtis and Kathleen LeBlanc, are old-timers on Grand Isle and veteran fisherfolk. People who come to the island to wet a line often drive up and down Rte. 1 looking for their brown Ram as a sure sign of a hot fishing spot. Their five apartments are among the nicest on the island. Most come with a couple of double beds and a few cots. They rent for $60 for four people and $5 each additional guest. There is a cottage with two double beds and five cots for $80. The best feature of Bill's is the shady lawn. There is a full set-up to cook fish or boil crabs, picnic tables, and a swing. Turn off Rte. 1 beside Blue Water Sports. (504) 787-3170.

★Bruce Apartments Landry Street, one block off Rte. 1.

The cottages are from the forties and some of the coziest on Grand Isle. Each camp is a double house with screened-in front porch and camp-style furnishings. Turn off of Rte. 1 by the supermarket on Landry Street, and look for Bruce's white wood-frame cabins on the left. Doubles cost $50 (less by the week or in off season). (504) 787-3374.

Gulfstream Apartments. (504) 787-3566.

Kirkland's Cove Apartments. (504) 787-3412.

Ocean Beach. (504) 787-3169.

Camping: There are quite a few small lots on the island with full hookups for RV campers (none of which take reservations). Cigar's Marina and the Offshore Campground are two of the more popular among the camp-and-fish crowd.

Elmer's Island Rte. 1 west of Caminada Bay Bridge.
See description under Recreation and Fishing section.

★Grand Isle State Park Rte. 1, east end of Grand Isle.
See description under Recreation and Fishing section.

NORTH BAYOU LAFOURCHE

For 50 miles between U.S. 90 at Raceland and its headwaters in the town of Donaldsonville on the Mississippi River, Upper Bayou Lafourche is adjoined by cane fields that slope gradually into swamp. The bayou has been dammed at its intersection with the river, and plantation homes along its banks look out on a sluggish stream choked with water hyacinths. Small sugarmill towns like Labadieville, Supreme, and Napoleonville form an almost continuous "line village" on the western side of the stream. This is a historic route traveled by early settlers as they moved down the bayou from the Mississippi River.

Similar to the Mississippi and Bayou Teche, many early land grants on Lafourche went to Acadians but were bought up by Anglo planters during the antebellum sugar boom.

Like the waters of the bayou, the towns along Upper Lafourche are quiet and darkly reflective. Even Thibodaux, a college town and the biggest population center on the bayou, seems more like an old trading post and mill town than a social or economic hub. The small farming communities of the area offer little in the way of food and entertainment, but Rte. 1 provides a good look at the "sugar bowl" of Louisiana and the unleveed bayou offers a scenic route between River Road and Bayou Country. The Acadian Cultural Center in Thibodaux and nearby Laurel Valley Village plantation are easy side trips from U.S. 90.

Lafourche Parish Tourist Commission Rte. 1 just south of U.S. 90.

The Lafourche Visitors Center has information on all the attractions of Bayou Lafourche. There are always French-speaking staff on duty and brochures in French are available. They have a brochure with self-guided driving and walking tours and maps of local towns. The Visitors Center is south of the U.S. 90 Bridge over Bayou Lafourche, so folks planning on traveling Upper Lafourche will have to make a very short detour south. The center is open Monday through Friday from 9 to 4 and Saturday from 10 to 3. (504) 537-5800.

Raceland

Three miles north of U.S. 90 on Bayou Lafourche, Raceland (population about 5,000) allegedly got its name from horse races that were held on the surrounding meadows in antebellum times. Nothing so exciting as horse racing transpires here now. The business area on the west bank is almost entirely closed. During the summer months, this is a good area to find farmers selling fresh vegetables from the backs of pickups or at roadside stands.

★Rouse's Bakery Local Fave. 3880 Rte. 1.

Rouse's Supermarket is one of few places where you can still purchase a *tarte à la bouillee*. The *tarte à la bouillee* is a traditional Cajun confection that I have not found sold anywhere except Bayou Country. It is rich boiled milk custard in a sweet-dough pie shell. I would stack this up against any similar poor boy's dessert in the South. Although Rouse's is a chain grocery with several locations in the region, don't let that put you off; they prepare all their baked goods fresh on the premises. The best time to get your *tarte à la bouillee* is in the morning when they are still hot from the oven and are more

easily eaten with a spoon than a fork (num-num). If you are not up
for sweets at breakfast, pick one up for dessert; get a fork from the
deli department and scarf down in the car! An eight-inch pie costs
about $3. Rouse's is one mile north of U.S. 90. It is open daily from
7 A.M. to 9 P.M. (504) 537-6666.

Thibodaux

Thibodaux, 20 miles north of U.S. 90 and 30 miles south of the Mississippi River, is the largest town on Bayou Lafourche, with a population of 15,000. The site was originally settled in the mid-1700s by
French and German people moving down from the river. It grew into
an important trading post at a time when goods traveling between
New Orleans and the Teche frontier moved to and from the Mississippi by way of Bayou Lafourche. The town became the seat of government in 1808 and was incorporated as Thibodauxville (after local
planter Henry Schuyler Thibodaux) in 1830.

Thibodaux is one of several cities in Cajun Country that proudly
claim to be a former home of Jim Bowie. Today, the old downtown
area, with its two-story businesses and iron balustrades, looks like a
weary French Quarter. New motels, fast-food restaurants, and shopping centers stretch along Canal Boulevard (Rte. 20) to the east and
west, away from the old bayou-side community. The center of activity,
however, is Nicholls State University on the southern edge of town.

Thibodaux Chamber of Commerce 1048 Canal Blvd.

You can get a walking-tour map for Thibodaux at the Chamber
offices about five blocks from downtown. Hours are Monday through
Friday from 8:30 to 4:30 and Saturday from 9 to 3. (504) 446-1187.

ATTRACTIONS

Old Thibodaux Walking Tour

The Thibodaux Walking Tour (map available at Lafourche Tourist
Commission or Thibodaux Chamber of Commerce) emanates from
the downtown area at Rte. 1 and Green Street. There is plenty of free
and inexpensive street parking in the area. Even without the
brochure, which lists only bare-bones information for about 50 buildings, you can enjoy a walk through the downtown area, which sports
a mixture of antebellum and turn-of-the-century homes and businesses. Most of the listed structures are in a 10-block swath stretching
west from the bayou between Narrow Street on the south and Jackson Street on the north.

The eastern edge of the tour is highlighted by the *Lafourche Parish*

Courthouse (at the corner of Second and Green streets), built in 1861. It is one of a handful of antebellum Louisiana courthouses still in use. Cornerstones of the western edge of the tour are two old churches. *St. Joseph Cathedral* (at Canal Boulevard and E. Seventh Street) was built in 1819 and was originally housed in a wood building, which burned in 1916. The "new" building was constructed in 1923 using many details copied from churches in Europe, including a vaulted ceiling and stained-glass window modeled after the rose window of Notre Dame Cathedral in France. Most unusual is the wax figure of St. Valerie on display (see description below). *St. John's Episcopal Church* (at 718 Jackson on the corner of Seventh Street) is the oldest Episcopal church in Louisiana and one of the oldest west of the Mississippi. It was consecrated in 1845 and is a rare example of Georgian church architecture. Visitors are admitted to the sanctuary, where they can see an old slave gallery, which now functions as a choir loft.

★St. Valerie Shrine St. Joseph Cathedral, Canal Boulevard at E. Seventh Street.

The St. Valerie Shrine is an ornate glass and wood casket containing a wax statue embedded with the actual severed arm of St. Valerie. Valerie was born in Rome and became a virgin Christian martyr when she was tortured and beheaded in the Roman Coliseum in the late second century. Fr. Charles Menard obtained Valerie's arm for St. Joseph Cathedral on a visit to Rome in 1867. Interestingly, he was offered a

St. Valerie Shrine at St. Joseph's Cathedral. (Photo by Macon Fry)

choice of relics by Cardinal Parizzi, either this arm or the severed head of St. Prosper. Father Menard decided the virgin's arm would best "increase among parishioners the spirit of piety and religion." When I called for more information on the relic I was informed that it was collected at the same time as a similar relic of St. Faustine (on display just up Bayou Lafourche in Plattenville), and rumor held that the two may have been inadvertently switched in transport. The shrine is located near the entrance to the cathedral. There are votive candles for religious pilgrims and descriptive information for the curious. The cathedral is usually open from 6 A.M. to 6 P.M. daily. (504) 446-1387.

Laurel Valley Village Two miles south of Rte. 20 on Rte. 308.

Laurel Valley Plantation is described as "the most intact turn-of-the-century sugar plantation complex in the country." This is one of very few places where you can actually see a variety of plantation outbuildings. The land here was deeded to an Acadian in the late 1700s but was subsequently bought by a wealthy planter from Mississippi. Laurel Valley was the most productive sugar plantation in the parish prior to the War Between the States. After the war it rebounded to become a nearly self-sufficient village by 1900. Cane was carried to a mill located on the premises via 15 miles of private (small gauge) rail.

All but one of the outbuildings are closed. The general store serves as a visitors center, museum, and gift shop. Volunteers provide

General store at Laurel Valley Village. (Photo by Julie Posner)

information on the history of the plantation, and you will find photographs and old farm equipment on display. There is local honey and cane syrup for sale. In a shed behind the store several dugout pirogues, a 27-foot lugger, and several other boats are on display.

Drive down the two-mile plantation road, which leads past rows of century-old laborers' cabins. At the end of the road are the wooden schoolhouse, blacksmith and cooperage shops, overseer's cabin, one-room school, and the crumbling mill, built in 1845. Although these buildings are preserved, they have not undergone substantial renovation and thus are closed to foot traffic. A visit to the store and grounds takes 45 minutes. There is no admission charged. Hours are from 10 to 4 weekdays and from noon to 4 weekends. (504) 446-7456.

Nicholls State University One mile south of Thibodaux on Rte. 1.

Nicholls State University, with its 166-acre campus overlooking Bayou Lafourche, is the biggest employer in the city of Thibodaux. The school was founded in 1948 and named for Thibodaux resident and two-term governor Francis T. Nicholls (1834-1912). The school has grown to encompass 88 degree programs offered through four senior academic colleges.

Allen Ellender Memorial Library: The Louisiana Collection, located on the third floor of the library, contains over 200,000 volumes pertaining to the people, geography, and history of the state. It is open during the fall, Monday through Thursday, from 7:30 A.M. to 11 P.M., Friday to 4:30 P.M., Saturday from noon to 4 P.M., and Sunday from 3 to 11 P.M.

Center for Traditional Boat Building: The Center for Traditional Louisiana Boat Building is located in the Allen Ellender Memorial Library at Nicholls State University. The Center conducts research on wooden boat building throughout South Louisiana and has a small exhibit in the first floor lobby of the library. Several boats are on display, along with a case full of pictures, artifacts, and models. Fishermen and outdoorsmen are constantly turning up old craft or portions thereof in the swamps of Cajun Country. The Center accepts donations, provides information, and will often send out personnel to examine artifacts. There are several boats from the Center on display at Laurel Valley Village, however the bulk of the Center's dugouts, luggers, and skiffs is housed in a barn on campus. Tours may be arranged on a day's notice. (504) 448-4626.

★Wetlands Acadian Cultural Center 314 St. Mary St., Thibodaux.

This is one of three Acadian Centers operated by Jean Lafitte National Park. Anyone with an interest in Cajun culture should visit this facility, which includes several permanent and rotating displays. Among the permanent exhibits are those dealing with the immigration of the Acadians, boat building, Cajun music, and the fishing and oil industries. There are many videos available for viewing in the comfortable theater. Ask for a list of titles. If no one is waiting you may request a screening of your choice. Videos with local interest include *Haunted Waters, Fragile Lands* (directed by Glen Pitre), and *Hidden Nation,* about the Houma Indians. I recommend the excellent *Anything I Catch,* about Cajun hand-fishing (unbelievable!). The Center bookstore has a collection of titles in both French and English. At the time of this writing there is a free Cajun music jam session on Mondays from 5:30 to 7 P.M. The Center is open Monday from 9 to 7, Tuesday through Thursday to 6, and until 5 on Friday through Sunday. (504) 448-1375.

Drive-by Plantations

There are several private antebellum homes on the banks of Bayou Lafourche just south of Thibodaux. *Acadia Plantation* is comprised of three cottages (later joined into one home) built in the 1820s by members of the Jim Bowie family. It is located south of Nicholls State University on Rte. 1. *Rienzi Plantation,* two-tenths of a mile south of Rte. 20 on Rte. 308, was built in 1796. Legend has it that it was constructed by order of the Spanish queen, Maria Louisa, as a possible sanctuary in the event of her defeat by Napoleon.

RECREATION

Torres' Swamp Tours Rte. 307, 17 miles northeast of Thibodaux.
  See New Orleans to Lafourche section.

Zam's Swamp Tours Rte. 307, 17 miles northeast of Thibodaux.
  See New Orleans to Lafourche section.

FOOD

Try not to get hungry in Thibodaux. You will find plenty of fast food here and a couple of local favorites, but the choices are very limited. On a cool day, I recommend stopping at Rouse's Grocery to get picnic fixings from the deli and a *tarte à la bouillee* from their bakery (*see* description at Raceland store).

Boudreaux's Restaurant Down Home, $. Rte. 20, seven miles north of Thibodaux.
  See New Orleans to Lafourche section.

★Bourgeois Meat Market $. 519 Rte. 20 (Schriever Highway), Schriever.

This meat market has been in the Bourgeois family for three generations, long enough to develop a loyal following throughout Bayou

Country. They have a variety of fresh and smoked meats, but their specialty is the chewy strips of spicy Cajun beef jerky (smoked for 10 hours each day). This isn't the leathery, hard jerky you find on the snack rack at your neighborhood convenience store, but a thicker and more tender meat. It is a well-seasoned treat, so be sure to get a cold drink to go with it. Also be sure to get twice as much as you think you want because it will likely disappear in a hurry. The jerky costs around $15 a pound, and Bourgeois will ship it UPS anywhere in the states. They are open from 7 A.M. to 5:30 P.M. weekdays and until 1 P.M. Saturdays. Bourgeois is located just south of Thibodaux. (504) 447-7128.

Bubba's II Restaurant & Sports Lounge Local Fave/Seafood, $-$$. 764 Bayou Rd. (Rte. 308), Thibodaux.

In 1997 *Sports Illustrated* declared Bubba's II the "top sports lounge in the nation." The place has hundreds of donated items from helmets to autographed photos. Most prized is the championship ring that former Dodgers manager Tommy Lasorda donated after enjoying dinner at the restaurant. Owner Neil Swanner, who attended Nicholls State in Thibodaux, has gotten a trove of Louisiana college athletic memorabilia to surround the eight big televisions in the sports area. The big surprise here is that the food is quite good. The menu is huge, but the few things I have tried (stuffed soft-shell crab, steaks, and fried seafood) are all competently prepared and very inexpensive. Bubba's is located on the east bank of Bayou Lafourche, across the bayou from the Acadian Cultural Center. Hours are 11 A.M. to 2 P.M. and 5 to 9:30 P.M. daily. (504) 446-5117.

Doug's Restaurant Local Fave, $. 201 N. Canal Blvd., Thibodaux.

I recommend one thing here, the sandwiches on homemade bread. That's right, this little restaurant in the Howard Johnson motel actually bakes fresh loaves each day! Pillowy white bread is delicious stuffed with fried crawfish and Doug's own mustard slaw. Doug's is open 24 hours Tuesday through Saturday and until 9 P.M. on Sunday and Monday. (504) 447-9071.

Nubby's Country Kitchen Down Home, $. Rte. 1, nine miles northwest of Thibodaux.

See Labadieville section below.

Politz's Local Fave, $-$$. 535 St. Mary N. (Rte. 1), Thibodaux.

Politz's is the favorite lunch spot in Thibodaux. They serve everything from plate lunches to seafood, burgers, and gumbos. The big drawing card is Le Petit Menu, offered at lunch. Few items on the "little menu" are over $3, including a selection of salads, po' boys, and gumbos. Fried okra or garlic bread is under a buck. Politz's gives the almost exclusively local clientele what they want—large servings at low prices. I can't highly recommend the food, but Politz's offers a good value. They are open for lunch Tuesday through Friday from 11 to 1:30. Dinner is served Tuesday through Saturday from 5 to 9. (504) 448-0944.

★Rouse's Bakery Local Fave. Rte. 1 N., Thibodaux.

Rouse's Supermarket has a full-service deli and is one of a few places where you can purchase a *tarte à la bouillee*, a traditional Cajun confection indigenous to Bayou Country. For details see description of Rouse's in Raceland. Rouse's is open from 7 A.M. to 10 P.M. daily. (504) 447-5998.

Utopia Cafe Sweets/Sandwiches, $. 601 Third St., Thibodaux.

Utopia offers a cool reprieve for those walking through downtown Thibodaux. They serve light fare including pecan pancakes at breakfast, cold sandwiches and salads at lunch, and grilled entrees. Pastries and coffee are served all day. Utopia is open Monday and Tuesday from 7 A.M. to 5 P.M. and Wednesday through Saturday until 9 P.M.

MUSIC

La Pirogue Lounge Cajun Dance/Lounge. 201 N. Canal Blvd., Thibodaux.

Every Saturday from noon until 3 P.M. La Pirogue Lounge at Howard Johnson hosts a French dance. This is one of the few places to hear Cajun music in Bayou Country. You can tell by the hours that this show caters to an older crowd. (504) 447-9071.

Wetlands Acadian Cultural Center Cajun. 314 St. Mary St., Thibodaux.

Every Monday from 5:30 to 7 P.M. the Center stages a Cajun jam session. Call ahead to make sure this event is still happening. For more information on the Acadian Cultural Center see the review above. (504) 448-1375.

LODGING

Hotels and Motels:

Holiday Inn 400 E. First St., $60 to $65 double. (504) 446-0561, (800) HOLIDAY.

Howard Johnson 201 N. Canal Blvd., $65 to $70 double. (504) 447-9071, (800) 952-2968.

Bed and Breakfasts:

Lovell House Bed and Breakfast 221 W. Seventh St., Thibodaux.

Charlene Elmore speaks fluent French and German. Charlene and

Richard rent out one bedroom with double bed in their Victorian home in downtown Thibodaux. The bath is "down the hall." Breakfast is served on a porch overlooking the backyard. The house is within walking distance of the historic downtown district, Acadian Cultural Center, and restaurants. Double rate is $60. (504) 446-2750.

McAnn's Bed and Breakfast 450 Easy St., Thibodaux.

Ann McDonald rents a three-room suite in her large brick home in a quiet suburban subdivision. The suite has a private bath, small refrigerator, and everything needed to make coffee or tea. A queen-size sleeper-sofa is available. Double rate is $55 (cash or traveler's check). (504) 446-0005.

Labadieville

This village of about 2,000 residents and the surrounding area were the site of the first settlements on Bayou Lafourche. The town, nine miles north of Thibodaux, was originally called Star, for nearby Star Merchandise and Red Star Plantation. It was later changed to Labadieville in honor of the plantation owner, a French colonist named Jean Louis Labadie. The town landmark is the spire of St. Philomene Church, built in 1888.

More unusual are the several little lunch counters advertising "Choupic Burgers." Elsewhere, choupic (known under the euphemism "cypress trout") is considered a "trash" fish. It is, however, plentiful in the freshwater streams around these parts, where it is served chopped, seasoned, made into patties, and fried.

Another unusual characteristic of Labadieville is the three old card bars that line Rte. 1. Here the most popular card game is not the traditional bourré, but a variant similar to spades called Pedro.

★Nubby's Country Kitchen Down Home, $. Rte. 1, Labadieville.

Nubby's has the misfortune to be located in an old fast-food building. Their name is not exactly a zinger either, but this is my favorite eatery on Upper Bayou Lafourche. Fried chicken is the self-proclaimed specialty at Nubby's. I go for their meaty jambalaya and plate-lunch specials. Jambalaya is always served on Saturdays but is sometimes available during the week. It is dished out in mountainous scoops for under a dollar or as part of a monumental plate lunch with chicken, salad, beans, and dessert for about $5. On Sunday you can get a big midday meal of baked chicken with cornbread dressing. They are open from 2:30 A.M. to 8 P.M. (504) 526-8869.

Madewood Plantation Rte. 308, two miles south of Napoleonville.

Madewood Plantation was built in 1846 for Col. Thomas Pugh and took eight years to complete. The 21-room, columned Greek Revival structure was built of wood gathered exclusively from the plantation's 3,000 acres. It has a huge, free-standing staircase carved from walnut and 25-foot-high ceilings. Mr. and Mrs. Harold Marshall bought the house in 1964, completely restored it, and installed period antique furnishings. Since that time it has been featured in two films, *Sister, Sister* and *A Woman Called Moses*. The Marshall family has opened Bed and Breakfast accommodations in the main house, an outbuilding, and another small house built in 1820. Tours are offered daily from 10 to 5. Admission is $5 for adults and $3 for kids. (504) 369-7151.

Madewood Plantation Bed and Breakfast
Brace yourself for pampered luxury should you decide to stay at Madewood. The glamor experience is a night in the main house, which includes a candlelight dinner and full breakfast. A bell is placed on the dinner table and guests are instructed to ring it if they need anything. Because the house is on tour, the rooms are available only from 5 P.M. to 10 A.M., but in the evenings guests have the whole house to themselves. Accommodations are also available in two smaller antebellum outbuildings. Guests receive a wine and cheese tray and personalized tour of the house. The entire package goes for the princely sum of $190 a couple. (504) 369-7151.

Napoleonville

Although it has scarcely more than 1,000 residents, Napoleonville (18 miles north of Thibodaux) is the seat of Assumption Parish government. This can probably be explained by looking at a map and noting that there are only five other towns listed in the entire parish. The town of Napoleonville was first settled by Spanish and Acadians moving down the bayou from the German Coast of the river.

Glenwood Sugar Factory Tour 5065 Hwy. 1006.
Glenwood will sometimes give tours of its facility during sugar season (roughly mid-October to mid-December). Tours are not regularly scheduled, so call in advance to make sure someone can show you around. Glenwood markets a unique, partially refined, brown sugar product sold locally under the name Cajun Crystals. (504) 369-2941.

Cajun Corner Cafe Down Home, $. 201 Franklin St., Napoleonville.
When it is not being used as a location for a video or movie shoot, the Corner Cafe serves plate lunches and sandwiches. The main attraction is the place. The exterior is pure Norman Rockwell, with a corner-facing entrance that sucks you in. Built as the Bank of Napoleonville in 1895, the tellers' windows have been replaced with

a huge mahogany bar and the lobby filled with four tables. The most unique use of space is the vault, which houses a couple of video poker machines. Among the movies shot here are *Fear Is the Key* and *Heaven's Prisoners* starring Alec Baldwin. Hours are Monday through Friday from 6 A.M. to 1:30 P.M. (504) 369-6625.

Plattenville

St. Faustine Relic and Bier Assumption Catholic Church, Rte. 308.

It struck me as a little unusual that a glass-sided casket containing a wax figure with human hair and embedded with a real body part was displayed in a church. Then I discovered there was another almost identical bier and wax figure (of another virgin) just 28 miles down the road at St. Joseph's in Thibodaux! One account has it that Father Menard brought back both from a visit to Rome in 1867. Another account has Father Menard traveling with a fellow priest who brought back the Faustine relic. To complicate matters, a rumor persists that the relics were accidentally switched. Both St. Faustine and St. Valerie were virgins beheaded by cruel monarchs. Many parishioners of both churches have reportedly had their prayers answered by intervention of the respective saints. The bier is located just inside the entrance of the church, which is open to the public. (504) 369-2130.

TRAVEL TIP

Above Plattenville, Rte. 1 intersects Rte. 70 east. Travel east on 70 to cross the Sunshine Bridge at Donaldsonville (10 miles) and to reach I-10 (20 miles). These areas are covered in the River Road chapter of this book.

Paincourtville

St. Elizabeth's Gothic Church Rte. 403, Paincourtville.

St. Elizabeth's has some of the most beautiful stained-glass windows in the state, imported from France. It also reputedly has a fantastic mural on the ceiling. The priest informed me that visitors who called ahead were welcome, but on two different occasions, after calling I found no one in the church or rectory. You may have better luck. The late-19th-century building lost its twin spires in a hurricane in 1903 and they were never replaced. The church is two blocks east of Rte. 1. (504) 369-7398.

★Rte. 70 to Morgan City

At the town of Paincourtville (pronounced "Pankerville"), about 2

miles north of Plattenville, Rte. 70 veers southeast to Pierre Part and follows the Atchafalaya Basin to Morgan City. This is one of the most interesting drives in Cajun Country. It is the main road between the fishing
and industrial center of Morgan City and Baton Rouge but is seldom
seen by tourists. On both sides of the road, land quickly turns to swamp
or open water. I highly recommend timing your drive to catch some
music at one of the rustic dance halls of Pierre Part, 13 miles west of Rte.
1 (see below). Shortly after Pierre Part, Rte. 70 crosses Belle River and
follows the East Atchafalaya Basin Levee south to Morgan City. This area
produces much of the state's wild (noncultivated) crawfish harvest.
From Rte. 1 it is only 33 miles to Morgan City and U.S. 90.

Pierre Part

Pierre Part is about 30 miles southwest of I-10 at exit #180 (Sunshine Bridge/Donaldsonville). Because Pierre Part is only 20 miles
north of Morgan City (the closest accommodations), it is reviewed
under the North of Morgan City section in the Teche chapter.

Houma

Located at the geographic center of Bayou Country, about an hour
and a half southwest of New Orleans by way of U.S. 90, Houma calls
itself the Venice of America. Bayou Black, Little Bayou Black, Bayou
Terrebonne, and the Intracoastal Waterway all converge on this city of
bridges. Houma (population 37,000) is the seat of the Terrebonne
Parish government and the economic and social hub of the bayou
region. Here plantation and farm country abuts the marsh and provides visitors a look at the varied economy of Cajun Country. The city
has a large number of bargain-priced accommodations, including
several Bed and Breakfasts, as well as major motel chains.

Houma was established on the banks of Bayou Terrebonne in 1834
and incorporated in 1843. The earliest recorded denizens of the
region were Houma Indians, for whom the town is named. The
Houma (which means red) use the red swamp crawfish as their tribal
emblem. They made their way into the area in the early 18th century
and were followed shortly by a wave of Acadian immigrants, who
pushed the Indians into the wetlands to the south (where most still
live). Early settlers relied largely on hunting, fishing, and trapping
for sustenance. When the process for refining and granulating sugar
was perfected in 1794, sugarcane became the predominant crop. Several antebellum sugar plantations may still be seen in the Houma area,
and the stately Southdown Plantation Home is open to visitors.

While thousands of acres of sugarcane still fill the landscape, since

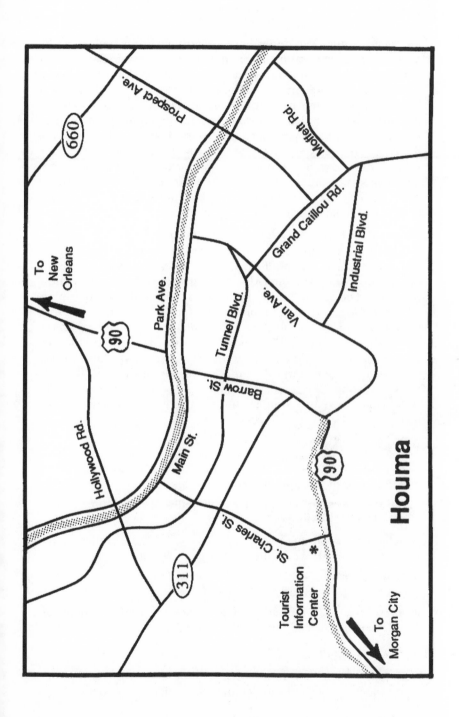

the 1930s Houma's fortunes have been inextricably tied to the oil and gas industry operating in the wetlands to the south. Barges, crew boats, and other petroleum vessels make their way down the Houma Navigation Channel and southern bayous to rich coastal oil fields. Like other oil centers in South Louisiana, Houma was economically pounded by the collapse of oil prices in the eighties. In the late nineties the economy boomed again, spurred by a renewed health in the oil patch and expanding health-care and tourism industries. The shops of downtown have reopened, as have a host of chain restaurants. Most visitors will want to explore the wetlands paradise below Houma. (Visit the Houma-Terrebonne Tourist Center to get a driving-tour map of the wetlands or to arrange a swamp tour.)

Houma-Terrebonne Tourist Center U.S. 90 and St. Charles.

This is the first place to visit before exploring the Houma area. You will find walking-tour info, maps, brochures, and listings of special events. Most helpful is the "ABC Driving Tour of Coastal Wetlands" brochure. The staff will map out wetlands tours to the south or plantation country to the north, make reservations for swamp tours, or connect you with a fishing charter. If plantations are your bag, drive a few blocks north on St. Charles Street to Rte. 311, which has some elegant old homes. To get to the tourist center from New Orleans, you must drive through downtown on U.S. 90 before turning north on St. Charles. From the west the center will greet you before you enter town. Hours are 9 to 5 Monday through Friday and until 3:30 on Saturday. (504) 868-2732 or 1-800-688-2732.

RECREATION

The main forms of recreation in the Houma area are swamp tours and fishing in the surrounding wetlands.

Annie Miller Swamp Tour Located eight miles west of Houma on U.S. 90. See Houma to Morgan City.

★Atchafalaya Basin Backwater Adventure Located 21 miles west of Houma on Rte. 20. See Houma to Morgan City. Pirogue rentals.

★A Cajun Man's Tour Located 10 miles west of the Houma tourist center on U.S. 90. See Houma to Morgan City.

Munson's Swamp Tours Located eight miles northwest of Houma off Rte. 311 or Rte. 20. See Attractions on Rte. 311 below.

ATTRACTIONS

Before you tour downtown, budget time to see the outlying wetlands, which are the main attraction of the region. There is not a lot to see in downtown Houma, but there is no denying the charm of this town that tangles like a child's first Etch-A-Sketch drawing along the banks of a half-dozen or so streams. Many streets are one-way avenues split down the middle by bayous. The main streets are Rte. 24 (Main Street), which follows Bayou Terrebonne, and U.S. 90 (Barrow Street), which traces the banks of the Intracoastal Waterway.

Walking Tour of the Houma Historic District Rte. 24 and U.S. 90.

A map of historic buildings on the downtown walking tour is available at the Houma-Terrebonne Tourist Center. The tour can be completed in half an hour if you park near the intersection of Rte. 24 and U.S. 90. A metered parking space here costs five cents an hour. From this corner you can scope out the odd mixture of Victorian and turn-of-the-century storefronts and the Art-Deco-style *Parish Courthouse.* One good reason to stop here is to grab a lunch at *Bayou Vue Cafe,* where you can eat on a deck overlooking Bayou Terrebonne (*see* review in the food section). A Wetlands and Seafood Museum is under construction on the banks of Bayou Terrebonne beside Bayou Vue Cafe. Among the scenic buildings are the *Old Post Office* on Main Street, which was used for the clandestine burial of Union soldiers killed in an ambush during the War Between the States (it now houses a restaurant), and the Art-Deco *People's Drug* building.

ATTRACTIONS ON RTE. 311—HOUMA TO THIBODAUX

Rte. 311 arcs northwest from Houma to Thibodaux following the natural levee of Little Bayou Black. From a point just north of the tourist center, it skirts a couple of the city's main attractions before blazing into the cane fields of plantation country.

Southdown Plantation/Terrebonne Museum Rte. 311 and St. Charles.

Southdown is the only plantation house in Bayou Country open to individual visitors (as opposed to large groups/bus tours) and is conveniently located within the Houma city limits. The plantation was constructed in 1859, with a second floor added in 1893. There is a room full of historical photos and artifacts of local industries such as fishing, seafood packing, shrimp drying, lumber milling, sugarcane, and petroleum. The Senator Allen J. Ellender Room on the second floor houses a replica of his senate office packed with souvenirs of a 36-year tenure (a record) in the U.S. Senate. Ellender was born in the tiny community of Bourg, south of Houma. His career stretched from days as floor leader in the State House during the Huey Long administration to a term as President Pro Tempore of the U.S. Senate before his death in 1972. The Ellender Room is filled with autographed pictures of political figures and celebrities received during his 36-year reign. There are a couple of super shots of President Kennedy and Jackie. Southdown is just a few blocks north of the Houma-Terrebonne Tourist Center. Admission is $4 for adults. The plantation and museum are open Tuesday through Saturday from 10 to 4 (except holidays). (504) 851-0154.

Munson's Swamp Tours 979 Bull Run Rd., Schriever.

I thought I had the wrong place when I saw miles of sugarcane and a distant tree line. However, the canal from Munson's headquarters to the swamp is infested with gators and a good spot to watch birds on the wing. On my visit a heron was nested by the water and I edged up to see hatchlings.

Once in the woods, the tour winds down three dead-end logging canals. Though not deep swamp, the area is packed with wildlife that enjoys Munson's handouts. He adds a twist to gator feeding by throwing doughnuts. These have two advantages over chicken: they cost less and they float. Nutrias and raccoons also wait for the chuck wagon and hurry forth at the sound of the boat. My guide had a gift for spotting wildlife and found an owl staring from the shadows as well as the biggest snake I have ever seen twisted among some tree roots. The canals are privately owned and maintained by Munson so you do not see other boats or litter on this tour. Munson's is 4.2 miles northwest of Rte. 311 (5.8 miles south of Rte. 20) on Bull Run Road. The tour costs $15 for adults and $10 for children (6-12) and lasts about two hours. Call for reservations. (504) 851-3569.

Drive-by Plantations

Between the tourist center in Houma and the town of Schriever, 15 miles to the north, there are four plantation houses that are privately owned but may be viewed from the road. *Crescent Farm Plantation,* 4 miles north of Houma, was built in 1834. *Ellendale Plantation,* about 7 miles above Houma, was built in the early 1800s and has an old brick sugar house on the grounds. *Ardoyne Plantation* (a mile north of Ellendale) is an ornate, high-Victorian gingerbread mansion built in 1897. *Magnolia Plantation,* 12 miles north of Houma, is a Greek Revival-style structure built in 1854 and used as a hospital by Union soldiers.

FOOD

A-Bear's Restaurant Down Home, $$. 809 Bayou Black Dr. (Rte. 311 at U.S. 90).

You won't find any bears lurking about the entrance to this tiny cafe; "A-Bear" is the phonetic spelling of Hebert, the proprietor's last name. The food here is hearty fare. Po' boys, red beans with sausage and potato salad, plate lunches, and bowls of gumbo for under $5 are recommended. To enjoy A-Bear's at its good-timing best, stop by on a Friday night for "all you can eat" fried catfish, which is served to the strains of Cajun music. The music and catfish are popular among locals, so be sure and get there before 7 P.M. or you may not get a seat! Don't pass up a chance to sample the heartbreakingly good icebox pies. The lemon and coconut are refreshingly chilled cream pies, while the pecan is served hot with ice cream. You can get a lunch to go or a slice of pie and coffee and enjoy them at neighboring Jim Bowie Park on the Intracoastal Waterway. A-Bear's has good breakfasts, too. It is located at the south edge of town near the tourist center. Hours are Monday through Friday from 7 A.M. to 3 P.M., Saturday from 11 A.M. to 2 P.M., and Friday for dinner from 5:30 to 9:30. (504) 872-6306.

Bayou Delight Restaurant Seafood/Cajun/Creole, $-$$. 4038 U.S. 90 W.

Bayou Delight offers standard fried seafood and soups. However, this is one of the few places in the area where you can hear live music. Bands play from 6 to 10 P.M. Friday and Sunday. Restaurant hours are 10 to 9 Sunday through Thursday and until 10 on Friday and Saturday. (504) 876-4879.

Bayou Vue Cafe Cajun/Creole, $ (lunch)-$$. 611 E. Main St., downtown.

This is the best place in downtown Houma to get a hot lunch or light supper. The shrimp and okra gumbo is delicious (I like mine with a cool scoop of potato salad right in the middle). On Fridays the lunch special is a spicy crawfish etouffée with salad and bread for $5. Bayou Vue also sells sandwiches at lunch. These are best consumed on the outdoor deck (weather permitting), which extends over Bayou Terrebonne. Dinners are $10-$15 and feature several grilled choices. Hours are Monday through Wednesday 6 A.M. to 6 P.M., Thursday through Saturday until 9:30 P.M., and Sundays (buffet brunch) from 11 to 3. (504) 872-6292.

Bubba's II Restaurant and Sports Lounge Local Fave, $-$$. 724 High St.

I haven't eaten at this Bubba's II, but if it is as good as the one in Thibodaux it is certainly worth a try. It is one of the most popular seafood places in town and folks praise their steaks too. (504) 868-2299.

Copeland's Cajun/Creole, $-$$. 1534 Martin Luther King Blvd. (Rte. 3040).

Al Copeland went national with his chain of moderately priced Cajun eateries in the nineties, and for folks who want food with a regional flair and predictability, this is the spot. Copeland's opens at 11 A.M. daily. It closes at 11 P.M. Monday through Thursday, at midnight on Friday and Saturday, and at 10 on Sunday. (504) 973-9600.

Dave's Cajun Kitchen Seafood, $-$$. 6240 W. Main St. (Rte. 24).

Dave LeBeuf dishes up generous servings of fresh fried seafood at moderate prices. All of LeBeuf's seafood dishes and platters (except the "large," which serves two) are priced around $10, including a soft-shell platter of two crabs with salad and fries. My favorite is the fried catfish, which is cooked so that the center is just tender and the edges are crisp. Try one of the seafood po' boys or a lunch special. One recent lunch plate featured a softshell crab, white beans, beets, and a salad for $6. After the weather cools down, try the chicken andouille gumbo, redolent of smoked sausage and seasoned to warm more than your soul. Dave's is located just northwest of town. Hours are 10:30 A.M. to 9 P.M. Tuesday through Saturday and Monday for lunch only until 2. (504) 868-3870.

Dula and Edwin's Seafood, $-$$. 2426 Bayou Blue Rd. (Rte. 316 N.).

The boisterous level of conversation and visiting between tables marks D&E's as a favorite among the locals, who line up for boiled crawfish, seafood gumbo, and the special seafood-stuffed potatoes. On Tuesday nights there is a Cajun band and dancing from 7 until 10. Dula and Edwin enjoy sitting down and demonstrating how to peel those crawfish and get into the hard-shell crabs. You know the boiled seafood is coming to you directly from the pot because you can see Edwin dumping the baskets of steaming crustaceans into serving bins at the rear of the dining area. D&E's is located just north of Houma. Hours are Tuesday through Friday and Sunday from 10 to 10 and Saturday from 11 A.M. (504) 876-0271.

★Rouse's Supermarket Bakery Local Fave. 2737 W. Main St.

This is the only place in Houma where you can still purchase a *tarte à la bouillee*. The *tarte à la bouillee* is a traditional Cajun confection that I have not found mentioned or sold anywhere except Bayou Country. It is a rich boiled milk custard in a sweet-dough pie shell. See description in Raceland section. The Rouse's "superstore" is at the corner of West Main Street and Martin Luther King Boulevard. It is open from 7 A.M. to 11 P.M. daily. (504) 868-5033.

NEARBY FOOD

Sportsman's Paradise Seafood, $-$$. See South of Houma.

Co-Co Marina Seafood, $-$$$. See South of Houma.

Harbor Light Restaurant Seafood, $. See South of Houma.

La Trouvaille Restaurant Down Home, $$. See South of Houma.

★Chester's Cypress Inn Local Fave, $-$$. See Houma to Morgan City.

MUSIC

Houma is not known for its music scene. Several new venues are planned, but for now if you want to hear or dance to Cajun music, you will have to go to a restaurant. The Cajun bands here usually play with a country edge. A new club has opened downtown featuring roots music, rock and roll, and blues (see review of Smoky Row below).

A-Bear's Restaurant Cajun Food/Music. 809 Bayou Black Dr.

This little restaurant features Cajun music with a country flair every Friday night from about 7 to 9:30. There is no room to dance. There is barely room to move, so get there early. Eat some fried catfish and a slice of pie (see food reviews). A-Bear's is located just south of town. (504) 872-6306.

Dula and Edwin's Cajun Food/Music. 2426 Bayou Blue Rd. (Rte. 316 N.).

This is about the best seafood place in Houma, a place that gets rockin' even when there is no band. Cajun music is a recent and popular addition. Get there early and eat (see review in food section). The band plays from 7 to 10 on Tuesday nights. (504) 876-0271.

Bayou Delight Food/Music. 4038 U.S. 90 W.

Bayou Delight, eight miles west of Houma, is best known as the dock for the Annie Miller Swamp Tour. There is not much room to dance. Bands play country and oldies on Friday and Sunday nights from about 6 until 10. (504) 876-4879.

Smoky Row Blues Emporium Blues/Rock and Roll. 314 E. Main St., downtown.

There are few more dramatic signs of the rehabilitation of Houma's fortunes and its downtown in particular than the opening of this roots music club in an old brick building near the courthouse. A young crowd comes to see acts from New Orleans and Lafayette. There is a house blues band every Sunday. Shows start at 9. Call for more information. (504) 868-6399.

Harbor Light Restaurant Country/Cajun. Rte. 56, Cocodrie.

The oldest marina south of Houma serves sandwiches, cans of beer, and country or French music most Fridays and Saturdays from 9 P.M. "until." Call first. (504) 594-4183 or 594-7369.

The Jolly Inn Cajun Dance Hall.

Ask at the tourist center about this dance hall scheduled to open soon.

LODGING

Hotels and Motels:

Holiday Inn Holidome 210 S. Hollywood Rd., $75 to $85 double. (504) 868-5851, (800) 465-4329.

Plantation Inn 1381 W. Tunnel Blvd., $40 to $45 double. (504) 868-0500.

Quality Inn 1400 W. Tunnel Blvd., $55 to $60 double. (504) 879-4871, (800) 228-5151.

Red Carpet Inn U.S. 90 West, $45 to $55 double. (504) 876-4160, (800) 251-1962. Located in southwest Houma across from the tourist center.

Bed and Breakfasts:

Cajun-French Bed and Breakfast Association

This association specializes in finding Bed and Breakfast accommodations with French-speaking hosts. It is able to place singles, couples, or entire busloads of guests in homes around the area. Not only do all hosts speak French but (for better or worse) they house guests in their own homes rather than private cottages, cabins, or guesthouses. All hosts offer dinner for $10 with advance notice. You sacrifice some privacy in exchange for getting to know a local family. Most houses are not old homes but typical suburban and country residences. Doubles cost about $60. Contact Audrey George, (504) 879-3285, for reservations or more information.

Amanda Magenta Plantation B&B 1233 Rte. 55, Montegut.

Amanda Magenta was constructed circa 1820. Michael and Eva Keen modernized the long-neglected house considerably when they moved in. The downstairs kitchen and family room, which are shared by guests, are large and well lit. Upstairs there are four guest rooms with carpet and big-screen televisions. Two have private baths in the rooms. The owners stay on the first floor. The double rate is $65. (504) 594-898 or 594-9686.

Bayou Cabins 4326 Grand Caillou Rd. (Rte. 57), south Houma.

Owner Lawanda Boudreaux said that when she was constructing one of the cabins, work was temporarily halted because an alligator was "hissin' and cavortin'," depriving workers of access to the place. One cabin is close to the road but when you walk through and onto the porch you will feel as though you are in another world. There are two rockers and a porch swing facing directly onto Bayou Grand Caillou about 15 feet away. To get a closer look guests may use a pirogue and paddles. The cabin is rather rough with single beds in a loft and a full bed downstairs. It has a TV, phone, and furnished kitchen. Smoking is allowed. Munson's Swamp Tours used to depart from next door and there may be plans to convert their old restaurant to a tavern; ask Lawanda about these plans, which might disturb the future serenity. Also be sure to request the cabin on the bayou, not the road. The double rate is $75 but ask about weekly and off-season specials. (504) 879-1328.

★**Le Jardin Sur Le Bayou** 256 Lower Country Dr. (off Rte. 24), Bourg.

Le Jardin is a truly special place, and for bird watchers the best place to stay in the Houma area. Owners Dave and Jo Ann Coignet custom built their two-story house on a huge lot that extends into a cypress swamp and 26-acre wildlife refuge. Guests are lodged in a private suite on the second floor with firm bed, television, telephone, and small refrigerator. The hosts stay on the first floor.

The house is comfortable but the grounds are amazing. Dave is president of the Houma-Terrebonne Bird Club and maintains several acres of gardens (primarily native plants) designed to attract birds and butterflies. A 20-minute walk down a maintained path leads from the gardens to a cypress swamp. Another 15 or 20 minutes into the swamp, visitors will find a cypress tree with 8.5-foot-tall knees (six inches shy of the state record). I recommend you take Dave up on his offer of a guided tour or perhaps his unique nighttime "flashlight tour." Save a private walk for the following morning after breakfast. The double rate is $80. For a group of four the sitting room upstairs converts to a second bedroom ($15 for each additional person). Traveler's checks, checks, or cash are accepted. (504) 594-2722.

★**Wildlife Gardens Cabins** U.S. 90, Gibson (16 miles west of Houma).

If merely watching alligators is old hat, try sleeping with them. They do not come inside, but there is no question what the chicken wire on the porch railing is for. The four cabins sit over a pond that is brimming with fish, turtles, frogs, and gators. Surrounding the pond are 35 acres of swamp, trails, and gardens, which form the backyard of owners James and Betty Provost. The pond is small, but the cabins are well spaced for privacy. They are simple one-room structures with baths, air conditioning, and porches. They have no televisions or phones, so stretch out and listen to the sounds of the swamp.

The Provosts, who conduct walking tours through the compound, built the cabins after fielding requests from folks who wanted to stay in their model trapper's camp. They raise alligators, turtles, emus, and guinea hens, the sound of which gives overnight guests the feeling they have awoken on the set of a Tarzan movie. Wildlife Gardens is surely one of the most unusual and charming places a visitor could

A Bed and Breakfast cabin at Wildlife Gardens. (Courtesy of Wildlife Gardens)

possibly stay. Take the walking tour and try the sunset swamp cruise offered by Joseph Provost. A cabin for two costs $70 a night ($12 for an extra child under 12) and includes a big breakfast. (504) 575-3676.

Camping: There are a number of campgrounds in the Houma area. Those to the south tend to be small lots with recreational fishermen in mind. Others in town seem to be paved and permanent mobile-home communities. The few mentioned here are ones I would recommend.

Carriage Cove Mobile Home Park 3204 E. Park Ave. (Rte. 659 S.).
$12 for RVs with full hookups on slabs. (504) 872-2756.

Whispering Oaks 2706 E. Main St. (Rte. 24 S.).
Located on the southern fringe of Houma. It is small, sometimes crowded, but very shady. 20 sites with full hookups, washateria. $13 for two people. (504) 879-2075.

Linda's Campground 5427 Bayou Black Dr. (U.S. 90), Gibson.
17 sites with full hookups and laundry. RV rate is $12 for two people, $10 for pop-ups/vans, $14 for campers over 24 feet. Tents are welcome. (504) 575-3934.

Hideaway Ponds Resort 6367 U.S. 90, Gibson.
KOA-type quality. Full hookups, clubhouse, bath facilities, security, indoor/outdoor swimming, jacuzzi, putt putt, and cable. $25 per night. (504) 575-9928.

Grand Bois Park 470 Rte. 24, Bourg.
44 sites with full hookups and water. Rest rooms with showers. Picnic area, nature trail. Tents are welcome ($7). RV rate is $10. (504) 594-7410.

Lapeyrouse Campground 6890 Hwy. 56, Chauvin.
39 sites with full hookups. Boat launch and fishing. $20 per night. (504) 594-2600.

SOUTH OF HOUMA
(COASTAL WETLANDS TOUR)

The area south of Houma is true Bayou Country. Four main bayous radiate out in a crow's-foot pattern through the coastal marsh. (Maps and brochures are available at the Houma-Terrebonne Tourist Center.) These carry shrimp and oil industry boats to the Gulf and support long, narrow communities on their banks. Each bayou has a distinct character and set of family names and loyalties. In some places there is friction between folks on one side of a bayou and those on "the other side." The west side of Bayou Grand Caillou is settled mainly by Houma Indians and had no paved road until recently, while the east has been paved for decades and is inhabited predominantly by Cajuns. The diverging pattern of settlement has preserved many of the customs and much of the Cajun dialect of the region. Linguists have found different varieties of French spoken on neighboring streams and the Houma Indians have a variety all their own.

Most residents south of Houma extract a living from the marsh in the form of oil or seafood. Driving south you will see seafood-processing plants, shrimp boats, and miles of rozo cane (tall marsh cane) under mottled Gulf skies. The towns here are line villages that stretch for miles but are often only one block deep. It takes half a day to drive the bayous below Houma if you stop to eat lunch and stretch your legs. A tourist center brochure traces the bayous from west to east; this book reverses the direction. To the east Bayou Pointe Aux-Chenes (Rte. 665) offers fabulous scenery. To the west on Bayous du Large (Rte. 315) and Grand Caillou (Rte. 57) one can find Indian communities, burial mounds, and the haunted "cypress cemetery." The best lunch stop is in the middle on busy Bayou Petit Caillou (Rte. 56). Little backtracking is required since the bayous are intermittently connected by east-west routes. There are several Bed and Breakfasts south of Houma, including the excellent Le Jardin Sur Le Bayou in Bourg and a few Cajun-French B&B participants (*see* Houma Lodging).

Bayou Pointe Aux-Chenes (Rte. 665)

This is the easternmost bayou in the crow's foot south of Houma and perhaps the loveliest of all the streams in Bayou Country. Take Rte. 55 south to Rte. 665 (about 4 miles south of Bourg). Turn left on Rte. 665. From this point the road follows the natural levee of Bayou Pointe Aux-Chenes for 14 miles before ending abruptly at the old Indian community of Isle de Jean Charles. Along the side of the bayou you will see small herds of unfenced cattle grazing by the water in the shade of gnarled oak trees. There is a gas station, convenience store, and bait shop along the way.

The most spectacular leg of the drive begins 8.5 miles from the turnoff at Rte. 55. Here you turn right on *Isle de Jean Charles Road.* Until the early seventies there was no road here at all and the Houma Indian community at Isle de Jean Charles was isolated from "civilization" by 6 miles of marsh and water! At high tide the road is covered with four to eight inches of brackish water and fishermen pull in shrimp, crabs, trout, and redfish from the roadside. During a hurricane, the water could be well over the roof of your car. At the end of the road the homes of Isle de Jean Charles rise 15 and 20 feet above permanently flooded "yards" on the spindly support of telephone poles. As you drive past you can look up at the floorboards of these camps and trailers, but it is hard to imagine the storm surge they await. A boat launch is located near the end of the Isle de Jean Charles Road. If the wind

Isle de Jean Charles Road at high tide. (Photo by Julie Posner)

is down, there are hundreds of acres of pristine wetlands that may be explored by small, flat-bottomed boat, canoe, or rowboat. To return to Rte. 55 you have no choice but to backtrack.

Bayou Terrebonne (Rte. 55)

Rte. 55 veers south from Houma and hugs the east side of Bayou Terrebonne for about 20 miles before literally submerging in the marsh. From the junction of Rte. 55 and Rte. 665 (the Pointe Aux-Chenes road), it is a mile south to the fishing community of Montegut. Below Montegut, it is 8 miles to the end of the road. The last 2 miles are dirt and the last ¾ mile is submerged. The road actually resembles a canal at this point, and some folks near the end have jonboats tied by the road to carry them across "front yards" to their doorsteps! You can often find seafood for sale at the docks here. To continue your bayou tour, cross Bayou Terrebonne on Rte. 58 in Montegut and head west about 1.5 miles to the town of Chauvin on Bayou Petit Caillou.

Amanda Magenta Plantation B&B 1233 Rte. 55, Montegut. See Houma Lodging.

★Le Jardin Sur Le Bayou B&B 256 Lower Country Dr., Bourg. See Houma Lodging.

Bayou Petit Caillou (Rte. 56)

This is the busiest of the streams south of Houma and the corresponding road, Rte. 56, is the most settled and commercially developed of the bayou routes. The road skirts the west side of Bayou Petit Caillou, or "little stones," a name reportedly derived from a pile of ballast stones that developed at the mouth of the bayou, left here by boats that had to lighten the load to make it through the shallows. It connects with Bayou Terrebonne and Rte. 55 via Rte. 58 at Chauvin and with Bayou Grand Caillou via Rte. 57 at Cocodrie in the south. Chauvin or Cocodrie are the best places to find a meal south of Houma.

CHAUVIN

Rte. 58 intersects Rte. 57 in the middle of the line village of Chauvin. The town was founded by a French hunter who settled on the high ground here and it was dubbed Petit Caillou after the adjacent bayou. In 1912 a post office was built and the town was named after the postmaster. Like in other bayou towns of the region, shrimping became the primary industry in the 20th century. Since the thirties, Chauvin has celebrated the bounty of the sea and its main industry with an annual blessing of the shrimp fleet.

La Trouvaille Restaurant Down Home, $$. Rte. 56, Chauvin.

In the early eighties Wylma Dusenberry bought this little Cajun cabin by Bayou Petit Caillou, two miles north of the Rte. 58 crossover, and began cooking for neighborhood folks. Today visitors from around the world arrive by tour bus to join throngs of locals eating at La Trouvaille (which means "lucky find"). Cotton tablecloths adorn simple wood tables and the dinnerware is mix and match. The best seats in the house are the four tables in the kitchen, where you can watch the family at work. Wylma and two of her five daughters do all the cooking and you will hear cries of "Hey, Mama!" coming from the stove.

The food is simple "blue plate" fare like pork roast, dirty rice, gumbo, and vegetables for a set price of about $8. The servings are not very large, but folks don't come here for the food so much as the country ambiance, the Dusenberry hospitality, and the singing. On the first Sunday of each month during the fall, a large contingent of the Dusenberry family gathers outside after lunch and sings to accordion and guitar accompaniment. The Dusenberrys are a Cajun Von Trapp family. Their music is far from traditional, but they perform favorites in back-porch sing-along harmony for the folks who gather on lawn chairs and benches. La Trouvaille is open for lunch on Wednesday, Friday, and Sunday between October and May, but the best time to stop by is for the singing on the first Sunday of each month during the fall. Call for reservations. The restaurant is five miles south of Houma. (504) 594-9503 or 873-8005.

Sportsman's Paradise Restaurant/Marina/Motel Rte. 56, Chauvin.

The restaurant at Sportsman's Paradise Marina is a casual setting for a fried seafood dinner. The bargain-priced fried seafood platter is among the best I've eaten. By lunchtime, sunburned fishermen are returning from half-day charters with big smiles and big appetites. The food and supercold beers keep 'em smiling. Behind the restaurant is a small fisherman's motel (no-frills lodging for anglers who want to leave early, get back late, or have a place to wash the salt off). Hours are 5 A.M. to 9 P.M. daily. (504) 594-2414.

Lapeyrouse Seafood, Camping, and Fishing Rte. 56 south of Chauvin.

This is a hangout for commercial and recreational fishermen (in other words, just about everyone down here), who stop by for a drink at the bar and some tall tales. You can get bait, fishing tips, and groceries in the store. A flat fee of $20 covers a camping space with hookups, boat launch, and bank-fishing privileges. Day use costs $2. The store and bar are open from 4 A.M. "until." Lapeyrouse Seafood is located on Rte. 56 at the Old Robinson Canal (one mile north of the Rte. 56 and 57 *T*). (504) 594-2600.

Lapeyrouse Store Junction of Rte. 57 and Rte. 56, south of Chauvin.

This community gathering spot has been in the Lapeyrouse family since the 1910s. Current owner Cecil Lapeyrouse used to work offshore, but when the oil industry bottomed out he took over the store. Now he dispenses fishing tips, bait, fuel, dry goods, and other essentials from the back room of the old grocery. Lapeyrouse relates stories that have been passed down through the family, like the time that water was four feet deep inside the store and waves crashed against the roof during the mighty storm of '26. In addition to groceries and fishing stuff, the shelves at Lapeyrouse Store are laden with products from its decades in business, like a shiny Bakelite radio, fiesta-ware plates, and sundries whose practical purposes have been obscured by age. The store is five miles north of the Co-Co Marina.

COCODRIE

Cocodrie is at the southern end of Rte. 56 about 35 miles south of Houma. The name means alligator in French, but the main attraction down here is fish, not reptiles. Whether you like your fish cooked and served with savory side dishes, swimming in an aquarium, or struggling at the end of a fishing rod, Cocodrie is a prime destination.

★**LUMCON** Rte. 56, Cocodrie.

LUMCON is an acronym for the Louisiana Universities Marine Consortium, a marine research facility in Cocodrie with a free display

Louisiana Marine Conservatories Research Center. (Courtesy of LUMCON)

and video presentation on the wildlife, history, and development of the Gulf coastal wetlands. You can't miss this sleek structure rising from the waving patches of marsh grass beside Rte. 56, just south of the Rte. 57 intersection. LUMCON is an essential stop for anyone who was curious enough about Louisiana's lovely wetlands to drive all the way down to Cocodrie. In addition to the Gulf exhibit, there are aquaria displaying the fauna of the salt and freshwater marshes as well as the tropical fishes that live around many offshore oil platforms. Eighty feet above the exhibition hall is a public observation tower with a panoramic view of the surrounding delta. There is a a short board-walk into the marsh. LUMCON is open daily until 4:30, but the security guard will allow you inside until dark. (504) 851-2800.

Co-Co Marina & Motel Rte. 56, end of the road in Cocodrie.

This is the ultimate fishing facility. Here you find nice motel rooms, classy and moderately priced condominiums, fishing charters, boat hoists, supplies, and a seafood restaurant. The restaurant sports a wood bar with all types of fishing lures shellacked into the surface. Rooms in the Co-Co's deluxe condo cost $150 a day for six, and some have jacuzzis. Rooms in the less luxurious, but comfortable, motel are $50 a night for four persons. Rates are lower in cool-weather months. (504) 594-6626.

Lighthouse Restaurant Seafood, $-$$. Rte. 56, Cocodrie.

A sunset dinner at the Lighthouse is recommended, even if the view is often better than the food. From the second-story dining room one can gaze through a wall of windows and watch the sun fall over a patchwork of marsh and water stretching south into the Gulf of Mexico. Fishing videos play quietly on the television over the bar, providing the rare opportunity of watching fish being caught while eating them. As evening darkens, fishermen who are staying at the Co-Co Marina trickle in and stand at the bar to trade stories and plan the next day's excursion.

The Lighthouse serves the freshest seafood anywhere. The broiled tuna I had on one visit tasted as if it had been caught that morning. Delicious po' boys are available at $5 for shrimp (grilled or fried), oyster, or fish and $8 for softshell crab. The restaurant is located in the marina on the right at the end of Rte. 56 (five miles below the intersection of Rte. 57). (504) 594-6626.

Harbor Light Restaurant Seafood, $. Rte. 56, Cocodrie.

This is the oldest marina/restaurant on the bayou. It is open from 6 A.M. until 2 or 3 A.M. daily. Sandwiches, cans of beer, and fried food are the staples. On most Fridays a country or French band plays from 9 P.M. "until." (504) 594-4183 or 594-7369.

Bayou Grand Caillou (Rte. 57)

Grand Caillou has two very distinct communities stretching along its east and west banks. On the east side, Rte. 57 breezes past miles of tidy bayou-side homes and shrimp boats belonging mainly to Cajuns. Twenty miles south of Houma, Rte. 57 intersects Rte. 56 in Cocodrie. On the west side a smaller road, known as Shrimper's Row, passes homes and stores owned by members of the United Houma Indian Nation. There is no reservation, sign, or boundary denoting the presence of Louisiana's largest Indian tribe, but the greatest concentration of these people live between Houma and Dulac on the west side of Bayou Grand Caillou.

Bayou Cabins 4326 Grand Caillou Rd. (Rte. 57). See Houma Lodging.

Coastguard Road/Indian Settlement

Below Dulac, Rte. 57 turns east to join Rte. 56 on neighboring Bayou Petit Caillou. To the south, Rte. 57 becomes Rte. 3011. Within a mile you will come to an old Houma Indian settlement. Though not as large as the community across the bayou, it is home to the Houma Nation tribal leader, Kirby Verret, and a number of fine artisans (including

Houma artisan Mary Verret with moss doll. (Photo by Macon Fry)

Mrs. Verret) who make cane baskets and moss dolls. The 17,000 members of the Houma Nation have not yet been federally recognized as a tribe; thus, you will not find a reservation, visitors center, crafts display, or casino. Verret ascribes the lack of recognition to the fact that the Houmas never waged a war against whites and, thus, never entered into a formal treaty with them. The Indians just kept moving southward and were mainly ignored until oil and gas were found in the area. Francophiles delight in visiting the area, as a large number of Indians, including many children, still speak an archaic variety of French.

Clanton Chapel/Dulac Music Center Coastguard Road.

These are good places to inquire about Houma tribal news, craftsmen, and events. (504) 563-7497 or 563-2549.

Bayou du Large (Rte. 315)

Rte. 315 follows Bayou Du Large south through the communities of Theriot and du Large. The Falgout Canal Road intersects Rte. 315 at the Bayou du Large Fire Station and provides a scenic link to the Indian community on lower Bayou Grand Caillou.

Cypress Cemetery Falgout Canal Road.

The Falgout Canal Road crosses the Houma Navigation Channel and a five-mile swath of eerie wetlands. As far as the horizon, bleached and blackened trunks and limbs of dead cypress protrude from the water. When the navigation channel was dredged out, salt water rushed into this freshwater swamp. The salinity destroyed sweetwater plant life and painted the ghostly landscape you see today.

HOUMA TO MORGAN CITY

The main east-west route in Houma is U.S. 90. Construction is inching along on a four-lane Houma bypass, which will cut a direct path to Morgan City north of the existing highway. The current course of U.S. 90 dips to the south as it follows the natural levee of Bayou Black. After crawling through downtown Houma, it passes a few old sugar plantations, rows of modest bayou-side homes, and a large number of decrepit shacks and houseboats. The road is shadowed by immense arms of ancient oak trees. Settlements along Bayou Black are only as wide as the small ridges of high ground along its banks. Several swamp tours depart from Bayou Black west of Houma.

Wildlife Gardens U.S. 90, 16 miles west of Houma, near Gibson.

In 1975, James and Betty Provost had six parakeets and a new home with a natural swamp in the backyard. Now their swamp is a sculpted garden with raised trails, and houses a spectacular collection of native Louisiana wildlife. There are bobcats, red fox, otter, nutria, and alligators. Mrs. Provost explains, "You just don't have a tourist attraction in this area without alligators." Depending on when you visit, you may have an opportunity to handle baby alligators. In the late summer you can see alligators on their nests. More impressive than the gators are the nearly 100-year-old Loggerhead turtles (now an endangered species), the great horned owls, and an extremely rare albino nutria.

The 20-acre garden includes 3 acres of preserved swamp, enclosed animal habitats, a simulated trapper's cabin (originally created for a movie set), and a duck pond. According to Provost, the zoo has been a learning experience for her as well as her guests. It took her a while to discover it was not a stray gator gobbling up her ducklings but giant largemouth bass that lurk in the pond! Provost explains the difference between her "Cajun zoo" and a big-city zoo this way: "At those big-city zoos the animal-identification plates provide the scientific and the common names for each animal. Here we provide the given name and the recipe!" Guided tours begin at 10, 1, and 4 daily except Sunday. For a wild time, spend a night in one of the Provosts' guest cabins (see review under Houma Lodging). The gardens are on the north side of Bayou Black about 16 miles west of Houma. Cross the bayou on the bridge at Greenwood School and continue west a couple of miles. Admission is $8 for adults and $3.25 for children. (504) 575-3676.

Annie Miller Swamp Tour U.S. 90, eight miles west of Houma.

No doubt about it, this is the most popular swamp tour in South Louisiana. If your main objective is to see alligators fed hunks of rotten chicken, you won't be disappointed. Annie Miller has been running this tour for a long time and her gators are well conditioned. She makes a show of calling them "by name," but when those guys hear the rumble of the outboard motor at the same time each day, they come like cats at the sound of a can opener. Annie Miller is a certified character; just listen to her warn passengers as the boat glides beneath an overpass, "This bridge would not only knock your head off, it would knock your brains out!" The problem with her tour is that it spends half of its duration getting to and from gator holes, which aren't located in the swamp at all but in man-made canals cut through marshland near the Intracoastal Waterway. Miller offers bilingual tours for French-speaking guests and her dock is conveniently located on U.S. 90 about eight miles west of Houma. She has three large party barges (with uncomfortable center seating), which go out every day. Call for tour times and reservations. The 2½-hour trip costs $15 for adults and $10 for children ages 3 to 12. (504) 879-3934.

Cajun Man guide "Black" Guidry and Gator Bait. (Photo by Julie Posner)

★A Cajun Man's Tour U.S. 90, 10 miles west of Houma.

How does the idea of cruising the swamps and marshes of the Houma area with a Cajun musician and his Catahoula cur (the state dog) named Gator Bait strike you? Whether he is holding forth while piloting a comfortable party barge through the marsh, or picking and singing a Cajun favorite like "Big Mamou," "Black" Guidry is a consummate entertainer. Once Guidry gets past cautioning everyone that the tour fee is only "one way" and reminding folks to keep track of which way they are heading, he comes up with the comforting assurance, "If you have any questions, I'll answer them. If I can't answer them, I'll make something up!"

Kidding aside, Guidry is a conscientious and knowledgeable guide who makes sure everyone enjoys the trip as much as he so plainly does. The wetlands south of Houma are not the most scenic in Cajun Country, but Black has a good route, twisting through natural bayous draped with Spanish moss and blazing down wide oil-field canals. He edges up to tupelo swamps tangled with the white flowers of elderberry vines and red muscadine grapes and slowly skirts open marsh where thousands of waterbirds coat the distant horizon like snow.

Black carries a bag of old chicken, which he dangles over the side at intervals for alligators that await his regular visits. This is the part of the trip that really excites the dog Gator Bait, who charges fearlessly to the railing, snarling and flashing his blue Catahoula eyes at the oblivious reptiles below. If you have never seen a Catahoula hound, or "spotted leopard dog," as they are sometimes called, the playful Gator Bait is one of the down-home attractions of this trip. The climax of the Cajun Man tour comes at a lost bend of a bayou where Guidry cuts the engines and unpacks his guitar and homemade accordion for a set of Cajun tunes. The shade is cool under the boat awning as Guidry winds up a song with "son of a gun, we'll have big fun on the bayou!" Cajun Man leaves from a dock 10 miles west of Houma on U.S. 90. Several tours go out each day for 1½ to 2 hours. Call to confirm times and availability. For two people, the cost is $20 each, but usually there is a group to join and the fee is only $15 for adults and $10 for children. (504) 868-4625.

Rte. 20 to Morgan City

After decades of bickering among engineers, politicians, and environmentalists, a four-lane U.S. 90 bypass (temporarily designated Rte. 3052) is completed above Houma as far west as Rte. 20. Rte. 20 connects with U.S. 90 again about 24 miles west of Houma, offering a faster route for travelers between Morgan City and New Orleans who wish to bypass the city. This route also passes the best restaurant and swamp tour in the Houma area.

★**Chester's Cypress Inn** Local Fave, $-$$. Rte. 20, Donner.

Nestled in a stand of cypress trees halfway between Houma and Morgan City, this little hideaway has the best fried chicken this side of Grandma's kitchen table. A sign boasts, "If the Colonel had our recipe he'd be a general." You won't find any nouveau Cajun cuisine here, just plates piled high with fried chicken, fish, froglegs, and mounds of crispy onion rings. Chester Boudreaux has passed away, but his children, Calvin Boudreaux and Bobbie LaRose, have kept the Inn much the same as it was when he opened in the forties. The tables are still covered with plastic, and the waitresses still carry cardboard plates laden with golden fried food from the adjacent building that houses the kitchen. Crowds drive the 20 miles from Morgan City and Houma (past dozens of new fast-food franchises) to eat in the homey dining room that once housed a dance hall. The onion rings, which arrive in towering portions that will serve three, are sweet and sliced to order. The Cypress Inn is a perfect stop after a weekend swamp tour. Chester's is on Rte. 20, about 3.5 miles east of the intersection with U.S. 90 (25 miles west of Houma). Their hours are Friday and Saturday from 5 P.M. to 10 P.M. and Sunday 11 A.M. to 10 P.M. (504) 446-6821.

Chester's Cypress Inn. (Photo by Julie Posner)

★Atchafalaya Basin Backwater Adventure North Bayou Black Drive, Gibson.

Among tours for the seriously adventurous, Atchafalaya Backwater is in a class by itself! While other "swamp" tours in the Houma area wend through the open marsh, canals, and navigation channels to the south, Backwater Adventure operates solely within the commercially unnavigable waterways of the Great Chacahoula Swamp. Tours are limited to six, the most that will fit in a small swamp boat. Guide Jon Faslun won't bend your ear with pat jokes and rehearsed hospitality, but his knowledge of the history, wildlife, and waterways in this part of the Basin is awe inspiring. You get the feeling that no two trips with him are going to be alike.

The tour I took began with a brief bayou tour of the historic village of Donner before spinning into the swamp. About 30 minutes away from the launch, Faslun beached the boat on a narrow wooded levee and helped his guests ashore. Ensconced on a tiny strip of land in a quiet backwater of the Chacahoula Swamp, Faslun settled in like Br'er Rabbit in the briar patch. In a quarter-mile nature hike, he casually explained what type of snake was hanging overhead, plucked berries to taste, and crushed leaves to smell. Of the plants he commented, "A few are good to eat, a few aren't, and a few are here in case you eat the wrong thing." The climax of the tour was a short trek to the abandoned site of a century-old cypress mill (the second largest in the state in its heyday). It's overgrown with vines and still littered with artifacts of the lumbering operation.

Atchafalaya Backwater offers an experience that is more an adventure than a tour. It is a trip that will leave you talking as much about what you have done and learned as what you have seen. If you want to explore on your own, you can rent a pirogue, pack a cooler, and paddle about 45 minutes to the old mill site. The 2½-hour tour of the swamp surrounding Donner and Gibson costs $20 per person, with a $40 minimum. Tours are offered at 11 and 3 daily. Pirogue rental is $10 for a 12-hour day (maps and instructions are furnished). From Houma take U.S. 90 west to the bridge by the water tower in Gibson. After crossing the bayou, double back east two blocks on North Bayou Black Drive. The fastest way to get there from New Orleans is by way of Rte. 20. About 150 yards past the Gibson sign on Rte. 20, turn left (south) on Caroll Street. Turn left again on North Bayou Black Drive. Atchafalaya Backwater Adventure is .2 mile down on the left. (504) 575-2371.

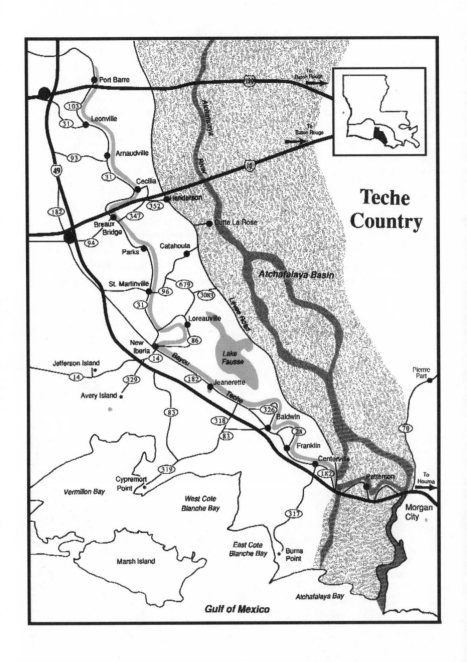

Teche Country

12

Teche Country

For centuries the main route for transportation in the Teche region was the bayou from which it derives its name. From headwaters in Port Barre, Bayou Teche (pronounced "Tesh") travels 130 miles through canopies of live oaks and acres of gleaming cane fields before pouring into the Atchafalaya River above Morgan City. The area was once occupied by the reputedly cannibalistic Attakapas Indians, who were eradicated when the first Europeans arrived. The name Teche was derived from the Indian word *tenche* (snake), which accurately describes the stream's twisting course through the geographic center of South Louisiana. The stream formed the main channel of the Mississippi River until about 3,000 years ago when the river jumped its banks, seeking a shorter outlet to the Gulf. The quiet bayou now divides the soggy regions of the Atchafalaya Basin from the prairie to the west and marshes along the coast. Thanks to

Morning mist on Bayou Teche. (Photo by Greg Guirard)

179

the poetry of Henry Wadsworth Longfellow, the region surrounding the bayou is often referred to as Evangeline Country in deference to the poet's Acadian heroine.

Although the Teche long ago faded from preeminence as an arterial highway, the romanticism of Longfellow only begins to scrape the surface of the diversity of attractions in the area today. The main route through the region is the Old Spanish Trail (U.S. 90 and Rte. 182), which mostly follows the course of the bayou. Teche Country is divided into two subregions that roughly reflect the different cultures and terrain along its banks. The Lower Teche (below St. Martinville) is dominated by the Anglo sugar culture that blossomed in the early 1800s. The less navigable Upper Teche (between St. Martinville and Port Barre) is a swampy area settled primarily by Cajuns and Creoles in the 18th century. The Europeans who settled the Upper Teche enjoyed a life of opulence and high culture when the rest of Cajun Country was a wild frontier. Teche Country remains an area largely disconnected from the Mississippi River and the rest of the nation, isolated by miles of swamp and marsh. A drive along the bayou on U.S. 90 and Rte. 182 provides a longer (3.5 hour) but more scenic route between New Orleans and Lafayette.

THE LOWER TECHE

From the industrial port of Morgan City west to Jeanerette, the Lower Teche is dominated by the sugar culture. Miles of cane fields reach the horizon and the temple-like edifices of sugar plantations grace the higher west bank of the bayou. With the Louisiana Purchase and arrival of steamboats in the early 1800s, a wealthy planter class supplanted the few Cajun ranchers and farmers who had settled here. The Anglos established lumber mills and leveled thousands of acres of land for cane cultivation. They built massive houses and populated mill towns and trading posts along the bayou, which was the major route of transportation at the time. The dominance of Yankee settlers on the Lower Teche is evident today in the succession of decidedly non-French towns like Patterson, Franklin, and Baldwin. Anyone but the hurried traveler will want to forsake the four-lane rush of U.S. 90 for a drive down Rte. 182 (the Old Spanish Trail), which closely follows the bayou. On this venerable oak-shaded highway you will pass through the heart of the sugar belt, see turn-of-the-century towns and antebellum homes, and find opportunities for short side trips to coastal recreational areas and the Chitimacha Indian Reservation.

Downtown Morgan City from the river. (Photo by Macon Fry)

Morgan City

Located at the confluence of the Atchafalaya River, Bayou Teche, and the Intracoastal Waterway, Morgan City (the Shrimp and Petroleum Capital of Louisiana) is a bustling Gulf port with a huge oil and fishing fleet. This city of 16,000 is an interesting if atypical gateway to the enchanting world of Teche Country. Entering from the east, one is greeted by miles of shipyards and oil-industry facilities. Offshore oil platforms, hundreds of feet tall, rest on their sides on barges, awaiting transport to the Gulf. You will pass mounds of shredded steel at Southern Scrap Yards, stacks of massive wooden spools at Hercules Wire Rope Company, and hundreds of jackup barges docked at McDermott Industries.

This is not the place to look for traditional French folkways. The town's founding fathers were Thomas Berwick (of Pennsylvania), Dr. Walter Brashear (of Kentucky), and Charles Morgan (of New York). The city was incorporated in 1860 after the arrival of the rail line from New Orleans and named for Dr. Brashear, who owned the vast Tiger Island sugar plantation, which occupied the site. When Charles Morgan purchased the railroad and steamship lines after the War Between the States, Morgan City was renamed in his honor. It was an honor well bestowed, as Morgan's dredging of the Atchafalaya Bay in 1872 opened the city to major industrial traffic. The port became a hub for fishing and lumbering interests. Although Morgan City dubbed itself "Shrimp

Capital of the World" following the first harvest of jumbo Gulf shrimp in the 1930s, the most significant economic development was the drilling of the nation's first producing offshore oil well nearby in 1947. The city celebrates its twin industries in the unusual Shrimp and Petroleum Festival. For an exotic glimpse of these industries, visit the old riverfront and Mr. Charlie Oil Rig, which can be toured in a couple hours. Folks interested in exploring a hidden corner of Cajun Louisiana should take a short drive up Rte. 70 to the watery communities of Stephensville and Pierre Part (see North of Morgan City [Rte. 70] section below).

Morgan City Visitors Information Center 725 Myrtle St.

Despité the heavy industry here, there are several worthy attractions and lovely wetlands vistas in the Morgan City area. The best place to get brochures is from the Morgan City Visitors Center, but for a knowledgeable and helpful staff, call or visit the St. Mary Parish Tourist Center (see Patterson). The Morgan City Center is a block north of U.S. 90 beside Swamp Gardens. It has rest rooms, maps, and brochures on important local events and sites. It is open from 8 to 4 Monday through Friday and from 9 on weekends. (504) 384-3343.

RECREATION

Atchafalaya Basin Airboat Tours Rte. 70, Russo Memorial Launch.

Capt. Bob McHugh has spent much of his life working and playing in the Atchafalaya Basin, visiting his family camp, and traveling to their various holdings in the swamp. He can show you places that no other operator would find and can give a personal account of how the Basin has changed. Let him know what you wish to do, whether it is to see historical sites, wildlife, ancient cypress or miles of floating wildflowers, or to disembark and walk through an abandoned cypress mill. If your interest is fishing he can tell you plenty about that, too. Not only is McHugh the only tour operator in the Lower Atchafalaya Basin, but he has the advantage of operating by airboat. These craft are extremely fast and can travel in shallow ponds and overgrown streams. They are also very loud. Captain Bob provides protective headphones and lifejackets. Tours are available by appointment only. The boat can accommodate up to five at $30 per person (two-passenger minimum). Cash only. (504) 384-4258.

★Lake End Park Rte. 70, Morgan City.

Since the late 1800s, this cypress-studded area on Lake Palourde has been a popular picnic and swimming site. Palourde is nearly six miles long and four miles across from north to south. Its sweet and cool waters provide the best swimming in all of Cajun Country. Thirty acres were donated to the park in the 1930s by the Morgan City Land Company, and it has since grown into a fully equipped recreation area with rest rooms, showers, sheltered picnic pavilion, camping, and a small sandy beach. On summer weekends, the park gets very crowded. The best time to wheel in is at the close of day or during midweek. There is nothing like a quiet dip in the lake after a day touring in the Louisiana heat (*see* Lake End Park Campground in the Lodging section of this chapter). Admission to the park is $2 per car for up to four people. (504) 380-4623.

Scully's Swamp Tours Rte. 70, Stephensville (5.3 miles above Rte. 182).

From a position at the edge of a wonderfully unspoiled region of lakes, swamps, and bayous, Capt. Bob Scully is perfectly situated to offer one of the best tours in the state. The swamp above Morgan City was once part of the natural drainage system of the Atchafalaya Basin but was lopped off by new levees. The area is unscarred by the oil and gas industry and features a profusion of wildlife, sweet water, and fresh air. Scully was born and raised in the swampy area around Stephensville, where his grandfather was an original settler. He builds his own boats, fixes his own motors, and knows the smallest bayous and their histories by heart.

Daily tours are scheduled on a 49-passenger, covered pontoon barge, but the best trip is in Scully's small skiff. By skiff, Captain Bob can get you quickly to the largest cypress you are likely to see anywhere. Some of the trees on the skiff route are 200 to 400 years old. Back at the launch there is a bar and restaurant where you can relax in one of two dining rooms and order the best seafood in the Morgan City area (*see* review below). A two-hour tour costs $20 each for two people and $15 each for groups of three or more. Typically Scully goes out once in the morning and twice in the afternoon. Call first to verify rates, times, and availability of the small-boat excursion. (504) 385-2388.

ATTRACTIONS

Swamp Gardens and Wildlife Zoo

In the tradition of the Dells of Wisconsin and Dinosaur World, Swamp Gardens is a genuine fifties-style attraction where the simulated does battle with the natural. In one end of the Gardens a loudspeaker plays the sound of frogs croaking while real frogs respond from the surrounding pond. At one point during my tour the guide decided that a sleeping alligator should show its teeth for the tourists, so she gave it a nice poke with a stick! The Gardens and tour are dated enough to be a museum piece themselves and are quite enjoyable as such. A side exhibit of swamp boats and an antique swamp buggy is quite interesting. Guided tours are offered on the hour Monday through Saturday from 11 to 4 and Sunday from 1. Tickets must be purchased at the Visitors Center across the street at $3 for adults and $1.50 for children. (504) 384-3343.

★**Mr. Charlie Oil Rig Tour** Riverfront, Morgan City.

Do not miss this rare opportunity to climb onto and into a real off-shore drilling rig. Mr. Charlie is tethered to the mainland at the Morgan City riverfront by a steel ramp. From atop the heliport deck you may look across the rooftops of the historic district, view commerce on the busy Atchafalaya River, and, towards the Gulf, spy the shores of Avoca Island.

The giant rig was the first portable offshore oil platform and operated from 1954 until 1989, drilling as many as 500 wells in the Gulf of Mexico. Tour guide Bob Cockerham, a 40-year-veteran of the offshore oil industry, worked on Mr. Charlie in 1958. He explains how the rig was floated around the Gulf on a barge that would be raised or sunk at each drilling site to provide a stable foundation for the crew quarters (accommodating 50 workers), engine rooms, and derrick above. Climbing the maze of stairs and ladders, Cockerham drifts from technical talk to tales of life on board rigs, blowouts, rig fires, and the time he was asked to appear in the 1952 movie *Thunder Bay*. Mr. Charlie is used as a training center for offshore workers, offering visitors an accurate picture of operations. To get to the rig take old U.S. 90 west past the ramp for the new bridge. Turn left on Second Street and

Mr. Charlie Oil Rig. (Photo by Macon Fry)

follow the signs to Mr. Charlie. Tours are offered Monday through Saturday at 10 and 2 for $5. Call the rig office to be sure that tours are running. (504) 384-3744.

Avoca Island Ferry

I'm a sucker for ferries, often opting to wait in line for the chance to glide across a stream rather than drive over it, so it was natural to make the five-minute detour from the Morgan City Visitors Center to check this one out. The Avoca Island Ferry holds four to six vehicles and is propelled by a steel cable cranked through a pulley. The ferry crosses the intracoastal canal and drops passengers on the small, privately owned marsh island just south of the city. The west side of Avoca (where the ferry lands) is occupied by a private hunt club. On the east side at the end of a nine-mile dirt road, a handful of residents live in a muddy cluster of ramshackle homes and trailers. Through some mystifying political machinations, the public ferry (operated by St. Mary Police Jury) provides free service to the private island daily. The ferry runs every half-hour except at lunchtime. To get to the Avoca Ferry from U.S. 90, turn south onto Myrtle Street. Follow Myrtle past the old cemetery and across the railroad tracks. The road bends and ends at the ferry landing.

Brownell Memorial Park and Carillon Tower Rte. 70, Morgan City.

The Brownell Memorial Park is a 9.5-acre tract of swampy land on the banks of Lake Palourde just five minutes north of Morgan City. The park was donated by Mrs. Claire Horatio Brownell as a quiet, nondenominational retreat and place of contemplation. There is a short elevated trail that leads to a 106-foot-tall bell tower and a garden. The swamp is filled with cattails, palmettos, ferns, and flowering plants. The park is open Monday through Saturday from 9 to 5. The bells in the Carillon are rung (mechanically) on the half-hour. Admission is free.

★Johnny's Time In A Bottle Rte. 182, Bayou Vista (four miles west of Morgan City).

Museum of ships and scenes in bottles. (*See* Bayou Vista and Patterson section.)

DOWNTOWN ATTRACTIONS

The historic district of downtown Morgan City runs along the Atchafalaya riverfront south from the Rte. 182 Bridge four blocks to Railroad Avenue, and stretches away from the river four blocks to Federal Avenue. It was developed during the lumber boom, so most of the buildings date from the early 1900s. The commercial section is concentrated on Front Street facing the Atchafalaya, while the turn-of-the-

Fishing on the Morgan City riverfront. (Photo by Anna Graham Hunter)

century residential district rambles away from the river on numbered streets. Rita Mae's Kitchen at 711 Federal is a great breakfast or lunch stop (*see* Food section). If you are traveling west on U.S. 90, do not get on the bridge ramps but stay right on Brashear Avenue until you reach the flood wall.

The Great Wall Front Street.

Standing below the 21-foot-tall "great wall" is a fine place to appreciate the awe with which man faces the floodwaters of the Atchafalaya River. Constructed by the Corps of Engineers, the walls in Morgan City and across the river in Berwick are designed to withstand a flood of truly unimaginable proportions. Morgan City lies directly below the Atchafalaya Basin floodway at the very mouth of the river. When the Corps channels water from the Mississippi River into the Atchafalaya to prevent flooding in New Orleans, those waters wind up lapping the walls here. Climb the steps that scale the wall at regular intervals and you are in for a real surprise. Upriver from the bridge a number of businesses and most of a neighborhood were left to God's protection. Some houses sit in several feet of water each spring, and there are places where fishermen dock their boats and walk down ramps into their homes.

Despite the immensity of the flood-control project, engineers predict total devastation of the city on the day that the Mississippi River makes its anticipated jump and begins to course down the Atchafalaya. Steps and viewing stations are located at the downtown section of the wall near Brashear and Front Street.

Historic Commercial District Front Street, east of Brashear Avenue.

Since the 1960s the old commercial district has suffered the same flight and blight as other downtown areas. It has also weathered direct hits from a couple of hurricanes and the collapse of oil prices in the eighties. Several businesses still remain including **Shannon Hardware** and the bizarre **Kahn's Women's Clothing,** which specializes in clothes that have "come back in style." Its shelves are well stocked with items from the sixties and seventies. About the only new clothes are a large selection of glittery and gauzy costumes sold to exotic dancers. For an immersion in local color, visit the half-dozen bars that line the first block of **Railroad Avenue** heading away from the river on the south side of the historic district. The clientele is mainly shrimpers and oil-field workers (the shrimpers are identifiable by their white rubber boots). My favorites are the Kabooze and the Blowout Lounge.

Petroleum Museum Front Street.

Wherever you go in the region you are likely to see some evidence of the quest for oil and this is a logical place to put it in perspective. Though the Petroleum Museum was not quite finished at my last visit, it will house a collection of photographs, models, equipment, and explanatory information relating to the oil industry in Louisiana. Be sure to visit the Mr. Charlie Oil Rig operated by the museum, about a mile farther down the waterfront. Information on the museum may be obtained by calling the rig at (504) 384-3744.

Turn-of-the-Century House 715 Second St.

The oldest neighborhood in Morgan City is located southeast of the Atchafalaya Bridge, where the U.S. 90 upramp begins its ascent. Most of the homes here, like the commercial district beside the river, were built in the early 1900s during the halcyon days of the lumber industry. The Turn-of-the-Century House was built in 1906 and lay squarely in the path of the new U.S. 90 Bridge, constructed in 1970. It was disassembled and moved a few blocks to its present location, where it operates as a small museum. Most of the mill work in the house is cypress, but the floors are long-leaf yellow pine. The first floor is decorated exclusively with period furniture of mahogany and oak, while the upstairs houses a display of Mardi Gras costumes and photographs. The house is open weekdays from 10 to 5 and weekends from 1. Admission is $3 for adults and $1.50 for students. (504) 380-4651.

MORGAN CITY ON FILM: *TARZAN* AND *THUNDER BAY*

The first film adaptation of Edgar Rice Burroughs' *Tarzan of the Apes,* starring Elmo Lincoln, was filmed in the swamps around Morgan City in 1916. Like the book, the film was hugely successful. Claimed by

Elmo Lincoln as the first film Tarzan, shot in Morgan City. (Courtesy of Burroughs Archives)

some to be the first movie to gross over a million dollars, *Tarzan* spawned a host of other jungle films. The National Film Corporation, which produced the picture, called the silent epic "a mastodonic monopoly embracing all that the mind of man can possibly conceive, suggest or imagine" and "the most stupendous amazing film production in the world's history." (Take that, Steven Spielberg!)

Thunder Bay was shot in 1952 on one of the early offshore oil rigs south of Morgan City and on the shrimp docks in Morgan City and Berwick. It stars Jimmy Stewart, Joanne Dru, and Dan Duryea. The film depicts an actual feud that developed between Cajun shrimpers and the men who came to explore for offshore oil. A similar feud has exploded again between fishermen and geologists using seismic devices in the Atchafalaya Basin.

SPECIAL EVENTS

Louisiana Shrimp and Petroleum Festival Labor Day weekend.

After the first offshore oil well started producing in 1947, the former Louisiana Shrimp Festival (the oldest chartered harvest festival in the state) was renamed the Shrimp and Petroleum Festival. The idea of a shrimp and petroleum fair calls to mind images of jumbo crustaceans steeping in vats of crude, but the two products are never actually mixed. The main events are the coronation of the court and a Sunday blessing of the shrimp fleet. These are surrounded by a weekend of free outdoor music and carnival rides.

Much of the festival takes place in the shadow of the Atchafalaya Bridge ramp. This is not a picturesque setting, but if you have ever been in Morgan City during a steamy September, you understand the value of any scrap of shade. Bands play in Lawrence Park (near the bridge). (504) 385-0703.

FOOD

Morgan City may be the "Shrimp Capital of the World," but the title is industrial not culinary. The flow of oil-field and industrial workers through town has not bolstered the restaurant scene except to assure a good number of fast-food franchises. My local favorite is the recently opened Rita Mae's Kitchen.

D&B Seafood Market Boiled Seafood (to go). 1601 Rte. 70, Morgan City.

D&B is a seafood market, grocery, and gas station one mile north of U.S. 90 on Rte. 70. A line forms on Friday and Saturday afternoon in the summer when steaming seafood is sold right out of the boiling pot. The crabs and crawfish are both excellent. D&B is convenient to Lake End Park Campground and the wetlands around Stephensville. The store is open daily from 5:30 A.M. to 9 P.M. Hot boiled seafood is sold from 3 P.M. on weekdays and 1 P.M. on weekends until 7 P.M. (504) 385-5833.

Duffy's Restaurant Seafood, $-$$. Rte. 70, Pierre Part.

Like neighboring Landry's, Duffy's (20 miles north of Morgan City) is a convenient place to eat if you are visiting the dance halls of Pierre Part. It is very popular with locals, who feed on the fried seafood and steaks. You can build a nice sampler out of the appetizers here. Turtle, crawfish, crab, and shrimp stews are all available in $3-$4 servings, as are the fried alligator and softshell crab. Hours are 10 A.M. to 9 P.M. weekdays and until 10 P.M. weekends (closed Mondays). (504) 252-9936.

Fisherman's Inn Seafood, $-$$. 1255 Stephensville Rd.

Fisherman's Inn is a local hangout so you are likely to get a helping of local color with your food. There is a good Country and Swamp Pop jukebox in the corner and a pool table in another room. The food is standard South Louisiana fare: fried seafood, stews, gumbos, and sandwiches. Plate lunches are served on weekdays. From U.S. 90 take Rte. 70 north 5 miles. The place is located 1.3 miles east of Rte. 70 on Stephensville Road (just past the Doiron Canal Bridge). The kitchen is open Monday through Saturday from 9 A.M. to 8 P.M. (504) 384-9266.

Landry's Restaurant Seafood, $-$$. Rte. 70, Pierre Part.

If you are driving to Pierre Part (20 miles north of Morgan City) for a dance at the Rainbow Inn or Chilly's, this is one of two places to eat in the area. It is quite popular with locals. The menu features familiar South Louisiana seafood favorites from gumbos and stews to fried-seafood platters and sandwiches. Somewhat more unusual are the alligator and turtle sauce piquants, fried froglegs, and fried alligator. Hours are Tuesday through Thursday and Sunday from 9 A.M. to 9 P.M. Friday and Saturday they stay open until 10 P.M. (504) 252-6909.

★Rita Mae's Kitchen Down Home, $. 711 Federal Ave.

Along with the Mr. Charlie Oil Rig, Rita Mae's Kitchen is a good reason to stop in Morgan City. Ms. Mae knows what she does best and that is red or white beans and stewed pork chops (about $5). I could find no fault in her hearty shrimp or crawfish stews (under $8) either, though most locals seem to go for the hefty hamburgers. Try a hot fruit cobbler for dessert. Breakfasts range from large to huge, but the basic $4-$5 model includes eggs, pork chops or steak, grits or hash browns, and a biscuit. A couple of biscuits with rich white sausage gravy is my pick. This soulful food is served in a tidy converted house in the center of the historic district, just a few blocks from the Turn-of-the-Century House and a short drive from Mr. Charlie. Another Rita Mae's is opening on Second Street in the historic district to serve the growing clientele. To get to Rita Mae's take old U.S. 90 west past the ramp to the new bridge. Turn left on Federal Avenue. The restaurant is a few blocks down on the right. Hours are 8:30 A.M. to 9 P.M. on Sunday and until 10 P.M. Monday through Saturday. (504) 384-3550.

Scully's Restaurant Seafood, $$. 3141 Rte. 70, Stephensville.

Some of the best eats we got in Morgan City were not in town at all but 5.3 miles north at Scully's Restaurant. Not only were our platters of fried food and gumbo substantial, but the place was a lot of fun and has a water view. Try appetizer-size crabmeat and crawfish stew with the salad bar, or go for a bowl of shrimp and okra gumbo with potato salad. Scully's is open Monday through Saturday from 10:30 A.M. to 9 P.M. (504) 385-2388.

MUSIC

There are a couple of fantastic 1930s dance halls featuring Swamp Pop and Cajun music most weekends, but you've got to make the 20-minute drive up to Pierre Part. Otherwise Morgan City is more of a Country-music place, with no options for live entertainment.

★Chilly's 17 miles north of Morgan City.

Highly recommended 1930s dance hall over Lake Verret! Cajun

dance on Sunday afternoon, Swamp Pop on Saturday night. *See* Pierre Part section below.

Club Country Country dance hall. Rte. 182, Berwick.

Club Country (formerly Randy's) is a big Texas-style dance hall, over the bridge in Berwick. They are open Thursday through Saturday. Specials may change but they have been offering $5 "all the beer you can drink," free drinks for ladies, dance lessons, and free pool on Thursdays. On Fridays and Saturdays local Country bands like Kid Sonnier and the Hurricanes take the stage at 9:30. (504) 385-2272.

Light House Lounge Country/Swamp Pop. 180 Canton St., Berwick.

The Light House has been a fixture on the Berwick riverfront for many years, at one time featuring French dances on Sundays. There is still music most weekends and Sunday afternoons, performed by local Country combos. The lounge is an interesting place, with nautical and oil-patch photos on the walls and a couple of miniature wooden boats reputedly crafted by Johnny Carbonell (*see* Johnny's Time In A Bottle below). (504) 384-4258.

★Rainbow Inn 20 miles north of Morgan City.

Highly recommended 1930s dance hall! Occasional Swamp Pop dances. The bar is usually open Wednesday through Saturday. *See* Pierre Part section below.

LODGING

Houseboat Rental:

★Cajun Houseboat Rentals Rte. 70, 6.3 miles north of Morgan City.

Connie Thomas's houseboat *Magnolia* is not only the best place to stay in Morgan City but a worthy destination in itself. This retreat on the banks of Bayou Long near Stephensville has central air conditioning, cable TV, phone, stereo, washer and dryer, barbecue grill, full kitchen, and comfortable furnishings. You can actually have a ball for two days without ever getting back in your car. Take a short walk up the bayou to Charlieville (see review), fish or swim from the deck, or kick back with your feet up and read. The perfect antidote to Morgan City's heat is a dive into the cool water of Bayou Long. Guests retire to a chorus of frogs and hoot owls and wake to the sun rising over moss-covered cypress on the east shore. One evening as I ate crawfish on the covered porch a huge owl descended on a nearby post.

The *Magnolia* is part of an old houseboat and camp community that was once called Bayou Long, an excellent base for visiting the dance halls of Pierre Part and exploring Stephensville. *See* the North of Morgan City (Rte. 70) section for more on this area. Most of the folks along this stretch are permanent residents so, except for the sound of occasional fishing boats or cars on Rte. 70, the place is quite serene. The house is permanently moored to the shore so you can park in the driveway and walk in. It is just across the levee from the Atchafalaya Basin and less than three miles from two swamp tours and a couple of good eateries. The basic rate is $95 plus $10 for each occupant. Children under 12 stay free. With two bedrooms and a futon sofa in the living room there is space to sleep eight. (504) 385-2738.

Motels and Hotels:

Acadian Inn 1924 U.S. 90 E., $64 double. (504) 384-5750.

Holiday Inn 520 Roderick St., $65 double. (504) 385-2200.

Camping:

★Lake End Park Campground Rte. 70 North.

This is a beautiful campground that combines proximity to the highway with a great natural setting, lake swimming, fishing, laundry, and camper pavilions. There are 141 camper spaces with complete hookups, and room for dozens of tents on the cypress-shaded lawn overlooking Lake Palourde. The best time to camp here is on weeknights in the fall or spring, when the grounds are quiet and the white sand beach is empty. My favorite meal in Morgan City was fresh shrimp grilled beside Lake Palourde during a camping trip. It costs around $10 for both tents and RVs. (504) 380-4623.

North of Morgan City (Rte. 70)

One of the least visited and most interesting areas in Bayou Country is the watery region heading north on Rte. 70. This small highway is actually the main route connecting Morgan City to I-10 near Baton Rouge. For about 16 miles, the Atchafalaya Basin levee forms a verdant wall on the west side of the road occupied by grazing cattle and egrets. On the east side, Rte. 70 is lined with the houseboat and camp communities of Stephensville, Bayou Long, and Belle River. At Belle River Rte. 70 curves northeast across some beautiful swamp on its way to the Mississippi River Road and I-10. A real treat awaits those who make the 20-mile drive to the 1930s dance halls in Pierre Part (see reviews below).

STEPHENSVILLE

Stephensville is a community of houseboats and camps radiating out from the intersection of Rte. 70 and Stephensville Road (about five miles north of Rte. 90 in Morgan City). Only an outsider would describe it this way; better to say the community radiates from the confluence of Bayou Long and Doiron Canal. Once part of the Atchafalaya Basin, the place has little to do with roads and everything to do with water and boats. For more than a century folks have lived in boats and camps in these wetlands near the juncture of Lake Verret and Lake Palourde and there are plenty of fourth-generation fishermen and boat builders there now. To see the area by boat, enlist the services of Scully's Swamp Tours. There are many places you can reach by car. For an immersion in local color I recommend a visit to Charlieville and T-Man Bailey's. If you have a little more time consider staying on the houseboat *Magnolia* (*see* Morgan City Lodging) and taking in the night life of Pierre Part (reviewed below).

★T-Man Bailey's Bar and Grocery 12 miles off Rte. 70.

T-Man's family has lived in and run this store and bar (let's just call it a hangout) at the intersection of Bayou Long and Four Mile Bayou since the 1930s (way before there was any road). The place is a wood-frame building with double screen doors that swing open onto the bayou (which is where most visitors arrive from). There is a sparse selection of groceries; primary nourishment here is cold cans of beer. T-Man holds forth from behind the long checkout counter, which doubles as a bar and divides the grocery (hangout area) from the pool room. When he got back from World War II T-Man anticipated the road and built a modern home with a garage. The road arrived but the garage opens onto the bayou (oops). Getting to T-Man's can be fun if you are not in a hurry. From Rte. 70 head east on Stephensville Road. Cross the Doiron Canal Bridge at the Lil Country Store. Make a left after crossing the bridge. The road turns to gravel and winds treacherously through the swamp for about 10 miles before terminating at T-Man's. T-Man's is open most afternoons until dusk, the time when people are winding up a day on the water. (225) 635-4512.

★Charlieville 2941 Rte. 70, 6.5 miles north of Morgan City.

Charlieville is ostensibly a barroom but, as its name would suggest, this place founded and governed by the colorful Charlie Estay is a whole lot more. After working oil-industry jobs all over South Louisiana for 40 years, Estay retreated to his trailer on the banks of Bayou Long and "incorporated" the bar next door in his own name. The bar has become a social center for the former community of Bayou Long, a gathering place for family, storytellers, lie swappers, and others who come to enjoy the good-natured atmosphere of Charlieville. I won't go through a litany of the quirky features of this bar or its host. Visit and discover for yourself! (504) 384-9646.

Charlie Estay at the Charlieville bar. (Photo by Anna Graham Hunter)

PIERRE PART

Pierre Part is little more than a charming stop in the road, but it is home to two quintessential 1930s dance halls (*see* reviews below). Anyone seeking out Cajun culture, local color, or a great time at a South Louisiana dance should visit Pierre Part. It is about 20 miles from Morgan City and 20 miles from River Road at Donaldsonville (I-10 exit #182). Pierre Part grew from fishing village to cane-raising community to lumber town. During the lumbering days, hundreds of loggers arrived on weekends, escaping the confines of their floating dormitories. This influx spawned the growth of the town's legendary dance halls. Now the biggest employers are refineries along Rte. 70 East and River Road. French is still spoken by many residents and understood by nearly everyone. The center of the community is the little bridge over Bayou Pierre Part where the Virgin Mary stands guard and the Rainbow Inn beckons thirsty travelers. Here you will also find a grocery, marina, and church. Two restaurants just south of the bridge are very popular with locals.

Statue of Virgin Mary Rte. 70, Pierre Part Bridge.

In the 1940s a tornado destroyed the Pierre Part Church and this statue was moved to its present spot on an overgrown island just north of the Rte. 70 bridge. Since then many storms and floods have threatened Pierre Part but the water has never gone above the statue's feet, the point at which the community would flood. Locals have come to view the statue as a protector of the town.

★**Chilly's** Shell Beach Road, Pierre Part.

This is just a great place, a hidden treasure! How could such a wildly popular dance hall exist since the 1930s on a tiny scrap of sinking land 2.5 miles off the Baton Rouge to Morgan City highway? It helps that the dance hall actually sits on stilts over tranquil Lake Verret and that hundreds of recreational fishermen back their boats in here on weekends. Slow dancers can gaze out the window at moonlight and moss reflecting on the water. The place does not look very old; according to current owner "Chilly" Russo, grandson of the original builder, it was 75 percent obliterated by Hurricane Andrew and a few years earlier 50 percent destroyed by Hurricane Juan. After each storm a new plywood floor was placed on the old pilings. A young crowd shows up for the Saturday-night Swamp Pop shows by local singer Don Rich, but the big event is the Sunday-afternoon Cajun dance. Folks drive from Morgan City and Baton Rouge or come by boat from around Lake Verret to dance, drink, and hang out on the patio by the lake. During cool-weather months the Sunday dance begins around 5 but in the summer the band starts as early as 3. Saturday shows begin around 9:30. Call ahead to find out who is playing and when. (504) 252-6891.

★**Rainbow Inn** Rte. 70, Pierre Part.

The Rainbow is perhaps the quintessential South Louisiana barroom and dance hall. Built in the late thirties, it is a wooden structure with a broad stucco face that sports two round Coke signs and its

Rainbow Inn. (Photo by Julie Posner)

name in bold red lettering. An old kitchen and dining area in one side is now unused, but the main room with its long bar and wide dance floor still gets action. Bands are scheduled intermittently but usually on Thursday night. The favorite performer is Don Rich, a young local Swamp Pop singer. In its heyday the Rainbow got top Country acts as well as South Louisiana stars like Johnny Allan and Warren Storm. The bar is officially open Wednesday through Saturday, though it seems to be pretty much whenever they feel like it so call before visiting. (504) 252-8069.

Bayou Vista and Patterson

West of Morgan City, U.S. 90 begins its snake dance with Bayou Teche. In some places the bayou is nearly visible from the road, and in others it kinks as much as four miles north. The road that most closely follows these capricious bends is scenic Rte. 182. (If you want good scenery and good food, drive Rte. 182 instead of U.S. 90; it only takes a few minutes longer.) Located on two adjacent oxbow bends in Bayou Teche are the little old lumber towns of Bayou Vista and Patterson. For about 30 years at the turn of the century, Patterson boomed around the Red Cypress Company of Frank Williams, "Cypress King of the World." Few of the old mill towns of Louisiana bear reminders of the once booming trade. The companies came, got all the timber, and left. Patterson (population about 4,500) might have been just another quiet bayou town, deserted by the lumber barons and living off the seafood industry, were it not for nine glorious years between 1928 and 1936, when it was home to the world-famous Wedell-Williams Air Service. Today the city is the site of a fantastic museum commemorating the pioneering work of Wedell-Williams' engineers and its daredevil pilots (*see* review of museum below).

St. Mary Parish Tourist Center Rte. 182 (Main Street), Patterson.

Here you will find rest rooms, a well-informed staff, and brochures for attractions throughout St. Mary Parish (Morgan City through Franklin). The shaded lawn that slopes gently to Bayou Teche is a perfect spot for a picnic. The center is four miles west of Morgan City on Rte. 182 at a point where it is plainly visible from U.S. 90, sitting beside Cajun Jack's Swamp Tours. The center is open daily from dawn to dusk but is only staffed on weekdays. 1-800-256-2931.

ATTRACTIONS

★Johnny's Time In A Bottle 193 Rte. 182 E., Bayou Vista.

Johnny Carbonell has never sold his carefully crafted scenes-in-a-bottle. He has given quite a few away since he began tinkering and

Time In A Bottle artisan Johnny Carbonell. (Photo by Macon Fry)

teaching himself the skill in 1947, but most have been added to the now huge collection in his tiny shedlike museum in Bayou Vista. Detailed outriggers, towboats, shrimp boats, and crew boats appear to have sailed miraculously through the necks of bottles, but the most amazing creations are tiny scenes of stores with miniature produce on the shelves and replicas of plantation homes such as Nottoway and Oaklawn. Among the oddities is a New York tableau of the Statue of Liberty. Carbonell's most complicated creation has 1,795 pieces. He builds his models inside bottles and streetlight bulbs by inserting each tiny piece through the neck with a sharpened coat hanger. Most pieces, like ladybug-size block and tackle, are hand carved using a utility knife. Ship rigging and wheels are fabricated from fishing leaders and washers. Johnny is an engaging character who clearly loves his craft and loves showing it. The museum and workshop are located in a shed beside Bayou Teche in Johnny's backyard. It is open daily but visitors should call in advance. There is no admission. Johnny's house and museum are visible from U.S. 90, just a few doors east of the St. Mary Parish Tourist Center in Patterson (about 10 minutes west of Morgan City). (504) 395-3011.

★Wedell-Williams Memorial Aviation Museum Rte. 182, Patterson.
Harry Williams was mayor of Patterson in 1926 when speed pilot

and contraband runner Jimmy Wedell landed his plane in a field on the outskirts of town. The two got together and a partnership was born that built the fastest aircraft of the day, supplying top long-distance and pylon racers. In an era when aircraft were just beginning to be used commercially, the Wedell-Williams Air Service secured airmail contracts between New Orleans and Texas and put wings under dozens of barnstorming daredevils. The pair loved speed. Williams reportedly raced one of his mechanics to the airport each morning, and Wedell became the first pilot to record a speed of 305 miles an hour. Much has been made of the early astronauts who had the "right stuff," but the individuals commemorated at the Wedell-Williams museum were test flying planes at a time when preflight test technology was virtually nonexistent.

It is not surprising that these men who lived in the air died in their planes, but it was a crushing blow to the business in Patterson when their top pilot, top engineer, and main financier all died in crashes within two years. Before his death in an air crash at Patterson in 1934 (at age 34), Jimmy Wedell held more air-speed records than any man. With Wedell, Wedell's brother Walter, and Harry Williams all dead, Mrs. Williams (a silent-movie star who owned the Latter Library mansion in New Orleans) sold their lucrative airmail routes to fledgling Eastern Airlines. The parts of Wedell-Williams record-breaking aircraft were dumped into Bayou Teche.

Although the Wedell-Williams museum is responsible for preserving and documenting all of Louisiana's aviation history, the real attractions here are the aircraft parts and displays regarding the operations of Wedell and Williams. The museum, located on the site of the famous air service, houses replicas and original craft manufactured by the team, along with pieces of #44, the famous speed-record holder of 1933 (raised from the muddy bottom of Bayou Teche). A video is shown depicting the careers and antics of Wedell, Williams, and many of the pilots of the barnstorming era. An adjacent collection displays trophies and clippings documenting the achievements of these brave men. The museum is one of the hidden treasures of Cajun Country and a must-see whether you are an aviation buff or not. Admission is $2 for adults and 50 cents for kids. It is open Tuesday through Saturday from 9 to 5. Take Rte. 182, which branches north from U.S. 90 in Patterson, and look for the signs. (504) 395-7067.

Cajun Jack's Swamp Tours 112 Main St. (U.S. 90), Patterson.

Captain Jack takes groups by party barge (accommodates 25) into the lower reaches of the Atchafalaya Basin. This is a beautiful area, but the best parts of the tour are unreachable during low water. Jack can show you where the local cypress company had its camps and made its cuts and where parts of the first Tarzan film were shot. Best of all, he offers a "sunset cruise" (5:30 to 8) during the summer. This later trip is recommended, as the air is cooler and the water is less crowded with fishermen. Cajun Jack's is on U.S. 90 in Patterson, beside the St. Mary Parish Tourist Center. Tours normally leave at 9 and 2:30 daily. Call first to make sure tours are running. (504) 395-7420 (after 6, 384-6828).

Cypress Sawmill Festival Mid-April, Patterson.

The sawmill festival is not big but has plenty of information and artifacts relating to its theme. A video is shown that was made from old film footage shot during the boom days of the logging era. 1-800-256-2931.

LODGING

Lonely Oak Campground Rte. 182, Bayou Vista.

This small, private, RV campground is literally on the banks of Bayou Teche, affording a perfect view of the sunset over its wide waters. There are chairs, picnic tables, and a sheltered patio at the water edge. Rates are $10 a night. Lonely Oak is located in the middle of an oxbow bend of Bayou Teche about six miles west of Morgan City. (504) 395-6765.

Kemper Williams Park U.S. 90, Patterson.

Kemper is a 290-acre recreation and camping facility located off U.S. 90 and adjacent to the Lower Atchafalaya River near Patterson. The park has five baseball/softball fields, six lighted tennis courts, a picnic area with playgrounds, pavilion structures, and a golf driving range. There are 26 RV sites with full hookups and rest rooms with showers. It costs $12 to camp and $2 for day use (up to four people). The park is across U.S. 90 from the St. Mary Parish Tourist Center in Patterson. (504) 395-2298.

Calumet to Franklin

All but those in a hurry will want to get off U.S. 90 in Calumet and take Rte. 182 west. The 45-mile section of Rte. 182 between Calumet and New Iberia follows Bayou Teche closely and provides the best views of its waters, sugar mills, plantations, and small towns.

Centerville/Burns Point Turnoff

Don't blink or you may miss this former steamboat landing on the bayou. Centerville is the turnoff for Rte. 317 to Burns Point, a coastal recreation and camping area about 18 miles south (*see* description below). There are several (private) antebellum homes along the bayou in Centerville. Bocage on Rte. 182, 1 mile west of Centerville, is open by appointment only, Monday through Friday. (318) 828-0132.

Burns Point Recreation Area Camping/Fishing. Rte. 317 South.

This coastal park is also known as Pointe Salé (French for Salt Point). From Rte. 182, Rte. 317 follows Bayou Salé 18 miles south along one of three arable ridges in St. Mary Parish. The road passes miles of sugarcane and the Ellerslie Plantation (1839, private) before dead-ending at the Rabbit Island Texaco Plant, the site of an ancient Indian burial mound (not open to public). A mile before the end of the road you will see a sign and turnoff for Burns Point Recreation Area. The narrow shell road to the point emerges from a tangle of reeds onto a spit of grass and sand on Cote Blanche Bay.

The area is dotted with picnic tables, campsites, a shelter, and a boat ramp. Typical of Louisiana's coastal fringe, the beach is not beautiful for swimming but is great for fishing. This was the site of an old fishing camp, and there are plenty of places to catch redfish and trout from the shore. If you are looking for camping away from the hubbub, you will find it in the waterside sites. Tent campers will appreciate the hot-water showers but bemoan the lack of shade. Camping costs $7 for RVs, $5 for pop-ups, and $3 for tents and vans. There is a $1 entrance fee for day use. (318) 836-9784.

City of Franklin

A lasting impression of Lower Teche Country is the sight of huge cane trucks rumbling through the grand entrance to the town of Franklin, 25 miles west of Morgan City. Known locally as the Great White Way, East Main Street (Rte. 182) in Franklin is shaded by dual rows of oaks, split by a grassy neutral ground, and lined with a half-dozen Greek Revival plantation homes. Cast-iron street lamps adorn the neutral ground. The lamps, which have become a symbol of the city, have a branching top portion that may be rotated during the sugar harvest to prevent cane-laden trucks from smashing the round, glass globes.

The city grew westward in a linear fashion along the higher southern side of Bayou Teche. Heading in this direction down Main Street, you first pass antebellum homes, a turn-of-the-century commercial and railroad district, and then the new suburbs of West Franklin, where Rte. 182 sports fast-food franchises and discount department

Cane truck on Main Street in Franklin. (Photo by Julie Posner)

stores. Park near the intersection of Willow and Main Street to stroll the historic district.

As you might guess from its name, Franklin is a community with stronger Anglo than French roots. During the 18th century it was known as Carlin's Settlement. In 1800, Guinea Lewis arrived from Pennsylvania, donated property for a courthouse, and laid out a street plan. The city was renamed in honor of Benjamin Franklin. When St. Mary Parish was established in 1811, Franklin became the seat of government. Until the War Between the States, it functioned as an important interior port city, shipping its sugar harvest on the waters of Bayou Teche. The arrival of the railroad and lumber industry after the war prompted growth of the business district west of Willow Street (a walking tour of this area is available from the Franklin Visitors Center). Today petroleum and carbon black are important industrial products, but sugar remains the main crop. During the fall, smoke drifts in from surrounding cane fields and the city resounds with the rumble of passing trucks, which spill loose cane onto the otherwise tidy streets as they make their way to the old Sterling Sugar Mill.

Franklin Visitors Center U.S. 90 at Northwest Boulevard (Rte. 3211).

The staff at this new information center on U.S. 90 can provide information on old homes, antique shopping, and where to find good food. During the fall they will help arrange a tour at the St. Mary Sugar Co-op. Be sure to pick up a *Walking Tour Guide to the Franklin Historic District.* The center is open 8:30 to 4:30 in the winter and 9 to 5 in the summer. (318) 828-2555 or 1-800-256-2931.

ATTRACTIONS

★Walking Tour of Franklin Historic District Main and Willow St.

The oak-shaded Main Street of Franklin will make you want to stop and abandon your vehicle even on the hottest South Louisiana days. It may even put you in mind to hook up a buggy and clatter about town. The Franklin Historic District was first listed on the National Register of Historic Places in 1982 and contains over 400 significant buildings. You won't find any buggies (although the street lamps still bear No Hitching signs), but the area is easily viewed on foot in less than an hour. Once you have gotten a copy of the walking-tour guide (free) at the Franklin Visitors Center on U.S. 90, the best place to start a tour is near the intersection of Willow and Main Street. Even without the guide, you can find grand homes and quaint turn-of-the-century cottages by walking a five-block area bounded by Main (on the north), Willow (on the west), Morris (on the east), and Second Street (on the south). Stop at Polito's Cafe for a cold drink or hot lunch. For a look at the early-20th-century businesses and residences of Railroad Town, walk the five-block area west of Willow Street between Second and Main.

Arlington Plantation 56 E. Main St. (Rte. 182).

This mansion just east of Franklin was built in the 1830s by the Carlin family, original settlers in Franklin. A circular driveway curves past flowering shrubs, live oaks, and formal gardens. The front and bayou sides of the house are graced with large, columned porticos, while smaller identical porticos adorn the sides. The house is lit by bronze and crystal chandeliers and decorated with period antiques. Arlington is open for viewing by appointment Tuesday through Saturday from 10 to 4. Admission is $5 for adults and $2 for students; children 12 and under are admitted free. (318) 828-2644.

Grevemberg House Sterling Street (Rte. 322).

The Grevemberg House is a Greek Revival home constructed in 1851 and the only house in Franklin open for walk-in tours (no appointment necessary). The house was nearly destroyed by fire in

1983 and has been thoroughly restored by the local chapter of the Louisiana Historic Landmark Society. The floors are original, but most of the details, like the painted "faux bois" cypress, wallpaper, and draperies, are meticulous reproductions. The house is furnished with period furniture. Its grounds are partially occupied by Franklin City Park. Traveling west on Main Street (Rte. 182), bear right on Sterling Road (Rte. 322) and Grevemberg is about a half-mile ahead on the left. The house is open Monday through Friday from 10 to 4. Tours cost $3 for adults and $1.50 for children 12 and under. (318) 828-2092.

Sterling Sugar Mill Rte. 322.

Sterling no longer offers tours but is still a good drive-by attraction in the late fall when the trucks are bringing sugar in. Take Rte. 182 west and bear right on Sterling Road. The mill is located just past the Grevemberg House. (318) 828-0620.

FOOD

Charlie's Meat and Deli Down Home, $. 1803 W. Main St.

Charlie's serves weighty plate lunches and suppers from their deli counter. Specials change daily, but there is always a choice of two main dishes. Friday there are seafood plates, like shrimp stew with rice and gravy, potato salad, fried bread, and bread pudding. Weekday choices include meatloaf, chicken stew, and crab and shrimp etouffée. These are served with rice, cornbread or rice dressings, or potato salad. Lunches are $4 and supper is $5. Charlie's Meat sells whole, deboned chickens stuffed with a variety of fillings. Toss one in the cooler and throw it on the smoker when you get home. Charlie's is located on Rte. 182 in the west end of Franklin. The deli and lunch counter are open from 11 to 2 Monday through Saturday. The meat market is open weekdays from 8 to 6 and Saturdays until 2 P.M. (318) 828-4169.

Forest Inn Restaurant Cajun/Creole, $-$$. West Main Street.

The Forest Inn is the most popular restaurant in the Lower Teche Region. The restaurant and motel have been a family-run business since the 1960s and they pride themselves on their own crawfish and gumbo recipes. Their crab and okra gumbo is thick and spicy, while the oyster and crab gumbo is light and flavored with a splash of sherry. A bowl of gumbo or rich crawfish bisque in a nutty gravy makes a hearty meal by itself. In addition to soups and stews there is a broad selection of seafood entrees (mostly fried), steaks, and sandwiches. I began hearing about the Mississippi Mud Pie at the Forest when I was still 60 miles away in Houma. A thick butter crust packed with chopped pecans is topped with a sweet cream-cheese filling, homemade chocolate pudding, whipped cream, and more crumbled pecans. Several lunch specials are available for under $10. The Forest Inn is located on Rte. 182 in the west end of town. It is open Monday through Saturday from 5:30 A.M. to 9:30 P.M. (318) 828-1810.

Iberia Street Cash Grocery Local Fave, $. 501 Iberia St.

A gas-station attendant directed us to this country grocery for "the best hamburgers in town." I can't remember the sandwiches, but the Iberia Cash Grocery offers time-warp dining at its most primitive. The one-room country store has wood-plank floors, walls lined with household goods, and a corner with two powerline-spool tables and wooden benches. The place seemed to be most popular among the kids, who paused to study the "new" prices scrawled over the candy rack. There are quite a few items that have been around the store so long that they are no longer for sale but are on display. While you are waiting for a motherly ham and cheese sandwich on cross-cut white bread or a griddled burger, check out the newspaper clippings on the wall: "Bomb Dropped," "Titanic Sinks," and "Lindburgh Killer Electrocuted." The grocery is open from Monday through Friday, from 8:15 A.M. to 6 P.M., and Saturday until noon. (318) 828-0392.

Polito's Cafe/Bar and Grill Local Fave, $. 710 Main St.

For breakfast, lunch, ice cream, or cold beer, this is the best place downtown to cool your heels. When I asked the waitress if Polito's had changed any over the years she allowed, "We got hit pretty bad by Hurricane Andrew, and if you stand across the street you can see that the building is kind of crooked." Despite a slight face-lift in the nineties and a few hurricanes, Polito's probably looks much the same as it did in the fifties, with its old beer coolers, stainless-steel bar, and sizzling grill. Most welcome additions to the menu are the ice cream, malts, and shakes. At midday the place fills with courthouse workers looking for a hearty lunch or an irregularly shaped burger, but when the crowd thins it assumes the aspect of a sleepy barroom. I can't imagine what goes on on Fridays (when they are open all night); Franklin does not seem like an after-hours kind of town. Plate lunches are served Monday through Friday for $5-$6. Burgers, sandwiches, and breakfasts are available anytime. Hours are 5 to 9:30 Monday through Thursday, all night on Friday, and until midnight Saturday. (318) 828-0242.

LODGING

The Hanson House Bed and Breakfast 114 Main St.

The Hanson House is an antebellum home in Franklin's historic district built by a ship captain who traded on the Teche. It was subsequently bought and renovated by mill owner Albert Hanson. The house has remained in the family for five generations and current owner Col. Clarence Kemper, Jr., is the great-great-grandson of Albert Hanson. Rooms are large and furnished in antiques. A plantation breakfast is served. Double rate is $125. (318) 828-3217 or 823-7675.

Best Western Forest Motel Rte. 182 West, $60 to $70 double. (318) 828-1810, (800) 528-1234.

Side Trips Between Franklin and Jeanerette

It is only 13 miles from Franklin to Jeanerette by way of U.S. 90 or the more scenic Rte. 182, but there are several short and scenic side trips along the way. Among the most interesting detours on the Lower Teche are two oxbow bends that wind through vast cane fields and sugar settlements. The first of these oxbows begins on the west end of Franklin and is followed by Irish Bend Road (Rte. 322), named to honor Alexander Porter, a wealthy Irishman who settled there in the early 1800s. In the middle of the bend, Porter built the massive *Oaklawn Plantation* (open for tours). A second horseshoe bend in Bayou Teche begins in Baldwin, a few miles west from where Irish Bend Road rejoins Rte. 182. The second oxbow, known as Indian Bend, is an 8-mile kink followed by Rte. 326. This route passes through the *Chitimacha Indian Reservation* in Charenton. A third interesting side trip is not an oxbend at all, but a 20-mile detour through the cane fields and marsh southwest of Baldwin that terminates at the coastal community and state park at *Cypremort Point.*

Medric Martin Grocery Irish Bend Rd. (Rte. 322), west of Franklin.

Medric Martin has operated this rustic grocery, bar, and lounge since the 1930s. As the cane industry became more mechanized, fewer and fewer customers remained along Irish Bend Road. Martin still mans the rough-hewn wooden counter and bar, but there isn't much to buy except cold drinks. His brother wanders in every day to keep him company, and the two can tell of very different days in sugar country. The now silent juke joint beside the store is testimony to the changing times. The Medric Martin Grocery is not only the best place to stop for a soda, it is the lone commercial establishment on Irish Bend Road. It is located six miles from Rte. 182 in Franklin and two miles east of Oaklawn Plantation.

★Oaklawn Manor Plantation Irish Bend Road (Rte. 322).

This luxurious Greek Revival mansion is the home of Louisiana governor Mike Foster. The place was built in 1837 by Irish immigrant and U.S. senator Alexander Porter. It took over three years to build,

The Martin brothers at Medric Martin Grocery. (Photo by Julie Posner)

Oaklawn Plantation. (Courtesy of Oaklawn)

using bricks made from Bayou Teche clay and local cypress. The house looks down an elegantly sloping, landscaped yard towards the bayou. An apiary, old dairy house, and live-oak grove are located on the estate's 35 sculpted acres.

The history of Oaklawn is one of wealth and romance. C. A. Barbour, a wealthy steamboat captain, passed the house in his trips piloting lumber boats on the bayou. In 1926, he bought and restored the crumbling structure, only to see it burn down just before completion! Unflaggingly, Barbour rebuilt it from the ground up. Although the reconstruction was done from drawings of the original, the house now has many features of Barbour's conception. Marble floors were installed using material from the old St. Louis Hotel in New Orleans. Tons of Italian marble, French glass, and other exotic materials were shipped up the bayou. The top two floors are closed to the public, but regular tours are conducted on the lavish first floor. Governor Foster's huge collection of Audubon prints and books is on display. From Rte. 182 in Franklin, head west on Sterling Road, which becomes Irish Bend Road (Rte. 322). The entrance to Oaklawn is 8 miles from Franklin and 3.5 miles from the junction with Rte. 182 in the west. Tours cost $6 and are offered daily from 10 to 4.

Chitimacha Indian Reservation Rte. 326, Charenton.

The Chitimacha are the only Indian tribe native to South Louisiana still living on a portion of their original territory. In 1925, their numbers decimated to 50, a reservation was established, and the Chitimacha became the first federally recognized tribe in Louisiana. Native customs and lore, as well as the Chitimacha language, are virtually extinct. A handful of artisans still weave split-cane baskets, which are the crowning artistic achievement of the tribe. Until the sixties, these baskets, which are among the finest in the world, were widely available and inexpensive. Following visits by folklorists and writers, demand for the tightly woven (some double-weave varieties can hold water) buff, red, and black baskets soared. They may still be ordered for about $20 a square inch from tribal craftspeople, but there is a waiting list.

A *Visitors Center* housing the tribal offices and a display on the history and crafts of the tribe is in the heart of the reservation. The museum portion is operated by the Jean Lafitte State Park Service. Here you can see photographs of past chiefs and tribal members, elaborate specimens of old and new split-cane baskets, and other artifacts. The center also will provide a list of tribal craftspeople. The Visitors Center is located in the middle of the Charenton oxbow, four miles from Rte. 182 in either direction. It is open Tuesday through Friday from 8 to 4:30 and Saturday from 9 to 5. (318) 923-4830 (museum and Visitors Center), (318) 923-4973 (tribal offices).

Cypress Bayou Casino Bobtown Road, Charenton, Chitimacha Reservation.

With a nod from the Louisiana legislature, casino gambling supplanted bingo as the cash cow on the state's Indian reservations in the midnineties. Cypress Bayou is a serious gaming operation with all the customary tables but dominated by several rooms of slots. It is not named for a natural feature nearby but for the man-made bayou that runs through the heart of the place. The scene is even more bizarre than most gambling parlors. Stuffed gators, nutrias, and raccoons laze around the fake stream while neon lights gleam through the hanging moss. Cypress Bayou charges no admission; gamblers drink free and may purchase food at two restaurants on site. There are 12 acres of free and secure parking and free valet service. Cypress Bayou is open 365 days a year—weekdays from 10 A.M. until 2 A.M. and Friday, Saturday, and some holidays until 4 A.M. 1-800-284-4386.

Cypremort Point State Park Rte. 319, 20 miles southwest of Baldwin.

This is one of two places in Lower Teche Country where travelers can reach public recreation facilities on the coast. The drive southwest from U.S. 90 crosses 20 miles of sparsely populated fields and open marsh. At Cypremort Point you will find a grocery, bait shop, restaurant (not recommended), and bar. Once nourished by fresh water, the area was named Cypremort (French for "dead cypress") after the cypress trees were killed by saltwater incursion.

Several miles before reaching the end-of-the-road community, you will pass Cypremort Point State Park. Most of the 185-acre park is covered with cordgrass, but there is a man-made beach on the shore of East Cote Blanche Bay. The sand reaches about four feet from shore before giving way to mud bottom, but the park is a popular spot for swimming, boating, and crabbing. Facilities include a boat launch, a covered pier for crabbing, picnic shelters with grills, and clean rest rooms with outdoor showers. This is a wonderfully desolate spot, but be advised that shade is at a premium (bring bug spray and sun screen). Camping is not allowed inside the park. The park is open from 7 A.M. to 10 P.M. Admission is $2 per car for up to four people. From U.S. 90, take Rte. 83 southwest about 12 miles. In the town of Louisa follow Rte. 319 south another 8 miles to Cypremort Point. (318) 867-4510.

Bayview Inn Restaurant & Bar Local Fave, $$. Rte. 319, Cypremort Point.

This is the only place to eat within 25 miles and it is located right on the water. After a hot and shadeless visit to Cypremort Point Park you may want to stop here just to get out of the sun! The food is mostly fried. Locals rave about the softshell-crab po' boys. Bayview is open Tuesday through Thursday from 11 to 8 and Friday and Saturday until 9 (closed Mondays). (318) 867-4478.

Sugar mill in Jeanerette. (Photo by Macon Fry)

Jeanerette

Although Jeanerette is grouped for geographic reasons with the nearby Anglo communities of the Lower Teche, this city of 7,000 has strong French roots. Names like Patout, Broussard, and LeJeune on turn-of-the-century businesses on Main Street are the first indicator that the town has a very different ethnic mix than Baldwin and Franklin to the south. Jeanerette is located on the bayou about 8 miles northwest of Baldwin and 10 miles southeast of New Iberia. The town got its name from John Jeanerette, who founded a community at the site and became its first postmaster in 1830. Cajuns as well as Creole French came to the region, along with a few Anglo planters. In 1870, the railroad arrived and Jeanerette bloomed as a marketplace and shipping point for cane and lumber products. Petroleum has supplanted lumber as a mainstay of the local economy, but the sugar industry owns the landscape. Visit Jeanerette in the fall and you will find the streets bordered by piles of spilled sugarcane and the air rich with the scent of burning sugar fields.

ATTRACTIONS

★**Le Beau Petit Musée** 500 E. Main St.

After spending years driving through cane country, it took a stop at "The Pretty Little Museum" to finally understand exactly what is involved in the planting, harvesting, and processing of sugarcane. In addition to a 25-panel display on "200 Years of the Louisiana Sugarcane Industry," the museum shows a 20-minute video entitled *Sugarcane to Sugar*, produced by the USL Center for Louisiana Studies, which traces the production of sugar from seed to mill. Among artifacts on display are a collection of cypress patterns from Jeanerette's Moresi Foundry. These patterns were used in the 1800s as models in the creation of gears for sugar and rice mills and steamboats. There is a room filled with mounted swamp animals and sundry items pertaining to many facets of life on the Teche. Le Beau Petit Musée is open Monday through Friday from 10 to 4. Regular admission is $3, seniors $1.50, and students 50 cents. (318) 276-4408.

City Park Wormser Street at Bayou Teche.

Jeanerette's City Park is a good place to unpack a picnic beside the bayou. There is a covered pavilion and several barbecue pits. To get to the park, turn towards the bayou on Wormser (just west of LeJeune's Bakery).

★Justin's Observatory 125 E. Main St.

It's easy to miss the sign that announces Justin's Observatory, but it is almost impossible to miss the three-story silver-domed structure towering over a garage in the background. It is owned and maintained by self-taught astronomer Justin Lerive, who built the dome in 1984. Lerive lives next door but spends most of his time in the garage/observatory poring over astronomy magazines and entertaining guests.

Next to looking at stars, Lerive likes best to talk about them. A question about solar flare-ups led to talk of the sun, the solar system, and the creation of the galaxy. His explanation ended with the cosmic proclamation, "Everything starts out round." In a part of the country where scientists are generally occupied with such earthly concerns as squeezing oil out of the ground and keeping the Mississippi out of the Atchafalaya Basin, Lerive's perspectives are delightfully expansive. His advice: "People need to take some time and look at the sky." Justin's Observatory is located on Main Street (Rte. 182) in east Jeanerette. (318) 276-6220.

St. Mary Sugar Co-op Rte. 182 at Rte. 318, east of Jeanerette.

The St. Mary Sugar Co-op offers informal tours during sugar season (the fall). If you get there and a tour is not available, you can still pull over and witness the general 24-hour-a-day hubbub of harvest time. You will see more during the day but at night the glare of the factory and flickering of truck lights reflected in clouds of steam create a monstrous, bristling specter. (318) 276-6167 or 828-2555.

(Photo by Julie Posner)

FOOD

★LeJeune's Bakery Local Fave. 1510 W. Main St.

Now in its third generation here, LeJeune's has been a Jeanerette landmark since 1884. There are few things tastier than a loaf of their crusty French bread, hot from the oven. Stop by the bakery on any weekday around 11:30 A.M. and you can buy a loaf before it has a chance to move from the brick oven onto the cooling rack. The storefront is closed, so all business is transacted at the side entrance, where you can see the bakers at work. LeJeune's only makes two items—French bread and gingerbread "stageplanks." The stageplanks are my favorite but must be eaten hot to be truly appreciated. These faintly sweet, breadlike cookie-cakes emerge from the oven on Tuesday and Thursday between 10:30 A.M. and 2 P.M. Plan your trip around this event, and whether you are buying French bread or gingerbread, be sure to have a little cream cheese or butter to spread on top. Before leaving, grab a couple of extra bread wrappers (suitable for framing), which sport the original LeJeune's logo and slogan, "The proof of the pudding is in the eating." You can also purchase the same graphics on a T-shirt. (318) 276-5690.

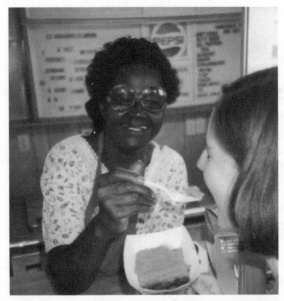

Sampling Lil's sweet-potato bread. (Photo by Macon
Fry)

★**Lil's Kitchen** Sweet-Potato Bread, $. 521 E. Main (Rte. 182).

Don't be put off by Lil's cinder-block exterior or lack of a sign. The
sweet-potato bread here is simply to die for! Sure, you can get plate
lunches and sandwiches, but the show starts and finishes with those
amazing slices of bread, available only on Wednesday and Friday. The
bread is taller and more solid than a sweet-potato pie, with a texture similar to a sturdy New Orleans bread pudding. It has no crust, but during
baking the edges get firm. Lil learned the unique recipe from her
father, William Richards, Sr. Although it remains a family secret, enough
of her 23 grandchildren know how to make it to keep the tradition alive.
Enjoy a slice at one of the booths inside where you can see pictures of
the grandchildren. Lil's is open weekdays and serves the sweet-potato
bread from 11 A.M. to 1 P.M. on Wednesday and Friday. It is a good idea
to call first and have Lil save you a few slices. (318) 276-9600.

LODGING

Alice Plantation Bed and Breakfast 9217 Old Jeanerette Rd.,
Jeanerette.

Alice Plantation is an antebellum (circa 1796) mansion located on
the north side of Bayou Teche, just across Old Jeanerette Road from

the stream. The upper stories of the house were moved from Baldwin by barge and installed on a new foundation. Accommodations are in two new private cottages constructed behind the antebellum home, overlooking a small swimming pool. The cottages are furnished with large comfortable couches and chairs, huge televisions, wall-to-wall carpets, and small refrigerators. Hosts Rachael and Stan Rodgers offer a big breakfast of items like quiche, crepes, hashbrown casserole, stuffed French toast, and an assortment of egg dishes. Cottages start at $125 for two. A room is also offered upstairs in the main house for $100. (318) 276-3187.

THE UPPER TECHE

Just below New Iberia, the eastern edge of the Upper Teche region, Bayou Teche turns north and is followed by Rte. 31. The land becomes more moist and broad fields begin to give way to forest. Limbs of live oaks meet over the road in moss-draped archways. This region between the Cajun Prairie and the Atchafalaya Basin is a historical center of Cajun, French, and Creole culture. The earliest settlers were French, who arrived in the early 18th century. In 1762 a Spanish military garrison was established at the Poste de Atakapas (named for the Indians who once inhabited the region). The community that grew around the post went on to become St. Martinville, a hub of opulent

Byway in Upper Teche Country. (Courtesy of Louisiana Wild Life & Fisheries Commission)

Creole culture on the wild frontier. Most of the countryside was given to farming and ranching, but the city was the westernmost bastion of high culture on the continent.

When Cajuns began arriving on the Upper Teche in 1765, they were not always greeted warmly by the established Creole society. Shunning the high society of St. Martinville, these rural people moved up the bayou, east towards the Atchafalaya, and west onto the prairie to set up their own farms and communities. While the rich Creole society has all but disappeared, Cajun culture remains strong. Drive up the bayou on Rte. 31 through towns like Breaux Bridge and Henderson and you will find Cajuns processing crawfish and continuing the traditional pursuits of fishing and farming. You will also find a plethora of Cajun and Zydeco dance halls, and restaurants serving dishes prepared with "wild" Basin crawfish.

New Iberia

New Iberia calls itself Queen City of the Teche, but during its first half-century this active trade and industrial center of 36,000 played second fiddle to an older and more established neighbor, St. Martinville. The name "Iberia" was appointed by Spaniards and Canary Islanders who settled there and took up ranching in the late 1700s. Prosperity did not visit the community until the sugar industry and steamboats arrived in the 1820s. Wide and fertile fields around New Iberia, the discovery of salt on nearby Avery Island, and the cultivation of fiery peppers signaled the economic ascendance of the Queen City. After the War Between the States, New Iberia became the seat of government for newly formed Iberia Parish. With the discovery of oil and natural gas nearby and a connection with Gulf shipping lanes at the Port of Iberia, New Iberia boomed in the 20th century.

Today, New Iberia is a busy city whose suburban fringe supports a collection of supermarkets, malls, and fast-food franchises. The historic downtown area is nestled on the banks of Bayou Teche at the intersection of Rte. 182 (Main Street) and Rte. 14 (Center Street), about 20 miles southwest of Lafayette. Here travelers can tour Shadows Plantation, walk to nearby restaurants, and spend the night in a Bed and Breakfast within throwing distance of the bayou. Just a short drive from downtown, the historic Konriko Rice Mill has a visitors center and plant tours. Although the downtown area may be easily seen in a couple of hours, there is enough food, music (nearby), and interesting accommodations to make New Iberia a good choice for an overnight stop. A side trip to the coastal wetlands about 15 miles below New Iberia leads to a land of hot peppers, sugar, salt, and two of the most famous gardens in the South.

Iberia Visitors Center 2690 Center St. (Rte. 14) at U.S. 90.

Some pals visited this center and reported, "They were so friendly, it was scary!" The tourist information center, housed in an Acadian-style home, has rest-room facilities and plenty of information on city and parish-wide attractions. They can help with everything from finding accommodations to arranging a plantation or swamp tour. You can pick up parish and town maps, a brochure for a downtown New Iberia walking tour, and a map to sites mentioned in the work of local author James Lee Burke. The center is open daily from 9 to 5. (318) 365-1540.

RECREATION

★**Lake Fausse State Park** See St. Martinville Recreation section.

Boat rentals, picnic area, hiking trails, fishing dock, and camping in swamp setting.

★**Airboat Tours, Inc.** See Loreauville.

ATTRACTIONS

Downtown Walking Tour

In the heart of the city, Rte. 182 splits into two one-way roads, with Main Street carrying westbound traffic and St. Peter Street eastbound. The Downtown Walking Tour (map available from Visitors Center) covers a 12-block area centered at the intersection of Main Street and Center Street (Rte. 14). Park at this juncture and visit Shadows on the Teche Plantation before walking east through the shady old residential district with its mix of antebellum, Victorian, and steamboat gothic homes. Then stroll west a couple of blocks on Rte. 182 to New Iberia's turn-of-the-century business strip. Here you will find some great lunch spots among old storefronts facing the Teche. There is a public parking lot beside Bouligny Plaza.

★**Shadows on the Teche** 317 E. Main St. at Weeks St.

After visiting Shadows, writer Henry Miller scribed a note to his friend Weeks Hall, "I expect to be back and write a book here—the book of camelias and hallucinations." The rich family history of this mansion and the beauty of its grounds provide a dreamy, soft-focus view of the genteel life that flourished along Bayou Teche for more than a century. Shadows was built in 1834 by wealthy sugar planter David Weeks. More than 250,000 bricks were molded of clay from the banks of the bayou to construct the 18"-thick walls and lower floor of the mansion. Most striking to those unfamiliar with the antebellum homes of Louisiana are the exterior stairways, which connect wide first- and second-floor galleries. These stairs are the only way to move between the two main floors of the house. Inside there are no hallways

Shadows on the Teche. (Courtesy of Louisiana Office of Tourism)

or closets. Rooms are furnished with fine Empire and Federal antiques.

At one time, Shadows was the center of five sugar plantations and its grounds stretched from present-day U.S. 90 to the silent waters of the Teche. After Northern troops occupied it during the War Between the States, the house fell into disrepair. In the 1920s, William Weeks Hall, great-grandson of the original builder, restored Shadows and became the fourth successive generation of the family to inhabit the house. Weeks Hall entertained intellectuals and celebrities from around the country. Many of these were invited to sign an upstairs parlor door. This door, now covered with scrawled messages from Henry Miller, Tex Ritter, and Elia Kazan, is on display on the first floor, near the gift shop. Many visitors concur with the observations of Kazan, who scribbled, "The most beautiful house I've seen in all [the] South." Hall left the house to the National Trust for Historic Preservation, which now operates tours daily from 9 to 4:30. Tours cost $6 for adults, $4 for seniors, and $3 for children. The grounds, including a planned garden and sloping lawn beside the Teche, are open for free. (318) 369-6446.

Statue of Hadrian Corner of Weeks and St. Peter streets.

This is not what you would call an organic attraction in New Iberia, but it is a singular work of art by any standard. Hadrian ruled the Roman Empire from A.D. 117 to 138. This work, sculpted in A.D. 130, is the only full-length statue of Hadrian in the United States. Brought to England from Italy in the 19th century, the statue was purchased by Iberia Savings and Loan in 1961 and is now on display in a glassed-in viewing area outside the bank.

Bouligny Plaza Main Street between Iberia and French streets.

This sun-drenched plaza on the banks of Bayou Teche has restroom facilities, a gazebo, and a large parking area within walking distance of downtown attractions and restaurants. The plaza is the location of a historical marker and bust of Lt. Col. Francisco Bouligny, who brought several hundred Spanish settlers to the site of present-day New Iberia in 1779 and is generally credited as the town founder.

Books Along the Teche 110 E. Main St.

An excellent stop for book lovers, this store stocks the *New York Times Book Review* and participates in its best-seller survey. Books Along the Teche is small but has a superb Louisiana collection, including signed copies of books by local author James Lee Burke. You can pick up a free brochure here that lists some of the places mentioned in Burke's novels, pairing quotes from the books with numbered sites on a town map. The store is open Monday through Saturday from 9:30 to 5:30. (318) 367-7621.

Left Bank Gallery 206 E. Main St.

Left Bank Gallery joins Books Along the Teche in leading a rejuvenation of downtown New Iberia culture and commerce. The gallery shows works in all media by local artists. Recently it had a fine selection of paintings, drawings, jewelry, and ceramics, including paintings by local folk artist Paul Schexnayder. It is open Tuesday through Saturday from 11 A.M. to 3 P.M. (318) 364-0825.

METRO-AREA ATTRACTIONS

Konriko Rice Mill and Store 301 Ann St.

Founded in 1912 by Phillip Conrad (the company name is a phonetic contraction of Conrad Rice Company), this is one of the oldest continuously operating mills in the state and the sole manufacturer of unique Wild Pecan Rice. Tours originate at the Konriko Store (housed in the old mill office) and begin with a 20-minute video that tells more about the history of the region than the rice industry. Your guide will show samples of rice with the husk attached, milled, and polished. After the video you are invited into the mill to see bagging and packaging operations. You may want to skip the tour and browse around the store, where you can sample the daily rice dish, served from a steaming crock pot, and look at a large selection of books on local topics. There are postcards and regional food products for sale. I recommend getting a couple of boxes of Konriko's Wild Pecan Rice, which cooks firm and has a rich, nutty flavor. The store is open Monday through Saturday, from 9 to 5 (free of charge). Tours are scheduled at 10, 11, 1, 2, and 3. The tour costs $2.75 for adults and $1.25 for children. To get to the store from Rte. 182, head south on Ann Street. (318) 367-6163 or 1-800-551-3245 (out of state).

Bunk Johnson's Grave Corner of French Street and Dale Street.

Many legendary performers of the early jazz era have roots in Cajun Country. Foremost among these was William Geary ("Bunk") Johnson, a black trumpet player who reportedly taught Louis ("Satchmo") Armstrong how to play. Johnson was born to former slaves in New Orleans in 1879. For 30 years he played with famous jazz groups like Buddy Bolden's band. Bunk faded into obscurity in the early 1900s and settled in New Iberia, where he taught music in the public schools, worked at Shadows as a yard man, labored at the Konriko Rice Mill, and drove a cane truck. He enjoyed a brief return to the limelight when a jazz writer contacted Weeks Hall looking for him. Hall told the writer to "look in the Harlem Grill [a local hangout], but he will probably be incoherent." Bunk Johnson died in New Iberia in 1949 and was

Bunk Johnson's grave. (Photo by Julie Posner)

buried in this small cemetery. Enter the French Street gate and follow the path into the cemetery about 30 yards. The grave of Willie ("Bunk") Johnson is three rows over to your right.

City Park Parkview Drive, north bank of Bayou Teche.

We can't all enjoy mint juleps on arbor-covered verandas beside the bayou, but anyone can partake of the beauty of the Teche at this serene park. Whether you are making a picnic out of a plate lunch from Victor's or Theriot's (*see* food section) or wetting a fishing line, this is probably the most relaxing spot on the water. To get to the park, head west on Rte. 182 from Rte. 14. Cross the bayou at Bridge Street (here you will see the *Mount Carmel Convent,* built in 1830). Turn right on Davis Street, left on Pollard, and right again on Parkview Drive.

Justine Antebellum Home Rte. 86 (Loreauville Road) four miles from New Iberia.

This antebellum home (1822) is a convenient stop on the way to the Basin town of Loreauville. The house has a Victorian facade, added in the 1890s, and was moved to this site in the sixties. Justine is known for its fine collection of antebellum furniture, Louisiana antiques, and primitive pieces. To get to Justine, cross the bayou on Rte. 87 and turn right on Rte. 86. The mansion is four miles from New Iberia on Rte. 86 (Loreauville Road). Tours are available by appointment and cost $4. (318) 364-0973.

Louisiana Sugarcane Festival Last weekend in September.

See the Sugar Cane Queen and "King Sucros." This festival is worth a visit if you happen to be in Teche Country during sugar season.

Avery Island, Tabasco Factory, Jungle Gardens, and Salt Dome

Located about 30 minutes south of New Iberia on Rte. 329. See South of New Iberia section.

★Jefferson Island and Rip Van Winkle Gardens, House, and Boat Tour

Located about 30 minutes southwest of New Iberia off Rte 14. See South of New Iberia section.

FOOD

Boiling Point Boiled Seafood, $$. U.S. 90, four miles east of New Iberia.

What's in a name? In this case the name tells the whole story. Boiled crawfish and crabs are all anybody bothers to order at this diminutive seafood joint. The hand-washing sinks in a corner of the dining area and a long line outside the door on weekends during Lent are the marks of a classic boiled-seafood haven. Crawfish are large and well seasoned throughout spring and early summer. Other months try the large, spicy, blue crabs. The Boiling Point is open Monday through Friday from 10 A.M. to 10 P.M. and Saturday and Sunday from 3:30 to 10 P.M. The Boiling Point is located about four miles west of Rte. 14 on U.S. 90. (318) 365-7596.

★**Bonin's Boudin and Cracklin's** Meat Market, $. 210 Robertson, New Iberia.

Waldo ("Nook") Bonin makes some mouthwatering boudin with the perfect blend of tender rice, pork, and seasoning. Bonin modestly attributes the burst of flavor to the fact that he heats his boudin in the oven rather than steaming it. If pressed further he will tell you that his wife is the secret ingredient! Dispensing boudin is a habit deeply ingrained in Bonin, who started selling his father's boudin door to door before opening his own shop in 1952. Since then he has narrowed his production to just boudin and cracklins, of which he dispenses free

Nook Bonin with a heap of his famous boudin. (Photo by Mary Tutwiler)

samples (and good conversation in French or English) to anybody who walks in the door. Watching a young boy slip into the store and stretch on tiptoe to receive a sample before darting out, I realized that Bonin is not just running a business but performing a public service. Where would folks go for boudin on Sunday after church if he did not open from 8 to noon? To get to Bonin's from Center Street (Rte. 14) go west on Main Street (Rte. 182) .4 mile and turn left on French Street. Travel five blocks south on French and make a right on Robertson Street. Bonin's is a half-block down on the right. He will be glad to speak French with you. Hours are 8 to 5 Monday through Saturday and 8 to noon Sunday. He sometimes closes for an hour at midday. (318) 369-3432.

★**Brenda's** Down Home/Soul Food, $. 409 W. Pershing, New Iberia.

Brenda Placide dedicates her restaurant to her mother (who taught her how to cook) and employs a variety of family members. No wonder the place has such a warm vibe. The dining room is impeccably clean and service responsive. Most important, the food is wonderful, rib-sticking fare. There is a choice of two hot lunches, served with vegetable and starch for under $5. Gumbo, fried chicken, fish, crawfish etouffée (very spicy), or barbecued ribs are served daily for around $6. Friday is seafood day. Monday's fried chicken special (with homemade apple pie) and Thursday's barbecue special (with warm fruit cobbler) are highly recommended. The cobbler arrives in a bowl and has a soft bottom crust and lightly crisp topping resting on the fruit. This is the essence of down-home cooking. In the evenings the jukebox plays Bobby Bland, Johnnie Taylor, and the Staple Singers. To get to Brenda's from Center Street (Rte. 14), take Main Street (Rte. 182) .8 mile west and turn left on Jefferson Street. Go about four blocks on Jefferson and turn right on Pershing Street. Brenda's is one and a half blocks down on the left. She is open for lunch and dinner, and most specials are available through the evening. Hours are Monday through Thursday 9 A.M. to 8 P.M., Friday and Saturday until 4 A.M., and Sunday 10 A.M. until 8 P.M. (318) 364-6820.

★**Danna's Bakery** Local Fave/Bakery. 317 Hopkins St., New Iberia.

This is the spot to stock up on sweets for a morning brunch or afternoon dessert in City Park or nearby Avery Island. You won't find fancy pastries here, just moist pecan macaroons, fresh blackberry tarts, and luscious sweet-dough pies. I can't leave Danna's without a bag full of thumbprint cookies and nut bars. This bakery is a few blocks off the beaten path but has been attracting customers from all over New Iberia since 1921. To get to Danna's take Rte. 182 west past the old commercial district and turn left on Hopkins Street. Danna's is open Tuesday through Saturday from 5 A.M. to 5:30 P.M. and Sunday until noon. (318) 364-7341.

Dave's Quality Meats 802 E. Dale St., New Iberia.

Dave's is a full-service butcher shop selling everything from beef jerky and andouille to cracklins, boudin, and fresh meat. The unique items here are stuffed breads and birds, ready to be taken home and thrown in the oven. Whole deboned chickens are stuffed with cornbread, seafood, and crawfish dressing and sold for $8 to $9. These are good cooked outside on a kettle grill. Dave also sells turducken (a deboned chicken is stuffed into a deboned duck, which is stuffed into a deboned turkey). The breads are filled with crawfish, meat, or boudin and sold frozen. Bring a cooler. Dave's is open from 8 to 6 Monday through Saturday. (318) 364-3441.

★Guiding Star Boiled Seafood, $-$$. U.S. 90, west of New Iberia.

The Guiding Star has the biggest and cleanest crawfish east of Lafayette and the best seasoning anywhere! Owner and boil chef Ralph Schaubert seasons his water with Tabasco mash, purchased in casks from the McIlhenny hot sauce company in New Iberia. Cayenne and salt are added for what may be the perfect blend of strong and hot flavors. Schaubert uses only select rice-field crawfish. The tail meat pulls easily from the shell and the heads are laden with golden fat. The Guiding Star had a reputation as a "wild place" for 30 years at its former location over on Rte. 14, where the parking lot was literally paved

Eating crawfish at the Guiding Star. (Photo by Julie Posner)

with beer-bottle caps. The new restaurant is not what you would call "wild" (the mayor of Erath was dining there with his family on my last visit), but it is definitely rustic. There are a couple of pool tables in a side room, but everything else is vintage boiling-point decor, from the hand-washing sinks in the dining area to the wooden tables covered with newspaper.

Crawfish are the big attraction from January to May. After May, huge "sweetwater" crabs from Lake Fausse arrive. These are blue crabs like those popular in New Orleans and the Chesapeake Bay, but they come from freshwater lakes and are incredibly large! The same pepper-mash seasoning is thrown into the pot, and the seasonings would probably be enough to cook these crustaceans without boiling. The Guiding Star is open seven days a week from 3 to 10 P.M. It is located in a small cinder-block building on U.S. 90, about three miles west of Rte. 14 in New Iberia (beside the Country Truck Stop). (318) 365-9113.

★Lagniappe Too Local Fave, $ (lunch)-$$ (dinner). 204 E. Main St., New Iberia.

This popular downtown eatery (easy walking distance from Shadows on the Teche) would be too cute if the food weren't so good. "Lagniappe" is a South Louisiana term for "a little something extra." In this case that something extra is the attention that goes into every dish. Everything is made from scratch, including croutons on the soups, dressings on the salads, and a few flavors of ice cream. Elaine Landry, who owns the restaurant, creates food with flair, whether it is a chicken salad spiked with olives and pecans or a tasty dinner salad of spicy mixed greens. Her soups, bisques, and gumbos are fantastic. The menu includes fish, poultry, and beef selections (and amazingly for this region, none are deep fried). For dessert get the self-proclaimed "world's best" bread pudding *and* the homemade ice cream. The bread pudding is almost as fluffy as its meringue topping, and the ice cream is the texture of just-whipped cream. Lagniappe Too also serves breakfast on weekdays. Try coffee and Cajun-style biscuits with pecans and cane syrup for a genuine South Louisiana eye opener. In 1996 Lagniappe Too won awards in the *Daily Iberian* for Best Steak, Best Bread Pudding, Best Sandwich, and Best Wait Staff. Enough said! It is open Monday through Friday from 8 A.M. until 2 P.M. and Friday and Saturday evenings from 6 until 9. (318) 365-9419.

Le Rosier Cajun/Creole, $$ (lunch)-$$$$$. 314 Main St., New Iberia.

New Iberia got its first upscale restaurant and inn when Chef Hallman and Mary Beth Woods opened Le Rosier in the midnineties. Woods and his restaurant have won accolades from *Food & Wine, Southern Living,* and the *Houston Chronicle.* Le Rosier is in fact elegant, and the ambiance in this 19th-century home-turned-restaurant across from Shadows on the Teche is romantic. Entrees like grilled and marinated duck and oven-roasted lamb are well prepared as are the four or five appetizers offered nightly. Le Rosier is expensive compared to restaurants serving similar fare in New Orleans and Lafayette. If you are looking for a splurge in New Iberia you might consider dining here and spending the night in the reproduced Acadian cottage behind the restaurant (see review under lodging). You can sample from Le Rosier's lunch menu and escape for around $20. It is open for lunch (no reservations accepted) Monday through Friday from 11:30 to 2. Dinner (reservations recommended) is served Tuesday through Saturday from 6:30 to 10:30. (318) 367-5306.

Theriot's Grocery and Meat Market Down Home, $. 330 Julia St.

Theriot's serves traditional plate-lunch fare from a window in the back of a country-style grocery. Daily specials include roast pork and beef, meatloaf, and baked chicken with a choice of three veggies and dessert. Seafood is served on Fridays. There is also a choice of sandwiches and fresh boudin or cracklins. Plunk down less than $5 for a plate and take it over to City Park for a lunch on the bayou. Theriot's is located on Julia (a pretty side street two blocks west of Center Street) at the corner of Pershing. Lunch is served from 10:30 to 1 on weekdays. (318) 369-3871.

Vern's Barbecue $. 620 Hopkins St., New Iberia.

Vern Mitchell's barbecue joint is appropriately set in the heart of New Iberia's soul-food district. His barbecue is tender, sparsely sauced, and plenty spicy. I like the ribs and rabbit. The peach cobbler with a moist cakelike crust was delicious (the blackberry a little dry). To get to Vern's from Center Street (Rte. 14), head west on Main Street (Rte. 182) .8 mile. Turn left on Hopkins (Rte. 615) and go .6 mile. Vern's is in a brick building to the right (facing Lombard Street). Look for his barbecue pit in the lot. Hours are Monday through Thursday, 10 A.M. to 2 P.M. and 5 to 8 P.M., and Friday and Saturday, 10 A.M. to midnight. (318) 369-7300.

Victor's Cafeteria Local Fave, $. 109 W. Main St.

With the average age in America creeping upward, cafeterias are unlikely to die, but the small independent ones like Victor's have all but disappeared. Victor's is a plate-food haven with cafeteria-style service. By far the most popular items are stuffed bell peppers with white beans (usually served on Thursdays) and the homemade chicken pot pies. These pies (also available in meat and crawfish flavors) are served in individual pie pans and have flaky top crusts with forked edges. Chicken pies are usually served on Thursdays, but if you order one

45 minutes in advance, they can prepare it any day. Victor's is the lunch spot of choice with the older crowd. It is easy walking distance from Shadows on the Teche plantation house. It is open Monday through Friday from 6 A.M. to 2 P.M., Saturday from 6 to 10 A.M., and Sunday from 10 A.M. to 2 P.M. (318) 369-9924.

MUSIC

New Iberia is not a great spot for night life but is a short drive from dance halls in three neighboring towns. See the listings for St. Martinville and Breaux Bridge in this chapter and Erath in the Central Cajun Country chapter.

Clifton's Club Zydeco dance hall. Croche Lane, Loreauville.
See Loreauville (North of New Iberia).

Club Mon Amis Country/Swamp Pop/Zydeco. U.S. 90, Grand Marais.
Eight miles east of New Iberia (Rte. 14.) on U.S. 90. (318) 276-5494.

Double D Cotton Club Zydeco dance hall. Parks.
See Breaux Bridge.

★Rainbeaux Club Country/Swamp Pop. 1373 Rte. 182 W.
For over 30 years the Rainbeaux (that's Cajun for rainbow) was the destination of Cajun music lovers from all over Teche Country. It no longer has Cajun music but Sunday afternoon Swamp Pop and Country shows draw a big crowd of old-timers. Lending atmosphere are long strands of Christmas lights strung in a web across the ceiling. On Sundays bands play from 4:30 to 8:30. Admission is usually $2. From downtown New Iberia, head west on Rte. 182. The dance hall is on the bayou side of the highway on the far western outskirts of town. (318) 367-6731.

LODGING

Bed and Breakfasts:

Chez Hebert 5304 Shoreline Dr., New Iberia.
To call this private guest cottage on the Teche unusual would be an understatement. Designed and built as a retreat by Cong. and Mrs. Edward F. Hebert, the cottage is a single 1,000-square-foot room with vaulted ceiling. A second-floor balcony wraps around the room and houses the library and memorabilia of Congressman Hebert, who represented Louisiana's First District from 1940 to 1976. His political books and photos from this turbulent period and his collection of Louisiana titles are fascinating. There are large windows and doors that open onto a veranda with an expansive view of the bayou. Inside there is a kitchenette, bathroom, and couch. Unfortunately, the beds

are old Murphy beds, which fold out of the wall and are less comfortable than the average fold-out sofa. Dawn Hebert provides breakfast on the screened veranda. Rates are $125 a night for two (cash or check). (318) 367-6447.

★The Estorge-Norton House 446 E. Main St.

Built entirely of cypress in the early 1900s by Edward Estorge, this three-story home overlooks the Old Spanish Trail and the spreading oaks around Shadows on the Teche. The first floor of the house was once an antique shop and is filled with a hodgepodge of old furniture. On the second floor there is a quiet reading room stocked with books and brochures, and four distinctively decorated rooms. Manager Charles Norton displays Southern hospitality and a great knowledge of the area while remaining an "invisible host" to those looking for privacy. He will show you around and give you a ride on the antique elevator (the first in New Iberia). Norton serves a full breakfast in a sunny breakfast room. You can walk out the door, stroll the historic district, and get lunch at Lagniappe Too. Doubles cost $60-$70. Not all rooms have private baths. Call for reservations. (318) 365-7603.

Inn at Le Rosier 314 Main St.

Saveur magazine called Le Rosier "the perfect little Acadian Fantasy B&B." The rooms in this reproduction of a raised Acadian cottage are cozy and quiet but hardly a fantasy of mine! Couples planning to complete their Acadian fantasy by dining at the touted restaurant (located in the 1867 main house) can drop over $200 in a night. The rate for one of the four small rooms with private bath is $100. (318) 367-5306.

★La Maison Bed and Breakfast 8401 Weeks Island Rd. (Rte. 83), eight miles southwest of New Iberia.

If you want silence, seclusion, and privacy, look no further. Sixty acres of cane rustles outside the windows, and shade creeps slowly from one side of the porch to the other at this wonderful Acadian cottage near the farming community of Lydia. Actually "cottage" is too diminutive a term for this hacienda. The two-bedroom house has been modernized and is furnished with a TV, washer and dryer, and fully equipped kitchen where you will find an icebox stocked with juices. Owners Eleanor and Ron Naquin live in a brick rambler next door and dispense a generous breakfast along with "insider" travel tips in Cajun French or English. Ron is a recreational shrimper and will often take guests (who cover gas expenses) for a short shrimping expedition on Vermilion Bay. The rate for double occupancy in one bedroom is $75. To get to La Maison from U.S. 90, take Rte. 83 south about two miles. Call first to make arrangements. (318) 364-2970.

La Maison Du Teche 417 E. Main St.

La Maison Du Teche is only three doors away from the historic Shadows on the Teche (see review), in downtown New Iberia. It is a historic three-story structure with impressive woodwork and a private bath in each room. Hosts Tom and Mary Livaudais reside on the third floor. There are two guest rooms on the second floor. One has a window overlooking Bayou Teche; the other overlooks Main Street. Neither has furnishings or lighting suitable for reading or relaxing, but the beds are comfortable. A third guest room looks out on Main Street from the first floor. Double rate is $85. Visa, Mastercard, and checks are accepted. (318) 367-9456.

Pourtos House 4018 Old Jeanerette Rd.

You have a choice of a private cottage by the pool or one of several rooms in this modern mansion on the north bank of Bayou Teche. There is plenty of privacy in the main house, which rambles so much one could get lost in it. The David Eldridge Suite has a private entrance. All rooms are furnished comfortably (though they are short on windows). It is the amenities like the quiet bayou, swimming pool, billiards room, and tennis courts that make Pourtos unique. The host is John Nugent. (318) 367-7045 or 1-800-336-7317.

Hotels and Motels:

Best Western 2714 Rte. 14 (Center Street), $60 to $65 double. (318) 364-3030, (800) 528-1234.

Inn of Iberia 924 E. Admiral Doyle Dr. $40. (318) 367-3211.

Holiday Inn 2915 Rte. 14 (Center Street), $55 to $60 double. (318) 367-1201, (800) 465-4329.

Teche Motel 1830 E. Main St. (Rte. 182), $30 double.

This old motor-court motel on Bayou Teche, 2.5 miles east of Rte. 14, has charm but is a bit worn. (318) 369-3756.

Camping:

Belmont Campground Rte. 31 and Rte. 86, eight miles north of New Iberia.

Belmont Campground is located on Bayou Teche halfway between St. Martinville and New Iberia. The campground has 200 sites on 29 wooded acres. Swimming is permitted in the bayou and facilities include showers, full hookups, pay phones, and a pavilion. The fees are $10 for RVs and $8 for tents (two persons). Take Rte. 31 north from New Iberia about eight miles to the intersection of Rte. 31 and Rte. 86. (318) 364-6020.

*Lake Fausse Pointe State Park See St. Martinville Recreation section.

Camping with full hookups and cabins, boat and canoe rentals, picnic area, hiking trails, and fishing dock in a swamp setting. This is a great recreational facility and is highly recommended.

Sher-Mac Campground Rte. 90 and Curtis Street, New Iberia.

Sher-Mac has 160 camper sites, full RV hookups for $18, and partial hookups for $15. Showers and toilets are available for tent campers. (318) 364-4256.

SOUTH OF NEW IBERIA
Avery Island

Avery Island's 2,500 acres are a South Louisiana "feast of the senses," from the scent of thousands of blossoms to the searing heat of tabasco peppers and verdant vistas. Here you can visit the Jungle Gardens, Bird City egret sanctuary, and Tabasco hot sauce factory. The so-called island is not an island at all but the largest of Louisiana's five major coastal salt domes. The 90'-high dome was caused by the upwelling of an immense subterranean plug of salt. French settlers called it Petite Anse (little

Tabasco Pepper Sauce Factory. (Courtesy of Louisiana Wild Life & Fisheries Commission)

cove), after the bayou that wraps around it. Around 1800, the island became the property of John Marsh, whose descendants, the Averys and McIlhennys, have lived there ever since. Five miles from the outskirts of New Iberia, Avery is visible as a wooded hill above the surrounding plain of marsh. The drive southwest on Avery Island Road carries visitors through floating marsh and cane and rice fields. The island is bordered on three sides by marsh and on the fourth by cypress swamps thick with wildlife. Far to the south the marsh drops away to Vermilion Bay. From U.S. 90, exit on Rte. 14 north. Go a couple of blocks and turn right on Rte. 329, which doubles back under U.S. 90 to Avery Island. A $1 toll is charged to enter the island.

The Avery Island Salt Mine (No longer open for tours for insurance reasons. Thank the lawyers for that.)

The salt mine at the southeast edge of Avery Island is the longest-operating rock salt mine in the country, excavating a plug of salt estimated to be one-and-a-half times as large as Mount Everest. Fossil evidence indicates that during prehistoric times man and mastodon alike congregated around saltwater springs here. It was not until 1790, when John Hayes stumbled upon a salt spring while hunting, that modern man began harvesting the island's salt. In 1862, J. M. Avery began enlarging one of the springs to facilitate evaporation mining when he discovered rock salt only 13 feet below the surface! It was the first discovery of rock salt on the continent, and the resource was quickly put to use in provisioning Southern forces during the War Between the States.

During the first 35 years of operation, the mine suffered destruction by Northern troops, flooding, and transportation problems. In 1899, the International Salt Company began quarrying. They dug to a depth of 550 feet, employing teams of mules underground and rail lines above to ship the product to market. After almost a century of operation, the International Salt Company has created a salt city 1,000 feet deep and over a mile in diameter (some caverns have 100-foot-high ceilings) but has barely scraped a nick in the huge salt reserve. The industrial southeast end of the island is officially closed to visitors, but an inadvertent wrong turn down the road that runs between the Jungle Gardens Visitors Center and the Tabasco Factory will lead you into this fascinating area. Known as "the Tangle" for its web of roads once used by pepper-field and factory workers and salt miners, the south end still sports the white frame structures that housed company employees, schools, and store.

Tabasco Pepper Sauce Factory (Tours offered)

Tabasco sauce may be the ultimate Cajun Country product. It is hot, it is the red color of boiled crawfish, and it is made with fresh

Avery Island salt and peppers. The most famous hot sauce in the nation was patented by Edmund McIlhenny following the War Between the States. From a first batch of 150 bottles in 1868, it has become so popular that the trademarked name, Tabasco, is often used to refer to other products. Legend has it that the hot capsicum peppers used to make McIlhenny's sauce were brought to the area in the early 1800s by a soldier returning from the Tabasco region of Mexico. Today, the McIlhenny Company raises seedlings at Avery Island and each August harvests adult peppers in Mexico, Colombia, and Honduras, as well as locally. Following company tradition, the field supervisor ensures that peppers are the correct color by comparing them to a *petit bâton rouge* (little red stick). The peppers are taken to the factory, mashed with Avery Island salt, and fermented for three years in oak barrels capped with salt. Finally the pepper mash is mixed with vinegar, stirred for a month, and strained for bottling.

The McIlhenny folks have a planned tour and visitors center that attracts thousands of visitors each year. The tour begins in a gallery that houses historic photographs and artifacts from the island. There is a 10-minute promotional video that shows people pouring on the Tabasco. The big disappointment is the factory tour, which is a walk down a glassed-in corridor with a view of the packaging area. At the end of the walkway, you wind up in the gift shop. There you can sample McIlhenny products and purchase a few unique items, like Tabasco C-rations from the Second World War, small vest-pocket-size bottles of the sauce to carry "in case of emergency," and dozens of products with the Tabasco/McIlhenny logo.

The pepper-scented production area is not part of the tour, but there is a way to get inside. Ask where you can purchase bags of the pepper mash, which is left after the sauce is strained. You will be directed to the adjacent brick factory, where workers wander around fermenting casks of mash, oblivious to the choking fumes. The pepper mash is sold in bulk for use in red hots, Dentine gum, and as a seasoning for boiled seafood (*see* review of the Guiding Star restaurant in New Iberia). The mash costs less than 50 cents a pound and a little bit goes a very long way in making sauce piquant. The price of a three-pound bag is worth the chance to get a whiff (whew!) of the factory itself. The Tabasco Factory is on the left after you pass the toll booth entering the island. Tour hours are Monday through Friday from 9 to 4 and Saturday from 9 to noon. Closed Sundays and holidays. Admission is free. 1-800-634-9599.

★**Jungle Gardens** (Open to public.)

In the early 1900s, Edward Avery McIlhenny put the wealth of several family enterprises, and his experience as an explorer, conservationist, and naturalist, to work in developing the most exotic gardens in the South.

The 200-acre compound surrounding his estate on Mayard Hill is a patchwork of hollows filled with flowering shrubs, bushes, lagoons, sunken fern gardens, and hilltop shrines. A 14-acre live-oak grove welcomes visitors with a canopy of shade that is perfect for picnics (snacks are sold at the visitors center, but you will have to bring your own lunch provisions).

The true beauty of the Jungle Gardens awaits those who walk the miles of secluded pathways. For the less energetic, a gravel road winds through the gardens with parking areas convenient to such notable attractions as the Buddha Shrine, Camelia Gardens, and Bird City. Watch for the island's deer as you go through. The gardens at Avery Island are a kaleidoscope of native and imported plantings. They are not attended to on a frequent basis, but spread out naturally over the compound. McIlhenny brought in lotus and papyrus from the Upper Nile, hybrid grapefruits and finger bananas from China, and 64 varieties of bamboo, including a dense forest of 60-foot canes of Chinese Timber variety. The thousands of types of camelias and hundreds of azaleas are the main attraction here, painting the hillsides fantastic colors during late winter and early spring. There is always something in bloom. Camelias blossom from December through March. Azaleas and wild iris bloom from late February into April. Dogwoods begin to flower in April. By summer, water hyacinths, wisteria, and lilies are opening, followed by lotus and chrysanthemums. The Jungle Gardens and Bird City are open daily from 8 to 5:30. Visitors may stay until dark. Admission is $5.50 for adults and $3.50 for kids, and the cost covers both attractions. (318) 369-6243.

Bird City in Jungle Gardens

Located on the southeast edge of the Jungle Gardens is the largest egret colony in the United States. During the late 1800s, Avery Island

Rookery and viewing platform at Bird City. (Courtesy of Louisiana Office of Tourism)

was the last haven for these birds, which were prized by plume hunters for their showy "nuptial" feathers. When they disappeared from the island in 1892, E. A. McIlhenny searched out 7 young birds in the marsh and established this colony over a man-made lake on the eastern side of Mayard Hill. He built a nesting area of bamboo on pilings over the water and, in less than 25 years, nearly 20,000 egrets were nesting at the site each summer. The egrets begin nesting here each spring in February or March and remain into early summer. Many smaller birds join the flocks of egrets and make the observation deck and grounds surrounding Bird City a prime destination for bird watchers. The Jungle Gardens and Bird City are open daily from 8 to 5:30. Visitors may stay until dark. Admission is $5.50 for adults and $3.50 for kids, and the cost covers both attractions. (318) 369-6243.

★Jefferson Island

Like Avery Island six miles to the east, Jefferson is not actually an island but a large hill caused by the protrusion of an underground salt dome. Also like Avery, Jefferson Island is the site of some of the grandest public gardens in the state. What sets Jefferson apart as an attraction is the presence of 1,300-acre Lake Peignur, site of a major industrial/geologic disaster in 1980. Boat tours of the catastrophe site, lake, and surrounding region are offered. There is also a cafe with a view of the lake, and a luxury Bed and Breakfast cottage on the grounds (see reviews below). Jefferson gets its name from actor Joseph Jefferson, famous for his stage role as Rip Van Winkle. Jefferson, who purchased the island in 1865, used it as a winter retreat and constructed a grand Victorian mansion before selling out to John Bayless in the early 1900s. It was the late John Bayless, Jr., who began planting bright formal gardens inspired by those of E. A. McIlhenny on Avery Island. After hiring gardeners from England to help plant and landscape 20 acres with camelias, azaleas, hibiscus, and flower gardens, Bayless set 700 acres of the estate aside as a public attraction.

Rip Van Winkle Gardens, House, and Boat Tour

Jefferson Island underwent a face-lift in 1997 and is again one of the great attractions of South Louisiana. The extensive gardens are replanted, a new chef is running the cafe, a luxury Bed and Breakfast is open (see reviews below), and daily boat tours are being introduced. Most interesting is a recently produced video that has vintage footage of the great disaster. Guests may wander the gardens and oak-covered lawns before taking the cruise or touring the ornate Jefferson House. The house has many elaborate details but most memorable are the vistas from high-backed rockers on the front porch. To get to Jefferson Island take Rte. 675 south from U.S. 90 in New Iberia about six miles. Turn right on Rip Van Winkle Road. It is another half-mile to the parking area. Hours are 9 to 5 daily. Admission is $6.50 for the gardens and $8.50 for the house tour and gardens. No price was available at press time for the boat tour. (318) 365-3332 or 1-800-375-3332.

Disaster

There are other gardens, other historic homes, and other boat tours, but Jefferson Island lays sole claim to one of the most extraordinary geophysical events to strike South Louisiana in modern times. On November 20, 1980, Texaco Platform #20 was drilling for oil in the waters of Lake Peignur, a couple of hundred yards from the island. Sometime in the early morning hours, the drill pipe became jammed. A short time later the platform began to tilt precariously. Moments after being evacuated, the rig slipped beneath the water surface. At

Lake Peignur goes down the drain. (Courtesy of Rip Van Winkle Gardens)

about the same time, miners working 1,300 feet down in the Jefferson Island salt mine (which extended below the lake) noticed muddy water rising in the chamber floor. An alarm was sounded and the mine elevators began working nonstop to pull miners to the surface. The last of the miners arrived above ground to witness a startling event.

The oil rig had apparently punctured the mine and water was rapidly draining from the lake, forming a massive whirlpool as it poured into the underground caverns. Eleven barges disappeared into the maelstrom and two recreational fishermen abandoned their skiff and crawled through the mud to safety. A tugboat crew in the Delcambre Canal found the powerful craft being hauled backwards towards the lake and jumped ashore to watch it get sucked down! The spinning water collapsed surrounding banks, stealing 50 acres, five greenhouses, and a conservatory from John Bayless, Jr.'s estate.

Bayless watched and videotaped from the roof of his brick home as the floor of the lake collapsed, sending 3.5 billion gallons of water roaring into the mine below. Within seven hours the lake was empty. Local fishermen watched stunned as the Delcambre Canal, normally an outlet flowing into the Gulf, reversed its direction and, over the next two days, refilled the empty basin. Most of the barges bobbed back up to the surface, and no lives were lost in the event. Today the chimneys and columns of Bayless's brick home stand in the edge of the now deepwater lake.

Cafe Jefferson Cajun/Creole, $ (lunch)-$$$. Jefferson Island.

If a beautiful view of the gardens and lake is not enough, the cafe at Jefferson Island is home to Chef Pat Mould. One of the celebrated chefs of Cajun Country, Mould developed menus at Cafe Vermilionville, Charly G's, and the Hub City Diner before moving to Jefferson Island in '97. The lunch menu has simple sandwiches, salads, and soups. It's at dinner that Mould shows his stuff. Highlights of the menu include seared quail Acadie with sweet-corn pancake, smoked duck and andouille gumbo, grilled cowboy steak, and braised breast of guinea hen. On the light side there are a couple of good salads and a vegetable ragout. Lunch hours are 11 to 4 daily. Dinner is served from 6 to 10 Friday and Saturday. (318) 365-3332.

Rip Van Winkle Gardens Bed and Breakfast Cottage

A luxurious guesthouse at Rip Van Winkle Gardens opened just before this book went to press. The renovated turn-of-the-century cookhouse has a king-size bed with cotton linens, a Jacuzzi, wet bar, phone, TV, and refrigerator stocked with breakfast supplies. Of course the great thing about spending a night here is the opportunity to stroll the gardens while they are quiet and free of other visitors. If you are spending a Friday or Saturday night you will surely want to eat dinner at Cafe Jefferson. I have not been to this one, but it sounds great. Several more B&B cottages are planned. Double rate is $175 (major credit cards accepted). (318) 365-3332 or 1-800-375-3332.

Loreauville (North of New Iberia)

Few outsiders make it around the tight, 20-mile oxbow bend in Bayou Teche, north of New Iberia, to find this village of about 900. Most travelers between New Iberia and St. Martinville shave 14 miles off the trip by taking Rte. 182 west and cutting off the Loreauville bend. Those who take the extra few minutes can stop for lunch at a Cajun cafe on the bayou, see the Indian mound in downtown Loreauville, and visit the grave of the town's most famous resident, Clifton Chenier, the King of Zydeco. Plan in advance and you can take an airboat tour of the breathtaking Lake Fausse region or take in a show at Clifton's Club, a huge Zydeco dance hall owned by the musician's widow.

Indian Mound Main Street (Rte. 86), Loreauville.

At one time, a village museum with 40 historic structures and thousands of artifacts was open at this site. Upon the death of the proprietor, the buildings were auctioned off, but the mound remains. In fact, it is the only hill for miles around. North of the small downtown section of Loreauville on Main Street (Rte. 86), look for the mound in a grassy field, three houses above Bonin Street.

Patio Restaurant Seafood, $-$$. Main Street (Rte. 86), Loreauville.

How many other towns with a population under 1,000 and a location designed to thwart drive-through visitors sport an ambitious seafood restaurant? Half the fun of eating here is in finding good food off the beaten path. I must admit I *have* had better seafood, but seldom enjoyed it more than in this bright cafe. The salad bar and homemade bread pudding make for a great lunch on a hot day (especially after a swamp tour with nearby Airboat Tours, Inc.). Seafood-stuffed baked potatoes are very popular and there is a wide selection of grilled seafood and meat. The Patio is open Tuesday through Saturday from 11 to 2 and 5 to 11. (318) 229-8281.

Clifton Chenier's Grave Landry Road, Loreauville.

Zydeco fans who want to visit the unmarked grave of Clifton Chenier and the sprawling Clifton's Club Zydeco dance hall will find both less than 5 miles off Rte. 86 in the flat alluvial prairie outside Loreauville.

Take Rte. 86 into Loreauville. Just past the Patio Restaurant, turn west onto La. 3242 (a sign says "To Lake Dauterive"). Go 1.3 miles and take a left onto Landry Road. The cemetery is 1.5 miles down Landry. Take the second entrance. Go midway down and next to the drive on the right is the unmarked grave of Clifton Chenier. It is parallel to the Veret and Broussard graves.

Clifton's Club Zydeco dance hall. Croche Lane, Loreauville.

This is not one of those Zydeco halls where you walk in, are recognized as an outsider, and are asked if you are "from the film crew." The folks at Clifton's Club, including his widow, Margaret Chenier, whom I found sitting at a table in the back, seemed genuinely surprised that any outsider had found the secluded dance hall. The welcome was warm anyway, and the music by Edward Brown and His Zydeco House Rockers was downright hot. It is a tribute to the strength of the music that Clifton helped popularize that a huge dance hall (seats 700 and has two bars) in such a remote location can draw big crowds for bimonthly dances and trail rides. The music schedule here is quite unpredictable and not widely advertised, so you will have to call in advance to find out who is playing and when. Denise LaSalle recently played here for a $10 admission! To get to Clifton's Club, follow the same directions as those for his grave. Continue a half-mile beyond the cemetery and turn left onto Croche Lane (Parish Road 409). Go one mile and the club is on the right. (318) 229-6036 or 367-9912. If there is no answer at the club, try Hanks Records in New Iberia (367-7309).

★Airboats, Inc. Loreauville.

If I had to pick one swamp tour to go on based on natural beauty, profusion of wildlife, and great guide service, this would be it. Airboat Tours, Inc. has two big advantages over most other swamp tours. They access the grandest cypress swamp in Cajun Country, and their fast, air-driven craft can negotiate narrow passageways and barely wet sloughs that are favorite hangouts for a multitude of wild animals. The only complaint has been that airboats are loud. Airboat Tours, Inc. provides ear protection to wear while the boat is moving. The tour takes you to the pristine swamp around Lake Fausse (once part of the Atchafalaya Basin). Here you will see ancient stands of cypress and miles of water hyacinths (in the spring) and American lotus (in the late summer). Tours are conducted in French (with prior notice) or English by Lon Prioux and his family. These guys grew up in the area, building the first airboats in the Basin and hunting ducks. Their love of the swamp is apparent in each enthusiastic comment and bit of lore. Plan the trip for early morning or late evening, when the sun is low and mist is hanging over the Marshfield Boat Ramp. When Prioux brings your craft quietly to

Windblown travelers with Airboat Tours, Inc. (Photo by Julie Posner)

rest in a field of lotus that reaches to the horizon in all directions, take a deep breath of the oxygen exhaled by the surrounding forest.

The airboats can only accommodate five to six passengers, so this tour is more expensive than some others (if you are traveling alone ask if you can join a group), but the wild trip is worth every penny. Hour-long tours cost $10 a person, with a minimum charge of $50. Two-hour tours cost a bit more. Tours are offered daily. Call ahead to set up a time. Tours leave from the Marshfield Boat Ramp. From U.S. 90 in New Iberia take Lewis Street four miles to Rte. 86 (Loreauville Road). Turn right on Rte. 86 and travel five miles. Turn right on Black Line Road for one mile. Turn right again on the Marshfield Road and take it until it ends at the boat launch. For those spending a day or staying overnight at Lake Fausse Pointe State Park (*see* St. Martinville section for description), Airboat Tours, Inc. offers pick-up and drop-off service from the park boat launch! Call (318) 229-4457.

New Iberia to St. Martinville

Between New Iberia and St. Martinville, Bayou Teche turns almost due north. Rte. 31 parallels the stream on the west bank, and Rte. 347 on the east, as it cuts through the alluvial valley between the Vermilion River and the Atchafalaya Basin. Rte. 182 (the Old Spanish Trail), which had followed the bayou to this point, veers northwest to Lafayette.

St. Martin Square. (Photo by Julie Posner)

St. Martinville

St. Martinville, the seat of government for St. Martin Parish, is located 17 miles southeast of Lafayette and 10 miles north of New Iberia, at the intersection of Rte. 96 and Rte. 31. From Interstate 10 take exit #109 south (Breaux Bridge). From downtown Breaux Bridge travel 15 miles south on Rte. 31. Nowhere is Teche Country's spirit of quiet reflection more hauntingly exuded than in the once grand village of St. Martinville. Established as a military post in 1714, the town was settled by French expatriates, wealthy planters who fled a slave revolt in Santo Domingo, Spanish soldiers, and members of the French aristocracy who escaped the revolution in that country. When the first Cajuns arrived around 1765, they found a bustling Creole city centered around the Spanish military garrison, Poste de Atakapas. It is ironic that St. Martinville has become a veritable Cajun shrine whose "secular saint," Evangeline, has drawn tourists for most of a century. Few of the Cajuns who made the arduous journey from New Orleans to St. Martinville elected to stay there. When it was incorporated in 1817, the city, nicknamed Petit Paris, was a center of high culture and a resort for Creole families from New Orleans.

During the mid-1800s nearby New Iberia began to usurp St. Martinville as a steamboat port and trade center. Today there are few vestiges of the high life left in St. Martinville. Most visitors come to the former Creole capital to see such Cajun landmarks as the Evangeline Shrine, Evangeline Oak, and Evangeline State Commemorative Area (the best place in St. Martinville to get an unromanticized account of the Acadian settlement). Old St. Martin Square, the former site of the opera house, had fallen on hard times but is going through a revival with several shops opening across from St. Martin de Tours Catholic Church. The busiest night life is found in the old Zydeco halls (now featuring DJs) and soul shacks of South Main Street, where the smell of barbecue is the harbinger of a lively Saturday night. Unless you are interested in staying at the Old Castillo Bed and Breakfast, the town is easily seen in a couple of hours on the way to New Iberia, Breaux Bridge, or Lafayette.

RECREATION

★Lake Fausse Pointe State Park Atchafalaya Basin Levee Road.

Lake Fausse Pointe State Park is one of the newest and finest state parks in the South and a rare spot to experience the swamp on foot. The park occupies 6,000 acres immediately adjacent to the West Atchafalaya Basin levee (about 18 miles southeast of St. Martinville and 45 minutes southeast of Lafayette). Before the 20th century the Basin stretched westward to the banks of Bayou Teche. New levees built by the U.S. Corps of Engineers following the disastrous flood of 1927 reclaimed this section of the swamp and the adjacent lakes from the Basin. Lake Fausse is home to one of the oldest cypress groves in Cajun Country. The park includes a multitude of day-use facilities, including about 5 miles of hiking trails through junglelike forest, picnic and recreation areas on a bayou leading to Lake Fausse, a grocery store, bait shop, and paddleboat and canoe rentals.

On weekends during the summer, the park is abuzz with fishermen and recreational boaters. In the evening, day-use folks head home and those staying over can enjoy the perfect solitude of the swamp, catch a catfish off the dock, and take it back to cook while the birds and bugs set to singing. The park has 50 campsites with full hookups, laundry facilities, and a clean shower and rest station. There are eight air-conditioned cabins (and eight more under construction) with screened porches overlooking the bayou. Accommodating up to six persons, each is furnished with cooking and eating utensils, linens (except towels), and private baths. The alligators and snakes are generally friendly, but bring plenty of bug dope to fight ravenous mosquitoes and horseflies. Cabins cost $65 a night. RV and tent camping is $12 a night. Admission to the park is $2 per car for four people. Take Rte. 96 3.5 miles east from St. Martinville. Turn right on Rte. 679 and travel 8.3 miles. Make a right on the Levee Road and travel 8 miles to the park entrance. It takes about 40 minutes to travel the 20 miles from the intersection of Rte. 31 and Rte. 96 in St. Martinville. The park may also be reached by following the Atchafalaya Basin

Levee Road 27 miles south from Henderson at I-10 exit #115 (this route is gravel much of the way). The park is open during the summer from 7 A.M. to 10 P.M. Winter hours are 8 A.M. to 7 P.M. (318) 229-4764.

Lake Fausse Park Store/Canoe Rental Inside the state park.

This store within the boundaries of the state park is a good place to pick up essential camping supplies and one of very few places to rent a canoe in the area. You may rent the canoe here and take it elsewhere or put it in right in the park. A canoe (with paddles and life jackets) costs $25 a day or $5 an hour. Paddleboats are $6. If you want more than basic camp supplies, stock up at nearby St. Martinville. The store is open from 8 to 5 from late spring through early fall. Hours may change in the off season. They operate on short lease from the park service, so call first to verify information. (318) 229-6333.

ATTRACTIONS

St. Martin Square Rte. 31 and Rte. 96.

The spiritual and social center of St. Martinville is historic St. Martin Square, dominated by *St. Martin de Tours Catholic Church*. Around the square are a number of popular tourist attractions including the *Evangeline Oak, Acadian Memorial, Old Castillo Hotel, Evangeline Statue*, and *Petit Paris Museum*. Bordering the square on the side facing the church is a row of turn-of-the-century shops with balustraded galleries, which has recently benefited from the city's status as a "Main Street Community." I find these old commercial establishments and their largely French speaking clientele to be more interesting than the tourist industry that has grown around the Evangeline story. I usually spend more time in Thibodaux's Restaurant or on the boardwalk by Bayou Teche than chasing ghosts around the Evangeline Oak.

St. Martin de Tours Catholic Church 100 S. Main St.

Although the church was established in 1765 (one of the oldest churches in Louisiana), the current cement-covered brick building was built in 1832. Two wings extend from either side of the main chapel, one of which houses an 1870s replica of the famous French Grotto of Lourdes, which is surrounded by the votive candles of supplicants. The church is open to walk-in visitors who observe a reasonable decorum.

La Remise Coach House Beside the Evangeline Oak.

Despite the huge number of tourists visiting St. Martinville, this is the closest thing they have to a tourist information center. I was ready to walk by the coach house until I saw a sign: Inquire Inside About Air-conditioned Walking Tours. I never got an explanation of how a walking tour can be air conditioned but discovered a shop with hundreds of miniature ceramic Evangelines for sale. There are quite a few brochures and books with information on local attractions. This is also a place to buy tickets ($3) for the Acadian Memorial just two doors up the street. La Remise is open from 10 to 4 daily. (318) 394-2233.

Acadian Memorial
The memorial houses a mural of Acadian refugees arriving in South Louisiana, an eternal flame in tribute to the indomitable spirit of Acadian culture, and a list in bronze of the names of Acadian refugees found in Louisiana records. Admission is $3 (tickets available at La Remise Coach House). The memorial is open from 10 to 4 daily. (318) 394-2233.

Petit Paris Museum 103 S. Main St.
The dollar admission to the Petit Paris Museum could wind up being your worst entertainment investment in Cajun Country. That depends on whether you are interested in another exhibit of recent Mardi Gras costumes, out-of-date brochures, and trinkets for sale. Come to think of it, maybe it's worth it for a laugh. French or English tours of the church and square are also offered for $2 (with advance reservations), but anyone with two feet and 20 minutes can do that on their own. The Petit Paris Museum is open seven days a week from 9:30 to 4:30. (318) 394-7334.

Evangeline Statue (outside St. Martin de Tours Church).
Nowhere is the replacement of actual history by romance more apparent in St. Martinville than at the side of St. Martin de Tours Church, where a bronze statue of Evangeline has been placed on the site of the former Poste des Attakapas cemetery. Some folks around town have grown so accustomed to hearing local retellings of the Evangeline story that they will swear that this statue actually marks her grave. In fact, the statue was donated to the city by silent film star Delores Del Rio, who played the part of Evangeline in the 1929 movie filmed in St. Martinville.

Evangeline Oak Evangeline Boulevard at the bayou.
Not only has the St. Martinville Tourist Commission declared that the Evangeline Oak is the primary tourist attraction in town, they have also declared it the "most famous tree in America," an incredible feat for a tree that has never been poisoned or had anyone hung from it. It is located behind the town square beside Bayou Teche. Legend has it that townspeople stood in the shade of this tree greeting Acadian exiles who landed at the spot. There are a few blasphemers who point out that this is not actually the first "Evangeline Oak" and that others have been

destroyed by various natural causes. Even these skeptics refuse to doubt loudly that there was an original tree where Gabrielle probably waited many days for his lost love to arrive. The current Evangeline Oak has had so many visitors posing for photographs beside its trunk that it is suffering from soil compaction. A park with a raised walkway around the tree and along the bayou has alleviated the problem.

Guys under the Oak

Unless old age finally catches up with these raconteurs (as it recently did with their buddy Max Greig), or the bayou rages up and washes them away, you can count on finding the Romero brothers parked on chairs in the shade of the Evangeline Oak. Nothing reflects the pace of life in sleepy St. Martinville better than the fact that these old men, swapping stories by Bayou Teche, are one of the main attractions and most predictable events in town! In the best St. Martinville tradition, these guys effortlessly blend fact and fancy as they describe life on the Teche. If you are lucky, the Romero brothers will pull out the accordion for an impromptu bayouside serenade.

La Place D'Evangeline (Old Castillo Hotel), 220 Evangeline Blvd.

Constructed as a residence and trading post in 1792, this brick structure beside the Evangeline Oak is the oldest building in St. Martinville.

The Romero brothers perform under the Evangeline Oak. (Photo by Mary Tutwiler)

It operated as the elegant Castillo Hotel until purchased by the Convent of the Sisters of Mercy in 1899. The Sisters of Mercy ran the only girls' school in St. Martinville there for 87 years. Since 1987, the newly named Place D'Evangeline has reopened as a Bed and Breakfast, reviving the tradition of hospitality and classy accommodations it maintained during its days as a hotel (*see* Lodging section below). (318) 394-4010.

St. Martin Parish Courthouse 400 S. Main St.

This Greek Revival structure, four blocks south of the square, was built by slave labor about 1859. It is made of brick coated with cement and has four large Ionic columns. Historians may consult an extensive collection of French and Spanish documents from the Attakapas District dating back to the 1730s, which are kept on file here.

★Longfellow Evangeline State Commemorative Area 1200 N. Main St.

How strong was the spirit of Evangeline? It was strong enough for the normally prosaic state park service to make the 157-acre Longfellow State Commemorative Area the first state park in Louisiana in 1934. Locals claim that the house here was the property of Louis Arceneaux, the real-life counterpart of Longfellow's Gabrielle. Despite its poetic name and local legends surrounding the park, the Longfellow Evangeline Area has a museum and visitors center with the most clearly presented factual information (printed in French and English) available on the Acadian settlements in Canada and South Louisiana. Especially instructive is a series of maps depicting where and when Acadian settlements were begun and tracing their subsequent movements. There are displays of tools, artifacts, and handcrafted items from the colonial period, including items from both Acadian and Creole households.

The site was originally a *vacherie*, as the Cajuns called their ranches. In the early 1800s, the land was purchased by wealthy Creole planter Charles Olivier du Clozel, who built the raised Creole plantation home that is now open for tours. Typical of the way legend has colored "fact" around St. Martinville, this house, with its distinctive Creole features, is commonly known as the "Acadian House." Unlike mansions built by Anglo planters in the mid-1800s, it is of simple Creole design, raised off the ground, with the first floor constructed of brick and second-story walls of *bousillage* (a mud and moss mixture). An attendant at the house will show you around and clear up any rumors you picked up from the old men on St. Martin Square. A French-speaking guide is sometimes available. Most local visitors ignore the museum and house in favor of the recreational facilities. There are pavilions and grills (on the bayou), a boat launch, rest rooms, and crafts shop. The park is located on Rte. 31 (Main Street) about two miles from St. Martin Square. It is open from 9 to 5 daily. The house is open until 4:30. Admission of $2 a car (for up to four people) covers the museum and house tour. (318) 394-3754 or 394-4284.

★**Terrace Woodworks** 2085 Terrace Hwy. (Rte. 96).

Eddie Greig is the master of the porch swing and glider. Visitors come to Terrace Woodworks from around the country to purchase his basic, deluxe, and custom porch and patio furnishings. Greig is actually much more than a craftsman and woodworker. His shop has a cooler of homemade beer, a siphon water system fed from a rain cistern, and dozens of one-of-a-kind contraptions he designed. His creations range from nutty yard swings to elegant cypress furnishings made from his own supply of salvaged lumber. When a client needed a swing with a foot-pedal propulsion system, Eddie designed it. A double swing under a trellis? No problem! Eddie speaks French and is accustomed to visitors from around the globe. He has a rustic showroom with sample rockers, tables, and, of course, swings. Greig is often able to turn out a swing or table in a day. A standard five-foot swing is about $135 and a deluxe model is about $165. To get to the shop from

Craftsman Eddie Greig building a rocker. (Photo by Mary Tutwiler)

St. Martinville take Rte. 96 just over one mile west from the square. From U.S. 90 take 96 east toward St. Martinville. Shop hours are "whenever the door is open" (usually that means at least 9 to 4 Monday through Saturday). (318) 394-4485.

Way of the Cross

Along a nine-mile stretch of Rte. 96, northeast of St. Martinville, you will notice small birdhouse-size boxes posted on trees beside the road. Each box bears a Station of the Cross. On religious holidays, folks walk and drive the length of the route placing candles at each station.

Oak and Pine Alley Rte. 96, three miles northeast of St. Martinville.

Wealthy sugar planter Charles Durand planted a two-mile-long drive of alternating oak and pine trees here. Durand married off two of his daughters in a single glorious ceremony shortly before the War Between the States. Legend (a ubiquitous word around these parts) has it that, in an unmatched show of wealth, the trees along the drive were sown with spiders, which spun webs through their limbs. On the morning of the wedding, Durand dusted these webs with gold and silver dust, creating a sparkling passageway for the wedding procession. The plantation was burned during the war, the mill collapsed, and the spiders failed to thrive, but a mile of Oak and Pine Alley remains. When entering the alley you may notice a wooden figurine nailed to the first of the huge oaks. This is one of the Stations of the Cross found at regular intervals along Rte. 96.

St. Martinville to Breaux Bridge

Above St. Martinville the dry and arable land on either side of the bayou narrows. Off the beaten path of east/west traffic, the succession of small communities along the stream thins out and the landscape is dominated by groves of live oaks. The only town along this 14-mile stretch of Rte. 31 is the small, predominantly black Creole community of Parks, where you will find the Double D Cotton Club, one of the most down-home Zydeco dance halls in Cajun Country (*see* Breaux Bridge music listings for a description).

FOOD

Despite its reputation as a bastion of Cajun and Creole culture, St. Martinville is not a great place to eat. You are best off planning a visit between meals in nearby New Iberia, Broussard, Henderson, or Lafayette.

★Danna's Bakery Local Fave/Bakery. 207 E. Bridge St.

Danna's original location opened in New Iberia in 1921. They serve the same great cookies and pies here. Get a few to eat on the banks of the Teche, to take for a snack at Lake Fausse Pointe Park, or just to hold off the hungries on the road. Moist pecan macaroons, nut bars, thumbprint cookies, and sweet-dough pies are recommended. Danna's is open Tuesday through Saturday from 5 A.M. to 5 P.M. and Sunday until noon. (318) 394-3889.

Goulas Grocery Cracklins. Rte. 31 North.
See Breaux Bridge.

Josephine's Creole Restaurant Down Home, $. 830 S. Main St.
Josephine serves solid plate lunches with a punch of extra seasoning. Every day there is a different lunch menu with three or four main courses and five vegetables and starches to choose from. The cook, known as "Ms. Martha," conducted open-hearth cooking demonstrations at the Vermilionville theme park (see Lafayette section) for several years. It is no surprise that her cooked-down foods are excellent. I like the chicken or shrimp stews or the smothered chicken. Stuffed Turkey Wings appear on Wednesday and Creole Stuffed Bread is available daily. Josephine's is open for lunch from 10:30 until 2 every day. She stays open until 10 selling burgers and po' boys on Friday night. (318) 394-8030.

★Ms. Garret's Pie Kitchen Olivier Street, off Rte. 31.
Ms. Garret's homemade chicken and crawfish pies are a cottage industry that has gotten considerable attention. Everyone from the Lafayette *Daily Advertiser* to *Saveur* magazine has found time to rave about these simple treats. Before you get too excited, take note that the pies are sold uncooked (a good reason to stay at a Bed and Breakfast with a kitchen or a friendly host). Ms. Garret learned her pie recipe from her mother and is not sure how many generations it goes back, but the result is exquisite. The pies are irregular, hand-stuffed turnovers with egg crusts. The filling is not that of the typical Southern pot pie with carrots and potatoes and celery but a fricassee of chicken or crawfish in a brown gravy spiked with onion and garlic. To get to Garret's from St. Martin Square go north on Rte. 31 about .3 mile and make a left on Olivier Street. The pie shop is in the residential area just one block off of Rte. 31. Hours are Monday though Thursday 2 to 6 P.M. and Saturday 10 A.M. to 4 P.M. (318) 394-7507.

Old Castillo Hotel Restaurant Cajun/Creole, $-$$. 220 Evangeline Blvd.
This place is conveniently located right beside the Evangeline Oak on the banks of Bayou Teche and is popular with tour-bus patrons. There is usually French-speaking staff on duty. The menu, which is printed in French and English, includes a number of crawfish and shrimp preparations, gumbos, and froglegs in addition to fried

seafood and steaks. There are small cafes in town where you can find a better down-home Cajun lunch or supper, but this place is nice for families or those looking for something slightly more upscale. I recommend the Bed and Breakfast rooms here (see review under lodging). The restaurant opens at 8 A.M. daily. It closes at 2 P.M. Sunday, 5 P.M. Monday and Tuesday, and 9 P.M. Wednesday through Saturday. (318) 394-4010 or 1-800-621-3017.

Thibodeaux's Cafe Down Home, $. 116 S. Main (St. Martin Square).

Thibodeaux's looks as if it should be great. It is in an old storefront on St. Martin Square, facing the St. Martin de Tours Church. This tiny cafe fills up with locals conversing in French at breakfast and lunch. Unfortunately the food, which is standard grill and plate-lunch fare, just doesn't stack up to the ambiance. The coffee and conversation can't be beat, though. Thibodeaux's is open Monday through Saturday from 6 A.M. to 4 P.M. (318) 394-9268.

MUSIC

As with food, there is a notable dearth of music establishments in St. Martinville. The busiest scene is the black nightclub district on South Main Street. Those staying in the St. Martinville area may want to drive up the bayou to Breaux Bridge and Henderson or over to Lafayette to find more night life.

Tee's Connection Zydeco dance hall. 704 S. Main St.

Tee's alternates Disco and Zydeco on weekends. (318) 394-3870.

LODGING

Bed and Breakfasts:

Bienvenue House 421 N. Main St.

This large antebellum house is within easy walking distance to St. Martin Square and Bayou Teche. There are three guest rooms decorated with antique furnishings and good beds. Each has a private, connected bath. The grand room at the front of the house has a private balcony overlooking Main Street, a queen-size bed, and a large bath. A gourmet South Louisiana-style breakfast is served. Hostess Leslie Leonpacher proved her knowledge of hidden attractions by directing us to Ms. Garret's Pie Kitchen (see review above). Talk her into heating a pie up for you! Rates are $80-$105. Visa and Mastercard are accepted. (318) 394-9100 or (888) 394-9100.

Maison Bleu 417 N. Main St.

Maison Bleu is just a couple of blocks from St. Martin Square. Guest rooms are in the front of the house on the first floor, so street noise may bother some guests. One room has a connected bath; the other has a private bath down the hall. Maison Bleu is undergoing a change of ownership so further comments are not possible. (318) 394-1215.

★Old Castillo Hotel 220 Evangeline Blvd.

Whether you have dreams of Evangeline or nightmares of a schoolmistress grabbing you by the ear, the history of the Old Castillo coats its rooms like chalk dust. This was a colonial trading post, a hotel, and for most of the last century a Catholic school for girls. The first floor is now occupied by La Place D'Evangeline Restaurant. Five former classrooms on the second floor are crisply decorated overnight accommodations furnished with turn-of-the-century antiques.

Like the weary travelers who disembarked from steamboat or stage coach at the adjacent landing, you check in at the restaurant on the first floor, then climb steps to the seclusion of your room. On the bayou side, you can open a window and get a wake-up call from ducks quacking by the bayou. Breakfast of *pain perdu* or *beignets* is served beneath walls bearing class photographs of girls who suffered through history lessons in the very room you slept in. The restaurant (see review above) opens at 8 A.M. daily. Room rates are $50 to $80 for double occupancy. Host Peggy Hulin and several of her staff speak French fluently. (318) 394-4010 or 1-800-621-3017.

Motel:

Beno's Motel 7202 Main St. (Rte. 31).

Very clean, well-maintained rooms, comfortable beds, small pool. Two miles east of St. Martin Square. $32-$37 double. (318) 394-5523.

Cabin Rental:

Lake Fausse Pointe State Park 18 miles southeast.

See review in Recreation section.

Camping:

Harry Smith Lodge RV Park Rte. 96 near U.S. 90.

Harry Smith has huge facilities to accommodate RV rallies. They have 300 full hookups, 600 partial, two complete bath houses, and a 330'-by-30' covered pavilion. They are located in the quiet rural community of Cade, two miles east of U.S. 90. $16.50 for hookups. (318) 837-6286.

Lake Fausse Pointe State Park 18 miles southeast of St. Martinville.

One of the premier camping and recreational facilities in the state, the park has cabins and tent spaces and canoe rentals. See description under Recreation for details.

Café Des Amis, downtown Breaux Bridge. (Photo by Macon Fry)

Breaux Bridge

Breaux Bridge is the Cajun Capital of Teche Country and, by declaration of the state legislature, *La Capitale Mondiale des Ecrevisses* (the Crawfish Capital of the World). The city rests on the banks of the bayou near the intersection of Interstate 10 and Rte. 31, about 6 miles east of Lafayette and 13 miles north of St. Martinville. Breaux Bridge is an essential stop for anybody visiting the Upper Teche area, Lafayette, or just driving past on nearby Interstate 10 (exit #109). In the past few years the village has undergone a makeover in spirit, trading downtown biker bars and beer joints for a great restaurant, a couple of unusual B&Bs, and a half-dozen antique shops, most within easy walking distance of each other and the bayou.

Originally known as La Pointe, Breaux Bridge was settled by Cajuns who took up ranching and hunting on the high ground west of the bayou in the late 1700s. There are several accounts of how Breaux Bridge got its name. One holds that it was in honor of Agricole Breaux, the builder of an early bridge at the site. Others claim that it was named for large landholder Firmin Breaux. Regardless, a long succession of wooden and steel bridges has spanned the Teche here, including one that was torched by Southern troops as they fled the advancing Northern army.

Throughout much of its history Breaux Bridge has been known as a wild place. In the mid-1800s, it was the site of several vigilante lynchings, and during Prohibition was notoriously "wet." Main Street was lined with saloons, speakeasies, and a large cockpit, earning the city the nickname "Little Mexico." The basic character of Main Street in this village of 7,800 remained little changed until the 1990s, when locals began to renovate the old downtown area, and a number of artists (including renowned South Louisiana photographer Debbie Fleming Caffery) found homes and studio space by the slow-moving stream. Now the wildest Breaux Bridge gets is during the Crawfish Festival (see description below). Even the festival has been tamed, moving from the beer-washed streets of downtown to the confines of nearby Parc Hardy.

The local phone directory, packed with a handful of Cajun surnames like Breaux, Patin, Angelle, Thibodaux, and Melancon, provides testimony to the unregenerate Cajun character of Breaux Bridge. In fact, there are so many people of the same name that the city directory at one time accepted listings by nicknames like Tee Bob and Boo Boo to clear up confusion! Breaux Bridge remains one of the best places to sample the music and food of Cajun Country. With its excellent (and reasonably priced) Bed and Breakfasts, I recommend the town as a base for exploring the whole region.

Visitors Center/Chamber of Commerce 314 Bridge St.

The Visitors Center and Chamber have adjoining offices. I had a hard time prying any information out of the staff here but did find a few helpful brochures and guide to the city. The Visitors Center is right in downtown Breaux Bridge, so you can leave your car here and walk to all the attractions listed below. From I-10 take exit #109 south (Reese Street) to Bridge Street. Make a right on Bridge Street. The Visitors Center is on the left beside the Bayou Teche Bridge. (318) 332-8500 or 332-5406.

RECREATION

★Lake Martin/Cypress Island Swamp South of Breaux Bridge.

This beautiful swamp just 10 minutes from Breaux Bridge and 20 minutes from Lafayette has the densest population of water birds, nutrias, and alligators I have seen anywhere. Many of the alligators dozing along the edge are 10 to 15 feet long. One of the great things about Lake Martin is its accessibility. Three miles of shoreline can be traveled by car (including the rookery), and the entire seven-mile levee surrounding the lake may be hiked. (I recommend not allowing small dogs off their leashes.) Better yet, rent a canoe from Wiltz Landing in Henderson (see review). Naturally, the best time for bird watching and spotting wildlife is in the cool of the morning and evening.

A portion of the swamp owned by the Nature Conservancy contains the largest white-ibis rookery in the world. The ibis are joined by a variety of herons, egrets, cormorants, and beautiful roseate spoonbills. During spring and autumn, thousands of migratory birds flit through the cypress.

Guided swamp tours of the lake are reviewed below. There are no rest rooms or commercial facilities. From Bridge Street in downtown Breaux Bridge drive 2.7 miles south on Rte. 31. Turn right on Lake Martin Road (which becomes gravel). Two miles from the turnoff the road stops at the lake at a boat launch. A right turn from the launch takes you .75 mile to a dirt turnaround. A left turn at the launch runs 2 miles along Rookery Road (the section of swamp owned by the Nature Conservancy).

Atchafalaya Experience Swamp Tours Lake Martin, Breaux Bridge.

This is one of two tours operating primarily in beautiful Lake Martin (see description above). Lake Martin is one of the premier spots anywhere for observing wildlife, especially birds. A large portion of the lake is owned by the Nature Conservancy and includes the biggest shorebird rookery in North America! The sentinels of the rookery are alligators who consume many of the birds' natural predators. These gators are numerous and as big as any I have seen. Both operators at Lake Martin are knowledgeable of the flora, fauna, and history of the area and both have rather expansive personalities. French-speaking visitors may prefer this tour since Coerte Voorhies speaks fluent French. Voorhies also offers tours in other areas. Tours are offered by appointment. They are about one and a half hours and cost $30 per person. (318) 233-7816.

★de la Houssaye's Swamp Tours Lake Martin, Breaux Bridge.

Marcus de la Houssaye has one big advantage over most other tour

operators, and that is Lake Martin (see description above). This is one
of the great spots in South Louisiana for observing wildlife, particularly birds and alligators, since much of the lake is owned and pro-
tected by the Nature Conservancy. de la Houssaye breeds and trains
championship Catahoulas (the state dog) and a couple of these
accompany the tour. I found them amusing and they were usually the
first to spot alligators. (If you don't like dogs this is not the tour for
you.) de la Houssaye is extremely knowledgeable, but like his competition at Lake Martin, he has a very large personality. de la Houssaye
bumps his small craft through shallow places and over logs to where
you look into the eyes of alligators and nests of birds. Tours cost $20
for adults and $5 for children and are by appointment only. (318) 845-
5332.

ATTRACTIONS

★Downtown Breaux Bridge

The old downtown district, which runs for six blocks on either side
of the bayou on Bridge Street and as many blocks north and south
on Main Street (Rte. 31), can be easily enjoyed in a couple of hours.
From I-10 take exit #109 and head south on Rte. 328 (Reese Street)
for 1.7 miles. Turn right on Rte. 336-1 (Bridge Street) and cross the
bridge. Park at the Visitors Center or near the intersection of Bridge
Street and Main for a walking tour. You will find a half-dozen antique
shops and a couple of bars near the intersection. A block towards the
bridge in an old storefront is the fabulous Café Des Amis, a great stop
for a Cajun breakfast, a full-blown dinner, or a cup of rich coffee (see
review in Food section). The cafe has become the spiritual center of
the historic district, frequented by area artists and decorated with
their work. Most of the buildings in the district were built in the late
1800s and early 1900s. Among the interesting establishments are
Broussards Hardware Store (1922) at the corner of Main Street and
Bridge Street and the *Kidder Building* (1909) across the street, which
once functioned as a tavern, dance hall, and cockpit. The *O. Badon
House* (1869) on East Bridge Street, a half-block off Main, is one of the
few Acadian-style homes remaining in town. Two Bed and Breakfasts
on Bayou Teche beside the bridge (see Lodging section) afford visitors the chance to enjoy the pace of life downtown.

Parc des Ponts Bridge Street at Bayou Teche, downtown.

Parc des Ponts (Park of the Bridges) is a narrow green space along
Bayou Teche. There is a model of a Civil War-era bridge moored on
the waterfront, useful for picnics, fishing, or loafing. There are also
sheltered stone benches commemorating the various bridges that

have spanned the bayou and an engraved Indian legend of the bayou. Most impressive is a simple black line on a nearby flagpole that marks the height of the Mississippi floodwaters during the disaster of 1927. Parc des Ponts is tucked away behind Teche Liquors right beside the bridge. You can park at the Visitors Center and walk across the street.

Breaux Bridge Oaks Berard Fas and Courthouse streets, downtown.

A vigilante committee of 200 men reportedly lynched two outlaws on these oaks in 1882. The trees are now registered with the Live Oak Society.

★Crawfish Festival

This may be the most Cajun of South Louisiana's fairs and festivals. It celebrates a critter that has not only touched every life in the small towns of Upper Teche Country but has become a symbol of the culture itself. Breaux Bridge claims that the restaurant at the Hebert Hotel downtown (no longer standing) was the first eatery to serve crawfish preparations, bragging that Herbert Hoover ate crawfish there in 1927 when he was sent by President Coolidge to survey damage wrought by the great flood. Since the city was proclaimed Crawfish Capital of the World in 1959, the festival has been an annual event. In the mid-nineties a fondly remembered tradition died when the Downtown Merchants Association quit sponsoring a massive street party during the festival. (The handwriting was on the wall when antique shops began to outnumber barrooms.) The beer and music is now confined to Parc Hardy, where crawfish are sold in every form imaginable. Over 200,000 celebrants gather to compete in and watch crawfish-eating contests (the record is over 33 pounds in an hour!), crawfish races, and the crawfish parachute jump. In addition to carnival rides, there are live-music stages featuring some of the best Cajun and Zydeco bands. The festival is always the first full weekend in May, running from 5 Friday evening to 5 Sunday. Admission is $5. (318) 332-6655.

Rte. 94, Lafayette to Breaux Bridge

Before there was an interstate, Rte. 94 was the main road between the Hub City and its rustic neighbor, Breaux Bridge. The 8-mile stretch of road is still called "Lafayette Highway" by folks in Breaux Bridge and "Old Breaux Bridge Highway" by those in Lafayette. One and a half miles from Lafayette the road suddenly drops down the long, steep incline that was once the western bank of the Teche Basin. During the great flood of 1927, the combined flows of the Mississippi and Atchafalaya rivers formed a nearly unbroken sheet of water between this ridge and the state capital, 50 miles away in Baton Rouge. Evacuees from Breaux Bridge, Atchafalaya, and Pelba were brought by boat to this point for transportation to tent cities.

FOOD

★Bayou Boudin and Cracklin Local Fave, $. 100 Mills Ave. (Rte. 94) on the bayou.

If you are driving on the interstate and want a quick plunge into pure Cajun culture, pay a visit to Rocky and Lisa Sonnier at Bayou Cracklin. This is one of those places where the experience is greater than the sum of its parts! The store is in an authentic Acadian cabin by Bayou Teche. Get a snack and a homemade root beer or one of Rocky's tasty Sunday dinners and eat it on a screened porch overlooking the water. There are also tables inside where locals chat in English or French and listen to Cajun and Swamp Pop music on the radio. Rocky has won awards for his cracklins, but my favorites are the Sunday barbecue and fricassee, the boudin balls (floured and fried), and the crawfish boudin. You can sleep on the bayou in one of the Sonniers' six Bed and Breakfast cabins (see Bayou Cabins in the Lodging section). From I-10, take exit #109 and head south on Rte. 328 (Reese Street). Turn right on Rte. 94 (Mills Avenue) and Bayou Boudin is about a mile down on the right. Hours are 7 A.M. to 6 P.M. daily. (318) 332-6158.

★Café Des Amis Cajun/Creole, $-$$. 140 E. Bridge St.

This is the new culinary and social center of Breaux Bridge and one of the best restaurants you could hope to find within 10 minutes of Interstate 10. My favorite distraction while writing this book has been daydreaming about a breakfast of pastry-wrapped boudin and black coffee at Café Des Amis! All of the breakfasts here are just sensational, although lunch and dinner are no less dream worthy. Local ingredients like crawfish, catfish, andouille, cane syrup, and softshell crabs are used in a consistently good South Louisiana cuisine. Try seafood and corn soup or shrimp and okra gumbo (I like mine with a scoop of potato salad in it) as starters and move on to fried eggplant wheels topped with crawfish etouffée or crabmeat au gratin. A small salad accompanies each entree or may be purchased as an accompaniment to soup and sandwich. On a recent visit, dessert selections included three icebox pies and the Cajun specialty Gâteau Sirop (spice cake made with cane syrup). I tell pals to go to Café Des Amis and if they do not like it, dinner is on me. The atmosphere in this renovated store is so open and the wait staff so hospitable that wherever you are from, you will likely feel that you are dining among friends. The cafe is open Tuesday, Wednesday, and Sunday from 8 A.M. to 3 P.M. and Thursday through Saturday until 10 P.M. (318) 332-5273.

Goulas Grocery Cracklins. Rte. 351 at Rte. 31 South.

Goulas makes cracklins and fresh boudin every Saturday morning.

Get there early and you can get the cracklins hot out of the pot. They are small and moderately seasoned morsels. This little country grocery also sells cold drinks and beer to wash 'em down. Goulas is three miles north of St. Martinville, visible from Rte. 31. (318) 332-6006.

Mulate's Cajun/Creole/Seafood/Dance hall, $$-$$$. 325 Mills Ave. (Rte. 94).

For most of fifty years, Mulate's has been a restaurant and dance hall, but it was not until Kerry Boutte took over the place in 1980 that it became "the world's most famous Cajun restaurant." Although the food here is not special, you will find Cajun favorites like boiled crawfish, etouffée, jambalaya, and gumbo, served to the tune of live Cajun bands every night and at lunch on weekends.

The music can be excellent. Boutte established Mulate's reputation by bringing in up-and-coming bands like Zachary Richard and Beausoleil, who went on to stardom. You can still count on hearing good music and finding the dance floor that runs through the heart of the place filled with couples. Mulate's manages to be a tourist attraction without being a tourist trap and remains a good place to find music when the old-time dance halls are quiet. From I-10, take exit #109 and head towards Breaux Bridge. Turn right on Mills Avenue (Rte. 94) and Mulate's is about a mile down on the left. (318) 332-4648, 1-800-634-9880, or 1-800-42-CAJUN.

Mulate's. (Photo by Julie Posner)

Poche's Meat Market and Restaurant Down Home, $. Rte. 31 North.

Poche's meats and lunches are mighty good for a place with billboards on the interstate. You can get everything from a bag of cracklins and pound of boudin to go to sweet-dough pies and plate lunches at this modern stop-and-shop. There is plenty of indoor seating but most people buy to go. I usually stop for a few cracklins and a beer and to check the price of peeled crawfish meat (often on sale). Lunches (including the Sunday barbecue and crawfish etouffée) are under $6. From downtown Breaux Bridge, take Rte. 31 north (under the Interstate) two miles. From Interstate 10, take exit #109 north (Rte. 328). Go two miles and turn left on Poche Bridge Road. The restaurant is just over the bridge at the intersection with Rte. 31. It is open daily from 5:30 A.M. to 9 P.M. Lunch is served from 11 to 2, dinner from 5:30 to 8. (318) 332-2108.

MUSIC

Breaux Bridge is a Cajun and Zydeco bar-hopper's paradise. In most other places there are one or two dance halls that stand out as special places. The Breaux Bridge area has at least five that I would highly recommend.

Caffery's Alexander Ranch Zin Zin Road, Au Large (east of Breaux Bridge).

Talk about an obscure location! Half the people I asked in Breaux Bridge had never heard of the little Creole community about 6 miles southeast of town, much less Zin Zin Road. This club is worth hunting down. The dance hall is a huge screened patio with overhead fans for cooling. Dances are held on an irregular basis, so call in advance to find out what is going on. Actually, you may want to go out and see the place during the day. It is a beautiful drive and you can stop by the trailer next door and get a music schedule from Mrs. Caffery. A mark of this community's isolation is the super-rare Elvis Sun 45 I found at a little junk shop on Zin Zin Road (where it was being used as "money" by kids "playing store"). From I-10 go south at exit #109 (Reese Street) to Bridge Street. Take a left onto Bridge Street and go 1.4 miles. Take a right onto Doyle Melancon Road (Rte. 347). Go 1.7 miles on Doyle Melancon. At Zin Zin Road take a left. Go 2 miles on Zin Zin (the road curves to the left). Caffery's Ranch is on the left on the corner of Zin Zin Road and Latiolais Loop Road. (318) 332-5415.

Davis Lounge Zydeco dance hall. Rte. 31, Cecilia.

Like the Friendly Lounge, Davis has a very irregular schedule of dances and trail rides, and occasionally they have a soul DJ. Call first to get the scoop. From Interstate 10, take exit #109 north (Rte. 328). Go two miles and turn left on Poche Bridge Road. Cross Bayou Teche and make a right on Rte. 31. Davis Lounge is two miles north of the Poche Bridge. From downtown Breaux Bridge, take Rte. 31 north about three miles.

★**Double D Cotton Club** Zydeco dance hall. St. Louis Dr., Parks.

Also known as **Dauphine's Tuxedo Club,** this is a very funky dance hall "way out in the country." Parks is a small Creole farming community that grew just south of Ruth Plantation on the eastern bank of Bayou Teche (about 7 miles south of Breaux Bridge). Between the bayou and Rte. 347 (which follows the eastern bank) are rows of one- and two-room homes. According to Zydeco authority and DJ Herbert Wiltz, in the fifties and sixties Parks had a couple of clubs and used to get some of the major acts on the Chitlin' Circuit. This is surprising when you consider how rural the area is, but it all makes sense when you see the cars lining up for a Saturday-night dance at Dauphine's. People from scattered farms between the bayou and the basin drive for miles to get down at the Double D. From Breaux Bridge, take Rte. 31 south 5 miles to the town of Parks. At the *T* in the road turn left and cross the bayou

Double D Cotton Club dance hall. (Photo by Julie Posner)

on Rte. 350. Turn right onto Rte. 347 and go .3 mile. Turn left on St. Louis Drive (beside the large green church) and the club is a few blocks down on the left. (318) 394-9616 or 845-4880.

Friendly Lounge Zydeco dance hall. Rte. 31, Cecilia.

This building looks as if it only needs a good strong wind to fall down, but it withstands the pounding of dancing feet a couple of times a month. Call first to find out if, and when, there is a dance. From Interstate 10, take exit #109 north (Rte. 328). Go two miles and turn left on Poche Bridge Road. Cross Bayou Teche and make a right on Rte. 31. The Friendly Lounge is two miles north of the Poche Bridge. From downtown Breaux Bridge, take Rte. 31 north about four miles. (318) 667-8543.

Harry's Cajun dance hall. 519 Parkway Dr., Breaux Bridge.

From the outside Harry's looks more like a corrugated-steel warehouse than a dance hall, but step inside on a Sunday evening and you will find an enormous dance floor crowded with old-time dancers who glide when they waltz. The lighting is suitably dim, and with a warm glow from the bar, the place feels surprisingly cozy. Harry's is about two minutes from I-10. At exit #109 head south .5 mile on Rte. 328 (Reese Street). Turn left on Parkway. Harry's is about a half-block down on the left. A Cajun band plays every Sunday night from 5 to 9. Occasionally there is a Swamp Pop or Cajun band on Saturday night. Admission is $3. (318) 332-6852.

★La Poussiere 1301 Grand Point Rd. (Rte. 347 East).

Looking for a Cajun Saturday night? This is the real thing. Since the 1960s, Walter Mouton and the Scott Playboys have been playing the Saturday-night dance at this wide and low dance hall on the outskirts of Breaux Bridge. Unlike the young couples who twine like pretzels on the dance floors at popular "dine & dance" joints, the older crowd here dances light and close. Even the fast songs are danced chest to chest with amazing grace. Admission is only a couple of bucks, and the music starts early, so you can check out La Poussiere on the way to one of the neighboring Zydeco halls. From I-10 at Breaux Bridge take Rte. 328 south until it ends. Turn left on Bridge Street (Rte. 336-1). Make the first right, then the first left on Rte. 347 (Grand Point Road). La Poussiere is .25 mile east on Rte. 347. There is a Cajun dance every Saturday night from 8:30 "until." (318) 332-1721.

★Mulate's Cajun dance hall/Restaurant. 325 Mills Ave. (Rte. 94).

See description under Food section above.

Swamps Tavern Cajun dance hall. 2742 Grand Point Rd. (Rte. 347), Henderson.

See Henderson music listings below.

★Whiskey River Landing Cajun dance hall. Levee Road, Henderson. Sunday afternoon dance. See Henderson music listings below.

LODGING

Bed and Breakfasts:

★Bayou Cabins 100 Mills Ave. (Rte. 94), Breaux Bridge.

A night at Bayou Cabins is what you might call a Cajun immersion program. The six small cabins behind Bayou Boudin and Cracklin sit on the banks of Bayou Teche within walking distance of Mulate's dance hall. When you check in you get a complimentary boudin and cracklin tray with glasses of cold homemade root beer. You can eat these on the screened porch at the cafe, where host Rocky Sonnier is usually listening to Cajun music, or walk down the hill to your cabin and enjoy them on a private deck over the bayou. In the morning you get a full Cajun breakfast. The cabins are simple, containing little more than a double bed and small bathroom. The sheets are polyester and there is no mattress pad, but it is hard to argue with the romance of a cabin on the bayou. Rocky and Lisa Sonnier speak a little Cajun French and have employees at the store who are more fluent. Visa and American Express credit cards are accepted. At $50 to $60 the cabins cost less than most motel rooms. (318) 332-6158.

★House Boat Adventures Levee Road, Henderson.

See Henderson listings.

★Maison Des Amis On Bayou Teche, downtown Breaux Bridge.

Maison Des Amis is tastefully decorated, perfectly comfortable, and well situated for visitors to enjoy the sights (and flavors) of downtown Breaux Bridge. This B&B operates in a historic Caribbean Creole cottage on the bayou. Common areas used by all guests include an enclosed air-conditioned porch and a gazebo over the Teche. The porch contains a refrigerator, telephone, and coffee-making supplies. There are three guest rooms, each with private entrance, private bath, comfortable queen-size bed with luxurious pillows and cotton sheets, reading lamps, and cotton robes in the closet. Walls are adorned with folk art and the work of local photographers. Hosts Dickie and Cynthia Breaux do not live in but can be found around the corner at Café Des Amis (one of the best restaurants in Cajun Country). Guests are served breakfast at the cafe and it is a meal not to be missed (see review). Dickie and Cynthia speak French. A room for two costs $70-$85 and is payable with credit card, check, or cash. (318) 332-5273.

Country Oaks Bed and Breakfast Cabins 1138A Lawless Tauzin Rd.

The five "cabins" at Country Oaks are actually restored antique cottages. They were transported from around the area to a wooded 14-acre site just outside Breaux Bridge by hosts Jim and Judy Allen and now surround a fishing pond stocked with largemouth bass. Each cottage is furnished with kitchen, private bath, comfortable furniture, and barbecue grill. My favorite is "Little Cypress," which has laundry facilities and room to set things down and stretch out. In the other cottages I felt hemmed in by collections of stuffed animals, ornaments, and religious books. Jim Allen hosted a fishing show on the local CBS television affiliate and he is serious when he says the pond is fishable. (A former guest raved about catching an eight-pounder!) Fishing gear is available, as is the use of a small boat and paddles. In addition to the Bible verses on the walls and religious tracts in each room, guests should be prepared for the owners' Christian testimonial during the communal breakfast. (The breakfast is very good.) The Allens ask that guests refrain from consuming alcoholic beverages on premises. The double rate is $85 ($15 for each extra person). Cash or checks are accepted. (318) 332-3093 or 1-800-318-2423.

Hotel/Motel:

Best Western I-10 at exit #109, $65-$75 double.

Henderson

Henderson has the fortune (or misfortune) to be the first exit on Interstate 10 on the western side of the wide Atchafalaya Throughway. The town is located on the edge of the Atchafalaya Basin about 5 miles east of Breaux Bridge (12 miles from Lafayette). It is not surprising that most people who drive past see Henderson as a town of billboards, restaurants, and service stations. In fact, the town has two other distinct areas, the old "line village," which stretches east from near the interstate to the Atchafalaya Basin Levee, and a strip of Basin-side restaurants and recreational facilities that stretches 7 miles south along the Atchafalaya Basin Levee Road. The latter is a great place to rent a canoe or small motorboat for a self-guided spin through the Henderson Swamp or (for the less adventurous) to get onto one of the large tour boats that chugs through the area.

Henderson landed on the state map in 1971, when it incorporated and elected a mayor. The nucleus of the town, however, was born of disaster almost half a century earlier. Until the thirties, the site was little more than wide, moist fields pressed against the low levees of the Atchafalaya Basin. In 1927, the Mississippi and Atchafalaya rivers raged above their banks and destroyed the homes of those living in the interior Basin villages of Pelba, Atchafalaya, and Bayou Chene (as well as hundreds of other communities throughout the Mississippi Valley). Flood waters pounded the levee system and broke through just south of present-day Henderson, at what became known as the Cypremort Crevasse. From this and other levee faults, the water rushed into neighboring towns, reaching 12 feet in nearby Breaux Bridge. Evacuees lived in makeshift tent cities in Lafayette. Months later, when the water finally subsided, former residents of the Basin moved their houses by barge to new communities like Henderson, Catahoula, and Coteau Homes, which sprung up on the dry side of the new levee system.

For 40 years after the flood, Henderson (then called Lenora) remained isolated on the edge of the Basin. Residents engaged in their former pursuits, operating apiaries, boat building, fishing, and net making. Following the development of the first planned crawfish pond in 1959, the fields around Henderson were devoted to this new

Refugees from the flood of 1927. (Courtesy of Lafayette Court-house Archives)

and lucrative industry. The town grew slowly in a line from its nucleus near the Atchafalaya Basin levee westward. When the difficult Atchafalaya Throughway portion of the interstate was completed in the seventies (using the hard labor of many Henderson residents who had once lived within its banks), Henderson was at last linked with Baton Rouge and New Orleans. The town's crawfish harvest quickly found its way to the new restaurants that sprang up to feed hungry travelers, and the town found its way onto the map. There is plenty of good food near the interstate in Henderson, but the most interesting experiences await those who make the 10-minute drive to the restaurants, swamp tours, and boat rental facilities along the Levee Road.

To get to the Levee Road you must first get off the interstate in Henderson at exit #115. One block south of the highway turn left on Rte. 352. This route carries you three miles east through the old "line village" before ending at a stream known locally as Bayou Amy, which is actually the borrow pit from which the Corps of Engineers removed dirt to create the new levee system. Cross Bayou Amy and turn right atop the levee to reach the recreational facilities, restaurants, and wateringholes of the Levee Road.

RECREATION

The biggest recreational attraction in Henderson is obviously the Atchafalaya Basin Swamp. Whether you rent a boat, bring your own, or go on one of the commercial tours, any visitor to the area should see this watery region. Two of the biggest swamp tours in the state depart from Henderson; both accommodate tour-bus customers on their large pontoon boats. These operators have the advantage of being only 15 minutes off the interstate. Although this part of the Basin is lovely during the high water of spring, its accessibility makes it one of the most heavily trafficked areas. When the water goes down in the fall, you can see the cypress stumps left behind by a thoughtless lumber industry, and abandoned oil pipelines. Folks forging out on their own in a canoe or on an airboat can avoid these somewhat disturbing sights.

★**Wiltz Landing: Boat/Canoe Rentals and Bait** Levee Road.

This is the only canoe and boat rental operator on the Basin. Canoes are a great value at $12 a day, while jonboats with six-horsepower motors go for $35 (includes $3 of gas). There is a $1-per-day charge for paddles and life preservers. Neither the canoes nor the jonboats go fast, but some of the most beautiful scenery in the area is within 10 minutes of the launch. Pack a lunch, get bait and directions at the landing, and you can have a day to yourself in Henderson Swamp, or tie a canoe on your roof and drive over to Lake Martin (see

Henderson swamp tour. (Courtesy of Louisiana Office of Tourism)

Breaux Bridge Recreation). Wiltz Landing is less than a mile south on the Levee Road. (318) 228-2430.

Angelle's Atchafalaya Swamp Tours Whiskey River Landing, Levee Road.

Angelle's is one of the two big tour companies serving the Henderson Swamp in big, covered, party-barge-style boats. The Angelles are descendants of a family that once lived in the Basin town of Pelba. In fact, Murphy Angelle, born in 1910 and the oldest former resident of the village, can often be found hanging around the landing. The business is family run and the Angelles treat tourists to tales of the old life in the Basin and the destruction wrought by the oil, gas, and lumber industries. The tour offers a good view of this desecration as well as a "down under" view of the Atchafalaya Basin I-10 twin spans. Angelle's is popular with tour-bus operators so there is almost always a group to join. On slow days they will still go out for a minimum of $25. Follow the signs to Whiskey River Landing, which is the third exit on the Levee Road, 1.7 miles from the Bayou Amy Bridge. Tours cost $12 for adults and $6 for children. Advance reservations are recommended. French-speaking guides are available. Boats depart at 10, 1, 3, and 5. (318) 667-6135 or 228-8567.

McGee's Atchafalaya Basin Swamp Tours McGee's Landing, Levee Road.

McGee's is one of two tour companies operating large, covered pontoon boats in the Henderson Swamp. The Allemand family has been running a boat landing at this site since the fifties, and from the youngest to the oldest, they know the swamp by heart and offer tours in French and English. This slow, two-hour cruise covers a four- to five-mile radius from the launch, basically the same ground as the other local operators. You will pass under the I-10 spans, see oil and gas pipelines and platforms, and camp boats of part-time Basin dwellers. There is a lot of recreational boat traffic in this part of the Basin, but guides communicate by walkie-talkie to inform one another of where wildlife sightings are occurring, so you usually will see a good variety of animals. You may get a drink or dinner at McGee's Landing Restaurant when you get back to the dock. Follow the signs to McGee's Landing, which is 2.5 miles south on the Levee Road. Tours cost $12 for adults and $6 for kids. Boats leave at 10, 1, 3, and 5. (318) 228-2384, 228-8519, or 228-7555 (cafe).

ATTRACTIONS

Atchafalaya Basin Levee Road

The entire Atchafalaya Basin is surrounded by flood-protection levees. Along the base and the crest of these levees are narrow roads used by farmers, fishermen, and levee inspection crews. Most of these roads are gravel, but the first seven miles south of I-10 are paved. Nowhere is there more convenient access from the interstate to the swamps of the Basin than at the Levee Road in Henderson. Just 10 minutes from the highway, the Levee Road provides opportunities to visit the swamp by canoe, motorboat, or large tour barge. Driving south past McGee's Landing, the old flood-damaged levee is visible inside the new one, as is the huge gap of the Cypremort Crevasse. Those looking for a drink or a meal with a view of the swamp have a couple of good choices in the two-mile stretch of Levee Road immediately south of I-10. The road atop the levee is occasionally posted with No Trespassing signs, but in the seven-mile stretch between Henderson and the Butte La Rose Bridge (*see* Butte La Rose below), vehicles often ignore these postings and operate with impunity. From the top of the embankment, you can look east at the sparkling waters of

Henderson Lake and the houseboats along its shores. On the west, the clover-covered levee slopes down to Bayou Amy.

FOOD

Chicken on the Bayou Local Fave, $. I-10 exit #115.

Chicken on the Bayou is a small sandwich shop and seafood joint located in a tourist enclave beside I-10 at Henderson. It deserves a mention because it offers travelers a chance to hop off the highway and snag a unique taste of Louisiana like alligator, gator sausage, crawfish po' boys, crawfish etouffée, and boudin. The menu also lists "alligator wings," which I have not tried. It is located on Rte. 347 beside the candy shop (do not confuse it with Landry's) at the Henderson exit. Chicken on the Bayou is open from 9:30 A.M. to 8:30 P.M. daily. (318) 667-6073.

★Crawfish Town USA Boiled Seafood, $-$$. Rte. 347 north, Henderson.

For a place that was built with tourists in mind and seats 400, I was surprised by how good the crawfish were here. I was even more surprised by some of the other seafood preparations. This is a huge place that does large-volume business, but the gumbo and jambalaya are as good as those served at many of the small mom-and-pop places off the beaten path. They welcome crowds arriving by tour bus, but the vast majority of patrons are discriminating locals who can appreciate a gumbo in which the seafood is added at the last moment and cooked to firm perfection. The restaurant has become a gathering spot for state politicos from Baton Rouge, who are allowed to put up a poster on the wall if they stop by for dinner.

Crawfish and crabs are the main attraction. They are clean and perfectly seasoned. I recommend getting the extrahot, which are not very spicy by Cajun standards. If you like your food hot-hot, just let the waitress know and the kitchen can accommodate your fiery whims. At peak hours, Crawfish Town USA is a perfectly noisy place to go with a gang of pals or a big family group that likes to whoop it up and make a mess. After gorging on boiled seafood, you can wash at sinks located right in the dining room. Mosey over to the bar while waiting for the food and check out a jukebox packed with Cajun, Swamp Pop, and Zydeco obscurities. Call ahead to see if Crawfish Town is running one of their weeknight "all you can eat" specials. Take I-10 exit #115 and go north .5 mile on Rte. 347. Hours are 5 to 9 P.M. Monday through Thursday and until 10:30 on Friday and Saturday. (318) 667-6148.

Pat's Fisherman's Wharf Restaurant Seafood, $$. Levee Road.

Pat's is the oldest and most famous seafood restaurant in Henderson. It is popular with the tour-bus crowd. I sampled all of the seafood dishes and the highlight was a "camp-style" etouffée, which was a simple saute of crawfish tails and large chunks of onion and bell pepper in butter. A lot of people were ordering Pat's latest special, which is a plate of jambalaya, crawfish pie, and filé gumbo for around $16. Half the fun of eating at Pat's is the casual atmosphere (plastic tablecloths and porch seating) and bayou-side location. There could hardly be a more lovely place to dine than the porch at Pat's, which overlooks Bayou Amy. In the evenings, you will need a can of bug spray on your table to ward off marauding mosquitoes. Grab a window seat, order a beer, and select one of Pat's crawfish dishes (other than boiled). Pat's is open daily, 10 A.M. to 10 P.M. Off of I-10 take exit #115 south. Make the first left on Rte. 352. Pat's is at the end of the road, across the bridge, between Bayou Amy and the levee. (318) 228-7110.

Robin's Seafood, $ (lunch)-$$. Rte. 352.

Robin's is one of Henderson's oldest and most popular seafood restaurants. Crawfish preparations are the focus of the menu, and the crowning achievement of the kitchen is a superb crawfish bisque. This thin but richly flavored soup is the color of brazil nuts and is spiked with thinly sliced green onions. At the bottom of each bowl, soaking up the dark broth, are crawfish heads stuffed with seasonings, bread crumbs, and chopped tail meat. Nearly everything at Robin's is made on the premises, including some absolutely delicious desserts. Wherever you eat in the area, Robin's should be your dessert stop. There are four flavors of homemade ice cream, of which I highly recommend the smooth, rich, Belgian chocolate or fig. The bread pudding is made with French bread and is lightly browned in places for a delightful combination of chewy and soft parts. It is topped with a sharp lemon sauce. Robin's is a bit less expensive than nearby competitors (offering sandwiches at lunch and dinner) but still puts linen and real butter on the tables. From I-10 take exit #115 south and turn left on Rte. 352. Robin's is two miles down on the left. Hours are Monday through Saturday from 11 A.M. to 10 P.M. and Sunday until 4 P.M. (318) 228-7594.

McGee's Atchafalaya Cafe Seafood/Swamp tours, $-$$. Levee Road.

Built on stilts beside McGee's Landing Swamp Tours, this restaurant has big windows and open-deck seating with a panoramic view of the Atchafalaya Basin. McGee's serves a broad variety of Cajun food, including such exotica as fried alligator, frogleg etouffée, turtle soup, catfish *courtbouillon*, and crawfish *maque choux*. For those with less adventuresome tastebuds, there is a selection of po' boys for under $6 as well as fried food and standard Cajun fare. With such a huge selection, the preparations here are less than perfect, but the menu, like everything else in this rustic cafe, is a lot of fun. Even if you are not hungry, there is no arguing the pleasure of a window seat and cold drink here after a tour of Henderson Swamp (*see* swamp tour reviews under Recreation). Take exit #115 south off I-10. Turn left on Rte. 352. At the levee, turn right on the Levee Road and go 2.5 miles. (318) 228-7555.

Webster's Meat Market Meat Market. Rte. 347, Cecilia.

I found this place on a tip from Pat Huval at Pat's Seafood Restaurant and are mighty grateful. Theirs is some of the best boudin east of Lafayette. Also fantastic are the Sunday "boucherie dinners" and barbecue plates. The building that houses the time-worn meat market was formerly Webster's Dance Hall, a jumping joint that once featured big names like Jimmy C. Newman and Happy Fats. Since the sixties, the old wood dance floor has been given over to meat cases, racks of Evangeline Maid Bread, and snack cakes. If you are on the trail of the "best boudin," you will want to give Webster's a try. From I-10, take exit #115 at Henderson and head north about one mile on Rte. 347. Webster's is open Monday through Friday from 7 A.M. to 5 P.M., Saturday until 2 P.M., and Sunday until noon. (318) 667-6231.

MUSIC

Swamps Tavern Cajun dance hall. Rte. 347 North, Henderson.

Swamps has a somewhat erratic music schedule but has some great Saturday-night crowds for performers like Belton Richard. It is located about a mile north of I-10 at the Henderson exit. (318) 667-7590.

★Whiskey River Landing Cajun dance hall. Levee Road, Henderson.

During the day Whiskey River Landing serves as departure point for Angelle's Swamp Tours (see review under Recreation) and a Basin boat launch. Early on Sunday evenings they open the doors for a big Cajun dance featuring popular musicians like Steve Riley and Joe Douglas. The band room has a good dance floor and windows overlooking the water. It is great fun to dance, have a beer, and watch the boats pulling in from a day on the Basin. The mix of fishermen, Cajun-dance enthusiasts, and recreational boaters makes for a colorful crowd. There is usually someone grilling and selling hamburgers on the deck outside. The music starts at 4 and admission is $3. (318) 228-8567 or 667-6135.

Secluded site for a House Boat Adventure. (Photo by Macon Fry)

LODGING

★House Boat Adventures Access at Levee Road, Henderson (I-10 exit #115).

Whether you want to get away from it all or take an unforgettable trip with family or pals, House Boat Adventures offers a remarkable experience. Owner Doug Sebatier tows his houseboats to prime locations in the Atchafalaya Basin where guests can swim, fish, and relax in solitude. Each boat has full-size bunk beds in one room and a comfortable futon sofa bed in the living room/kitchen. Boats are equipped with full baths with hot showers, air conditioners, ceiling fans, TVs, and VCRs. Except for the hot showers you probably won't need all the amenities. I enjoyed sitting on the porch swing as the sun settled over the Basin and a fierce chorus of frogs welled up around us. One morning I drank coffee on the deck in the company of an egret not 10 feet away. To do the trip right you need at least two nights. A small boat and motor or pirogue are provided for recreational use. Doug's son Stephen is an aspiring fishing guide who specializes in taking novice anglers (everyone catches a fish). He will meet guests at their boat for a couple of hours' fishing for $10 per person. Departures are from Cypress Cove Landing, about seven miles south of Henderson on the Levee Road (20 minutes from I-10). The boats rent for $145 a night plus a $25 towing and gas fee. Prices are less for weeknights and the cool-weather months (the best times to be in the Basin). Visa, Mastercard, check, or cash are accepted. Advance reservations are required. (318) 824-4662 or 1-800-491-4662.

Lake Fausse Pointe Park Campground Levee Road, Catahoula.

See St. Martinville section for information on this fine recreational area about 30 miles south of Henderson on the Levee Road.

Butte La Rose Campgrounds and Camp Rental

See Butte La Rose (below) for additional accommodations in the Henderson area.

Butte La Rose

Located several miles west of Henderson on a patch of high ground beside the Atchafalaya River (actually inside of the Basin levees) is the town of Butte La Rose. This was the site of a fort during the War Between the States but is now covered with camps occupied by Lafayette weekenders and a few hardy full-timers. The strip of land has a couple of quiet campgrounds and a cabin for rent and offers a scenic loop route off of Interstate 10. Just take the Butte La Rose exit (about 20 minutes east of Lafayette) and head south on Rte. 105. Rte. 105 becomes Rte. 3177 and turns westward to join the Atchafalaya Basin Levee below Henderson. It is about eight miles from the interstate to the Levee Road. To complete the loop just drive north about seven miles on the Levee Road to Rte. 352, which will take you back to I-10 at the Henderson exit.

Frenchman's Wilderness Campground Butte La Rose, just off I-10.

Frenchman's Wilderness is on a large, verdant site just south of I-10 at the Butte La Rose exit. It has all the amenities, including a small swimming pool and clean showers. Rates for tents with partial hookups are $10; full hookups are $12.50. (318) 228-2616.

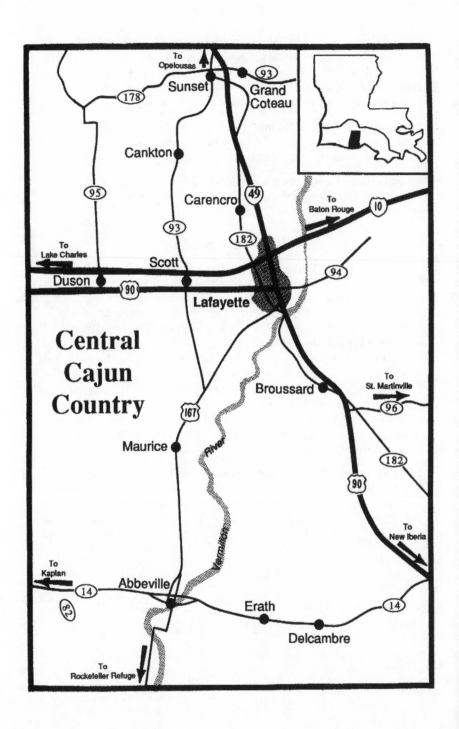

13

Central Cajun Country

Central Cajun Country is not a distinct geographic region but the name we've chosen to describe the hub city of Lafayette and the surrounding area. It includes the horse country and hills north to the tranquil village of Grand Coteau, farm hamlets that have become bedroom communities for Lafayette like Broussard and Scott, and historic Abbeville on the banks of the Vermilion River 15 miles south. The area was settled predominantly by Cajuns and remains a great place to seek out Cajun and Creole food and music. As it is the cosmopolitan crossroads of Cajun Country, most visitors will spend some time in the Lafayette vicinity. It is important when reading this chapter to remember that there are many attractions in other regions, especially Teche Country and Cajun Heartland, that are within 20 minutes and are logical destinations for visitors to Central Cajun Country.

LAFAYETTE

Known as the Hub City and Cajun Capital of South Louisiana, Lafayette (metro area population about 105,000) is the largest city in Cajun Country. It rests on the banks of Bayou Vermilion, with one foot beside the wild Atchafalaya Basin and the other on the rural Cajun Prairie. The seat of parish government, Lafayette is a world oil center, housing the offices of Louisiana's offshore petroleum industry. It is also the home of the University of Southwestern Louisiana (USL), whose students make up 20 percent of the population. Motorists entering town by interstate are heralded by a plethora of billboards, but behind the superhighway and suburban veneer you find small neighborhoods, great restaurants, and lively dance halls. Lafayette is remarkably safe and clean and has an attractive old downtown area that has managed to keep its shops open while avoiding cute remodeling.

Situated at the intersection of Louisiana's main north-south (Interstate 49) and east-west (Interstate 10) highways, Lafayette is within 90 minutes of most major attractions in Cajun Country. Its central location and wide variety of accommodations make it a great place to stay

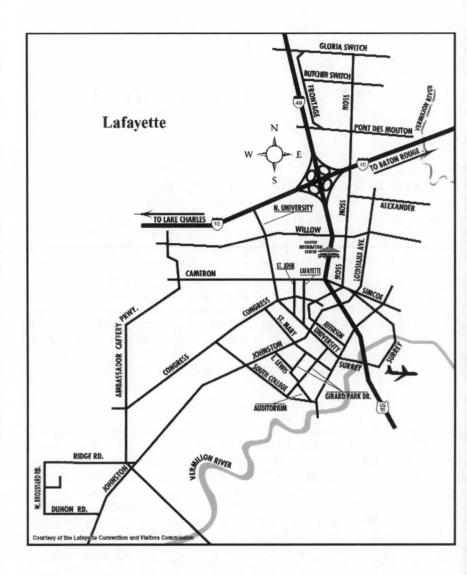

Lafayette

Courtesy of the Lafayette Convention and Visitors Commission

while exploring the Cajun hinterlands. You can become acquainted with the Cajun people and their culture by visiting the Cajun Cultural Center (operated by Jean Lafitte National Park), two Cajun historical theme parks and museums, and the Louisiana room at the USL library. Each spring the Festival International as well as the colorful blooms along the Azalea and Camellia trails draw thousands of visitors to the Hub City. The biggest event in Acadiana takes place in the fall, when Lafayette hosts the Festivals Acadiens, a free four-day celebration of Cajun music, food, and crafts.

History

EARLY SETTLEMENT

The first permanent white denizens of the area that is now Lafayette were Acadians who initially settled along Bayou Teche. Following conflicts with the aristocratic European Creole community around St. Martinville, they moved westward to the area of present-day Lafayette in the 1770s. A settlement of small ranches and farms grew just above the intersection of Bayou Tortue and the Vermilion River (generally called a river south of the city and "Bayou Vermilion" to the north). A dispute arose between Acadian landholder Jean Mouton and Anglo speculator John Reeves. Both were determined to establish the official town site on their holdings. Mouton won by donating the land on which a church and courthouse square were erected in 1812. In 1836, the town was granted a charter and named Vermilionville. In the 20 years prior to the War Between the States, Vermilionville prospered. The river was opened to steamboat navigation, providing a direct link to markets in Brashear (Morgan City). Rice became the main crop, and the city was on its way to becoming a hub of commerce and culture.

CIVIL WAR ERA

While Lafayette grew peacefully, things were not so placid on the surrounding prairie. With local police preoccupied by the fear of slave rebellions, outlaws terrorized the surrounding countryside. In 1859, vigilante committees were conscripted to stem the tide of lawlessness. Bands of armed men rode out of Lafayette, Broussard, and other nearby towns. Historian Carl Brasseaux described the vigilante movement as "unsurpassed in the history of the antebellum South." The movement rapidly outgrew the crime problem and became a tool for punishment and expulsion of those believed to be "undesirable." Although Louisiana's great war hero, Gen. Alfred Mouton of

Downtown Lafayette about 1930. (Courtesy of Lafayette Courthouse Archives)

Lafayette, was a Cajun, few of the local populace were slave holders,
and most had more heart for fighting outlaws than Yankees. Large
numbers of Cajun conscripts deserted or surrendered to Union forces
during the several Northern occupations of Lafayette.

REBUILDING

In 1880, the Louisiana and Texas Railroad arrived in Lafayette,
and by 1883, the line was complete to San Francisco. The following
year Vermilionville became Lafayette. Commerce and public education grew rapidly and the city began to attract many educated and
upwardly mobile Cajuns. The discovery of oil in Anse La Butte (near
present-day Breaux Bridge) and the bringing in of the Cankton and
Bosco fields in the early 1900s fostered the location of oil interests in
the city. South Louisiana Industrial Institute (now the University of
Southwest Louisiana) opened in 1920, and Lafayette became the educational center for all of Cajun South Louisiana.

OIL BOOM

A new era in Lafayette began in 1952 when local businessman Maurice Heymann opened an office complex targeting Louisiana's nascent
offshore oil industry. The complex of low-lying buildings, known as the

Heymann Oil Center, became a Mecca for the industry and, by 1959, housed 250 companies. This growth touched off cataclysmic changes in the character of Lafayette. Between 1960 and 1970 the population grew from around 40,000 to 70,000, with only 2 percent of the residents earning a living by farming. Many of the newcomers were Protestant oilmen and their families. Other new residents were students at USL, which began to attract scholars from around the country to its computer and engineering programs. Oil growth between 1950 and 1980 and the corresponding growth of USL led to a flowering of fine and popular arts in Lafayette. The city became a veritable boom town.

BUST

The collapse of world oil prices in the 1980s caused economic ruin in Lafayette since every sector of the local economy relied in some way on the influx of oil dollars. Small oil-related companies folded, and others slashed operations and closed offices. Unemployment reached double digits as thousands of untrained and poorly educated oilfield workers lost jobs and hit the streets. By 1986, the rate of bank failures exceeded that of the Great Depression.

PRESENT

The oil debacle of the eighties led to a diversification of the local economy, with tourism one of the fastest growing areas. The national interest in food, music, and all things Cajun has boosted an economic recovery and brought a new awareness among locals of the region's uniqueness. By the late nineties a resurgence began in the offshore oil patch. Local spirits are soaring, but nobody wants to hear the word "boom" again.

Getting There

BY CAR

Lafayette is three and a half hours from Houston, two hours from New Orleans, and an hour and a half from Alexandria by car. You will need a car in Lafayette to appreciate the city's position as a geographic hub of Cajun Country. All the major car-rental companies serve Lafayette. National, Thrifty, Avis, and Hertz have service at the Lafayette Regional Airport. You can also try one of the rental companies that claim to be discount agencies, Rent-A-Wreck, (800) 554-7433, or Easy Discount Auto Rentals, (318) 234-8716. Cab service is provided by Acadiana Yellow Cab, (318) 237-5701. For more on driving in Cajun Country see the introductory chapter "Transportation."

BY RAIL

Lafayette is served by Amtrak's Sunset Limited, which travels between Jacksonville, Florida and Los Angeles, California. See the "Transportation" chapter for more information.

BY AIR

Rates into Lafayette are sometimes better than they are into Baton Rouge, Houston, or New Orleans. The airport is served by subsidiaries of most major domestic airlines. See the "Transportation" chapter for more information.

Getting Around

You will need a good map in Lafayette (available from the Gateway Lafayette Visitors Center). Lafayette streets are an inscrutable jumble. Like in New Orleans, many streets radiate out from the river. On the south side, these streets meet at improbable angles with those of the old downtown area laid out by Jean Mouton. On the north, the old downtown intersects with a grid pattern based on the railroad line. Superimposed on these are ancient routes like the Old Spanish Trail (U.S. 90 and Rte. 182) and Old Abbeville Highway (Rte. 167). As if that weren't enough, it should be noted that some streets change names as they cross the Evangeline Throughway. To put it simply, Lafayette is the only city in which I have inadvertently driven in a complete circle!

Gateway Lafayette Visitors Center Rte. 167, Evangeline Throughway.

Gateway Lafayette is a park and visitors center located just southeast of Interstate 10 (exit #103) on the median of Rte. 167. Gateway has met the criteria to become a viable tourist attraction, having accrued a temporary resident alligator and permanent alligator story. Just a few months after completion, a four-foot gator appeared in one of the Gateway ponds. It was assumed that the reptile had not wandered across three lanes of traffic to get to his resting spot, but that he had had some human help. After a couple days' work he was finally trapped and removed, but not before he depleted the duck population in the pond.

The Gateway is a clearinghouse for information on activities and attractions not only in Lafayette but around most of the area. It has a knowledgeable and accommodating staff directing visitors to various points of interest, whether they are trying to find out who is playing at the Friday-afternoon street dances downtown or when the next cooking demonstration will be held at Vermilionville. Gateway is also a convenient place to pick up a copy of the *Times of Acadiana,* a weekly paper that features not only local news and commentary but an excellent entertainment and events calendar. Not the least of the services performed by the Gateway is orienting visitors to the mind-boggling and maze-like tangle of streets in the metro area. Detailed maps of Lafayette are available for a few bucks and a diagram of major roads is provided free of charge. The Gateway is open daily 9 to 5. If you have not already gotten a city map, buy one! (318) 232-3737, 1-800-346-1958, or in Canada 1-800-543-5340.

DOWNTOWN LAFAYETTE ATTRACTIONS

This 30-block area is the most walkable commercial district in Lafayette. You can easily stroll to all the attractions off Jefferson Street in a morning. From Interstate 10 take exit #103 south. I highly recommend the detailed map available for free from the Gateway Visitors Center (one mile south of I-10). A mile below the Visitors Center, Jefferson Street, the main street of downtown Lafayette, crosses the Evangeline Throughway (Rte. 167/U.S. 90). Heading south from the Throughway, Jefferson Street sports a turn-of-the-century shopping district, galleries, nightclubs, and a couple of the best plate-lunch joints in Acadiana. (*See* T-Coons and Dwyer's in the Food section.) The city's two major news publications have offices here as do CODOFIL, the Festival International, and the Centre International. A museum complex is in development in the old Heymann Department Store. I like to park at the south end where Jefferson crosses Johnston. There are free spaces nearby, or park in a metered spot on Jefferson (50 minutes for a quarter). All-day parking at Parc Lafayette garage is $2.50.

★Downtown Alive! Jefferson Street at Vermilion Street.

This old-time street dance is held on Friday nights from 5:30 to 8 during warm-weather months (April to June and September through November). Workers from downtown offices, students at nearby USL, and families from surrounding neighborhoods create a good-natured throng in the street; restaurants open their doors, and beer and hot dogs are sold on the sidewalk. The music varies from Zydeco to Cajun and rock and roll, usually performed by popular local groups. For information call (318) 268-5566.

Lafayette Museum/Jean Mouton House 1122 Lafayette St.

The Jean Mouton House was originally a two-room structure built by the Lafayette town founder in 1800 as a "Sunday house." He used the residence when visiting from his plantation in Carencro. One room of the old structure burned down. The remaining kitchen is an excellent example of early Acadian architecture and is stocked with artifacts used by Acadian settlers. The original room is now attached to a house constructed by Mouton's son Alexandre, the first Democratic governor of Louisiana. Another three rooms were added in 1849, creating a Greek Revival facade. Inside the main house are eight rooms of period furnishings and artifacts of 19th-century life in Lafayette. There is an obligatory Mardi Gras room displaying costumes of recent royalty. Among interesting Civil War pieces is a double-framed newspaper printed on the reverse side of wallpaper, the only printing material available at the time. The Lafayette Museum is three blocks west of Jefferson Street at Convent Street. It is open Tuesday through Saturday from 9 to 5 and Sunday from 3 to 5. Admission is $3. (318) 234-2208.

St. John's Cathedral, Oak Tree, and Cemetery 914 St. John St.

St. John's is the seat of the Diocese of Lafayette. This huge Dutch Gothic structure with flying buttresses was built in 1916 to replace the old wooden edifice completed in 1822. Beside the cathedral stands the 500-year-old St. John's Cathedral Oak, a member of the Live Oak Society. The tree has a girth of over 28 feet and limb span of 145 feet. It is estimated that the largest branch weighs about 72 tons! Behind the church, explore St. John's Cemetery. Here, in aboveground tombs, lie the remains of town founder Jean Mouton, his wife, Marie, their son Gen. Alfred Mouton, and Cidalese Arceneaux. Arceneaux is believed by some to be the daughter of "Gabriel" of Longfellow's "Evangeline." St. John's Cathedral is about five blocks west of Jefferson at Main Street. (318) 232-1322.

Photographic History of Lafayette Courthouse at 800 Buchanan St.

The Clerk of the Court in Lafayette has collected over 2,000 photographs of life in the Lafayette area over the last century. Many are on display in his office on the second floor of the courthouse. There are photos of the downtown area, important buildings from the turn of the century, politicians like Dudley LeBlanc and Huey Long, and images of the great flood of 1927. Most of the photographs have been donated from private collections and have never been displayed before. The courthouse is a block west of Jefferson at Main Street. The exhibit is free and open weekdays from 8:30 to 4:30. (318) 233-0150.

Artists' Alliance 121 W. Vermilion.

The Artists' Alliance is a contemporary art center founded by area artists in 1985 and is located in the historic Lafayette Hardware Building (Lafayette's oldest standing commercial structure). The center is financed by national and state endowments, memberships, and donations. A gallery features both local and traveling exhibits, performance art, and dance. One block west of Jefferson Street, it is open Wednesday through Friday from 11 to 5 and Saturday 1 to 5. (318) 233-7518.

Lafayette Hardware Building. (Photo by Macon Fry)

Maison du CODOFIL 217 W. Main St.

This building two blocks west of Jefferson Street was occupied by the Bank of Lafayette in 1898. After stints as City Hall and a public library, it was restored in 1981 and became the home of the Council on Development of French in Louisiana. CODOFIL was founded by James Domengeaux in 1968 with the goal of promoting French in Louisiana. Domengeaux's motto was "Make French the atomic bomb of Louisiana." Although his objectives have not been fully realized, CODOFIL has contributed to the explosion of regional interest in preserving the culture, heritage, and language of French South Louisiana. CODOFIL is not a tourist agency and not able to provide travel information. (318) 262-5810.

Le Centre International de Lafayette/Old City Hall 735 Jefferson St.

This proud Deco building at the corner of Lee and Jefferson streets once housed Lafayette City Hall. It is now home to the Centre International, an organization designed to promote international economic interests. There are representatives from France, Belgium, Montreal, Quebec, and Japan. The building also houses the offices of the Festival International de la Louisiane (*see* description under Special Events and Festivals). In the foyer you will find a number of helpful brochures published in French. (318) 291-5474.

City News Shop 535 Jefferson St.

You will not find a big selection of out-of-town papers at City News, but this is a convenient place to pick up a copy of the *New York Times, Wall Street Journal,* the local *Daily Advertiser* or to stock up on tobacco products. It is open Monday through Saturday from 8:30 to 5:30 and Sunday until 11:30 A.M. (318) 235-2665.

★Jefferson Street Market 538 Jefferson St.

The Jefferson Street Market has 17 vendors selling quality items by Louisiana artists and craftsmen. Several vendors specialize in unusual antiques; others sell photographs and signed prints. This market has the largest selection of quality Louisiana folk craft and art for sale in one place. The prices are reasonable and those wishing to take a bit of Louisiana home might consider a stop here instead of a trinket and T-shirt stand. You can purchase a beautiful hand-turned wooden bowl made by O. B. Lacoste of Lafayette or "Zydeco jewelry" by Rita Broussard.

The artists represented at Jefferson Street Market change. On my last visit I found cypress model boats, cornhusk dolls, bent-willow furniture, and paintings by New Iberia folk artist Paul Schexnayder. Most impressive were the blankets and other items by Gladys Clark of Judice, Louisiana. Ms. Clark picks, gins, cards, spins, and weaves her own cotton in the old Acadian way, learned from her mother. The market is open from 10 to 5 on weekdays and 10 to 4 on Saturday (closed Sunday). (318) 233-2589.

The Times of Acadiana 201 Jefferson St.

The *Times* is a weekly newsprint magazine that contains regional news analysis, magazine-style reporting on local issues and events, and a very good arts and entertainment listing. It is published on Wednesdays and is available free from the box out front and from the Gateway Lafayette Visitors Center. (318) 237-3560.

Daily Advertiser 221 Jefferson St.

The *Advertiser* is Lafayette's only daily newspaper and a good place to catch up on local and regional events as well as the latest news. On Friday the paper contains the *Weekend!* arts and entertainment guide, an essential source of information on nightclubs, bars, dance halls, and restaurants in Acadiana. Despite the *Weekend!* name, the music listings cover the entire week and include times, addresses, and phone numbers. (318) 289-6300.

Children's Museum of Acadiana 201 E. Congress.

The Children's Museum is behind the Old Heymann Building on Jefferson Street. Kids age three to six should have a blast here. There is a banking kiosk where young-uns can create their own automated-teller bank account and access it with a secret code. They may take all that money down to the museum store, get a cart full of items, and practice ringing them up on cash registers. There is a TV studio where future newscasters get in front of lights and camera with a microphone. Scariest is the hospital operating room, where a mannequin is strapped to a table. The museum fielded so many questions from returning kids about why he (the mannequin) was still sick, they now take pains to explain that it is not a real boy. Hours are Tuesday through Saturday from 10 to 5. Admission is $5. Age five months and under are admitted free. (318) 232-8500.

UNIVERSITY AREA ATTRACTIONS

University of Southwestern Louisiana University Avenue (I-10 exit #101).

USL is the second largest university in the state, with 16,000 students. Formerly known as Southwestern Louisiana Industrial Institute (SLII), it opened as a preparatory school in 1901. By 1920 it was operating as a four-year college and had become the educational center of Cajun Country. Construction on 15 buildings began during the governorship of Huey Long, so the school has a distinctly Art Deco look, contrasting with its oak-shaded streets and walkways. The campus, located just south of the old downtown area, is relatively small and easy to walk. On the south edge, it is bounded by Girard Park, on the east by the low-lying buildings of the Oil Center, and to the west (across Johnston Street) is a neighborhood known as "The Saints" (because many streets are named for saints). The Saints and the area around Girard Park are the best places to look for parking. The center of activity is the student complex surrounding Cypress Lake on Hebrard Boulevard between St. Mary Boulevard and University Avenue. From I-10, head south about four miles on University Avenue. (318) 482-6940.

Elderhostel Program at USL

I had never heard of Elderhostel until I began traveling extensively in Cajun Country. It seemed as though everyplace I went (even the Cajun Mardi Gras celebration in tiny Church Point), I kept running into small groups of senior citizens having a blast! I talked to a few and discovered that they were participants in the University of Southwest Louisiana's Elderhostel Program. Elderhostel operates at universities throughout the world, providing senior citizens with an opportunity to expand their horizons through intellectual, recreational, and social activity as well as travel. The program offers a week of activities, classes, room and board, and local transportation at participating institutions for the incredible price of around $350.

Classes are offered on Cajun and Creole food, music, and other subjects of regional interest. Attendance is required at one class a day. Classes are taught by leaders in the field from the USL French, Louisiana Studies, and Folklife programs. The best part of the program is participatory food and music events. Hosts guide hostelers to places on the Cajun Prairie that elude even diligent travelers. For the price folks would be hard pressed to find as much good food, music, and company on their own. The fall program is timed to end just as the Festivals Acadiens (*see* description below) is beginning, so that hostelers may linger in the area for these festivities. Hostelers must be 60 years or older (but may bring a companion 50 or over). Lodging in Lafayette is provided in a nearby hotel with shuttle service to campus twice a day. Meals are taken in the campus cafe, but there are several planned opportunities to enjoy great regional food in the countryside. For more information on the Elderhostel Program at USL call (318) 482-6344, or contact the national office at ELDER-HOSTEL, P.O. Box 1959, Dept. TN, Wakefield, MA 01880-5959.

Cypress Lake Hebrard Boulevard between St. Mary Boulevard and University Avenue.

Cypress Lake is the best-known landmark on the USL campus.

Cypress Lake at USL. (Photo by Julie Posner)

Shaded by feathery cypress branches hung with Spanish moss, the lake is home to crawfish, fish, turtles, frogs, and reportedly several alligators. The lake was originally a dry cypress grove and was the scene of USL commencements until World War II, when it was flooded for use as a reserve water supply. It now darkly reflects the facade of the new Student Union building.

University Art Museum Fletcher Hall, East Lewis and Girard Park Circle.

The University Art Museum occupies two buildings on opposite sides of Girard Park. The permanent collection is housed in the USL Foundation Building, a replica Greek Revival-style mansion at 101 Girard Park Dr., on the corner of East St. Mary Boulevard. Works in the permanent collection are shown on an annually rotating basis. The main draws to the museum are the contemporary, decorative, and special interest exhibits at the museum in Fletcher Hall. The museums are open Monday through Friday from 9 to 4. Fletcher Hall is also open on Sundays from 2 to 5. Both are free except for special shows. (318) 482-5326.

USL's Dupre Library St. Mary Boulevard at Hebrard.

Even if you are not planning on using the research facilities, stop by and check the changing exhibits in the library lobby. One recent exhibit displayed old newspaper articles and photographs of Louisiana hurricanes. Inside, the walls are decorated with large photographic images of early life in Cajun Country. The *Jefferson Caffery Louisiana Room* houses materials of all types pertaining to Louisiana. It is one of the best sources of information on subjects relating to Cajun and Creole culture, the oil industry, local history, and genealogy. The collection includes books, magazines, government documents, maps, newspapers, and more. Specific topics may be referenced in vertical files of newspaper clippings and pamphlets.

Adjacent to the Louisiana Room are the offices of the *USL Press* and Center for Louisiana Studies, which publishes and sells a number of books relevant to the history, customs, and people of Acadiana. The library is open Monday through Thursday from 7:30 A.M. to 11 P.M., Friday until 6, Saturday from 10 to 6, and Sunday from 2 to 11 P.M. Hours change for the summer sessions. (318) 482-6039 or 482-6025.

Girard Park St. Mary Boulevard and Girard Park Circle.

One of the loveliest city parks in Lafayette, Girard Park, with its spreading oaks and small streams, is a great place for a walk or picnic. It is the site of the music stage during the Festivals Acadiens. The park faces St. Mary Boulevard and is encircled by Girard Park Drive. It is flanked on two sides by the USL campus and lies just a few blocks from the Heymann Oil Center complex. At the back of the park is the Lafayette Natural History Museum and Planetarium.

Lafayette Natural History Museum and Planetarium 637 Girard Park Dr.

This small but modern museum features changing exhibits that interpret the region and explore the environment. The exhibits are fascinating for adults, and kids will enjoy several "hands on" displays in the Discovery Room. Recent exhibits have been "Our Gulf Of Mexico: Handle With Care" and "Louisiana Creoles of Color." The museum has a planetarium with programs every Monday and Tuesday followed by an opportunity to gaze through the eight-inch telescope. The museum also operates the Acadiana Park Nature Station (*see* Lafayette Recreation). A new site in downtown Lafayette is under development. It is open Monday through Friday from 9 to 5 (until 9 on Tuesday) and Saturday and Sunday from 1 to 5. Admission is free. (318) 268-5544.

Heymann Oil Center University Avenue.

In terms of architecture and blend of office and retail space, the Oil Center is vintage fifties. The 16-block area near the USL campus and Girard Park became the center of the Louisiana offshore oil industry and the local economy when businessman Maurice Heymann converted his nursery to oil-company office space in 1952. By 1959 the sprawling collection of rambling single-story offices was home to over 250 companies. Hundreds more followed, only to abandon town when oil prices collapsed in the eighties. There are still many oil and gas industry offices here, but there is even more retail space. The Oil Center Renaissance Association (OCRA) has published a brochure that maps out the many upscale shops and restaurants in the area; pick it up at the Gateway Visitors Center.

LAFAYETTE METRO AREA ATTRACTIONS

★Acadian Cultural Center Surrey Street near the airport.

This is one of three Acadian Cultural Centers in South Louisiana operated by Jean Lafitte National Park. The centers are among the best places to learn the history and folkways of Cajuns and black Creoles of the region. They have displays (some interactive) on Cajun music, food, and traditional pursuits. There is a bookstore with French and English titles and a 200-seat theater. A romanticized 40-minute feature on the history of the Acadian people (narrated in French) is shown throughout the day. Several documentaries may be viewed upon request. I recommend *Anything I Catch,* an amazing study of hand-fishing. Admission to the center is free. The Acadian unit is located on the eastern edge of town across from the airport beside Vermilionville theme park. Take exit #103 A from I-10. Go southeast on the Evangeline Throughway for four miles. Turn left onto Surrey Street by the Lafayette Regional Airport. Hours are 8 to 5 daily. (318) 232-0789 or 1-800-346-1958.

Vermilionville 1600 Surrey St., across from the airport.

Vermilionville, the newest of Lafayette's two Cajun theme parks, is set on 22 acres between the Vermilion River and the Lafayette Airport (beside the Acadian Cultural Center). It is a condensed version of an early Acadian town (unusual since most Acadians did not live in towns during the period represented), with replicas of a plantation home, overseer's cottage, cotton gin, chapel, schoolhouse, and more. The park is a "living history attraction." Host employees are costumed in period clothing and engage in continuous demonstrations and explanations of Acadian life and crafts. Most employees speak French. Demonstrations by visiting artisans can be excellent. Lectures, storytelling, and music by Cajun musicians is scheduled daily in the performance center.

A cooking school offers short demonstrations of Cajun and Creole cooking methods followed by a tasting session. If you want a full meal, *La Cuisine de Maman* restaurant serves traditional Cajun fare for under $10. The food is good and unpretentious, but you can do better in town. Festivals and special events such as Cajun weddings and *Courir du Mardi Gras* are frequently staged. Allow about two hours to see everything. Bands play weekdays from 1:30 to 3:30 and weekends from 3 to 5. Call to see what events are taking place. Admission is $8 for adults, $6.50 for seniors, and $5 for students. Children under six are admitted free. You may leave the grounds and return the same day for no additional charge. See directions to the Acadian Cultural Center above. Vermilionville is open from 9 to 5 Monday through Thursday, and until 9 Friday through Sunday. (318) 233-4077 or 1-800-99-BAYOU.

Acadian Village 200 Greenleaf Rd.

Like Vermilionville, Acadian Village is a historical theme park modeled on a condensed 19th-century Cajun town. A mark of the authenticity of the village is its use in dozens of films depicting the life of early Acadian immigrants. All but three of the dozen buildings at the Village are restored and correctly furnished period homes that were moved to the site. There is a special event, festival, or demonstration at the park nearly every weekend but, unlike Vermilionville, it is not a "living museum." Unless you are there on a special occasion, there will not be a costumed host or vendors hawking Cajun food.

Acadian Village has several excellent permanent exhibits (with printed material in French and English), including the home of Dud-

Acadian Village. (Courtesy of Louisiana Office of Tourism)

ley LeBlanc. A senator, author, and spokesman for the Cajun people, LeBlanc was a hero in South Louisiana. To the rest of the country, his fame lay in the invention and mass marketing of the vitamin tonic Hadacol (12 percent alcohol). The house is packed with memorabilia from the life and times of the man known affectionately as "Couzan Dud." There are displays on Cajun music and a Doctor's Museum that is an authentic restoration of a late 1800s doctor's office. Although there is no food or beverage concession at Acadian Village, the lawn and pavilion are open for picnics and barbecues. Bring your own food and beer. Call for a special-events schedule. The Village is a project of the Lafayette Association for Retarded Citizens. Proceeds go towards the ARC and maintaining the park. Admission is $6 for adults, $5 for seniors, and $2.50 for children 6-14 years old. From I-10 take Ambassador Caffery (exit #100) south 4 miles. Go right on Ridge Road. Travel 1.5 miles and turn left onto West Broussard Road. The park is a half-mile down on the left. It is open from 10 to 5 daily. (318) 981-2364 or 1-800-962-9133.

★Acadiana Park, Nature Station, and Hiking Trail (*see* Recreation section)

Floyd Sonnier's Beau Cajun Art Gallery 1012 St. Mary St., Scott.
   Noted Cajun artist Floyd Sonnier has a gallery and studio in this classic Old-West saloon. The saloon was built beside the railroad tracks

in 1902 by a Mr. Borque, who coined the phrase "Scott: where the west begins." The phrase has been co-opted by the Scott Bar, which sits across the tracks, but many of the old interior fixtures remain. An old stand-up bar with foot rails and no stools supports boxes of Sonnier's prints. In one corner you will see an original gaming table from the saloon. This was a rough and tumble place in its day and attracted a good number of farmers and oil workers. Respectable ladies would not have entered. Today everyone is welcome to browse through Sonnier's work, which is primarily pen-and-ink drawings depicting scenes of rural Cajun life and the countryside. The gallery is located two blocks north of U.S. 90 in Scott (three miles west of Lafayette), on the corner of St. Mary and Delhomme streets. It is open weekdays from 10 to 5 and Saturdays 10 to 4. (318) 237-7104.

Louisiana Museum of Military History I-49 Service Road.

Glenn Thibodaux began collecting military paraphernalia the way other kids collect baseball cards. He now has a 25,000-square-foot warehouse full of stuff. Visitors may wander though rows of jeeps and Bradley vehicles or climb inside a Huey Helicopter or tank to operate the controls. Field radios crackle to life and pick up a station in Colorado (950 miles away). While kids enjoy climbing on the heavy equipment, I found the exhibit on antipersonnel mines to be fascinating. More unusual was an exhibit of field communication devices that included secret transmitters disguised as a pile of dog-doo. Choose from a collection of hundreds of war videos, ranging from documentaries to Desert Storm training films, available for viewing on one of several screens. Surplus gear and dog tags are sold in a small Quartermaster's Store. From I-10 take I-49 north (exit #103 B) to the Pont des Mouton exit. Head north on the east service road. (318) 235-4322.

★Zoo of Acadiana 116 Lakeview Dr., Broussard.

No one would expect a zoo of this quality in such a location! Over 500 animals reside here, most in lush and spacious surroundings. Part of what makes the zoo so much fun is the thick canopy of pecan and oak trees shading its paths. At midmorning in the summer it is 10 degrees cooler at the zoo than on the streets of Lafayette. The monkeys love it here and I found the siamangs (native to Sumatra and Malaysia) swinging wildly in the top of a very tall pecan tree. Most of the exhibits are connected by raised walkways. The two-acre aviary is entered through a bird-proof gate. Here you will find a large family of fruit bats in a cage with two-toed sloths. Among the more disturbing creatures were a pair of warthogs. Visitors may participate in feeding the giraffes, llamas, and baboon. Feeding times are at 11, 1, and 3. To get to the zoo from I-10 take exit #103 (Evangeline Throughway) south. The zoo entrance is on U.S. 90, one mile south of the Rte. 182

intersection below Broussard. The zoo is open daily from 9 to 5. Admission is $6.50 for adults and $2.50 for kids. Wagon rentals cost $2.50. (318) 837-4325.

Evangeline Downs Racetrack (*see* Recreation section)

LAFAYETTE RECREATION

★Acadiana Park Nature Station and Hiking Trail East Alexander Street.

Acadiana Park is a 120-acre facility on the northeast edge of town with picnic tables, tennis courts, a beautiful city campground (*see* Lodging), and 3.5 miles of nature trails. The trails wind through bottomland forest in a 42-acre area that abuts the Vermilion River. A

Acadiana Park Nature Station. (Photo by Philip Gould)

three-story nature station has interpretive exhibits on flora, fauna, and geography of the region. Naturalists are available to answer questions and give guided tours (call in advance for a guide).

In South Louisiana high ground is at a premium, so there are not many undeveloped places to put on your walking shoes, unwind, and work off all the calories. The Acadiana Nature Station is one of those places, a natural jewel in Lafayette. From Rte. 167 (Evangeline Throughway), go north on Louisiana Avenue to Alexander Street. Turn right on Alexander and look for signs to the nature center. The Nature Station is open Monday through Friday from 9 to 5 and Saturday and Sunday from 11 to 3. Trails are open from sunrise to sunset. (318) 261-8348.

Canoe Rentals/Wiltz Landing Levee Road, Henderson.
See Teche Country chapter.

Crepe Myrtle/Wilderness Trail
This 26-mile route is a pleasant day trip by bike or short drive by car. It leaves from the northern suburbs of Lafayette and after a few turns joins Wilderness Trail Road. The Wilderness Trail portion of the circuit follows the upper reaches of the Vermilion River through shady wooded areas and green pastures of horse country and past the homesite of Louis Arceneaux (believed by many to be the real-life fiancé of Longfellow's Evangeline). The route was officially dubbed the Crepe Myrtle Trail in 1990 for the many plantings along its course. Bikers will find flat terrain, little traffic, and arrows painted on the pavement at most turns.

Evangeline Downs I-49, two miles north of Lafayette.
"Ils sont partis!" ("And they're off!") is the cry that marks the raising of the gate at Evangeline Downs. Horse racing and wagering are two time-honored traditions in Cajun South Louisiana. Eddie Delahoussaye (a two-time Kentucky Derby winner), Randy Romero, and Ray Sibille are just a few of the great jockeys who have ridden at Evangeline Downs. (Aside from being home to great jockeys, Evangeline Downs has been the residence of a number of alligators over the years. These reptiles make their home on the moist infield, occasionally wandering onto the track or into the parking lot.)

All it takes to join the excitement and tradition at Evangeline Downs is a couple of bucks for parking and admission (outdoor bleacher seating). Food and drink are available inside. Folks with kids park close to the fence and watch the races over tailgate picnics. If you want to sit in the climate-controlled grandstands, it costs an extra $2 for a seat or table. No minors are allowed. From I-10, head north on I-49. The season runs from late April through early September. Races are run Monday, Thursday, Friday, and Saturday. Post time is 6:45. (318) 896-7223.

Pack & Paddle 601 E. Pinhook.

Whether it is bicycling, canoeing, or hiking, the one-stop information center and equipment store in all of Cajun Country is Pack & Paddle. The staff here, including owner Joan Williams, has hiked or biked just about every byway in Acadiana. They are generous in sharing advice on routes and itineraries for local excursions. You can purchase detailed maps to roads, trails, and waterways in the area, as well as any type of gadget an outdoorsman could want. For longer trips in the region, Ms. Williams has published a biking guide, *Back-Road Tours of French Louisiana*, that will be a big help to the two-wheel enthusiast. Pack & Paddle sponsors day trips on weekends and overnight bike excursions throughout the year (fees charged). (318) 232-5854.

Swamp Tours (*see* Breaux Bridge and Loreauville in the Teche Country chapter)

Wild Birds Unlimited 137 Arnould Blvd.

Wild Birds Unlimited is a meeting place for bird watchers and backyard hobbyists from all over the region. It has a big library and resource center for both groups, with videos for sale and for in-store viewing. There is a large selection of optics, accessories, bird feed, and birdhouses. Owners Rose and Jack Must are serious bird enthusiasts and they can tell you where the prime birding areas are when you are there. They also are informed of the activities of local bird groups. I was invited to join a group going to watch the bird-feeding frenzy that accompanies the draining of a large crawfish field south of town. The shop is in a small shopping center beside Johnston Street about a half-mile south of Bertrand. Hours are Monday through Friday from 10 to 6:30, Saturday from 9:30 to 6, and Sunday from noon to 4. (318) 993-2473.

SHOPPING

Foreign visitors may purchase goods at many area stores (including quite a few at Acadiana Mall) free of state taxes. Vouchers are available for tangible goods that leave the state. To get a refund, visitors must show a foreign passport at time of purchase and request a refund voucher. The tax must be paid but is refunded upon submission of vouchers by mail or at the New Orleans Airport refund center. For more information call 1-800-346-1958.

Acadiana Mall Johnston at Ambassador Caffery (I-10 exit #100).

This is the premier shopping place in South Louisiana, easily competing in size and selection with malls in New Orleans. In fact, you would have to go to Houston or Atlanta to find a more mind-numbing collection of stores. The anchors are Dillard's, J. C. Penney, Maison Blanche, and Sears. There are eight sporting goods and athletic footwear shops, dozens of jewelers and apparel outlets, and two music stores. If one member of your party hates malls, he or she can hide out in the huge Barnes and Noble bookstore next door. Hours are Monday through Saturday from 10 to 9 and Sunday from noon to 6. (318) 984-8240.

Antiques and Gifts:

An Acadiana Antiques brochure is available from the Gateway Visitors Center that lists 45 shops and flea markets in Acadiana. The following are a few of the more interesting shops in Lafayette.

Cajun Country Store 401 Cypress St., downtown.

The Cajun Country Store has a good selection of tourist gifts, cassettes, alligator heads, T-shirts, books, Cajun food items, and Tabasco neckties. The store also sells a few quality craft items. It is located at the intersection of Johnston and Cypress, about two blocks south of the Evangeline Throughway and three blocks east of Jefferson Street. It has a catalogue and sells many more items by mail. The store is open daily from 10 to 6. (318) 233-9689 or 1-800-252-9689.

Gateway Antiques 200 Northgate Dr.

This old flea market is behind Northgate Mall, just off the Evangeline Throughway near the Lafayette Visitors Center. Gateway has a good mixture of trash and treasures to sort through. (318) 235-4989.

★Jefferson Street Market 538 Jefferson St.

Several vendors sell antiques and quality items by Louisiana artisans. See Downtown Lafayette Attractions. Hours are 10 to 5 on weekdays and 10 to 4 on Saturday (closed Sunday). (318) 233-2589.

Lafayette Antique Market 2015 Johnston, University area.

Located just four blocks from USL on Johnston, this place has 1,800 square feet and over 50 dealers. They have a huge selection of small items and glassware as well as furniture. They are open Tuesday through Friday from 10 to 6, Saturday from 10 to 5, and Sunday from 1 to 5. (318) 269-9430.

Books/Newsstands:

Barnes and Noble 5705 Johnston, south Lafayette.

Most folks are familiar with Barnes and Noble, the literary superstore. Besides having a huge selection of books, it also has Lafayette's biggest selection of magazines and newspapers. Many of the papers are a day or two out of date. There are benches and easy chairs sprinkled around the store for reading and a small cafe on the premises. Barnes and Noble is located on Johnston at Ambassador Caffery, in front of the Acadiana Mall. Take Johnston from downtown or get off I-10 at exit #100 and take Ambassador Caffery south. (318) 989-4142.

Oil Center News Stand 1518 South College Rd., Oil Center.

Oil Center News carries the Lafayette, Baton Rouge, and New Orleans dailies as well as the *New York Times*. It has a small selection of magazines. Hours are Monday through Friday 8 to 5 and Saturday until 2 P.M. (318) 235-9295.

Acadiana News Stand 4416 Johnston, south Lafayette.

Acadiana News stocks the best selection of current daily papers in Lafayette. It usually has the Houston, Dallas, Baton Rouge, and New Orleans papers. It also stocks quite a few magazines. The newsstand is in a strip mall on a busy stretch of Johnston near South College. Hours are Sunday 9 to 6 and Monday through Saturday until 9. (318) 988-2727.

LAFAYETTE SPECIAL EVENTS AND FESTIVALS

Azalea Trail, Spring Tour

The Azalea Trail is a 20-mile, self-guided city driving tour that passes some of the lovely manicured lawns and ornamental stands of azaleas for which Lafayette is famous. The azaleas usually bloom sometime between mid-March and mid-April. A map of the tour and up-to-date information on what is blooming are available from the Gateway Visitors Center or Chamber of Commerce. (318) 232-3737, 1-800-346-1958, or in Canada 1-800-543-5340.

★Downtown Alive!

Jefferson Street in downtown Lafayette is the scene of a free street dance every Friday night from 5:30 until 8 during warm-weather months (April to June and September through November). This is a great way to begin a weekend of music and food in Cajun Country. Families take to the streets, vendors sell beer and hot dogs on the sidewalk, and a festive street party unfolds. For information call (318) 268-5566.

★Festival International de la Louisiane Last week of April.

Billed as the biggest Francophone festival in America, the Festival International is a cultural baptism into the food, music, film, and crafts of French-speaking nations and communities from around the world. Over 400 artists from Africa, Canada, the Caribbean, Europe, and the Americas join regional South Louisiana musicians on bandstands scattered through historic downtown Lafayette. Crowds have been dazzled by local heroes like Zydeco star Boozoo Chavis as well as by the rhythms and dancing of the Drummers of Burundi and the Jamaican calypso band the Jolly Boys. There are hundreds of performances, dozens of art and craft exhibitions, and activities for kids. The whole thing is one big, free, and orderly street fair. Stages are located far enough apart so there is no bleed over or overcrowding. Even the lines at food booths move quickly. For more information, contact Festival International de la Louisiane, P.O. Box 4008, Lafayette, La. 70502. (318) 232-8086, 1-800-346-1958 (Visitors Center), or 1-800-543-5304 (in Canada).

★**Festivals Acadiens** Third week of September.

The Festivals Acadiens is a celebration of regional music, food, and crafts that attracts over 100,000 visitors. The event is actually a combination of festivals that begins in the middle of the week and culminates with food, crafts, and plenty of free Cajun and Zydeco music in Girard Park on the weekend. In addition to the main festivals, there

Canray Fontenot and Dewey Balfa at Festivals Acadiens. (Courtesy of Louisiana Office of Tourism)

is an extended Downtown Alive street dance on Friday and lots of music in the city's nightclubs. If you enjoy the New Orleans Jazz and Heritage Festival but are fed up with tow trucks, crowds, a shortage of toilets, and lines at food booths, visit the Festivals Acadiens and breathe a sigh of relief. Shuttle service is available every 15 minutes to Girard Park from a free lot at the Cajundome. For up-to-date information, contact the Lafayette Convention and Visitors Commission, P.O. Box 52066, Lafayette, La. 70505. (318) 232-3808, 1-800-346-1958, or in Canada 1-800-543-5304.

Festival de Musique Acadien is one of the two major weekend events (along with the Louisiana Native Crafts Festival), running from about 10 to 6 on Saturday and Sunday. I would highly recommend this event to any fan of South Louisiana music. It is a free concert that takes place on a stage erected near St. Mary Boulevard in the picture-book setting of Girard Park. Dozens of the best new and traditional Cajun and Zydeco musicians appear in an unending stream, providing 16 hours of great outdoor listening and dancing. Overcrowding has not been a problem, as folks spread out blankets and lawn chairs on the grass while others join the dancing in front of the bandstand. In the shade of spreading oaks there are plenty of beer trucks, food booths from local restaurants, and port-o-lets. The festival crowd includes plenty of families and elderly attendees and is orderly (even the USL students!). Golf carts provide transportation for the physically impaired to the nearby *Native Crafts Festival.*

The **Louisiana Native Crafts Festival,** just a short walk from the music and food area of the *Festival de Musique Acadien*, remains the best-kept secret of Festivals Acadiens. For a $3 admission one can see demonstrations of alligator skinning, decoy carving, net and trap making, and many other regional crafts. Representatives of Louisiana's Indian tribes demonstrate the weaving of native cane, rush, and pine-needle baskets. There is a pavilion that features instructional seminars, musical demonstrations, and appearances by storytellers and humorists. Best of all are the food booths! My favorite is an exhibit called "How Men Cook." In South Louisiana, "men cooking" does not mean burgers on the grill; at this booth you will find the whole range of regional cuisine, with an emphasis on wild game and pot food. Demonstrations, free samples, Cajun humor, and advice are generously dispensed. Among the other food exhibits are a *cochon de lait* (roast pig) and cracklin pot, each offering samples of the finished product.

Zydeco Extravaganza Last weekend in May.

Held the last weekend in May (the Sunday before Memorial Day) at

Blackham Coliseum, this is the biggest event on the Zydeco calendar in Lafayette. Twelve hours of continuous Zydeco music featuring South Louisiana's best bands can be heard. I prefer the outdoor settings of Festival International and Festivals Acadiens to the cavernous Coliseum, but there is no arguing with the great talent and low price tag for this event. Admission is only $5 for adults and $2 for children. For more information call (318) 234-9695 or the Visitors Center at 1-800-346-1958.

Lafayette Mardi Gras Late winter (dates vary).

Downtown: Lafayette lays claim to the second-largest (behind New Orleans) celebration of Mardi Gras in the nation. Most of the parades wind down Jefferson Street downtown. Here there is a small-town carnival atmosphere. The biggest parades are the Krewe of Bonaparte at 6 P.M. on the Saturday before Mardi Gras, the Queen's Parade at 6 P.M. on the Monday before Mardi Gras, and the King's Parade at 9 A.M. on Mardi Gras. For the Queen's Parade, families and students arrive early to enjoy amusements, rides, and food booths. The celebration in Lafayette is not as protracted as that of the Crescent City and offers a respite from the crush of huge crowds. Consult the index for information on the traditional *Courir du Mardi Gras* celebrations held in small towns of the surrounding Prairie. For up-to-date information contact the Tourist Commission at (318) 232-3808 or 1-800-346-1958.

Acadian Village Courir du Mardi Gras: Acadian Village has held an enactment of the traditional *Courir du Mardi Gras* on the Saturday before Mardi Gras since 1982. One can wander through the theme park, see the demonstration, hear a full day of music, and get some regional eats at food booths. When the festivities wind down at the village, you will still have time to head downtown and catch the Queen's Parade. For more information call (318) 981-2364.

Vermilionville Courir du Mardi Gras: Vermilionville hosts an enactment of the *Courir du Mardi Gras* two weeks before Fat Tuesday and another the Sunday before Mardi Gras. The usual admission is charged. For more information call (318) 233-4077 or 1-800-99-BAYOU.

FOOD IN THE DOWNTOWN AREA

★Borden's Ice Cream Local Fave, $. 1103 Jefferson.

This is the kind of old-fashioned ice-cream parlor that would set any child nagging his or her dad relentlessly. The facade is Art Deco,

Borden's. (Photo by Derick Moore)

with glass bricks and stucco, supporting a neon BORDEN'S sign. Inside, at a counter facing a row of booths, are the most wonderful counter ladies since the school lunchroom. Of course, those are just trimmings; the main event is the ice cream, which is available in a host of flavors and combinations. Borden's specializes in the really gooey stuff like splits and sundaes made with fruit toppings and wet nuts (in syrup). What knocks me out are the ice-cream drinks. Here, at last, is a place where people know the difference between a shake, float, soda, and freeze and serve definitive versions of each! Try the "Flip" (sherbet blended with carbonated water and milk) to cool off a hot day. There is no place better than Borden's to fight the South Louisiana heat. Located just off Jefferson Street on Johnston in downtown Lafayette, Borden's is within walking distance of downtown attractions. It is open daily from 11 to 10. (318) 235-9291.

★**Cedar Deli** Local Fave/Mideastern, $. 1115 Jefferson.

Too bad the Cedar Deli is not open for dinner; this is the best light food in town. The deli is located in the front of a small imported-food market, so you can sit at one of the half-dozen tables or at the window counter and enjoy the appetizing sights and smells of the grocery. Mideastern salads and dips with pita bread are under $2. The heart of the lunch menu is a creative list of sandwiches with Mideastern, Greek, and Italian flair. Several are suitable for vegetarians, including the falafel, farmer's paradise (feta, olives, and tabouli), labani (condensed yogurt, mint, tomatoes, and olives), and a tasty grilled cheese. A number of sandwiches are served with the Cedar's own olive salad and a combination of high-quality and imported meats and cheeses. Sandwiches are available on pita bread or fresh French bread from Poupart's Bakery. Try the Greek shrimp sandwich or veggie muffaletta if they are available. Cedar Deli is easy walking distance from downtown Lafayette, about 12 blocks south of the Evangeline Throughway (Rte. 167), at the corner of Jefferson and Johnston. Hours are Monday through Friday 9 to 6 and Saturday until 4 P.M. (318) 233-5460.

★Dwyer's Cafe Down Home, $. 323 Jefferson St.

One of two very popular lunch counters downtown, Dwyer's is proving that Main Street, U.S.A. is still alive. It has been a fixture on Jefferson Street since the thirties. That's the son of the original owner and cook wearing the tall chef's hat and greeting everybody from behind the serving counter. Dwyer's has good breakfasts (five omelets under $4) and the best coffee in the city. The coffee doesn't have a chance to get burnt because the morning crowd keeps the pot flowing. At lunchtime, ceiling fans stir air that is thick with the smell of pot roasts, gravies, and stewed chicken. The service is cafeteria style and by noon there is a 15-minute wait for plates that are heaped with rice and cornbread dressings, mashed potatoes, and vegetables. A full meal is about $5. Dwyer's is a few blocks off the Evangeline Throughway (Rte. 167) and easy walking distance to downtown attractions. Hours are Monday through Friday from 4 A.M. to 4 P.M. and Saturday until 2 P.M. (318) 235-9364.

★T-Coons Down Home, $. 740 Lafayette St. (at Jefferson St.).

This is one of the two great lunch places downtown and my favorite. T-Coons goes beyond typical plate lunches with dishes like smothered rabbit (Monday and Tuesday), stuffed pork chop (Wednesday), and stuffed chicken breast (Thursday). There are three or four different main-course choices each day served with two vegetables and rice for $3.75 to $6.50. Unless you are planning to sleep all afternoon, I recommend getting the half-plates. If these sound too heavy, try the excellent soups and gumbos and order off the sandwich menu. A good time to visit is on Thursday afternoons, when locals gather in the back room to sing, tell jokes, and chat in French. It is an informal gathering and all are welcome to join in or lend an ear. T-Coons is easy walking distance from all downtown attractions. Take exit #103 south (Evangeline Throughway) two miles and turn right on Jefferson. Hours are 11 A.M. to 2 P.M. Monday through Friday. (318) 232-3803.

FOOD IN THE UNIVERSITY AND OIL CENTER

★**Cafe Vermilionville** Cajun/Creole, $$$-$$$$. 1304 W. Pinhook Rd.

This restaurant, in the colonial Vermilion Inn, is a great spot to splurge on a meal that combines Cajun, Creole, and French cooking with the freshest local ingredients. The menu varies daily, but some unique dishes that frequently appear are snapper andouille, bronzed shrimp, and the award-winning Kahlua grilled shrimp. Common throughout is a reliance on light but flavorful sauces, ultra fresh ingredients, and top-quality seafood and meats. In the spicy crawfish bisque, the crawfish were huge, and the corn and crab soup was thick with select lump crabmeat. Cafe Vermilionville has the richest, thickest, and most pungent soups in Cajun Country. The smoked turkey and andouille gumbo is simply paradisiacal. The value here is not the greatest; you can easily spend $20 to $30 at lunch! Lunch hours are 11 to 2 Monday through Friday. Dinner is served Monday through Saturday from 5:30 to 10. (318) 232-3803.

★**Country Cuisine** Down Home/Barbecue, $. 709 University Ave.

Country Cuisine has very good barbecue and at least one plate lunch every day. There is no mistaking the specialty here. Drive by and you will see the smoke billowing from the big-screened barbecue pit. The barbecue might be called soul style, cooked tender and lightly basted with a very dark and very spicy sauce. It verges on incendiary and is well accompanied by the icy-cold potato salad (one of the specialties here). When I am looking for some hearty and spicy cooking in the evening (long after the plate lunch joints close) this is where I go. Country Cuisine is about two miles south of I-10 at exit #101. Hours are 10 until 6 on Tuesday through Thursday, until 8 on Friday, and until 7 on Saturday. On Sunday and Monday it is open from 11 until 3. (318) 269-1653.

Dean-O's Pizza Local Fave, $. 305 Bertrand Dr.

When I die let it be at the hands of a Cajun Executioner! Sooner or later someone was bound to come up with a "Cajun pizza." If your idea of Cajun is spicy, try the Cajun Executioner. This aptly named pie will show no mercy, pounding the innards with a combination of hot sausage, jalapeños, fresh onions and bell peppers, shrimp, and pepperoni. There are several good pizzas in the sub-atomic heat category, the best of which are the fresh seafood pies. The Marie LeBeau is topped with piles of fresh lump blue crabmeat (seasoned but not hot). The Seafood Seizure combines shrimp, scallops, and broccoli sauteed to perfection and may include crab meat. These pies resemble pizza only in general shape and construction. Dean-O's is one block north of Johnston (Rte. 167), near the Cajundome. It is open Monday through Saturday from 11 A.M. to 11 P.M. (until 1 A.M. on weekends) and Sunday from 4 P.M. (318) 233-5446.

★**Hub City Diner** Local Fave, $-$$. 1412 South College.

Just before opening his fifties-style (I am talking olde-tyme) eatery in 1990, owner George Graham described the menu as being "diner fare with Louisiana flair." The Diner is one of the only places you can get home-style Louisiana cooking at breakfast, dinner, and late at night. The menu offers such standard diner fare as meatloaf and gravy, chicken-fried steak, and vegetable plates as well as local items like Catfish Louisiana (topped with shrimp etouffée) and Pain Perdu Po-boy (French toast stuffed with sliced ham and topped with Steen's cane syrup—don't knock it 'til you've tried it). Breakfast specials include the Hub City Special Omelet (with tasso, shrimp, and ro-tel tomato) and banana-pecan waffles. Breakfast costs $3-$6; lunch and dinner are $5-$10 (no single item is over $7). There is a full-service soda fountain in front with vintage appliances. The Diner is open Monday through Saturday from 7 A.M. to 10 P.M. and 8 A.M. to 9 P.M. on Sunday. (318) 235-5683.

★**Judice Inn** Local Fave, $. 3134 Johnston (Rte. 167).

This tiny hamburger stand has been operated by the Judice family since 1947, when kids used to drop by for a bag of burgers to take into the drive-in theater across the street. The theater is gone, but you can still get curb service on weekends by pulling up and honking your horn! I doubt if anything significant has changed at the Judice Inn except maybe the addition of air conditioning, which, along with the beers and soft drinks (Cokes served in six-ounce bottles), ranks as the coldest in town. If you don't like burgers, you are outta luck here. The menu has hamburgers, cheeseburgers, potato chips (in small bags from a rack behind the counter), cold drinks, and beer. That's it (no fries). These are not thick gourmet burgers but tasty irregular-shaped patties served with mustard sauce on a toasted bun. To complete an authentic 1950s dining experience, top off the tank at Borden's Ice Cream parlor (*see* review in downtown section). The

Judice Inn is about a mile south of University Avenue. Hours are Monday through Saturday from 10 A.M. to 10 P.M. (318) 984-5614.

★Old Tyme Grocery Local Fave/Po' Boys, $. 218 W. St. Mary.

Old Tyme Grocery wins all the polls for "best sandwiches and po' boys outside New Orleans." I live in New Orleans and will testify; the shrimp (highly recommended) and roast-beef po' boys here are as good as any. Old Tyme has been serving po' boys since the 1970s and I don't know why they still call it a grocery, since no one ever buys anything but sandwiches, chips, and drinks. The lines at lunch are frightening, but they have a system that gets customers through very quickly. In the back there are several tables and a counter to sit at. Some po' boys are offered at reduced price in the evening. Small sandwiches are around $3 and large are around $5. Old Tyme is a block north of Johnston at the university. Hours are 8 A.M. to 10 P.M. Monday through Friday and 9 A.M. to 7 P.M. on Saturday. (318) 235-8165.

Whole Wheatery Health Food/Lunch, $. Harding and Travis.

The Whole Wheatery, Lafayette's oldest health-food store, has a comfortable little cafe where you can order vegetarian, chicken, or fish sandwiches, salads, or hot lunch specials. Nothing is over $5. They make some tasty desserts and have a wide selection of juices, teas, and protein drinks. The Wheatery is located in the heart of the Oil Center at the corner of Harding and Travis. From University Avenue, take Johnston (Rte. 167) south to St. Mary. Turn left on St. Mary, go seven blocks, and turn right on Harding. Hours are Monday through Friday 9:30 to 5 and Saturday to 4. (318) 269-0144.

FOOD IN THE METRO AREA

A. B. Henderson Gator Cove Boiled Seafood, $-$$. U.S. 90 East.

Gator Cove has the best boiled crawfish in Lafayette and some of the biggest I have ever eaten. They are pond raised, clean, and filled with bright yellow fat as sweet as creamery butter. This is not a tourist joint, so the crawfish are seasoned for the local palate (plenty hot). They are boiled with cayenne and salt, then dusted with pepper after cooking. A heaping serving of 3½ pounds goes for about $9. At the peak of crawfish season, they serve as many as 10,000 pounds a week! Crabs and shrimp are also available.

Although the Cove is primarily a "boiling point," they have a menu of fried seafood and a few pot dishes. You are likely to run into the local softball team downing brews. Henderson's is open daily, 4 to 10. From Lafayette, go east on U.S. 90. The Cove is just past the airport on the north access road behind Henderson's BBQ Lodge. (318) 264-1374.

Blair House Restaurant Cajun/Creole, $ (lunch)-$$$. 1316 Surrey St.

Since opening in 1950, Blair House has won accolades in *Travel and Leisure* and *Gourmet* magazines. I like a place that stakes at least part of its fame on homemade bread. Jim and Janet Blair serve up small, slightly yeasty white loaves with each meal. The main focus of the menu is local seafood. From the dozen or so seafood preparations on the regular menu, my favorite was the fried stuffed catfish topped with mousseline sauce ($18). It was wonderfully light and had a filling that melded perfectly with the fish. Salads are simple and fresh. The house dressing is a creamy ranch with a hint of garlic and chives. At lunch, the adjacent Blair House Cafe serves delicious soups (try the alligator and sausage gumbo), salads, and po' boys for a good bit less than the restaurant. Blair House is just around the corner from Vermilionville. Weekday hours are 11 A.M. to 2 P.M. and 5 to 10 P.M. Saturday hours are 5 to 10 P.M. (318) 234-0357.

★**Café Des Amis** Cajun/Creole, $-$$. Seven miles east.
See Breaux Bridge in Teche Country chapter.

★**Catahoula's** Cajun/Creole, $$-$$$. 11 miles north.
See Grand Coteau below.

★**Charley G's Seafood Grill** Local Fave, $$ (lunch)-$$$. 3809 Ambassador Caffery Pkwy.

A dinner at Charlie G's can be a full night of entertainment. Get started with the "sampler" of Cajun sausage (made in-house), bay shrimp, and softshell crawfish, or try the grilled Creole tomato slice (hot) topped with feta cheese (cool) and roasted peppers in olive oil (warm). Plenty of people just share an appetizer, duck and andouille gumbo, or superb Southern Caesar Salad over a drink in the lounge. Others come after a show to indulge in the best desserts in the city. The casual dining room offers a view of the grill, where flames leap as catfish and softshells are gently turned. Charley G's accommodates shameless eaters with just-made crab cakes in thickened béchamel sauce, softshell crab topped with lump crabmeat and meunière sauce, and smoked fried Gulf shrimp. Every day there is a lunch special for under $10. From I-10 take Ambassador Caffery south (exit #100) about five miles. Lunch is served daily from 11 to 2. Dinner hours are Monday through Thursday from 5:30 to 10, Friday and Saturday until 11. (318) 981-0108.

★**Creole Lunch House** Down Home, $. 713 12th St.

The specialty at the Creole Lunch House is chef/owner Merline Herbert's patented stuffed bread. A rich filling of Creole sausage, meat, cheese, and peppers (optional) is wrapped in homemade

Proprietor of Creole Lunch House, Merline Herbert. (Photo by Derick Moore)

French-bread dough and baked to a crusty perfection. Take a friend so you can split some bread and have room for Herbert's soulful specialties like baked chicken (stuffed with spices and herbs) served with dirty rice. Herbert also fixes a mouth-watering plate of black-eyed peas served with sweet cornbread. They are seasoned to warm the palate and put a sweat on the forehead. Equally spicy is the Sausage Creole, which comes in a sauce piquant over rice, accompanied by a corn muffin.

Herbert opened her first shop in a wood-frame house at 713 12th St. in 1985, when she retired from her job as a public school principal. If they had put her in the cafeteria, no one would have wanted to graduate. At the 12th Street location, you can eat in the tiny six-table dining area or on an outdoor patio. If you want supper or a Saturday meal, you will have to visit the Northgate Mall shop, which leers across the shopping promenade at the General Nutrition Center. Health-conscious folks can stop and pick up some vitamins and wheat germ before shoveling down some fried pork chops, dirty rice, and stuffed bread. The mall is just off I-10 (exit #103 south) on the Evangeline Throughway. The mall shop is open Monday through Saturday, 11 A.M. to 7:30 P.M. The 12th Street shop is a couple of blocks east of the Throughway. Hours are Monday through Friday from 11 A.M. to 2:30 P.M. (318) 232-9929.

★**Edie's** Plate Lunch, $. 1895 W. Pinhook Rd. at Kaliste Saloom.

Edie's claims to be "Lafayette's favorite lunch house" and they might be right. After 11:30 you are going to wait in line. Folks who feel uncomfortable at an old lunch counter can enjoy bringing the family to Edie's new and spacious dining room. Monday, crisp fried chicken is accompanied by real mashed potatoes. Tuesday the special is chicken pie, a bulging turnover crust hand wrapped around delicious chicken fricassee. On Wednesday a large piece of tender pork roast is accompanied by sweet potatoes baked in their jackets, cut open, and doused with a warm brown-sugar and butter sauce. On Sunday you can choose from all three. Thursday and Friday specials are hamburger steak and seafood. Lunches cost $5.50 and include a salad and vegetable selection. Two fluffy biscuits precede each dinner; I always save one to douse with honey for dessert. To get to Edie's take I-10 exit #103 (Evangeline Throughway) south 2.8 miles to Pinhook. Turn right on Pinhook and go 2.2 miles to Kaliste Saloom Road. Edie's is located in the strip shopping center to the left. Hours are Sunday through Friday from 11 A.M. to 2 P.M. (318) 234-2485.

Louisiana Pizza Kitchen Local Fave, $-$$. 1926 W. Pinhook Rd.

The Louisiana Pizza Kitchen is a regional chain serving authentic wood-fired pizzas. Individual-size pizzas are available with standard toppings and local specialties like tasso. This is one of a few places in Lafayette to go for a light meal. The mixed baby-green salad with blue cheese and toasted pecans and the spinach and tomatoes with balsamic dressing are the best salads in Lafayette. Homemade bread is served with seasoned olive oil for dipping. There is a full bar and decent wine selection. To get to the restaurant take I-10 exit #103 (Evangeline Throughway) south 2.8 miles to Pinhook. Turn right on Pinhook and go 2.2 miles. It is on the right just past the traffic light at Kaliste Saloom Road. (318) 237-5800.

★**Norbert's** Down Home, $. U.S. 90 and Ave. C, Broussard.

This little lunch counter is the oldest restaurant in Broussard and serves the best plate lunches and barbecue east of Lafayette. John Norbert and his wife, Lillie Mae, turn out definitive Creole dishes like crawfish stew, real "dirty" dirty rice, and tasty chicken or crawfish pies. They have a selection of three or four meats and five veggies (pick two) each day. Monday the special is chicken fricassee and red beans; Friday's special usually includes fried catfish and crab jambalaya. I recommend the Thursday barbecue plate. Pork ribs are slow cooked over a smoky fire until crusty on the outside and tender within. They are served with a moderately hot oniony barbecue sauce, creamy potato salad, dirty rice, and hot-hot corn. Norbert's chicken and crawfish pies, available daily, are his pride. It is a joy to sit at the counter and watch the Norberts turn out their lunches and to hear them talking in rich Creole accents. Lunch plates cost about $4. Norbert's faces U.S. 90 in Broussard, a few minutes southeast of Lafayette. They are open from 10:30 A.M. to 2 P.M. on weekdays. (318) 837-6704.

Prejean's Local Fave, $$-$$$. I-49 access road.

When Prejean's hired a chef from Montana, things started to look wildly appetizing. You can still get the same array of fried and richly sauced seafood, but Chef Graham's award-winning wild-game preparations are the new stars on the menu. I recommend the Whistling Dixie Venison appetizer ($7), a marinated venison tenderloin, grilled, sliced, and served in a browned butter and shiitake sauce with toasted pine nuts. Graham marinates and grills his game so that it is as tender as a good beef filet. Two people can split the Rocky Mountain Mixed Grill, which features an elk chop, a blackened deer chop, and a buffalo tenderloin, each grilled and sauced differently. Unfortunately the thick sauces fail to do justice to the perfectly prepared meats. For dessert Graham's wife creates a hedonist's chocolate cake and the famous Prejean's bread pudding with Jack Daniel's sauce recipe is still around. To get to Prejean's from I-10, take exit #103 B (I-49/167) north. Prejean's is on the service road on the east side just before the Evangeline Downs Racetrack exit. Hours are 11 to 10 daily. Prejean's has a Cajun band and dancing every night starting at 7:30. (318) 896-3247.

★Prudhomme's Cajun Cafe Cajun/Creole, $-$$. 4676 N.E. Evangeline Throughway, Carencro.

Year after year Prudhomme's gets voted the favorite Cajun restaurant in the state. I have driven up from New Orleans just to eat here. The cafe gets its name from proprietress Enola Prudhomme, sister of the state's most famous chef. Enola's son, "Sonny," runs the kitchen and turns out family favorites like blackened foods, etouffée, and eggplant pirogues. The latter is a crisply fried eggplant canoe stuffed with crawfish and shrimp and smothered in a buttery cheese sauce with a couple of large fried shrimp garnishing the top! The highlights are rich preparations of local ingredients like tasso, rabbit, and crawfish. Most dinners are under $15 and include vegetable, salad (with homemade dressings), dessert, and a homemade bread tray! Jalapeño cheese bread, white loaves, and spice muffins arrive fresh from the oven.

Prudhomme's lunch specials are as wonderful as the dinners. Despite dozens of medals for seafood preparations, Chef Sonny exclaims, "I was a welder. Give me a good round steak with potato salad. That's Cajun cooking. I got to have that blue plate." One of his tastiest lunches is a garlicky pork roast with cornbread dressing and sweet potatoes. We recommend the oyster loaf; French bread is hollowed out, brushed inside with oyster mayonnaise, and stuffed with perfectly fried oysters (be sure to specify the loaf, not the po' boy).

Why would anyone drive from New Orleans to eat here? Consider this: in the time you wait in line at K-Paul's you can probably drive to Enola's cafe and be seated. The food will blow you away and you can spend the money you saved to hear some live music, get a motel room, and return to Prudhomme's at 11 the next morning for lunch! Prudhomme's is seven miles north of I-10 on I-49. Take exit #7 and head south on the service road. Hours are Monday through Saturday from 11 A.M. to 10 P.M. (318) 896-7964.

★**Randol's Seafood Restaurant** Seafood/Dance hall, $$. 2320 Kaliste Saloom.

Randol's earns a recommendation on the basis of its lively Cajun dance scene rather than food. (Refer to Lafayette Music below.) Frank Randol claims to have earned a "Master's in Crabology." He steams his seafood Chesapeake Bay style rather than boiling it, for a firmer, more succulent meat. Fried seafood is popular, and there are beef and chicken dishes. About 30 percent of the clientele is tourists (many arrive by bus), who come primarily for the music and dance. The band starts around 8 P.M. and dancers often put on a show. Randol's is located in south Lafayette. From I-10 take Ambassador Caffery south (exit #100) about five miles to Kaliste Saloom Road. Turn left on Kaliste Saloom and look for Randol's on the left. It is open daily from 5 to 10 P.M. (318) 981-7080 or 1-800-YO-CAJUN.

Poupart's Local Fave/Bakery. 1902 Pinhook Rd.

Poupart's is your best bet for breakfast pastries, specialty cookies, and fresh French bread. The baked goods are not quite what you would find in fine cafes in New Orleans' French Quarter, but they are a lot less expensive and far above your standard commercial bakery fare. Chocolate peanut bars, brioche triangles, and filled croissants are under a dollar. There is a small cafe seating area in the front of the store. Poupart's is located on Pinhook near Kaliste Saloom Road. It is open Tuesday through Saturday from 7 to 6:30 and Sunday from 7 to 4. (318) 232-7921.

MEAT MARKETS

★**Best Stop** Meat Market. Rte. 93, one mile north of I-10.

Even though I am not partial to the liver-flavored boudin found in these parts, this is one of the "best stops" around. The heat factor is moderate and they get the seasonings and moistness just right. For something different try the nontraditional smoked boudin. The Best Stop is a great place to pack a cooler of meats to take home. Their tasso (available in turkey for nonbeef eaters) and smoked sausages are excellent and you will want to get a small bag of extraspicy cracklins to gobble in the car. The Best Stop is exactly one mile north of Interstate 10 at the Scott/Cankton exit. From U.S. 90, just head north on Rte. 93 and look on the left after you cross I-10. The Best Stop is open six days a week from 6 A.M. to 8 P.M. and Sundays until 6. (318) 233-5805.

★**Bruce's U-Need-A-Butcher** Cracklins, $. 713 Surrey Rd.

Bruce's makes a variety of popular meat products, including a very good (hot-hot) boudin. Their specialty, however, is cracklins, cooked fresh each morning. They are just the right size and have just the right amount of meat on the skin for texture and flavor. They are also highly seasoned with salt and pepper while still hot. The best time to get these is when they come smoking out of the pot at 9 each morning. Take 12th Street northeast from the Evangeline Throughway about six blocks. U-Need-A-Butcher is at 12th and Surrey. Hours are Monday through Friday from 7:30 to 5:30. (318) 234-1787.

Comeaux's Grocery Meat Market/Boudin. 1000 Lamar or 2807 Kaliste Saloom Rd.

Comeaux's is the most popular boudin maker in Lafayette. To my taste, the links are a bit heavy on the giblets (especially liver), but that is obviously the local preference. I like their hog's head cheese better. They sell a wide variety of specialty and smoked meats, shrink wrapped for travel. Comeaux's is open from 7 A.M. to 6 P.M. Monday through Friday and until 5 P.M. on Saturday. (318) 234-6109 and 988-0516.

LAFAYETTE MUSIC

While Lafayette attracts a variety of popular artists to its arenas and clubs, its most exciting sound is the indigenous music played nightly in bars, lounges, restaurants, and dance halls. Within the metropolitan area you will find Cajun, Swamp Pop, and Zydeco. For an up-to-date listing of who is playing, pick up a copy of the *Times of Acadiana* (available for free at the Gateway Visitors Center). Many people use Lafayette as a base to explore musical hideaways in surrounding towns like Breaux Bridge and Opelousas. Consult the music chapter in this book to get information on nearby night spots.

Zydeco:

★**El Sido's** Zydeco dance hall. 1523 Martin Luther King Dr.

The great thing about El Sido's is that you can pretty much count on them to have a dance every Friday and Saturday and some Sundays.

El Sido's (better known as Sid's) also enjoys a location only about a mile from downtown and a mile off I-10. Although it is relatively new, Sid's has the important things right, like a big dance floor and plenty of tables. It is a family-run business. Proprietor Sid Williams owns a grocery and lives nearby; on many Fridays, his brother Nathan performs with the Zydeco Cha Chas while Nathan's wife works the door. On Saturdays, Sid brings in the biggest names in Zydeco. The music usually starts around 10 P.M. If you get there early, walk across the street to Sid's One Stop and grab a cold drink and a bag of cracklins or link of boudin. To get to Sido's from I-10 take exit #103 A (Evangeline Throughway) south. About a mile down make a right on Willow Street. Turn right again on St. Antoine. El Sido's is at the corner of Martin Luther King Drive. (318) 235-0647 or 237-1959.

★**Hamilton's Place** Zydeco dance hall. 1808 Verot School Rd.

William Hamilton hosts dances a couple of weekends a month at this venerable old dance hall opened by his father, Adam Hamilton, in the twenties. Do not miss a dance at Hamilton's! In the style of many of the old country dance halls (and this was way out in the country when it was built), Hamilton's is an aging, wood-frame building in front of the family home. Mr. Hamilton, who has managed the hall since 1962, can be found out back during the day, tending some of his livestock. The crowd here is mainly black Creoles but Mr. Hamilton

A big dance at Hamilton's. (Photo by Julie Posner)

has hired a few local bands like the Blue Runners, so it is not unusual to find a few USL students on the dance floor. Hamilton's is on the southernmost edge of the city limits, where cattle outnumber buildings. From I-10, take the Evangeline Throughway south to Pinhook Road (Rte. 182). Go right on Pinhook. About three miles down take a right on Verot School Road. Hamilton's is on the right between Ambassador Caffery Parkway and Pinhook Road. (318) 984-5583 (home).

Washington Street Club Scene Washington Street, north Lafayette.

The neighborhood west of the Evangeline Throughway (Rte. 167), between Cameron Street (U.S. 90) and West Congress, is predominantly black and home to several Zydeco, Soul, and R&B nightclubs as well as a few soul-food places. **Club Spice** (237-1099) and **Blue Angel** are two of the better-known establishments. These clubs seldom advertise in the local entertainment listings. The neighborhood can be edgy at night.

Cajun Music:

Friendly Inn Cajun dance hall. 103 Gill Dr.

The Friendly Inn is a small prefab building that might be a double-wide trailer. It has low ceilings, chipboard walls, and a varnished plywood dance floor. When the lights dim, the beer signs click on, and the dance floor fills with old-timers, the atmosphere is vintage chanky-chank. If you are under 60 a visit here will make you feel young. The octogenarians come out in force for the midafternoon dances. The bar is aptly named, for you could not ask for a warmer environment. There is no bandstand, and a good bit of time is jawed away in conversations between the band and the patrons. The Friendly Inn is on the left, just two blocks west of I-49 at the Pont des Mouton exit (a couple miles north of I-10). There is no admission fee. Cajun bands play from 4 to 7 Saturday and from 3 to 6 Sunday. (318) 233-4599.

Prejean's Dine & dance. 3480 Rte. 167/I-49, north of Lafayette.

This family-style seafood restaurant gets a lot of locals as well as tourists by featuring live Cajun music and dancing seven nights a week. There is no admission. If the restaurant is busy, you will want to order dinner. The bands play for tips. Bands play from 7:30 to 9:30 P.M. on weekdays and until 11 on weekends. To get to Prejean's from I-10, take exit #103 B (I-49/167) north. Prejean's is on the service road on the right-hand side just before the Evangeline Downs Racetrack. (318) 896-3247.

★Randol's Dine & dance. 2320 Kaliste Saloom Rd.

Since 1985 Frank Randol has been serving up Cajun music along with his fresh steamed seafood. In recent years the place has become tremendously popular with Cajun-dance enthusiasts. No wonder—the music is good and the dance floor large. A couple of dance clubs meet here and they often try to get the novices out on the floor. The scene on the hardwood is a veritable Cajun Saturday Night Fever! Even if you don't dance, it is quite entertaining. If you're not hungry, grab a seat by the bar. Live music is featured seven nights a week, starting at 8. Randol's is located at the far south end of town. From I-10, take Ambassador Caffery Parkway south (exit #100) about five miles to Kaliste Saloom Road. Turn left on Kaliste Saloom and look for Randol's on the left. (318) 981-7080.

Club Scene:

★Grant Street Dancehall Mixed bag. 1113 W. Grant St.

Grant Street is Lafayette's premier night club for R&B, roots music, rock and roll, and the most popular Zydeco and Cajun bands. If you are familiar with the New Orleans club scene, Grant Street is more like the old Tipitina's than the House of Blues. It is located beside the Southern Pacific Railroad in an old brick warehouse. Grant Street has expansive wood floors, wooden beams, and no noticeable cooling or heating system. Nobody notices the temperature when the good times get rolling here. In the winter the crowd of students, professionals, and assorted locals is too busy making its own heat to worry about radiators. In the summer there is plenty of cold beer. Considering it is located right downtown, Grant Street Dancehall can be surprisingly hard to find. From I-10 take exit #103 A (Evangeline Throughway) south to Jefferson Street. Go right on Jefferson. Do not go under the railroad overpass, but stay to the right. The dance hall is two blocks off of the Evangeline Throughway at the corner of Jefferson and Grant streets. (318) 237-8513.

Swampwater Saloon Blues. North Bertrand Drive.

The Swampwater opened with a splash in the late nineties by featuring traditional and contemporary blues artists. In fact, the club has helped spawn a burgeoning blues scene in the Hub City. The Monday-night Cowboy Stew Blues Jam is a big event. Lil' Buck Senegal (Clifton Chenier's guitar player), Sonny Landreth, and Steve Riley are among the top-notch local musicians who have shown up with enough regularity to make this the place to be. There is a small dance floor and outdoor patio. The club also serves barbecue. Blues and R&B acts from Austin and New Orleans often play on weekends. The saloon is very smoky (from cigarettes, not the barbecue) and popular with USL students. Music often starts after 10 P.M. Take Ambassador Caffery (exit #100) south from I-10 and bear left when you get to Bertrand. A mile south of I-10, Bertrand Drive and North Bertrand Drive split. The Swampwater Saloon is on the left just before the split so you must keep your eyes open and cut back to get to it. (318) 269-9717.

Lounges:

When it comes to music, the term "lounge" has a pejorative connotation. It conjures up images of has-beens or never-were types doing Elvis and Tom Jones imitations in Reno. The lounge scene in Lafayette is something else entirely. For the dozens of accomplished session men and singers who have worked in the recording studios of Cajun Country, Lafayette is a Mecca. It is a place where R&B, Swamp Pop, and rock and roll grooves are still appreciated and where fine musicians can make a living playing the music they love. Artists like Warren Storm, Tommy McLain, Willie T, T. K. Hulin, and Little Bob draw faithful followings nightly. The crowds on the Lafayette lounge scene are generally middle-age folks who love to dance.

Swamp Pop legend Warren Storm at the Four Seasons Lodge.
(Photo by Macon Fry)

Back to Back Swamp Pop/Cajun/Country. Northgate Mall.

Where else can you listen to a Swamp Pop favorite like Lil' Alfred in one room, walk through a door, and find a Cajun band like Rodney Miller and Cajun Born sawing away in another? Back to Back is two lounges in one, and Thursday through Sunday they both feature live regional entertainment. Swamp Popper T. K. Hulin, local Country boy James Younger, and Kip Sonnier are just a few of the acts that appear on these stages regularly. Back to Back are modern nightclubs in a building behind Northgate Mall. Take I-10 exit #103 south and look for the mall on your left about one mile down. On Sunday there is Cajun music at 3:30 and another band at 6:30. Thursday through Saturday the bands start at 9:30. A separate admission (about $3) is charged at each club. (318) 232-9500 or 232-0272.

★Four Seasons Lodge Swamp Pop. 4855 W. Congress.

The Four Seasons, an old lodge-style log cabin, has been one of Lafayette's premier Swamp Pop lounge and dance halls since the sixties. Swamp Pop legend Warren Storm can usually be found singing white-soul and South Louisiana R&B Thursday through Saturday nights. Backing Storm is a tight band that usually includes a variety of other Swamp Pop greats. A fog of cigarette smoke hangs over the dance floor as couples get close during the ballads. To get to the Four Seasons take I-10 west to exit #100 south (Ambassador Caffery). Stay on Ambassador Caffery Parkway when it curves right; 5.5 miles from I-10 turn right on Congress. The Four Seasons is 1.3 miles down on the left. Admission is just a couple of bucks. Bands play from 9 P.M. to 1 A.M. (318) 989-2421.

Top End 2842 Evangeline Throughway.

The Top End lounge is a weird-looking adobe building on the I-49 service road just north of I-10. Music varies from Country to Swamp Pop and oldies. There are happy-hour food specials like free jambalaya or crawfish. (318) 233-4525.

Country Dance Halls:

Cowboy's Ambassador Caffery North.

This place is like a smaller version of Gilley's, an urban cowboy's delight. It has a huge dance floor, an army of pool tables, and two bars. The walls are decorated with Western-wear ads and ceiling fans stir the smoke about. Cowboy's features popular local Country bands (most of whom play the top hits of the day). It is located just north of I-10 at exit #100 (Ambassador Caffery). (318) 232-3232.

PROFESSIONAL SPORTS

Lafayette's professional hockey and indoor soccer teams play in the Cajundome, a modern facility with good traffic flow and easy interstate access. From I-10 take Ambassador Caffery south (exit #100) and bear left when you get to Bertrand. The dome is at the intersection of Bertrand and College Road.

Louisiana Ice Gators

The Louisiana Ice Gators professional hockey team debuted in 1996 and immediately started breaking league attendance records. They won plenty of games too, only to lose to South Carolina in the tournament championship. The team continues to fill or nearly fill the Cajundome's 11,700 seats almost every game. The East Coast Hockey League season runs from October through March and tickets range from $6 to $15. Tickets are available from the Cajundome at (318) 265-2100 or from Ticketmaster at 1-800-488-5252. For Ice Gators info call (318) 234-4423 or check out their web page.

Lafayette Swampcats

The year 1997 was the maiden season for the Swampcats and the Eastern Indoor Soccer League. Attendance was good considering nobody knew what indoor soccer was. It is more akin to hockey than soccer and scores can climb into double digits. The atmosphere at these games is youthful, with light shows and rock music as the teams take the field. The season runs June through August and tickets cost $5 to $12. For ticket information call the Cajundome at (318) 265-2100 or Ticketmaster at 1-800-488-5252. For Swampcats info call (318) 267-4390.

LODGING

Lafayette has over 30 hotels and motels, and there is seldom a shortage of rooms at a reasonable rate. Most are clustered near the intersection of Interstate 10 and I-49 (I-10 exit #103 A and #103 B). There are also a few at University Avenue (I-10 exit #101) and near the Lafayette Regional Airport on U.S. 90 east. Brochures listing accommodations in the city are available from the Gateway Lafayette Visitors Center.

Bed and Breakfasts:

There are several Bed and Breakfast accommodations in Lafayette. I recommend that visitors consider staying at some of the interesting ones in neighboring communities like Breaux Bridge, Carencro, Sunset, and St. Martinville. Within 15 minutes of the city you will find private cabins, deluxe guesthouses, and even an antique train car for rent! There is a list of nearby Bed and Breakfasts below the Lafayette reviews (consult the index to find more information on them).

Acadian Bed and Breakfast 127 Vincent Rd.

Lea LeJeune is connected to a network of French-speaking Bed and Breakfast operators, often placing entire busloads of visitors in Cajun-French homes around the area. These B&Bs are within the hosts' houses and many, like this one, are in typical suburban, brick ramblers. What the accommodations lack in uniqueness may be offset by the convenience (to French-speaking tourists) of having a French-speaking host to entertain and direct you on your way. It is also relatively inexpensive at $65 for a double. Several rooms are available. (318) 856-5260.

Alida's 2631 S.E. Evangeline Throughway (U.S. 90 East).

Alida's is a perfectly restored Victorian cottage east of the airport facing U.S. 90. The four guest rooms are mainly furnished with antiques but have all the modern amenities (comfortable queen-size beds, television, phone, VCR, and private baths). Hosts Doug and Tanya Greenwald live upstairs and share their lovely downstairs parlor and kitchen with visitors. They also enjoy sharing conversation with anyone so inclined. Though a builder by trade, Mr. Greenwald is an accomplished cook who is proud of his breakfast dishes. The rooms lack space and furnishings for spreading out and relaxing, but most visitors will want to spend their days exploring. Double rate for one night is $80-$90 and includes breakfast. Major credit cards are accepted. (318) 264-1191 or 1-800-922-5867.

Bois des Chênes Inn 338 N. Sterling St.

French-speaking hosts Coerte and Marjorie Voorhies rent guest quarters in the turn-of-the-century carriagehouse behind their house, the Charles Mouton Plantation (1820). They also have two Bed and Breakfast suites in the main house. Doubles start at $95 and include a full breakfast and tour of the plantation. The Bois des Chênes Inn is located in the Sterling Grove historic district, just two blocks east of the Evangeline Throughway and a short drive from downtown attractions. (318) 233-7816.

Country French Bed and Breakfast 616 General Mouton.

This place strikes me as rather bizarre. Jane Fleniken and her husband built their replica of a country French mansion in the seventies in an urban setting of small one-story homes. The downstairs houses Ms. Fleniken's Antiques and Interiors shop, which specializes in country French items. One guest room is located downstairs (fine if you do not mind price tags on the furniture). The tiny guest rooms upstairs are furnished with torturous-looking single beds. The upstairs rooms are $90 for a double. The downstairs room has a queen bed and costs $115 for two people. (318) 234-2866.

Maison d'Andre Billeaud 203 E. Main, Broussard.

Maison Billeaud is one of several huge houses in Broussard (five miles southeast of Lafayette) constructed around the turn of the century. There are two guest rooms in the house, each with a private bath and decorated with period antiques and comfortable beds. There is a spacious living room with TV for guests to share. Hosts Craig and Donna Kimball and their son live upstairs. The deluxe accommodations are in a separate structure to the rear of the house. This two-story cottage with stained-glass windows and small upstairs gallery is ideal for honeymooners. There's no TV or cozy reading chair, but the gallery overlooking the patio and fountain is wonderful. The cottage has a private phone, small refrigerator, complimentary bottle of wine, and a coffee pot. Craig Kimball is a chef and caterer so his afternoon snack and gourmet breakfast of fresh fruit and complicated egg preparations is something to look forward to. The B&B is less than 10 minutes from Lafayette. Rooms in the main house for two are $85. The cottage is $125. Major credit cards accepted. (318) 837-3455 or 1-800-960-REST.

Maison Mouton Bed and Breakfast 402 Garfield St.

Maison Mouton is a 14-bedroom B&B in downtown Lafayette. It is the only lodging within a couple of blocks of all the downtown attractions, and walking distance to the Amtrak train depot. All bedrooms in the old two-story house are furnished with canopy beds and other antiques and many have private baths. Doubles cost $45 to $75. The new manager is Karen Delauney. (318) 234-4661.

T' Frere's Bed and Breakfast 1905 Verot School Rd.

For 20 years French-speaking hosts Pat and Maugie Pastor operated Chez Pastor, one of Lafayette's popular Cajun restaurants. It is no surprise that tourists and visiting journalists have heaped praise on the breakfasts here, served on a lovely air-conditioned porch. The four guest rooms in this 19th-century Acadian Colonial home are upstairs. Each has a private bath (though not all are connected), coffee pot, and telephone. Although the rooms are comfortable, with king or queen beds, they are not large. I recommend the garçonnière, a recently built double cottage behind the main house. The cottage feels a bit more spacious, particularly if several of the rooms in the house are occupied. T' Frere's is located in suburban Lafayette just a short drive from most city attractions. Doubles cost $90, payable by Visa, Mastercard, or Discover. (318) 984-9347 or 1-800-984-9347.

Bed and Breakfasts within 15 minutes of Lafayette:

★**La Caboose Bed and Breakfast** (*see* North of Lafayette, Sunset)

★**La Maison de Compagne** (*see* North of Lafayette, Carencro)

Chrétien Point Plantation Bed and Breakfast (*see* North of Lafayette, Sunset)

★**Maison Des Amis** (*see* Breaux Bridge Lodging)

Country Oaks Bed and Breakfast Cabins (*see* Breaux Bridge Lodging)

★**Bayou Cabins** (*see* Breaux Bridge Lodging)

★**Old Castillo Hotel** (*see* St. Martinville Lodging)

Camping:

★**Acadiana Park Campground** 1201 E. Alexander.
This is one of the best urban campgrounds I have stayed at. It is quiet, wooded, and clean with a nature center and miles of forested hiking trails (*see* Acadiana Park in Recreation section), yet only minutes from downtown Lafayette. There are a few large pull-through sites, but Acadiana Park is best suited for medium to small rigs or tents. It has cold showers and full hookups. Cost $11 a night. (318) 234-3838.

Bayou Wilderness R.V. Resort 201 St. Clair Rd., off I-49 north.
Bayou Wilderness compares favorably with the KOA in Scott. It is quieter and closer to Lafayette attractions and has 120 full hookups and pull-through sites. There are heated/air-conditioned showers, laundry facilities, an enclosed pavilion, and store. Amenities include a pool, tennis courts, and Jacuzzi. To get to Bayou Wilderness from I-10, take exit #103 B and head north 2.5 miles on I-49. Exit east on Gloria Switch Road and go 2.5 miles to Wilderness Trail. The campground is 1 mile north on Wilderness Trail. A camp space for two is $16.50. Electric hookups are another $2.50. (318) 896-0598.

KOA Camping Right off I-10 at the Scott exit.
$18.50 for full hookups, $14.50 for a tent space. (318) 235-2739.

Maxie's Mobile Valley and Overnight Camping U.S. 90 East (6 miles east of Lafayette).
$14 full hookups. Laundry, rest rooms. (318) 837-6200.

NORTH OF LAFAYETTE

Heading north from Lafayette to Opelousas, I-49 is roughly paralleled by Rte. 182, which actually crosses the interstate twice and offers a closer look at the surprisingly hilly countryside. I-49 provides quick access to such nearby towns as Carencro (with its good restaurants and racetrack), Grand Coteau (known for the miracle that took place there and for Catahoula's restaurant), and Sunset in the heart of horse country. These small towns are all within 15 minutes of Lafayette and have some romantic guesthouses and Bed and Breakfasts. The exits on I-49 are numbered according to how far north they are from Lafayette. For example, Sunset, 11 miles north, is exit #11.

Carencro

Just above the funky suburbs of North Lafayette, seven miles outside the city limits, is the small town of Carencro. This village was first settled by ranchers in the mid-1800s. In 1874, land for a church was donated and for a short while the community was known as St. Pierre. Despite the arrival of the railroad in 1880 and the growth of Lafayette, this bedroom community of the Hub City is barely a stop in the road for travelers on the old route to Opelousas. There is still a large cattle-auction barn right on the main highway.

FOOD

Paul's Pirogue Cajun/Creole/Seafood, $-$$. 209 E. Peter St.

Paul's Pirogue has excellent versions of all the typical Cajun stews and soups, good boiled crawfish, and seafood platters, plus a few items you will not find anyplace else! This is the only restaurant that I know of in the area serving the traditional Gumbo Z'herbes, or "Green Gumbo." This gumbo is made with greens, onions, and tasso and thickened with bits of potato and beans rather than roux. Gumbo Z'herbes is a Creole dish that was often served during Lent. Legend has it that for each variety of greens used, the cook would make a new friend. I don't know how many different greens Chef Angelle threw in, but he won me over with this sharp, hot soup. The shrimp and crab etouffée was also fabulous. It is a mild stew with no roux but plenty of butter to thicken. Paul's is famous for its Cajun Mayonnaise, which is spiked with cayenne pepper and is a great accompaniment for anything consumable! Jars may be purchased to take home. For dessert try the Gâteau Sirop, or syrup cake, with a scoop of ice cream. This is a warm spice cake sweetened with Steen's cane syrup and filled with pecans. Paul's Pirogue is open seven days a week from 5 to 10 P.M. (Friday and Saturday until 11). (318) 896-3788.

LODGING

Bed and Breakfasts:

Bechet Homestead 313 N. Church St., Carencro.

The Bechet family has lived in this Victorian house seven miles north of Lafayette since 1904. The house is furnished with family antiques and photos. The hosts' quarters are downstairs and there are three guest rooms upstairs, each with private bath, TV, and VCR. Host Lucile Bechet Maroney speaks French, Spanish, and Italian. Ask about accommodations in several outbuildings under construction. Rates are $85. Visa and Mastercard accepted. (318) 896-3213 or 1-888-896-3211.

Belle of the Oaks Le Medecin Road, Carencro.

Belle of the Oaks is a meticulously maintained turn-of-the-century house on 11 acres in the countryside just outside Lafayette. Hosts Maxine and Gordon Perkins live on the first floor and have furnished three guest rooms upstairs with period antiques. Each bedroom has a private bath, but only the "blue room" (recommended) has a connecting bath. Each room has at least one comfortable reading chair, but most guests choose to relax in a rocking chair on the spacious gallery overlooking the grounds. A full breakfast is served on china in the formal dining room. Belle of the Oaks is right off I-49 at exit #7, about 10 minutes from Lafayette. Double rate is $85. Visa, Mastercard, and checks accepted. (318) 896-4965.

★La Maison de Compagne 825 Kidder Rd., Carencro.

No wonder La Maison de Compagne is popular with anniversary couples; this dream Bed and Breakfast sitting on nine manicured acres offers comfort, luxury, hospitality, and good food in a romantic setting. The main house (circa 1871) has three rooms with 13-foot ceilings, antique furnishings, and private baths. Two rooms in the house have king beds. My favorite, the Country Room, opens onto a common upstairs sitting area with sofas, coffee maker, and telephone. Hosts Joeann and Fred McLemore live in a private wing on the rear of the house.

The most comfortable nights I have spent in a Bed and Breakfast were a weekend in the 1907 Sharecropper's House out back! This cottage has a king bed with cotton sheets, laundry facilities, porch swing, furnished kitchen, and covered parking, plus room to spread out. It opens onto a full-size in-ground pool.

Maison de Compagne is on a quiet country road 10 minutes north of Lafayette and 5 minutes from Prudhomme's Cajun Cafe. Joeann McLemore provides delicious snacks and cold beverages upon your arrival. She cooks a colorful breakfast using fruit from her own garden and recipes from her award-winning cookbook. Alcoholic beverages are prohibited and openly unmarried couples may feel uncomfortable as the McLemores are active in the Christian Promise Keepers organization. Double rates range from $100 for the Sharecropper's House to $110 for the Magnolia Room. Add $7 during special events. Personal checks, Mastercard, or Visa. (318) 896-6529 or 1-800-895-0235.

Grand Coteau

Grand Coteau, 11 miles north of Lafayette on I-49, is the single most idyllic and tranquil village in all of Cajun Country. This community of 1,100 residents is nestled along a sweeping ridge that formed a western bank of the Mississippi River centuries ago (the name Coteau means "ridge" in French). Anyone visiting Lafayette for a couple of days should plan on spending an hour touring Sacred Heart Academy and Convent, the oldest school west of the Mississippi and site of the only miracle to occur in the United States (as certified by the Vatican). The room where the miracle occurred is now a shrine open to the public. Many of the homes on Grand Coteau's main street are on the historic register. There are superb examples of early Acadian architecture, Creole cottages, and turn-of-the-century commercial buildings. A fine example of the latter is now occupied by the highly recommended Catahoula's restaurant.

Shrine at the site of the miracle in Grand Coteau. (Photo by Macon Fry)

ATTRACTIONS

Academy of the Sacred Heart

For a quiet walk and contemplative moment amongst stately oaks, visit the Academy of the Sacred Heart. Hundreds of Catholics visit the academy and the convent of the Sisters of the Sacred Heart on retreats each year. The prestigious private school was founded in 1821 and had an initial class of eight students. A tour of the oldest structure and museum documenting the history of the school is available for $5. The tour includes the old chapel, a re-creation of a classroom full of school artifacts and photos, and a visit to the shrine. No fee is charged to visit just the shrine.

The miracle that took place at the academy in 1866 has been described as the "most dramatic event in American Catholic Church history." Without ruining the excitement of learning the full story of the miracle firsthand, here are the basics: In 1866, a young postulant at the convent named Mary Wilson became deathly ill. After struggling with the illness, she said novenas to John Berchmans. Berchmans appeared to her twice in visions at her death bed and Wilson was immediately cured (she went on to die eight months later; her grave may be seen in the Sacred Heart Cemetery). This confirmed miracle led to the canonization of Berchmans as a saint. The shrine is in the very room where the visions occurred. Although the shrine is open free of charge, the academy requests that visitors check in at the school office (parking lot in front of the main building). The office is closed on weekends so call ahead to make sure you can get in on those days.

Tours are offered Monday through Friday from 9 to 3, Saturday and Sunday by appointment. The fee for adults is $5, for seniors $3.50. From I-49, take exit #11 and turn onto Rte. 93 towards Grand Coteau. When you reach the traffic light, turn left onto Church Street. This road will take you to the academy. (318) 662-5275.

SHOPPING

The Kitchen Shop and Tea Room Martin Luther King Drive at Cherry.

The selection of greeting cards for sale (available in boxed sets) by local photographer John Slaughter is reason enough to visit the Kitchen Shop. This is not a typical gift shop smelling of potpourri and specializing in frilly, furry, or fuzzy objects. The shop, which is housed in one of the 70 local buildings listed on the historic register, carries gourmet kitchen supplies, regional cookbooks, and other books on Louisiana subjects. In another room you may escape the Louisiana heat over a cup of coffee or tea and fresh sweets made by pastry chef Nancy Brewer. Many of these same items appear on the dessert menu at Catahoula's (*see* review below). Try the orange scones or pecan na-na. The shop is open 10 to 5 Monday through Friday and noon to 4 on Sunday. (318) 662-3500.

FOOD

★**Catahoula's** Cajun/Creole, $$-$$$. 234 Martin Luther King Dr.

Catahoula's is one of a handful of restaurants in South Louisiana doing something different with Cajun food and succeeding (and at a very moderate price). In 1992 this was a store crowded with general merchandise; now it is packed with diners feasting on Crawfish Fettucine, Eggplant Coteau, and Chicken Catahoula. The latter is a sauteed boneless chicken breast accompanied by a maque choux mushroom sauce over penne pasta. There are vegetarian choices and plenty of typical items such as gumbo, etouffée, and grilled fresh fish. Many of the same entrees are available at lunch for a couple of bucks less, or you may choose from a half-dozen sandwiches. On Sunday several of the dinner and lunch items appear along with brunch specials like Grits and Grillades, Eggs Benedict, and Catahoula's Omelet. These are served with the best biscuits and preserves I have eaten since my grandmother quit baking! After lunch, stroll the grounds of Academy of the Sacred Heart and get dessert down the street at the Kitchen Shop Tea Room, where a number of the better desserts at Catahoula's originate. Catahoula's is open from 11 A.M. to 2 P.M. and 5 to 10 P.M. Tuesday through Saturday. Sunday it is open for brunch 10:30 to 2. (318) 662-2275.

Sunset

Sunset is a sleepy town of 2,600 just a couple of miles west of Grand Coteau on Rte. 182. From I-49 take exit #11 (Rte. 93) west. The village was originally called Sibilleville, after a local planter who introduced yams to the region. After the War Between the States, when the people of nearby Grand Coteau refused to allow the railroad to pass through their town, prominent planter Napoleon Robin (for whom Sunset's main street is named) gave the company the right-of-way across his property. With the arrival of rails, the town grew and changed its name to Sunset. This is horse-breeding and racing country. Until a few years ago there was a well-known "bush track" (as the small, dirt horse-racing tracks of Cajun Country are known) just south of town. Gambling is a popular pastime and the town is home to the Sunset Game Club cockfighting pit.

ATTRACTIONS

Chrétien Point Plantation

Built in the early 1830s, Chrétien Point is the oldest Greek Revival plantation house in Louisiana. It was the center of a 10,000-acre cotton plantation that was the site of armed conflict during the War Between the States. It has 12-foot-high ceilings, large windows for cross ventilation, and six fireplaces on interior walls with imported French-Empire-style mantels. Following the war, Chrétien Point fell into disrepair. Some rooms were used to store hay, while livestock roamed freely through others. The present owners have restored the manor and live there. They offer tours and Bed-and-Breakfast accommodations. Tours are scheduled daily from 10 to 5. The last tour starts at 4. The fee is $5 for adults and $2.50 for children. To get to Chrétien Point, turn off Rte. 182 just northwest of Sunset onto Rte. 93 south. Go 3.8 miles until you hit the Bristol/Bosco Road (Rte. 356). Turn right, go one block, and turn right again. Chrétien Point is one mile down on the left. (318) 662-5876.

Sunset Game Club Rte. 182, north of Sunset.

This cockpit has been labeled by local fight fans as "the Madison Square Garden of cockfighting." The pit is located on Rte. 182 just north of town. It is open January through June and has tournaments about once a month.

FOOD

Dugas Cafe Down Home, $. Rte. 182, Sunset.

With its Art Deco facade, I keep expecting to walk into Dugas Cafe and find Earl Long pontificating from a stool at the lunch counter. Old Uncle Earl would sure appreciate the sign reading "No personal checks cashed; we have a supply from last year." Mrs. Dugas runs the kitchen and counter as she has since the sixties. She fixes a different lunch special each day and turns out a top-notch Cajun meatloaf redolent of garlic, green peppers, and onions. (Mrs. Dugas had this to say about her seasoning: "We love garlic, grow it in our garden, and cook with it a lot.") Heaped on the side are mounds of rice and smothered potatoes swimming in gravy. The plate lunches come with a simple cobbler with biscuit crust for $4. You can't miss Dugas's; it is the green-and-white building beside the railroad tracks in the center of Sunset. They serve lunch from 10:30 until 2 on weekdays. (318) 662-9208.

★Rowena's Meat Market Boudin, $. Rte. 182, Sunset.

Since Enola Prudhomme told me about Rowena's boudin, I haven't passed by Sunset without stopping for a moist and meaty link. This is some spicy, hot boudin. You can see the red and black peppers in these sausages, and the skins sweat red bullets of steam. But it is not the heat that makes this boudin so great—it is the perfect mixture of rice and pork. There is no preponderance of giblets inside and the pork is just fatty enough to keep the whole thing moist. The boudin balls, which are deep fried with no batter, are also good.

Manager Kenneth Burleigh joked that today's boudin and cracklins just aren't as good as those that used to be cooked outdoors—"a little dust fell in it and gave it that taste." But his product is one of the best. In regards to the Prairie andouille, which is made with "guts stuffed in guts," Burleigh explained, "Once you get past the smell it's real good!" Rowena's is on Rte. 182 1.5 miles north of Rte. 178. It is open daily from 7 A.M. to 8 P.M. (318) 662-5630.

LODGING

Bed and Breakfasts:

Chrétien Point Plantation Bed and Breakfast

This B&B offers accommodations of rural gentility. There are three rooms for rent in the main plantation house, ranging from $125 (with private baths in the hall) to $200 (connected private bath). One room has a king bed and private entrance. Two upper rooms open out onto a gallery. Room prices include a tour of the house, use of the tennis court and pool, and plantation breakfast. All of the rooms are on tour, so check-in time is 5 P.M. and check-out is at 9 A.M. Directions to the plantation are provided above. Call for reservations. (318) 662-5876.

★La Caboose Bed and Breakfast 145 S. Budd St.

La Caboose may be South Louisiana's most unusual Bed and Breakfast. I always fantasized about living in a train car, so when I heard that Margaret Brinkhaus was offering overnight accommodations in a renovated 1930s caboose and turn-of-the-century train depot behind her home, I headed for Sunset. Sunset is less than 15 minutes from Lafayette and Opelousas and 2 minutes from beautiful Grand Coteau. The caboose and train depot share a deck in the shade of a large oak tree. Both have private baths, refrigerators, and coffeepots; neither has phone or TV. Ms. Brinkhaus stocks the kitchens with coffee and provides fresh fruit, homemade bread, and her own La Caboose brand jelly for breakfast (very good!). I loved the caboose, which was surprisingly spacious with two single beds, but opted for the train depot with its full-size bed. The depot is a romantic hexagonal room with wainscoting, walls, and ceiling all made of original unpainted beaded-board. A hallway, breakfast nook, and bathroom have been added to the rear of the depot. Ms. Brinkhaus's fine fruit jellies are available at gourmet shops around the area, but if you ask she will sell them to you directly. La Caboose is a minute off I-49, 11 miles from Lafayette and Opelousas. Rates are $65 to $75. Cash or check accepted. (318) 662-5401.

SOUTH OF LAFAYETTE

The road heading south from Lafayette Johnston Street (Rte. 167) is called the Old Abbeville Highway. This road follows the Vermilion River 15 miles down to the historic village of Abbeville, where it intersects Rte. 82, the Hug the Coast Highway. Once past the congested oil suburbs of south Lafayette, Rte. 167 passes quickly through the rice fields and cattle country of Vermilion Parish. You will see handsome riverside homes, small cabins, and lush fields. (*See* Western Cajun Country.)

Maurice

The first town heading south out of Lafayette on Johnston Street (Rte. 167) is Maurice. This little village of 550 is hardly a stop in the road (unless you catch a red light at the only traffic signal between Lafayette and Abbeville), but a couple of food landmarks make it a worthy destination.

★**Hebert's Specialty Meats** Meat Market, $. Rte. 167.

Lafayette is the southernmost outpost of Louisiana's "smoke belt." By the time you hit Maurice, just 12 miles south, you are in the province of fresh meats and stuffed fowl. Typical of the area, Hebert's (which serves Lafayette's finest restaurants) sells only fresh meat—no boudin or smoked products. Here you will find lean pork, turkey or mixed sausage, marinated pork, seasoned ribs, and rolled round steak (all for under $2.50 a pound!). Hebert's specialty is stuffed rabbit and chicken. Chickens are whole, deboned birds (a feat you will not want to try at home) stuffed with cornbread, shrimp and rice, or plain rice dressing. All of the dressings are superbly prepared. These birds are fantastic when slow cooked on the backyard grill or in the oven. I can't visit the Lafayette area without picking up a couple to bring home to roast on the barbecue. Each bird will feed five and costs under $10. Hebert's is open Monday through Saturday from 7:30 A.M. to 6:30 P.M. and Sunday until noon. (318) 893-5062.

★**Soop's Restaurant** Down Home, $-$$. Rte. 167.

In an old-fashioned diner adjacent to the meat market run by their father and brother, Rachel Hebert and her six sisters prepare some of the tastiest Cajun food you will find anywhere. Lunch often offers a chance to sample the stuffed chicken, prepared fresh daily in the meat market next door. Specials include vegetables and two or three starches and rarely exceed $5. At dinner, try the mouthwatering quail and sausage gumbo. All of the soups at Soop's are delicious. The crawfish bisque may be the best I have eaten and the seafood gumbo is laden with fresh crabmeat. Boiled crawfish also deserve special mention. They are perfectly cooked with a straightforward seasoning and are a real value. Soop's is open Monday from 11 A.M. to 1 P.M., Tuesday through Thursday until 9, and Friday and Saturday until 10. It is located on Rte. 167, just 15 minutes from Lafayette. (318) 893-2462.

Abbeville

Abbeville is a lovely village of 13,000 residents on the banks of the Vermilion River, just half an hour south of Lafayette and the same distance west of New Iberia. It is the seat of Vermilion Parish and center of the state's biggest cattle-producing region. In true South Louisiana style, however, the city's greatest reputation is culinary. Abbeville is home to three of the finest oyster bars anywhere, and a wonderfully rustic seafood patio. The town is noted for its two quaint downtown squares, which give it a distinctly Old World charm. The squares and historic center of Abbeville were laid out by the French priest Antoine Desire Megret, who founded the village and named it after his home in France in 1843. While Abbeville is beautiful year round, the best time to visit is in the fall and early winter when the city's famous oyster bars are open and the smoke from Steen's Syrup Mill flavors the air around St. Mary Magdalen and Courthouse

Downtown Abbeville. (Photo by Julie Posner)

squares. It is a great first or last stop when driving the scenic Hug the Coast Highway (Rte. 82), which begins just south of town. Abbeville is small enough to see in less than a couple of hours, but it will take many return visits to sample all of the good food.

Abbeville Tourist Information Center 7507 Veterans Memorial Dr. (Rte. 14 Bypass).

Stop here to view the small exhibit of artifacts and photographs of parish life around the turn of the century. The center provides public rest rooms, a parish map, and a street guide/walking tour to attractions in the old downtown area. The Visitors Center is in the same small building as the Chamber of Commerce about a mile east of Rte. 167 on Rte. 14 Bypass. It is open Monday through Friday from 9:30 to 4. (318) 893-4264.

DOWNTOWN ATTRACTIONS

Walking Tour of the Old Town Center

A map of downtown Abbeville attractions is available at the Visitors Center but is hardly necessary, as the area covers only about eight square blocks along the banks of the Vermilion River. Without any stops at the town's fine eateries, Abbeville may be toured on foot in an hour. Park near the Steen Syrup Mill (built in 1910) and stroll north around St. Mary Magdalen Square and Courthouse Square, which are surrounded by turn-of-the-century storefronts. A portrait of town founder Antoine Megret hangs in the courthouse. Walk south along the river to see the old cemetery and rice mills.

Steen's Syrup Mill 119 North Main St.

There used to be hundreds of syrup mills in Cajun Country. Many families made their own syrup at home by boiling the crushed cane from their fields. Steen's is the biggest remaining syrup mill and its strong but sweet product is a favorite topping for biscuits, cornbread, pancakes, and pain perdu (French toast) throughout the region. The mill began operations in 1910 when a hard freeze threatened to destroy C. S. Steen's sugar crop before he could get it to the local refinery. He built the makeshift mill to save the crop. The mill has remained in the Steen family and until recently offered plant tours. During the fall, huge trucks of cane can be seen unloading and the aroma of simmering sugar fills the air. Steen's is located just behind St. Mary Magdalen Square and Church Street.

Riviana Rice Mill Rue du Bas and First Street.

Walk about five blocks south of the Steen's Mill on Main Street and, at Railroad Avenue, you will see the huge Riviana, Water Maid, and

Mahatma rice mills. In late summer and early fall, trucks full of rice unload here and clouds of chaff rise from the refinery. Riviana was founded in the late 1800s and claims to be the "oldest existing mill in the state."

Godchaux Park South Main Street.

This little park is a good place for a picnic and to let the young 'uns unwind. There is playground equipment and benches. A sign on the grounds warns, "Prohibited: Gathering of persons which by nature, character, or size may forseeably disturb others." I assume that translates, "No hell-raisin'." The park is within walking distance of the downtown area on Main Street, about two blocks past the railroad tracks.

Celebration of the Giant Omelette First weekend in November.

The main event of this festival is the public preparation of a 5,000-egg omelet in a custom-designed 12-foot skillet. Before cooking, the eggs are paraded through downtown Abbeville. Of course there is plenty of omelet to go around when the cooking is finished. More prosaic, but with equally tasty results, are omelet toss contests, guest chef demonstrations, and plenty of hot pancakes doused in Steen's cane syrup. The affair has an international flavor, but there are also carnival rides and street food. The omelet is cooked on Sunday. (318) 893-6517.

AREA ATTRACTIONS

★Swamp Ivory Creations 1307 S. Henry (Rte. 355), Abbeville.

Kathy Richard uses dead alligators in ways that most people have never considered. Alligator jaws are piled in a pen to wash in the rain outside Richard's studio. Once they are clean she will remove the teeth and mount them on ingeniously crafted jewelry. No part of the gator jaws (which come from a local alligator farm) will be wasted. A friend takes the bones and hones them into knives and letter openers.

Those who visit Swamp Ivory Creations are in for a real treat. Kathy and her husband, Johnny Richard, live and work on the riverside compound where Johnny's grandfather Avery Richard set up a cattle auction and slaughterhouse in the 1930s. Johnny builds and repairs saddles in the old auction house, where tiers of wooden seats look down on the bidding platform. Kathy's studio is in the former slaughterhouse. If you call first and it is convenient, Kathy will not only show some of her latest pieces for sale, but will also offer a tour of the compound and auction house (which awaits historical recognition). The compound is one mile south of Rte. 14 Business on South Henry. Call for directions and to let them know you are coming. The Richards speak Cajun French. (318) 893-5760.

Clem's "Bush Track" Horse Racing Lafitte Road (Rte. 338 north).

This listing may turn out to be an obituary for a Cajun Country tradition. The track has "temporarily" ceased operations several times and was not operating when this went to press. Clem's was the last of several "bush" tracks in the region that offered quarter-horse racing on Sunday mornings. Many of the great Louisiana jockeys cut their teeth on the rugged bush circuit. The track is owned by Clement Hebert, who runs Hebert's Meat Market (see review) across the road. Check with him on the status of races at Clem's. The track and market are a mile north of Rte. 14 Bypass (Veterans Memorial Drive) on Rte. 338. (318) 893-8160.

Hebert's Cockpit Lafitte Road (Rte. 338 north).

The cockpit sits behind Clem Hebert's horsetrack, just across from Hebert's Meat Market. Tournaments are scheduled for Saturday nights into early summer. Try checking at the meat market for more information. The market, track, and cockpit are located a mile north of Rte. 14 Bypass (Veterans Memorial Drive) on Rte. 338.

★Gateway to Hug the Coast Highway Bird watching, scenic drive.

Rte. 82 drops south from south of Abbeville for nearly 45 miles before turning west at Pecan Island and hugging the coast. The scenic Hug the Coast Highway (Rte. 82) stretches along the Louisiana coast from Pecan Island to the Texas border. The road passes through miles of salt marsh, the Rockefeller Wildlife Refuge (55 miles), and endless acres of prime shorebird habitat. There are also several public beaches. Most travelers drive the 80-mile stretch from Abbeville to Creole or the 110 miles to Holly Beach before heading north to Lake Charles on Rte. 27 (the Creole Nature Trail). This takes at least three hours. For detailed information on Hug the Coast Highway and the Creole Nature Trail see the Scenic Wetlands section at the end of the Western Cajun Country chapter.

Intracoastal City/Leland Bowman Locks Bird watching, scenic drive.

The area below Abbeville is the province of cattlemen, fishermen, bird watchers, and businesses catering to the offshore oil industry. To get off the beaten path and see a little of all those pursuits, drive 11 miles south on Rte. 82 to Esther, and bear left on Rte. 333. Rte. 333 parallels the Vermilion River for 9 miles, past the oil docks at Intracoastal City, before terminating at the new Leland Bowman Locks. The old locks and the abandoned lock-keeper cabins are still standing. At this point, barge traffic drops from the Vermilion River into the Intracoastal Waterway. The gates are also opened and closed to control the flow of salt water into inland waterways. There is an observation tower with a shaded picnic table beside the lock house. (You can find a plate lunch to take to the locks at Roland's or G's, listed in the Food section below.) This is a good place to observe both barge and bird traffic. Brochures describing the lock history and operations are available inside. In the summer this is one of the hottest places in the universe and home to droves of dragonflies. The office is open to visitors Monday through Friday from 8 to 3. The observation pavilion is open during daylight hours daily. (318) 893-6790.

FOOD

I grew up near the Chesapeake Bay, have lived in New Orleans since 1982, and have eaten East Coast and Gulf oysters. I still put the ones at Black's, Dupuy's, and Shucks! in a class by themselves. They arrive fresh daily from the wetlands between Vermilion and Grand Isle. Folks used to eating at New Orleans oyster bars may be disappointed that the oysters are not opened before their eyes at the bar, but all apprehension will fade when the tray arrives. These babies are so firm, so cold, and so clear they will send oyster lovers to nirvana. They are also perfectly shucked, with never a nick or speck of mud on the oyster meat, which sits in a brimming shell of unspilled oyster juice (or liquor, as it is called by oyster heads). I am not trying to be diplomatic, but all these places are great! Abbeville has been the site of a veritable oyster war since the folks who had run Dupuy's

(Photo by Julie Posner)

for most of this century were displaced and opened Shucks! in '95. Many Dupuy's patrons have refused to forgive, and oyster lovers from across Acadiana are asking the question, "Which one are you going to?" Check the reviews to see which ambiance suits you, or better yet, try all three!

★Dupuy's Seafood/Oysters $-$$. 108 S. Main St.

Dupuy's has been an Abbeville tradition for over a hundred years. In 1896 Joseph Dupuy sold shucked oysters in this same location on the banks of Bayou Vermilion for 10 cents a dozen; the price dipped to 5 cents a dozen during the Second World War. The bivalves here are still an amazing inflation buster at $4 per salty dozen. I challenge anyone to find more perfect and more perfectly shucked oysters. They are served in a tiny, no-frills dining room on ice-laden trays with all the condiments. The room sports a wall of awards won by its famous oyster shuckers and a collection of newspaper clippings about the restaurant that date back to the early 1900s. Oysters are a cold-weather dish and the perfect accompaniment is a hearty bowl of Dupuy's delicious gumbo or oyster stew. Seafood po' boys are available for $4 and dinners for $5 to $10. Dupuy's always opens on the new moon in late August and closes in May. It is on the right after you cross the Vermilion Bridge, catty-corner to the church. Dupuy's is open Monday through Saturday from 11 A.M. to 9 P.M. Closed May through August. (318) 893-2336.

★Black's Oyster Bar Seafood/Oysters, $-$$. 319 Pere Megret St.

In business since 1969, Black's no longer has to call itself the newcomer on the Abbeville oyster scene (a new restaurant was added in '95). During the peak of oyster season folks line up for oysters here on Friday and Saturday nights. You can order any number of well-prepared seafood dishes (and even a burger or steak for the timid), but folks travel miles to eat the incredible bivalves! They arrive at your table or at the bar on a tray of ice with condiments for mixing your own cocktail sauce. They are so lovely that you may devour half a dozen before remembering to season them. A dozen of these epic morsels is under $5. If you are shy about raw seafood, Black's serves a knockout Chesapeake-style oyster chowder. Finely minced onion and celery are sauteed 'til limp, then the oysters, "oyster liquor," and milk are added and cooked just until the edges of each oyster begin to ruffle. Try Black's delicious fried seafood loaves for around $5. Black's is a brick building with large windows overlooking St. Mary Magdalen Church. It is open Monday through Thursday from 10 A.M. until 9:30 P.M. and until 10 on Friday and Saturday. It is closed on Sunday and in the months May through August.

★Shucks! Seafood/Oysters, $-$$. 701 W. Port St.

Shucks! became the third oyster bar in Abbeville in 1995, but it has a tradition much older than that. The place was opened by the family that operated Dupuy's (see review) for most of the past century. Loyalists followed them to Shucks!, where the oysters are as great as ever: cold, clean, and freshly shucked. The rest of the menu closely resembles the old Dupuy's, with excellent corn and crab chowder and oyster stew spiked with fresh oyster juice. Sandwiches and broiled or fried seafood platters are well executed. Unlike Dupuy's, which has a subdued interior of worn wood and historic photos, Shucks! offers the lively and informal atmosphere of a seafood patio. (318) 898-3311.

Bertrand's Local Fave, $. 400 Charity St.

Tired of fast-food franchises supplanting down-home eateries? Visit this former Kentucky Fried Chicken outlet turned blue-collar diner. Bertrand's not only has the best lunches in Abbeville but also the best breakfasts. It is open 24 hours and serves a very good cup of coffee. Everything but the desserts are made on premises, including the real mashed potatoes. If you are traveling the Hug the Coast Highway south of Abbeville this is a good place to begin or end your trip. To get to Bertrand's follow the signs for Rte. 14 Business. It is just east of the courthouse. Open 24 hours a day, seven days a week. Children 3-12 eat for half-price.

G's Bar and Grill Plate lunch, $. Rte. 333, Intracoastal City.

Unlike Roland's (just down the road), G's has an air-conditioned dining room and counter with an adjacent barroom. This can be a welcome amenity on a hot day in Intracoastal City. G's serves breakfast anytime except midday, when it serves plate lunches and sandwiches. It is 20 miles south of Abbeville. G's is open Monday through Friday serving breakfast at 7 and lunch from 11 until 1. (318) 893-0044.

★Hebert's Meat Market Red boudin. Lafitte Road.

Typical of the meat markets south of Lafayette, Hebert's specializes in fresh meat. One of the unusual items made here is Plantin, a well-seasoned pork sausage wrapped in a very thin veil of fat. According to Hebert, Plantin is often grilled, as it holds together well over the flame and bastes itself. Hebert's also sells both *Paunce* (stuffed calf stomach) and *Chaudin*, which is similar but made with pork stomach. Hebert's is one of few places I have found that carry the blood sausage, *boudin rouge*. This ready-to-eat delight is made with pork blood, giving the filling a more moist texture than beef blood. To get to Hebert's, turn north off of Rte. 14 Bypass onto Rte. 338 (Lafitte Road) and look for the meat market about a mile down on the left. Hebert's is open

Monday through Friday from 7 A.M. to 6 P.M. and Saturday until noon. (318) 893-5688.

★Richard's Seafood Patio Boiled Seafood, $$. South Henry (Rte. 355).

This is a classic boiling point. "Patio" is an oft-used term to describe the more rustic of South Louisiana's boiled seafood joints, and in this case, it is an appropriate one. The low-lying wood-frame structure with unadorned white wood walls, cement floors, and plastic-covered tables has all the ambiance of a front porch during a noisy family reunion. You won't find any tour buses down here, just folks from all over coastal Cajun Country who have come to sample the large, spicy crawfish. Getting to Richard's is half the fun, as it means driving down a narrow road along the lower reaches of the Vermilion River. Some diners arrive by boat and dock right in front of the restaurant. In typical boiling-point fashion, the crawfish arrive piled on trays in steaming 3½-pound heaps, and the beer flows liberally. The trays are a unique creation of Mr. Richard, who designed a pivoting divider to keep the shells apart from the uneaten crawfish.

Richard's is open (seasonally—mid-November through mid-June) seven days a week from 5 to 10:30 P.M. From Lafayette take Rte. 167 south. Follow the signs towards Rte. 14 Business. Turn right on Rte. 335 before crossing the Vermilion River Bridge (South Henry Street) and look for Richard's about three miles down on the right.

Roland's Supermarket Plate lunch, $. Rte. 333, Intracoastal City.

Roland's is one of two plate-lunch places in Intracoastal City (20 miles south of Abbeville). You can also buy po' boys, fried chicken, and breakfast. There is no dining room; lunches are sold to go. If the weather is cool, you can eat on the tower by the Leland Bowman Locks. Roland's makes and sells a very hot beef jerky. It is sliced almost as thin as a potato chip, layered with seasoning, and smoked until it is almost crisp. It goes very well with more than one beer. Roland's is open Monday through Saturday from 5 A.M. to 6:30 P.M. and Sunday from 7 A.M. to 7 P.M. (318) 893-3854.

MUSIC

★Levy's Place Zydeco dance hall. Lafitte Road (Rte. 338 N.).

Stumbling across a place like Levy's drove home the fact that it would be nearly impossible to compile a complete guide to the dance halls of Cajun Country. I was looking for Hebert's Meat Market on a Saturday afternoon when I saw the line of cars and heard the sound of an accordion coming from this white clapboard hall. I never made it to Hebert's that day, but got to sample their pork at what turned out

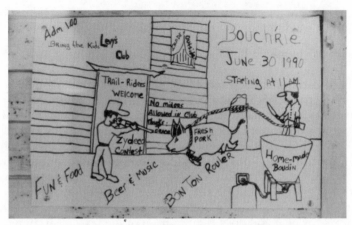

Levy's dance hall. (Photo by Macon Fry)

to be a big *boucherie* and Zydeco dance. Ms. Lernest Levy greeted friends and neighbors while the rest of her family stirred the cracklins and roasted the pig. The Levys occasionally host Zydeco dances. There is no phone so you will have to drive by to find out if anything is going on. From Rte. 14 Bypass (Veterans Memorial Drive) turn north onto Rte. 338 (Lafitte Road). Levy's is 2.5 miles ahead on the right.

Ponderosa Lounge Zydeco dance hall. 811 Nugier Ave.

The Ponderosa is in a neighborhood that's a bit rough for the casual tourist, but the crowd here is mellow. When I was trying to find the place, people kept telling me, "It's over in the Sticks" or "cross tracks," two names often used to describe the neighborhood. The Ponderosa has been bringing the top names in Zydeco to Abbeville since 1980. Manager Black Collins says, "I don't allow no trouble-makin' youngsters. You gotta be 21 or over." Look for music here one weekend a month during the summer. Go hungry so you can try out the barbecue next door. Turn south off Rte. 14 Bypass between the Sonic and the Taco Bell, onto Alphonse Road. Take the first left onto Nugier Road. The Ponderosa is two blocks down. (318) 893-2376.

★**Smiley's Bon Ami** Cajun dance hall. Rte. 14 between Erath and Delcambre.

See Erath listing.

LODGING

★**Kissinoaks Bed and Breakfast Cottage** Vermilion River.

Kissinoaks is the best place to stay in Abbeville. In the forties, owners Beverlee and Cecil Gremillion built this retreat on a bend in the

Vermilion River with over 1,500 feet of wooded frontage. Harkening back to the days when it was a party pad, the living room has a bar and the bedroom a hide-a-bed that folds into the wall. This is not one of those Murphy beds that threatens to fold you up! It is more comfortable than a sofa bed and has a headboard for nighttime reading. The bedroom features a desk, cozy chairs, and a glass wall opening onto a deck.

In the fifties the Gremillions found a plantation house on Bayou Teche, had it placed on a barge, and moved the structure 100 miles to a spot just behind the guest cottage. The story of the move (as related by Beverlee and Cecil) is worth the price of a night here! The Gremillions speak French. Kissinoaks is 1.2 miles north of the McDonald's at Rte. 14 Bypass, on Rte. 182 N. (If you come to the house with the Buick automobile hanging in the top of an oak tree, you have gone too far.) The camp has two guest quarters. The riverfront apartment rents for $95 a night; the back section costs $75. (318) 893-8888 or 893-7777.

Sunbelt Lodge Motel 1903 Veterans Memorial Dr. (Rte. 14).

The Sunbelt is the only decent motel in Abbeville. Some rooms are very nice and others are a bit worn. Beds are firm and there is a pool. The motel is on the highway (not downtown) right behind the Visitors Center, about a mile east of the Rte. 167 intersection. Double rate $45-$50. (318) 898-1453.

Sunnyside Motel Rte. 14, Kaplan (nine miles west of Abbeville).

This little fifties-style motel has clean rooms and comfortable beds. You get pine paneling, tile baths, a pool, a Jacuzzi, and a low rate. It is a convenient stopover for birders. A room for two costs $30 to $35. Sunnyside is 15 minutes west of Abbeville. (318) 643-7181.

Erath

There is not very much to this town of 2,250 stretching about 10 blocks along Rte. 14. Erath is, however, home to D. L. Menard, Cajun music's biggest living star, and the site of a great old-time Cajun dance hall.

ATTRACTIONS

D. L. Menard's Chair Factory Rte. 331 S.

D. L. (Doris Lee) Menard is Cajun music's biggest star and most distinctive voice. In the 1960s D. L. recorded "The Back Door," one of the great Cajun anthems of all time. It is not D. L.'s hit recordings, however, that have won him fans around the world. Menard's popularity

D. L. Menard, the "Cajun Hank Williams." (Photo by Julie Posner)

is born of charisma and love of life that busts through every time he smiles (which is most of the time).

D. L. doesn't waste much time when he gets back from an international tour, getting right back to making chairs in the shop beside his home in Erath. Menard explains that he decided to build chairs one day when he needed something to sit on. He works alone stacking lumber, turning wood on the lathe, and constructing sturdy platform and ladder-back rockers and dining chairs. When I suggested listing the D. L. Menard Chair Factory in a "crafts" section of this book, he protested, "This is not a craft but a factory!" Whatever you call them, D. L.'s chairs are built with a care and precision that defy their price. The joy of stopping at D. L.'s factory to order a chair and chatting with the "Cajun Hank Williams" is worth much more than the price of a chair. Be sure to get D. L. to sign your chair.

D. L.'s old factory, with many antique and handmade tools, burned down in October of '94. As we go to press he is just preparing to open a new one. Give him a call before you visit to make sure he is in. From Rte. 14 head south one mile on Rte. 331 (Kibbe Street). D. L.'s house and factory are on the left at the first bend in the road. (318) 937-5471.

FOOD

Big John's Seafood Patio Boiled Seafood, $$. Broadview Road.

Big John's is an old-style wood-frame boiling point located literally at the end of the road! The crawfish here are not the largest but are clean and tender. It is open from January until June daily, from 5 to 10 P.M. Take Rte. 14 to Erath. Go north on Rte. 339. Make a left on Broadview and follow it to the end. (318) 937-8355.

MUSIC

★**Smiley's Bon Ami** Cajun dance hall. Rte. 14, Delcambre.

When the venerable Smiley's Bayou Club in Erath closed in the midnineties, Wilbert ("Smiley") Menard moved his Cajun dances to the more expansive Bon Ami (also known as the Red Carpet). Located on the moist meadow between Erath and Delcambre, this big dance hall seems to be at the very edge of civilization, but on Friday and Saturday the parking lot gets packed beyond imagination as folks come to kick up their heels. Friday there is a free jam session from 8 P.M. "until." The big dance is Saturday night from 9 to 1 ($2). An older clientele shows up Sunday afternoon from 2 to 6. For information call Smiley at (318) 937-4591.

Delcambre

Delcambre (pronounced "DEL-come") is French for "community of meadows." This village of 2,000 located on Rte. 14 at the edge of Iberia Parish and Teche Country (20 minutes west of New Iberia and 45 minutes south of Lafayette) is home to one of the region's most productive shrimp fleets. The 200 shrimp boats docked beside the Delcambre Canal bring in over $14 million of shrimp annually. The shrimpers are honored and the shrimp fleet blessed each year at the August Shrimp Festival.

Shrimp Boat Landing

For a pleasant break from driving, and a look at the Delcambre shrimp fleet from up close, stop at the covered picnic area and fisherman's wharf just south of Rte. 14.

Shrimp Festival/Blessing of the Fleet Third weekend in August.

The year 1995 was the 45th anniversary of the Shrimp Festival. The four-day event is a typical small-town fair, with carnival rides and food. The highlight is Sunday, when the parish priest holds mass at the local community center and leads a procession to the dock for the "Blessing of the Fleet." The priest boards a decorated shrimpboat, which carries him through the harbor so that he may perform the rites. (318) 685-4462.

★**Rip Van Winkle Gardens, Jefferson Island** 15 minutes from Delcambre.

See South of New Iberia in the Teche Country chapter for complete details and directions.

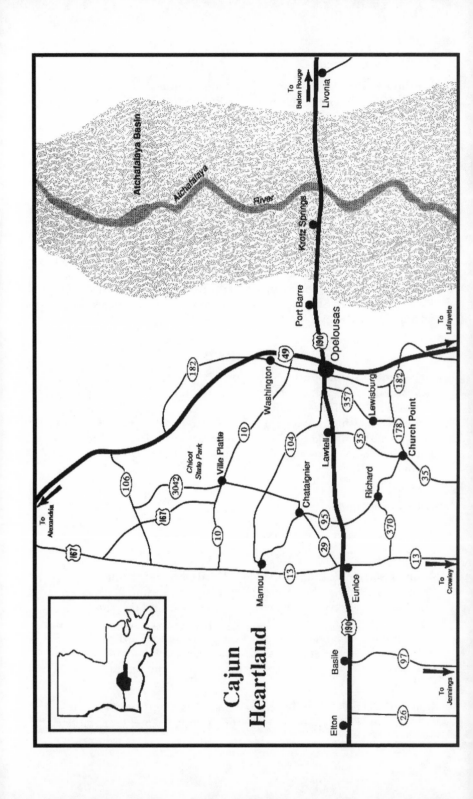

Cajun Heartland

14

Cajun Heartland

If food and music are used as a cultural barometer, the area at the northern apex of Cajun Country has every right to the title "Cajun Cultural Heartland" bestowed upon it by folklorist Alan Lomax. One has only to visit an old dance hall like Borque's or Slim's Y-Ki-Ki, or pry his or her eyes open at the live early-morning radio broadcasts from Fred's Lounge, to appreciate how integral music is to life on the northern Prairie.

The Cajun Heartland is a roughly triangle-shaped region defined by the richness of its culture more than distinct geographic boundaries. It includes most of St. Landry and Evangeline Parish at the top of the Acadiana triangle, with U.S. 190 (the Acadiana Trail) and the delightful Prairie outpost of Church Point forming its southern base. The land here reaches such heavenly elevations as 60 to 70 feet above sea level, but is generally flat. It rolls out in a majestic expanse of silver crawfish ponds and green rice and soybean fields, and is dotted with little railroad and cow towns.

The main east-west route through the region is U.S. 190, which begins in Port Allen just across the Mississippi River from Baton Rouge and enters Cajun Country at Bayou Gross Tete in Livonia. From Livonia the Trail carries travelers over the Morganza Spillway and Atchafalaya River into the historic town of Opelousas, where it intersects Interstate 49, the primary north-south highway in the state. Like the Old Spanish Trail to the south, this has been a major avenue of commerce and land transportation since the Indians used it as a footpath, but owes most of its character today to the Missouri Pacific rail line that was built along its course at the turn of the century.

BATON ROUGE TO OPELOUSAS

The portion of U.S. 190 that extends from Baton Rouge to Opelousas is the eastern gateway to the Cajun Heartland. For over 30 years, until the Atchafalaya Throughway on Interstate 10 was completed in the 1970s, this was the main route for motorists traveling

Crawfish pond in Cajun Heartland. (Photo by Julie Posner)

between Baton Rouge and Cajun Country. Were it not for dramatic elevated crossings at the Morganza and Atchafalaya floodways, this stretch of highway would resemble any number of old thoroughfares abandoned with the completion of interstate highways. There are lonely truckers' motels and Art-Deco-style white-tile gas stations, many now being reclaimed by vines and brambles.

Livonia

Located 17 miles west of Baton Rouge on U.S. 190 on the banks of Bayou Grosse Tete (French for "big head") at the junction of Rte. 77, Livonia has a population of about 600 and one of the best eateries in the state! I often get off the interstate and drive north on scenic Rte. 77 when traveling between Lafayette and New Orleans just so I can stop for a meal at Joe's.

★Joe's "Dreyfus Store" Restaurant Cajun/Creole, $-$$. Rte. 77.
This eatery is the best reason to travel U.S. 190 between Baton Rouge and Cajun Country. People come from all over the state to sample the recipes Joe Major perfected while working as a chef at New Orleans' prestigious Petroleum Club. Major offers everything from fried fish and po' boys to stuffed quail and catfish etouffée for under $14. All of the entrees come with a potato, vegetable, and hot French bread. The

The line forms outside Joe's "Dreyfus Store" Restaurant. (Courtesy of Dianne Major)

fancier preparations are as good as anything served in New Orleans' high-priced eateries, but Chef Major shines on country dishes like turkey pot pie with flaky homemade crust and po' boys with home fries.

The menu changes daily but always has a batch of regional favorites like roasted cornish game hen stuffed with cornbread dressing. Piquant corn and shrimp soup, oysters Bienville, and a slew of other appetizers are reverently prepared. I dream about Major's homemade white boudin smeared with pepper jelly. Top off the tank with sensual Creme Cafe Caramel, a custard topped with whipped cream and caramel sauce. Joe's is open Tuesday through Sunday from 11 to 2 for lunch and Tuesday through Saturday from 5 to 9 for dinner. It is .3 mile south of U.S. 190 on Rte. 77 in Livonia. From I-10 take Rte. 77 (exit #139) and travel north about 12 miles. (504) 637-2625.

Morganza Spillway

Eight miles west of Livonia, U.S. 190 crosses the lower guide levee of the Morganza Spillway. The spillway is one of several mammoth water-control projects initiated by the Corps of Engineers following the disastrous flood of 1927. At U.S. 190 there is a five-mile-wide swath of farmland that abuts the Atchafalaya River levee on the southwest and the Mississippi River on the northeast. When the Mississippi threatens to exceed its banks, the Corps of Engineers opens floodgates at the Mississippi and allows the turbid river water to pour into the Atchafalaya Basin. Crossing the great expanses of cultivated land on the five-mile-long overpass, imagine the scene in 1973 when the gates were opened and this verdant expanse was covered with a sheet of churning Mississippi River water. Continuing west on U.S. 190, the road crosses the Atchafalaya River Bridge (constructed by Huey Long in 1934) and drops down into the town of *Krotz Springs,* a small fishing village and notorious speed trap located squarely within the West Atchafalaya Spillway (consult the index for more information on the Atchafalaya and flood-control structures).

Krotz Springs

In the 1920s, entrepreneur C. W. Krotz arrived in the hamlet of Latania and drilled the first oil well in Louisiana. At 2,400 feet Krotz came up with a gusher of 100 percent pure artesian water (hence the new town name). Refusing to abandon the site, he marketed the water as a cure for "all kinds of stomach, kidney, and bowel trouble" and issued handbills proclaiming Krotz Springs to be "The Coming Health Resort of The South." Spring water was not to be featured in the future of the town (one local claims it had so many minerals that you gained 10 pounds by drinking a gallon). However, when Huey Long completed construction of the automobile bridge across the Atchafalaya, fish markets opened and a commissary was established near the foot of the bridge. After the flood of 1927 the Corps of Engineers constructed the West Atchafalaya Spillway (a western counterpart to the Morganza Spillway). In Simmesport (35 miles to the north) the Corps installed a "fuse plug levee" designed to give way if water reached a perilous level in the river. Under that scenario water would surge through the town of Melville and onto Krotz Springs. In response to this threat the city completely surrounded itself with levees in the 1950s. To visit old Krotz Springs one must drive south from U.S. 190 about six blocks.

Sherburne Wildlife Area Bird watching. Levee Road, Krotz Springs.

Sherburne is not a park, so it has few trails and no facilities. For exercise and incidental birding, try the 1.25-mile nature trail, which has several signs identifying different trees. Serious birders will do better atop the levee and at the Duck Lake egret rookery. To get to the nature trail take the Sherburne exit from U.S. 190 and head south 3 miles on Rte. 975 (the East Levee Road). To get to the rookery, go south about 8 miles and park beside the overhead power-line crossing. Walk the power-line right-of-way to Duck Lake Slough on the left. Follow the slough about .75 mile to the left. (318) 765-2999.

Country Store Bed and Breakfast 200 N. Main St., Krotz Springs.

The Dreyfus family has operated a commissary and general store in Krotz Springs since the 1920s. The Bed and Breakfast is over the "new" store, which was opened in the forties and is run by Sidney Dreyfus, son of the original owner. For folks who travel light, this is a perfect arrangement. If you need clothes or food, they are for sale downstairs. If you need fur traps, fishing gear, or hardware, they've got them too! The rooms are simple and comfortable, furnished much as they were when Sidney's parents lived over the store. There are two rooms with private bath and a suite with shared bath. Laundry facilities are available. Rooms for two cost $60 with a continental breakfast and $75 with a full breakfast. Visa, Mastercard, and Discover are accepted. (318) 566-2331 or 566-3501.

Port Barre

Twenty miles west of the Atchafalaya River and four miles east of Opelousas is the town of Port Barre (pronounced "Port Barry"). The town is best known as the "Birthplace of Bayou Teche," which springs from a brief confluence of Bayous Courtableau (cuh-tah-bluh) and Wauksha. Rte. 103 crosses U.S. 190 here, offering an opportunity to follow the bayou north to historic Washington (*see* index) or south through the old Creole settlement of Leonville and on to Breaux Bridge.

Birth of the Teche Park U.S. 190.

A historical marker and small picnic area on a bluff overlooking the black waters of the bayou are located on the north side of U.S. 190 on the east end of town.

Opelousas

Located 20 miles north of Lafayette and 56 miles west of Baton Rouge at the crossroads of Rte. 182 and U.S. 190 (just off Interstate 49), Opelousas (population 19,000) is the seat of St. Landry Parish, the largest town and main economic center in the Cajun Heartland. Opelousas (pronounced op-uh-LOO-sus) calls itself the Yam Capital of Louisiana for the luscious golden-orange sweet potatoes grown in the surrounding fields. Each year there is a Yam Festival (or Yambilee, as it is called) featuring performances by Cajun and Zydeco bands and a local group called the Yamettes. Opelousas's biggest cultural attractions are its Zydeco dance halls. While most residents are descendents of the Acadians, the city is a cultural capital for the large Creole population of St. Landry Parish. It is the birthplace of the late Zydeco king, Clifton Chenier, and home to colorful Slim's Y-Ki-Ki, one of the

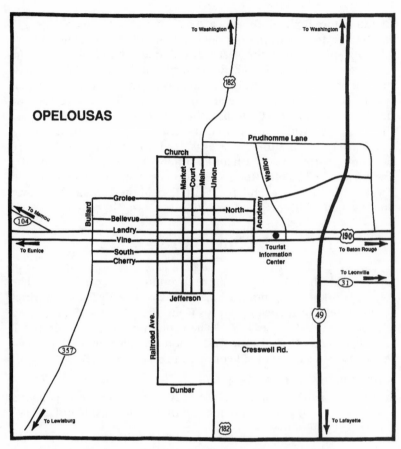

Opelousas. (St. Landry Tourist Commission)

best-known Zydeco dance halls in the state. It is also the ancestral home of world-famous chef Paul Prudhomme.

Opelousas, the third-oldest city in Louisiana, is located on a bluff 75 feet above sea level (a veritable mountain in these parts!). Founded as a French trading post in 1720, it functioned as a marketplace for *courriers du bois* (French traders and trappers). In 1769 a detachment of Spanish soldiers was stationed here to defend travelers between New Orleans and Nacogdoches and the settlement became known as El Poste de Opelousas, deriving its name from the local Indian tribe. When the first Acadian immigrants arrived in the late 18th century the post was a burgeoning trade center where whiskey and guns were traded for furs and skins and three-fourths of the population spoke French. In 1803, when the Louisiana Purchase was transacted,

Opelousas was named the seat of St. Landry Parish government and the town became a center for commerce in cotton, cattle, and later rice. A Methodist minister who moved to Opelousas from New Orleans complained in a letter dated 1803, "I have great difficulties in this country as there are no laws to suppress vice of any kind; so that the Sabbath is spent in frolicking and gambling."

Although no longer a wide-open frontier town, Opelousas still has its share of frolicking, with Cajun dances, Friday-night Zydeco blowouts, and several fairs like the Yambilee Festival, St. Landry Parish Heritage Festival, and Plaisance Zydeco Festival. Consider staying nearby at one of the B&Bs in historic Washington or Church Point.

ATTRACTIONS

The Jim Bowie Museum and Visitors Center U.S. 190 E., Opelousas.

This tourist information center greets travelers on the east edge of town. The first thing you are likely to notice is the tottering farmhouse that once belonged to a "free woman of color" in Prairie Ronde. The house, now open to the public, is partially restored and its billowing sides and roller-coaster floor resemble the fun house at an amusement park. Adjacent is an Acadian-style house that contains an information desk and the Jim Bowie Museum. At the information counter ask for the brochure that outlines a walking tour of historic Opelousas.

It is odd that this city, with its rich Spanish, French, Cajun, and distinctive Creole heritage, has claimed Jim Bowie as its favorite son, especially since it is unclear whether he actually spent much time there. Land records show members of the Bowie family arriving in the area in the early 1800s (when Bowie was not yet 10). There is a historical marker on Rte. 182 (Union Street) just south of town at the site where the Bowie family plantation stood. The collection of Bowie knives, artifacts, and news clippings housed in the Jim Bowie Museum gives an interesting glimpse of one of America's great frontier heroes. The Visitors Center and museum are open from 8 to 4 daily. (318) 948-6263 or 1-800-424-5442.

Historic District Walking Tour (Map available at Visitors Center).

U.S. 190, the main street in Opelousas, splits as it enters the city, with St. Landry Street becoming the primary westbound route and Vine Street handling eastbound traffic. There is plenty of free and inexpensive street parking around the intersection of Landry and Main (Rte. 182), where the walking tour begins. Whether you walk or drive, this tour can be easily managed in less than two hours. Although there are many historic homes on the tour (none of which are currently open to the public), the highlights are the old commercial establishments and public buildings around Courthouse Square.

Site of Clyde Barrow's last shave. (Photo by Julie Posner)

Across Court Street from the Deco-style *St. Landry Courthouse* is the *"New" Rexall Drug Store* (built about 1905). Around the corner on St. Landry Street is the old *Shute Building,* which housed the Star Barbershop. This is the site where Clyde Barrow, of the notorious outlaw gang Bonnie and Clyde, allegedly got his last shave (a close one?) before being gunned down two days later in an ambush on a dusty road in northern Louisiana's Bienville Parish.

Just a couple of blocks east of the courthouse at the corner of Main Street and Bellevue Street is the *Firemen's Museum.* The museum occupies one of the bays in the old Opelousas Fire Hall. Here you will find a mule-drawn fire wagon, a restored hook-and-ladder truck, and a roomful of antique firefighting paraphernalia. Don't wait for a guided tour; the two times I passed by, the collection was open but unattended.

No tour or cursory visit to downtown Opelousas is complete without a stop at the *Palace Cafe* on the corner of St. Landry and Market. This cafe was founded in the thirties and is the oldest restaurant in Opelousas. The best reason for stopping at the Palace Cafe is not its history but the homemade shakes, onion rings, and blue-plate or sandwich specials (*see* review in Food section).

★J. B. Sandoz Store 318 N. Main St. (Rte. 167).

I was not "born to shop," but I have spent hours prowling through the housewares and hardware at this most remarkable store. Sandoz has been a family-owned enterprise in Opelousas since 1878 (five generations). The current building was constructed in 1952 and covers most of a square block. It is packed with merchandise such as cookware, ceramics, freezing supplies, pressure cookers, and everything for the home or kitchen. The store stocks items that can be tough to find, like big-mouth glass cookie jars with screw-on lids, all manner of cruets and corked glass containers, kerosene lamps, drip coffee pots, well buckets, crock milk bowls, cast-iron cookware, and hardware for shutters. You will find yourself asking, "Do they really still make this stuff?" The last time I was there I picked up a cast-iron skillet with ridged bottom for pan grilling for around $15. Folks who have spent hours in Wal-Marts, Kmarts, and the other palaces of plastic can step back in time at Sandoz and shop a world of iron, galvanized steel, glass, and wood. I don't know where Sandoz finds all this stuff, but it is of impeccable quality at a fraction of the cost of what a chi-chi outlet like Pottery Barn might charge. If you are a shop-aholic be prepared to rent

Everything you could want, at Sandoz. (Photo by Macon Fry)

a trailer for your trip home. Ask at the counter for the Sandoz Centennial Brochure. The store is open from 7:15 to 5 Monday through Saturday. (318) 942-3564.

Opelousas Museum and Interpretive Center 329 N. Main St. (Rte. 167).

This new museum is building a collection of artifacts that provides insight into the history of the Opelousas area. There are exhibits on prehistory, Civil War activity, music, and food in the region. The most interesting things are displays of family and professional artifacts from local donors, including four generations of antique doctor's equipment and a reconstructed barbershop. The exhibits were a bit thin in 1997, but the museum is growing and admission is granted for a small donation. The museum is about five blocks north of U.S. 190 on Main Street. Hours are Tuesday through Saturday from 9 until 5. (318) 948-2589.

Savoie's Sausage & Food Products, Inc. Rte. 742, southeast of Opelousas.

Savoie's has one of the best "plant tours" in Acadiana, provided of course that you are not shy about raw meat. The wood-frame grocery tells the story of Eula Savoie's entry into business back in 1949 but belies the size of the sausage, sauce, and seasoning factory out back. Mrs. Savoie guides visitors through the spice-mixing room, roux-making area, and sausage-stuffing assembly line (which turns out over 10,000 pounds a day) before showing off the high-tech smokehouse. After the tour you can sit at an enameled table in the store and eat smoked sausage on a stick. It is important to go through with the sausage-eating part of the tour because seeing sausage made is a bit like falling off a motorcycle. If you are ever going to do it again it is a good idea to pick up and begin right away. Savoie's is open Monday through Saturday from 7 to 5. Tours are by appointment Tuesday through Thursday from 9 to 11. Go east on U.S. 190 and turn right onto Frontage Road after crossing under I-49. Go a couple of miles and turn left on Rte. 31. Go 1.5 miles to the fork and stay to the left onto Rte. 742. Savoie's is 3 miles farther. (318) 942-7241.

Tony Chachere's Creole Foods 533 North Lombard.

This small factory makes some of the state's most popular seasoning mixes and barbecue sauces. Tours are offered to individuals and groups who call in advance. There isn't a lot to see, but the smells range from delectable to sinus opening and there is an opportunity to buy products right off the assembly line. The factory is located near the downtown area. Call in advance. (318) 948-4691.

Runyon Products, Inc. Rte. 357, south of Opelousas.

The most interesting factory tour for the musically inclined is the workshop for Santy Runyon's Runyon Products, Inc. Runyon is an acclaimed musical and technical genius who has been manufacturing mouthpieces for horns and woodwinds since the early forties. Art Pepper, Ernie Shaw, and Harry James are just a few of the luminaries who have endorsed his handiwork. Runyon's creations have enabled musicians to get previously unavailable tones and volume from their instruments. In addition to producing 8,000 to 10,000 mouthpieces a month, octogenarian Runyon manufactures a slew of devices from neck straps to key raisers that help musicians get the most from their horns. The workshop at Runyon's is as amazing for its variety of custom-made machines that mold and cut plastics and metal as it is for its selection of specialized products. This cottage industry is a sax-man's dream. Runyon Products, Inc. is located on Rte. 357 one-half mile south of U.S. 190 on the right-hand side (leaving town). Call (318) 948-6252 to arrange for a visit.

SPECIAL EVENTS

★**"Here's the Beef" Cook-Off** Third weekend in March. Yambilee Arena.

A wall of smoke greets festival goers at the door to the Yambilee Arena. Somewhere behind the smoke a band is playing and people are dancing, but your sinuses will tell you right away that this is a barbecue blowout. Fans of mouthwatering red sauce, crusty ribs, and smoky-tender brisket will love this hoedown. No admission is charged, but beers and BBQ are sold at dozens of pits scattered across the dirt-floored arena. The festival grounds are behind the Yamatorium, on U.S. 190 in the west end of town. (318) 684-6751.

Yambilee Festival Last weekend in October. Yamatorium.

The Yambilee is the biggest and oldest harvest festival in St. Landry Parish. It features yam recipe and cooking contests and plenty of typical carnival-type foods. Bands perform and there is an amusement midway outside the festival hall. 1-800-210-5298.

★**Zydeco Festival** Labor Day weekend. Rte. 167, Plaisance.

This is the main event on the Zydeco calendar. The best bands from across Acadiana perform on stages set in the middle of the Cajun Prairie between Opelousas and Ville Platte. Always held the Saturday before Labor Day, this festival runs from 11 A.M. to midnight with continuous music and food. Labor Day weekend can be blisteringly hot, but the good times and copious quantities of beer and cold drinks wash all such earthly concerns away. Many of the bands appear at dance halls later in the evening, so you can plan on soaking up music and sun all day and eating at the Pig Stand in Ville Platte or the Palace

Cafe in Opelousas before going out for another round. Many visitors stay in the area and attend a big outdoor Zydeco party held at Richard's dance hall on Sunday. Hardcore Zydeco fans enjoy another full day of dance music at Boozoo's Dog Hill Day Zydeco Festival on Monday (*see* Lake Charles listings). The Zydeco Festival is held at the Southern Development Farm about 10 miles northwest of Opelousas. Take I-49 north to Rte. 167 (exit #23). The festival site is on the right about 8 miles from I-49. (318) 942-2392.

FOOD

Back In Time Sandwich Shop Local Fave, $. 145 W. Landry (U.S. 190).

This tiny sandwich shop and ice-cream parlor opened across from the courthouse and became an instant hit with the great legal minds and everyone else looking for a break from heavy stews and fried food. Don't let the cute nicknacks that clutter the place fool you; this place serves a dozen well-crafted sandwiches. The best salad is the chicken spinach with freshly made dressings. Thankfully the front of the menu looks healthy, because you will not want to leave without trying one of the excellent homemade desserts listed on the back. The lemon ice-box pie is very good with black coffee. If you want to overdo it, try the double-layer brownie with cream-cheese filling, topped with a scoop of ice cream and doused in fresh-made chocolate sauce (guaranteed to make you feel age seven again or kill you trying). Milkshakes are made on an old Hamilton Beach blender. Hours are 11 A.M. to 2:30 P.M. Monday through Saturday. (318) 942-2413.

★Catahoula's Cajun/Creole, $$-$$$. Grand Coteau (nine miles south).

See review in Central Cajun Country chapter (North of Lafayette).

Farmers' Market/Mikey's Donut King East Vine (U.S. 190).

If you cannot make up your mind about starting that health-food diet, this is the perfect breakfast stop. Use the same parking lot as the Opelousas Visitors Center (on the neutral ground of U.S. 190) in the east end of town. Mikey's serves piping-hot, freshly fried donuts from 4 A.M. to 1 P.M. daily. Right behind the donut shop is a pavilion where local farmers sell their produce from late spring to early fall. The farmers' market is open seasonally, Tuesday, Thursday, and Saturday at 6 A.M. until midmorning.

Kelly's Country Meat Block Meat Market. 1618 Union St. (Rte. 182 S.).

Kelly Cormier makes the best boudin in Opelousas, using large pieces of Boston butt pork that have been marinated, cooked down, and mixed with rice. It is mildly seasoned with a good meaty flavor. The Prairie-style andouille is not for everybody (casings stuffed with chopped, smoked hog chitterlings). Cormier learned how to cut meat during 13 years at a Church Point slaughterhouse, and he dispenses cooking tips that are worth even more than his steaks. The proof of his cooking advice is found next door at the Country Diner. The meat market is open Monday through Friday from 7 A.M. to 5:30 P.M. and on Saturday from 8 A.M. to 1 P.M. From U.S. 190, head south on Union Street (Rte. 182) about two miles. (318) 948-4170.

Kelly's Country Diner Down Home. 1618 Union St. (Rte. 182 S.).

Kelly's serves more than the typical plate-lunch fare. Sure, they have daily specials like beef cubes in gravy, pork chops, and chicken stews, but you will also find a good selection of grilled fish and seafood salads. All are served with two veggies, a dessert, and roll for $4.50. To settle down the young-uns, send them to the sno-ball window. See the directions to Kelly's Country Meat Block. The diner is open 11 A.M. to 9 P.M. Monday through Friday and until 1:30 P.M. on Saturday and Sunday. (318) 948-4170.

★The Palace Cafe Local Fave, $-$$. 167 W. Landry (U.S. 190).

This little diner built in 1954 is an essential stop on any visit to the Opelousas area, even if it's just to sit at the counter and down a cold milkshake created in an antique Hamilton Beach blender. In business since the thirties, the Palace is the oldest restaurant in Opelousas and the hands-down favorite among the Courthouse Square crowd, who flock there for Pete Doucas's (Mr. Pete, as everyone calls him) fried-chicken salad and homemade baklava. The salad is a cool combination of greens and tender chicken, well tossed in a light mayonnaise dressing and served on an oval dinner plate. Order a side of thin and crisp onion rings with your salad. Try the smoked sausage with rice and gravy, or calf's liver smothered in onions. At lunch (the best time to eat here), these and a selection of sandwiches are served with a choice of three vegetables for under $6. Wednesday's special is well-seasoned roast pork with rice and gravy, cornbread and dressing, and candied yams. Some good! The Palace is located at the corner of Market and Landry. It is open Monday through Saturday from 6 A.M. to 9 P.M. On Sunday it opens at 7 A.M. (318) 942-2142.

Ray's Boudin 889 E. Vine St. (U.S. 190).

Ray's sign shows a link of boudin wearing a cowboy hat and brandishing six-shooters over the proclamation "A Legend In Hot Boudin." The boudin here is good but not seasoned enough to my taste. Why do I go there? Ray's is just west of the I-49 exit at U.S. 190 and has a drive-up window. They sell as little as $1 worth of boudin, sliced and with a stack of napkins, and from I-49 the boudin-fueling process takes about two minutes! I also have to admit I am a sucker for the sign. Ray's is open from 8 to 6 Monday through Friday and until 5 on Sunday. If you want to park and go in, pull into the Visitors Center lot across the street. (318) 942-9150.

Soileau's Dinner Club Cajun/Creole, $-$$. 1620 N. Main St.

Soileau's has been in business on North Main Street since the thirties. The best bet is to order simple dishes. That means try the huge fried fresh Gulf shrimp ($13 a dozen) and U.S. Choice steaks ($15-$17). Most entrees come with salad and a choice of potatoes. The favorite of locals, who call in orders by the dozen each day, is the stuffed Idaho baked potato, filled with smoked sausage and cheese. Avoid the stuffed and sauce-smothered fish. For lunch or an economical dinner, order the shrimp po' boy, packed with large shrimp ($6). Head north on Rte. 167, which joins Main Street on the edge of town. Soileau's is open Sunday through Thursday from 11 A.M. to 10 P.M. and on Friday and Saturday until 11. (318) 942-2985.

★Steamboat Warehouse Restaurant Cajun/Creole, $$-$$$. Rte. 10, Washington (six miles north).

See review in Washington section.

MUSIC

Opelousas and the surrounding areas were a popular settling point for former slaves, free men of color, and other French-speaking black people during the late 18th and early 19th centuries. The present-day descendants of these early settlers, who call themselves Creoles, have made the region a veritable Mecca for Zydeco enthusiasts. Not only is Opelousas the birthplace of Zydeco's best-known practitioner, the late Clifton Chenier, but the area is home to C.R.E.O.L.E., Inc. (an organization promoting Creole culture and music), the annual Zydeco Festival, and two of South Louisiana's most venerated old Zydeco dance halls. A short drive southwest to Lewisburg uncovers two fantastic old Cajun dance halls. A good side trip is the jam session in Church Point, 15 miles southwest (see the section following Washington).

Zydeco:

★Slim's Y-Ki-Ki Zydeco dance hall. Rte. 167 N.

Slim's is one of the most popular Zydeco dance halls in the state, attracting the top bands and visitors from around the world. Slim (Arnold Gradney) opened the club back in 1947 and now runs it with the help of his son Tony. It is a place that puts out the welcome mat regardless of one's race or age. The dance floor, which cuts a wide

Poster from Slim's Y-Ki-Ki

swath between the bar and stage, is the center of attention. There is generally more competition for space on the floor than at tables, but it is wise to arrive by 9:30 or 10 if you want a seat. The choice seats are at the end of the club opposite the door, where huge airplane-propeller-size fans manage to move a little air. Beer and liquor are available at the bar, but the most popular drink configuration is a pint bottle of liquor, a bowl of ice, and some set-ups. The crowd at Slim's tends to be older and well dressed, with many of the same couples showing up every weekend. Slim's is on Rte. 167 (Main Street) in the north end of town. Dances are held most weekends on Friday or Saturday. Admission is $4 to $6. (318) 942-9980.

★**Richard's Club** Zydeco dance hall. U.S. 190 W., Lawtell.

Richard's joins Slim's Y-Ki-Ki as a true landmark on the Zydeco circuit. This rugged old place has been in business since the fifties. Prior to establishing itself as a Zydeco hall, it was a major stopping point on the Chitlin' Circuit, featuring some of the big names in R&B. Richard's got a lot of publicity when two albums featuring Boozoo Chavis and John Delafose were recorded there. The ambiance in the tattered wood-frame building is even more homey than Slim's and the crowd is a bit younger. They are used to plenty of visitors here; in fact, owner Kelvin Richard saw me jotting down notes and asked if I was with the "film crew"! Like at Slim's, you will find the best names in Zydeco here. Richard's is located on U.S. 190 just west of Opelousas in Lawtell. Dances are held on Fridays and Saturdays. For information call Mr. Kelvin Richard at (318) 543-6596 (home).

Offshore Lounge Zydeco dance hall. Just off U.S. 190, Lawtell.

Popular Zydeco accordionist and bandleader Roy Carrier runs this small wood-frame dance hall and lives in the adjacent trailer, and his son Chubby is a frequent performer. There is a Zydeco jam every Thursday and dances on some weekends. This location is a bit tricky, especially when the hand-lettered sign that marks the turnoff from U.S. 190 has been blown over, but it is just off the highway. Heading west on U.S. 190 into Lawtell, go a half-mile past the point where east- and westbound lanes split and make a right. This road is not marked, so check your odometer. Cross the railroad tracks and the red wood hall will appear in front of you. (318) 543-9996.

★Zydeco Festival Labor Day weekend. Rte. 167, Plaisance.

See Special Events listing above.

Cajun Music:

★Borque's Cajun dance hall. Lewisburg.

About eight miles southwest. Cajun dances every weekend. See Church Point section for review. (318) 948-9904.

★Guidry's Friendly Lounge Cajun dance hall. Lewisburg.

About eight miles southwest. Cajun dances every weekend. See Church Point section for review. (318) 942-9988.

★Train Depot Cajun Jam Session Main Street, Church Point.

See Church Point section.

LODGING

Hotels and Motels:

Best Western Opelousas 1635 I-49 Service Rd. S.

Doubles $65-$75. Located on the south edge of town. (318) 942-5540 or 1-888-942-5540.

Quality Inn Opelousas 4501 I-49 S.

Doubles $70-$80. Located a mile south of town. (318) 948-9500 or 1-800-228-5151.

Bed and Breakfast:

Opelousas has only one B&B operating. However, there are six excellent B&Bs in Washington (about 6 miles north), ranch-style cabins in

Church Point (about 15 miles southwest), and a caboose for rent in nearby Sunset (see North of Lafayette listings).

Maison de Saizan 412 Court St., Opelousas.

Louis and Donna Doucet speak French and rent three rooms with private baths and antique furnishings in their Victorian house. There is a TV and phone in each room and a porch overlooking the gardens. They are in the heart of downtown Opelousas within convenient walking distance of Courthouse Square and the Palace Cafe. Doubles cost $75-$130. (318) 942-1311 or 948-9898.

Camping:

Acadiana Wilderness Campground I-49 South, Opelousas.

This is a well-shaded campground with big spaces and full hookups. Camping costs $12 for RVs, $10 for pop-ups, and $8 for tents. From Opelousas head south a couple of miles on I-49 and take exit #15, then go south on the west Frontage Road about 1.5 miles. (318) 662-5154.

Washington

Walking through the small steamboat town of Washington is a remarkable experience. Eighty percent of the town is on the National Historic Register, yet there is no sense of self-conscious reconstruction or preservation like one gets in Williamsburg, Virginia. There is no designated "old downtown area"; it is as if the entire place was just frozen in time somewhere around 1880. Washington is about six miles north of Opelousas on Rte. 10 and only five blocks off Interstate 49 at exit #25 (about 30 minutes north of Lafayette). The town may be toured on foot in two and a half hours, but you may want to prolong your visit by planning a meal at the Steamboat Warehouse Restaurant or by planning a night at one of the several Bed and Breakfasts.

Situated on the banks over the River Opelousas, Washington is on hilly lands originally deeded to Jacque Courtableau, for whom the adjacent river was renamed Bayou Courtableau (pronounced "cuh-tah-bluh"). The land was subsequently granted to a "guardian of the Church," which began selling arpent (a bit less than an acre) lots in 1822. The settlement was called Church's Landing until it was incorporated in 1835 and renamed Washington. The first steamboat reportedly arrived in Washington in 1832 and the town rapidly grew into the largest steamboat port between New Orleans and St. Louis.

Washington is a place apart from the rest of Cajun South Louisiana. Settled by merchants and wealthy steamboat captains in greater numbers than Acadians, the bustling village had little in common with the tiny cow towns and pioneer settlements of the yawning Prairie. Tons of cotton, molasses, sugar, hides, and cattle were loaded at steamboat warehouses and exchanged for finished and manufactured goods unavailable on the frontier. There were operatic performances and all the vices associated with quantities of men and money.

With the arrival of the railroad in 1883, Washington's importance as a center of commerce declined. The last steamboat departed in 1900, leaving the town a veritable storybook land of antebellum and Victorian homes and plantations. Local merchants, Lafayette commuters, and retirees who call Washington home are proud of the village and its rich history.

ATTRACTIONS

Washington is a place that just begs you to stop the car and take a walk. Many of the most beautiful old homes and antique shops are located on a 10-block stretch of Main Street and in a hilly corridor 3 or 4 blocks wide on either side. The varied terrain makes Washington (especially the five miles of paths at Magnolia Ridge Plantation) one of the best walking spots in South Louisiana. There is unlimited free parking.

Washington Museum and Tourist Center Main Street and Dejean.

This is a fine place to begin poking around. Here you can watch a short video on the town history, look through a roomful of books, artifacts, and clippings pertaining to the old steamboat days, and get a town map and tour-guide brochure. The museum is open Wednesday

Last steamboat warehouse in Louisiana. (Photo by Julie Posner)

through Friday from 8 to 4 and on Saturday and Sunday from 9 to 4 (closed for noon lunch hour daily). (318) 826-3627.

The Historic Washington Walking Tour

This hike includes nine antebellum homes that are open to the public (map available at tourist center). They are generally shown by the homeowners ($5 fee), who make time for guests if possible, so it is essential to call ahead (you can use the phone at the tourist center) to make an appointment. You won't need a reservation to walk the paths at Magnolia Ridge Plantation and Cedar Hill Cemetery or to shop at the huge Old School Flea Market (*see* Shopping section below). You can begin the tour anywhere, but I recommend starting at the bayou on Main Street. Below are just a few of the highlights of the walking tour.

The Hinckley House 405 E. Dejean St.

This house is only a couple of blocks from the tourist center and is the one residence in Washington you should visit whether you are an old-house buff or not. Built in the late 1700s by trading-post operator Asa Norton, the house has remained in the same family for nearly two centuries. It is constructed of cypress beams and molding joined by pegs and square nails. The plaster walls are bound with deer and cattle hair. Throughout the years each generation has brought in "new" treasures and furnishings while preserving much of the old. Two of the more prominent family members were steamboat captains and there is an excellent array of steamboat memorabilia on display. Today the house is owned and shown by family historian Arthur Hinckley. (318) 826-3670.

Nicholson House of History Main Street and Vine.

If you are into spooks, call on Mrs. Nicholson; the dead come back to life as the lady of the house shows bloodstains in the attic, which once housed a Confederate hospital. The wounded who died were allegedly buried under the house, where Mrs. Nicholson points out a number of earthen mounds. If all this fails to get your imagination working, just ask Mrs. Nicholson if she has actually seen any ghosts. (318) 826-3670.

De la Morandiere St. John and Sittig Street.

On a hill overlooking Bayou Courtableau and the Steamboat Warehouse Restaurant is a two-story French Planter-style home built in 1830, with 5,000 square feet of airy rooms. One of the most elegant Washington homes, De la Morandiere is not open for tours but may be viewed from the adjacent streets. The present owners, Mr. and Mrs. Steve Johnson, operate a Bed and Breakfast for those who want to relax and enjoy the spacious grounds and perhaps dine at the adjacent Steamboat Warehouse Restaurant. (318) 826-3510.

Steamboat Warehouse Restaurant Main Street (Rte. 10) at Bayou Courtableau.

This is not just one of the best restaurants in St. Landry Parish; it is an authentic steamboat warehouse where goods were stored before export on one of the big paddlewheelers. Pass by for a drink at the bar, a listen at the jukebox, and a stroll along the dock (*see* review in Food section).

★Magnolia Ridge Plantation Hiking Trails Dejean Street (Rte. 103 W.).

One of the loveliest attractions in Washington is the five miles of paved paths that wind through 60 acres of landscaped grounds at Magnolia Ridge Plantation. Visitors may jog or walk along paths that wind from open fields and formal gardens to wooded hillsides by Bayou Courtableau. There is a cypress swamp with a small boardwalk and deck and a tropical fish pond showered by a fountain. The plantation house (built in the early 1800s) is the private residence of Anne and Tipton Golias, who bought the estate in 1985. It is not open for tours. Scattered around the property you will see small cottages and country houses bought by the Golias family and moved to Magnolia Ridge to save them from destruction. For a history of the main house (used as a headquarters by Southern and Northern forces during the War Between the States) and a small map of the trails, ask at the Washington tourist center. You can find your way around easily without the map. Magnolia Ridge grounds are open from dawn to dusk. There is a sign on the right side of Dejean Street (Rte. 103) pointing to the visitors parking about five blocks west of Main Street.

Cedar Hill Cemetery Vine Street and Wilkins.

Cedar Hill is located at the western end of the walking tour. This cemetery gains an ethereal feel from its odd collection of sunken and overgrown graves and the avenue of moss-hung cedars running through the center.

Arlington Plantation Dejean Street, 1.7 miles west of the tourist center.

Arlington (not close enough to be on the walking tour) was built in 1829 and is situated on a ridge overlooking the confluence of Bayous Boeuf (pronounced "buff"), Cocodrie, and Courtableau. Folks showing old plantation homes enjoy counting things like the number of bricks used in construction, and Arlington racks up some impressive numbers. At 8,000 square feet of floor space, it is the largest plantation in the area. It has nine fireplaces, three staircases, and a 40-foot-long schoolroom upstairs. The home is currently owned by Mrs. Robert Olivier, who gives tours by appointment but can be pretty hard to get ahold of on the spur of the moment. (318) 826-3298.

Elijah Harris crafts a basket in his shop outside Washington. (Photo by Macon Fry)

LOCAL CRAFTSMEN

Harris Split Oak Baskets White Oak Road, Washington.

Edward Harris learned how to make split oak baskets from his grandfather on their farm outside Washington in 1917, when he was five years old. Now he has a half-dozen sons who are accomplished basket makers. The most active of these is Elijah, who lives on the farm next to his father and makes baskets that by the elder Harris's admission are better than his own. They are made from white oak logs about eight inches in diameter, which are split with a wedge and mallet. The only other tool used is a sharp pocket knife. Edward recalls the first basket he made back in 1917, an egg basket that sold for 15 cents. Now the baskets start around $25, with a large part of the price increase due to the scarcity of white oak. You can examine and purchase Elijah Harris baskets at Kirt's Auto and Farm Supply on Main Street, but Elijah keeps a broad selection of baskets (at a better price) at his home. To meet Harris and purchase directly from him, call in advance at a reasonable hour. To get to the Harris farm from the intersection of Rte. 167 and Rte. 10, take Rte. 10 north towards Washington one mile. Turn left (west) on Prayer House Road and go about two miles. Make a right on White Oak Road. (318) 826-7267.

Soileau's Cowhide Chairs Rte. 363, Grand Prairie (eight miles west).

The Soileau name is well known when it comes to curing and stretching cowhide seats and backs for chairs. Joe Soileau learned the craft from his father, who learned it from his great-grandfather. Joe's father was "discovered" at a fair in Baton Rouge while conducting a moonshine-making demonstration. Folks from around the world have purchased Joe's covered chairs. He cleans the flesh and fat off raw cowhide, then stretches it in the rain and sun to wash and dry. In the final step, Joe binds the hide to chair frames with leather thongs. Joe has chairs you can choose from, but I recommend that you find them elsewhere and take them to Joe for custom covering. You may look through the hides and select the ones you like. Chair seats cost $25-$40 and backs are $50-$60. Driving to Joe's will take you through some beautiful countryside. From Main Street in Washington head west on Dejean Street (Rte. 103). Rte. 103 becomes Rte. 363; 8.3 miles from Washington you will arrive at a country store in Grand Prairie. Joe's home and shop are to the left, just off Rte. 363 beside the store. (318) 826-5818 or 826-3295.

SHOPPING

Kirt's Auto and Farm Supply Split oak baskets. 104 Main St.

Kirt's will remind you that as prim as downtown Washington is, this is still an agricultural region. The historic store is a good place to shop for split oak baskets by local artisan Elijah Harris (see listing above). Hours are 7 to 5 Monday through Friday and until noon on Saturday. (318) 826-3333.

★Old Washington Antique School Mall Flea Market Vine and Church Street.

Eighty-five dealers and over 20,000 square feet of antiques, junk, and esoterica make this a fascinating place to buy or browse. You will find some real oddities and bargains here, the kind that would make antique dealers in New Orleans weep. The old, two-story, wood-frame school is within easy walking distance from the Washington tourist center. It is open every weekend. (318) 826-3580.

Cajun Antique Flea Market 110 N. Main St.

This is another good place to find trash, treasures, bargains, and strange stuff on the walking tour. It is open Saturday and Sunday from 9 to 5.

The Acadian Connection 202 S. Main St.

Dot Mayer, who grew up at nearby Magnolia Ridge Plantation, operates this fine gift shop on the walking-tour route. In addition to work by local craftsmen, Dot stocks a big collection of books and brochures on regional subjects (harkening back to her days as city librarian). Behind the shop is La Chaumière Bed and Breakfast (*see* Lodging section below). The Acadian Connection is open Thursday through Sunday from 1 to 4 P.M. (318) 826-3967.

FOOD

Check the Opelousas and Ville Platte listings for a broader selection.

Charleen's Deli and Market Plate Lunch, $. 311 N. Main St.

Charleen's is the grocery store in Washington. They have a small lunch counter in front where they serve nice plate lunches to go. Even if it were not the only place in town, it is still a worthy lunch stop. If you are walking Main Street you can take lunch down to the banks of Bayou Courtableau for a picnic. A main dish (usually a choice of chicken fricassee, seafood stew, or fried chicken), rice, and two veggies costs about $4. (318) 826-3926.

Duo's Produce Rte. 10 at Rte. 167.

Duo's would deserve a mention for their herd of colorful hand-lettered signs even if they did not have the best produce in the area. The little roadside stand sells veggies, fruits, sweet-dough pies, local honey, cracklins, boudin, and cold drinks. If you are staying at a Bed and Breakfast in Washington, stop to buy your produce here, since you will not find any in town. Duo's is a couple of miles southwest of Washington at the intersection of Rte. 167 and Rte. 10. Hours are 8 A.M. to 7 P.M. (318) 826-3733.

★Steamboat Warehouse Restaurant Cajun/Creole, $$-$$$. Main Street.

The Steamboat Warehouse Restaurant is housed in the only remaining steamboat warehouse in South Louisiana. Huge cypress beams and raw wood dominate the decorating, while spinning ceiling fans and a great jukebox keep the atmosphere cozy. This is one of a few places where it pays to stretch out and order some of those nouveau Cajun dishes like fish blanketed and stuffed with seafood and sauces. The Catfish Palmetto, a fried fish topped with crawfish, tasso, and almonds in a cream sauce, won Chef Frankie Elder a gold medal for best seafood dish and is highly recommended. A less high-falutin' specialty is Elder's seafood gumbo (dark and pungent), which arrives at the table accompanied by a freshly baked St. Landry Parish yam! Another special finds the famous yams served up with succulent roast pork. Different desserts are prepared fresh each day. I had to get two helpings of the buttery apple cobbler with pecan-crunch crust. Hours are Tuesday through Saturday from 5 to 9 P.M. and Sunday from 11 A.M. to 2 P.M. (318) 826-7227.

MUSIC

Washington is *not* a music town. It is a quiet, mainly Anglo community that shares little in the *joie de vivre* that inspires French dances in Prairie communities half its size. However, it is only a short drive to the dance halls of Opelousas, Lawtell, and Ville Platte.

Willie's Campground Tavern Country/Oldies. By the bridge.

This raucous joint is not like anything you will find at your KOA-type campgrounds! Willie's features live Country and fifties music Friday and Saturday from 9 P.M. to 1 A.M. It is located by the bridge on the banks of Bayou Courtableau, just across from Washington. (318) 826-7227.

LODGING

Bed and Breakfasts:

Somehow the spell of Washington is broken if you must hop back in a car and drive out right away. Washington has six Bed and Breakfast or guesthouse accommodations among its lovely homes. You not only get to stay in a historic house but can go out in the morning or evening and walk the streets in the quiet and cool.

Camellia Cove 205 W. Hill St.

Annie and Herman Bidstrup are the owners of this beautiful two-story house (circa 1825) situated on two acres of camellia- and crepe myrtle-covered grounds. When the Bidstrups bought the place in 1982, they found a lot of old papers and artifacts in the attic, which have become part of the home's charm. Overnight guests can relax in large rocking chairs on the raised gallery and thumb through a book of before-and-after photographs of the Bidstrups' restoration. The house is conveniently located on the downtown walking tour. One room is furnished with period antiques and has a huge connected bath. The other room has a private bath in the hall. Beds are firm. Rates are $75. (318) 826-7362.

★La Chaumière 216 S. Main St.

Everyone who stays here has the same things to say: "What a great little place! What a great deal! I just couldn't believe how friendly Dot was!" Dot Mayer, the former head librarian of Opelousas, operates this quaint B&B in the small cottage built in the 1930s behind her own more modern home. The cottage has wood floors and a tin roof (perfect for rain storms!). It is decorated with antiques and homey artifacts like antique Mexican tin paintings. Dot stocks the fridge so you can make your own breakfast, but the food is basic (white bread for toast, preserves, and orange juice). (Some friends who stayed there on their honeymoon were treated to a bottle of wine.) La Chaumière is a real bargain and is one of the only B&Bs in Washington that offers the privacy of accommodations not connected to the owner's house. Spring through fall, Dot rents the cottage for $50 per couple! The rate may be a little lower in the cold-weather months. La Chaumière is located right on the downtown walking tour. (318) 826-3967.

The Country House Carriere Street at Anderson.

June Lowery rents out two guest rooms and a small cottage right behind her Victorian home on a quiet end of Carriere Street just a few blocks off Main. I recommend the cottage, if you do not mind the two single beds (which may be pushed together). The cottage was originally occupied by the inventor of the parking meter. When I suggested that this might give some urban guests nightmares Ms. Lowery scoffed that he only invented the meters, not the meter maids. The interior is detailed with pecky cypress and is very quaint without being too cute. A full meticulously prepared breakfast is served in the house at 8:30. A room for two costs $70 (checks or cash). (318) 826-3052.

De la Morandiere St. John and Sittig Street.

This is one of the grand homes of Washington. It was built in 1830 by a descendant of one of the first settlers of Poste Des Opelousas, Etienne Robert De la Morandiere. Guests share the house with the present owners, Steve and Kandi Johnson, who bought and restored it in 1987. Both guest rooms have private baths and guests are welcome to use the parlor and unwind on the spacious upper or lower verandas. The house is furnished with antiques, including a huge tester bed dating from the 1830s in the downstairs bedroom. This room also features a private entrance through French doors onto the veranda. Both bedrooms have working fireplaces, so consider staying here if you are traveling in the cold-weather months. The cost per couple is $60 to $75, which includes breakfast and a tour. (318) 826-3510.

The Elter Inn 603 S. Main St.

The Elter Inn is a large and beautifully restored guesthouse. The hosts, Mr. and Mrs. Bidstrup, live down the street at Camellia Cove. There are three bedrooms, thus space for three different guests at one time. Except during busy periods you are likely to have the place to yourself. The downstairs bedroom is actually a suite with sitting room and connected bath. The two upstairs bedrooms have attached private baths. All have very comfortable double beds. The bedroom furnishings are mainly antiques or reproductions, but there is plenty of comfortable furniture suitable for lounging in the common areas downstairs. Common areas include a completely furnished ultramodern kitchen (stocked with coffee and breakfast supplies), an informal living room with TV and VCR, and the grounds. The three acres may be enjoyed from a screened back porch or from the rocking chairs on the front porch. Two porch swings dangle from the large trees out front. You can easily walk the entire village from the Elter Inn. $70-$80. Call for reservations. (318) 826-7362.

★La Place d' deVille Guest House 217 W. Dejean.

La Place d' deVille is a private two-bedroom house right in historic Washington (at a great price!). This is not a historic home, nor is it packed with fine antiques; it is just a nice old wood-frame place with furnishings of the type you might really want to sit on. From the big country kitchen to the five rocking chairs, everything is familiar and comfortable, like countless grandmothers' houses that have been modernized over the years without losing their hominess. The rain sounds wonderful on the tin roof. La Place d' deVille is a quiet place to hide out and read, but you will also find it easy walking distance to the miles of trails at Magnolia Ridge (see review) or to the downtown historic sights. The two double beds are firm, and there is enough privacy for two couples traveling together (or a family) who are willing to share a bath. Your hosts, the Devilles, live just up the road in Grand Prairie. They speak fluent Cajun French and are very enjoyable to talk with. I am forever grateful that Ms. Deville tipped me to the Sunday barbecue at B&S in Ville Platte. Breakfast fixin's, coffee, and cold drinks are stocked in the kitchen. Towels and linens are provided. All of this comes at the price of $60 per couple ($10 for each extra person) or $200 a week. Visa, Mastercard, cash, or checks accepted. (318) 826-3367.

Camping:

Willie's Washington Campground Main Street beside the bridge.

If you are the type who likes to stay at the Holiday Inn so you don't get any surprises, this is not for you. Most campgrounds have a general store; this one has a tavern! This scruffy little campground is right on the edge of Bayou Courtableau. Walk over the bridge and you are at the Steamboat Warehouse Restaurant and Washington tourist center. There are picnic tables and shelters on the banks of the bayou. On Friday and Saturday nights Country and Oldies bands often play in the tavern from 9 P.M. to 1 A.M. RV camping costs $12 a night and $25 a week. Tent camping is $6 a night. (318) 826-9987.

Downtown Church Point. (Photo by Derick Moore)

Church Point

This Prairie outpost of 4,500 residents is a veritable bastion of Cajun French language and culture, claiming more resident Cajun musicians per acre than any other town in the state! Among its famous sons are Iry Lejeune, Shirley and Alphee Bergeron, and Cajun record man Lee Lavergne. For decades visitors came from around the world to visit with Lee at his Sound Center music store and recording studio. Sadly, he died in 1997. Although only 30 minutes from Lafayette, Opelousas, and Eunice, Church Point may owe some of its cultural integrity to isolation from major highways. It is 15 miles from Interstate 49 in Opelousas and U.S. 190 in Lawtell and 20 miles north of Interstate 10 at Rayne.

Church Point was originally named Plaquemine Point for the nearby stream, Plaquemine Brule. Jesuits from Grand Coteau built a church here in the early 1800s and the settlement became known as Church Point. Throughout the War Between the States the little town remained a popular gathering place for Prairie farmers who traveled miles in their buggies to attend church on Sundays. Buggies still roll down the streets during the annual spring Buggy Festival.

Church Point Information

For information on music and festivals in and around Church Point, call the Chamber of Commerce at (318) 684-3030 or give Cajun music enthusiast J. B. David a call at (318) 684-2023 or 684-5371. French is spoken at all these numbers.

ATTRACTIONS

Sound Center 329 Main St., Church Point.

The Sound Center was home to Lanor Records and recording studio. Lee Lavergne founded Lanor back in 1960 and was still recording and selling R&B, Soul, Cajun, Zydeco, and Swamp Pop from the small store until his death in 1997. Lee left the store packed with recorded treasures, and family members are considering reopening the business.

Shrine of Charlene Richard Rte. 1105, Richard.

See Eunice area attractions for more on the "Cajun Saint."

SPECIAL EVENTS

Church Point Courir du Mardi Gras

The *Courir du Mardi Gras* is run early in Church Point—Sunday—allowing participants and onlookers to enjoy Mamou's festivities (or New Orleans') on Tuesday. This is a super event for anyone interested in Cajun culture, food, and music. It is a heck of a party, too!

The whole family will be comfortable at the festivities here. Things can get a bit lively late in the day when everyone is tanked up and the riders have returned, but for the most part the Church Point run is a fascinating alternative to the crowded and boisterous celebration in Mamou.

All the participants mask and gather at 7 A.M., outside the Saddle Tramp Riders Club at 1036 E. Abbey. The Cajun band on the sound truck cranks up around 8, as horseback riders mill about the rodeo arena and other revelers board the flatbed trucks that will carry them to farms around the region. By 8:30 the procession is on its way. Once the riders have left, a couple of huge pots of gumbo are set to simmer and ladies of the community begin to arrive at the Saddle Tramp meeting hall with all manner of local goodies right from their home kitchens! A couple of radio stations broadcast from the hall over primitive remote kits, while everyone browses around and waits for the band to arrive.

The dance and food at the Saddle Tramp generally come together around 11 A.M. Admission is a paltry $2 and is good for the whole day. The food here is some of the best I have had at a small-town festival

Mardi Gras riders, Church Point. (Courtesy of Louisiana Office of Tourism)

anywhere. Heaping bowls of gumbo are about $3 and the tasty home-baked sweets are almost free. As the day wears on the dance floor gets more crowded, but there is no crush. Everyone seems to know there are plenty of good times and good food to go around. At 2 P.M., most folks leave the hall and line Main Street to watch the tired but jubilant (and drunk) riders return. The dance resumes in a more disorderly fashion when the procession arrives back at the Saddle Tramp with the playing of the traditional "Mardi Gras Song." (318) 684-5693.

FOOD

Church Point is really hurting for a good diner. There is no place that I would strongly recommend, but the grocery stores in town serve plate lunches to go. You can try the very popular **Sunny's Fried Chicken** on East Main Street.

Vautrot's Meat Market. East Main Street (Rte. 95) and Deanne Highway (Rte. 754).

I asked four people in Church Point about their favorite boudin and got four different tips. Vautrot's was my favorite. It is lean and well seasoned without being hot. It had tasty bits of green onion in it. Vautrot's is a meat market in a service station, but they make everything fresh and smoke their own meats. Try a little beef jerky too. Vautrot's is about a mile east of Rte. 35 on Main Street (Rte. 95). Hours are 6 to 6 daily. (318) 684-6164.

MUSIC

★Borque's Cajun dance hall. Lewisburg.

Drive 9 miles into the farm country south of Opelousas and on a narrow blacktop in the hamlet of Lewisburg you will find one of the most picturesque Cajun dance halls in Acadiana. Visiting Borque's is a bit like time travel. You won't find any tour buses in the tiny gravel parking lot, where the cry of a fiddle blends with the sounds of crickets and cicadas. You enter from a little wooden porch into the bar area, where there is a pool table and two card tables. The bar has two large windows and a door opening into the dance hall. In the old style, it is free to watch from the bar, but you will have to drop a dollar to get in and dance. The dance floor heaves as couples waltz and two-step to the puff of an accordion. From East Main Street in Church Point head north on Rte. 357 about 7 miles. From U.S. 190 W. in Opelousas head south on Rte. 357 about 7 miles. At Weston's Grocery in Lewisburg turn west on Rte. 759 and go .5 mile. Borque's has Cajun music every Saturday from 9 P.M. to 1 A.M. and every Sunday from 5 to 9 P.M. (318) 948-9904.

★Guidry's Friendly Lounge Cajun dance hall. Lewisburg.

It is amazing that an isolated farm community can sustain a dance hall at all, but the incredible fact is that Lewisburg has two of the most down-home Cajun nightspots on the Prairie! Little more than spittin' distance from Borque's is the even funkier Friendly Lounge. A young crowd hangs out at the pool tables, foosball game, and bar in the front, where Country and Swamp Pop tunes blare from the jukebox. A dollar or two buys entrance to the dance hall in back, where old-timers smooch over beers and crowd the dance floor. If you are lucky, Donald Thibodeaux (best known for his Saturday-morning performances at Fred's Lounge in Mamou) will be on the bandstand pumping the accordion and singing in French. Guidry's has Cajun music every Sunday from 5 to 9 P.M. To get to Guidry's follow the same directions as to Borque's. If you get to Borque's, you just passed Guidry's! (318) 942-9988.

Cajun Country Bar 829 W. Canal (Rte. 35).

This little barroom may be more local color than some folks really want. It can be stone quiet or rocking. The scene after the Buggy Festival or on Mardi Gras is unbelievable. If you see the street lined with trucks, drop in, have a cold drink, and enjoy one of the best Swamp Pop jukeboxes around. When the joint is hopping it is not unusual to find about 20 people playing every South Louisiana classic on the juke and singing along. (318) 684-9101.

★Train Depot Cajun Jam Session Main Street at Iry LeJeune Street.

Every Wednesday night from May through October there is an early-evening jam session at "Le Parc du Vieux Depot" featuring dozens of local musicians. It is a family affair that finds folks setting up lawn chairs and coolers under the old pavilion. Not only is the entertainment great (plenty of room to dance), but the session gives young musicians a chance to show their stuff in front of an audience. I have seen a 7-year-old girl playing raucous accordion on Nathan Abshire classics and a 10-year-old boy playing accordion and singing D. L. Menard weepers. Sometimes there are more musicians than listeners; at other times 100 to 200 people throng to the depot. The session starts at 6. For more information call organizer J. B. David. Mr. David, like almost everyone else attending the jam, speaks fluent Cajun French. (318) 684-2023.

LODGING

★Bob's Frontier Cabins Church Point.

There is no better place to enjoy the utter silence of the Cajun Prairie than at Bob's Frontier Cabins. The best cabin is a rustic cottage three miles out of Church Point, a mile off the road, and out of sight of anyone. It has two decks, a pond, and complete solitude (no phone). All the wood in the house is hand hewn and the comfortable furniture is made from tree limbs. There are two bedrooms with full beds, a loft, living room, and furnished kitchen (plenty of space for two couples). A second cabin behind Bob's commercial nursery in town has a small bedroom with full bed, a loft, and a split-log kitchen counter. (LuLu from the "HeeHaw" television show slept here.) The only comfort missing is mattress pads and cotton sheets.

Both spacious cabins were designed by Bob Thibodeaux and built of rough-cut lumber. They are works of craftsmanship, with board and batten interior, exposed beams, and log posts. Thibodeaux is a tree preservationist (a tree surgeon who refuses to wear a hat with a chain-saw logo) consulted statewide. Each cabin is a recycling project from felled trees. Despite the solitude, the cottages are convenient to the dance halls and restaurants of Opelousas and Eunice. Hosts Bob and Dot Thibodeaux speak fluent Cajun French. Bob's Nursery is on Main Street about .75 mile east of Rte. 35. The cabins are a deal at $55-$65. Major credit cards are accepted. (318) 684-5431.

Eunice

Located 20 miles west of Opelousas on U.S. 190 and only 45 minutes from Lafayette, Eunice (population about 12,000) is a hotbed of traditional Cajun music, food, and *joie de vivre*. Anyone interested in the folkways of Cajun Country must visit Eunice. The city (like several other towns in these parts) was founded by railroad man C. C. Duson. It is appropriate that Duson named it after his wife, as Eunice is a place where folks hold firmly to family and church traditions. The weeks after the city's big *Courir du Mardi Gras* celebration are quiet, but as Lent nears its end on Good Friday, backyards bustle with extended families and friends boiling crawfish and frying fish on outdoor burners. After Sunday Mass is over and Easter eggs have been found, folks get back to their usual enjoyment of all the food and music the region offers.

Once known as Faquetique Community, Eunice rightfully bills itself as the Cajun Prairie Capital. It has good accommodations, all the fast-food outlets and discount stores you could hope to find, and a location that allows quick access to the towns of Mamou and Ville Platte. It is the site of one of three Cajun Cultural Centers sponsored by the Jean Lafitte National Park and the location of the tremendously popular *Roundez Vous des Cajuns* Saturday-night broadcast.

Eunice Chamber and Information Center 220 C. C. Duson Dr. (Rte. 13).

Unlike the staff at many information centers, the folks here really know what is going on in the area in the way of food, music, and festivals. The center is located a couple of blocks from the Liberty Theater and Cajun Cultural Center, beside the Eunice Museum. From U.S. 190 turn south one block on Rte. 13 (C. C. Duson Drive). The Chamber is open Tuesday through Saturday from 8 to 5 (closed for lunch hour). (318) 457-2565.

DOWNTOWN ATTRACTIONS

All of the listings in this section are within four blocks of each other and there is plenty of free street parking.

★Acadian Cultural Center 250 W. Park Ave. at Third Street.

One of three Acadian Cultural Centers managed by the National

Park Service, the Eunice unit focuses on the life and history of Prairie Cajuns. The center includes museum exhibits, a kitchen for cooking demonstrations, and a craft area where local artisans stage demonstrations. Several videos are shown continuously throughout the day in a comfortable theater. These include excellent documentaries on Cajun and Zydeco music, crawfish farming, and, best of all, a feature on the highly unusual practice of "handfishing" called *Anything I Catch*. Time your visit for Saturday afternoon and see the *Roundez Vous des Cajuns* show at the neighboring Liberty Theater (*see* description in this chapter), or stop by on Sunday around 2 P.M. for the Cajun Jam Session. There are special events at the Cultural Center nearly every weekend, so call in advance to find out what is going on. The Center is open from 8 to 5 daily. (318) 457-8499.

Cajun French Music Association Hall of Fame 220 C. C. Duson Dr. (Rte. 13).

This long-overdue museum celebrating the legends of Cajun music had just opened when I visited last. It already had a good collection of donated and loaned accordions and other instruments, some belonging to legendary musicians. There are portraits of the first inductees and recent nominees on the walls with short biographies. The museum is adjacent to the Eunice Museum and Chamber of Commerce, just a block from the Liberty Theater. It is open Monday through Saturday from 8:30 to 4:30. (318) 457-6534.

The Eunice Museum 220 C. C. Duson Dr. (Rte. 13).

Located in the old train depot (beside the Information Center) at the site where C. C. Duson sold the first land parcels for the town, the Eunice Museum has a collection disproportionate to its size. There are old photographs of the city and an exhibit of artifacts and information on Prairie life at the turn of the century. You can view free exhibits and videos on Cajun music, instruments, and Mardi Gras. From Rte. 190 turn south one block on Rte. 13 (C. C. Duson Drive). The museum is open Tuesday through Saturday from 8 to 5 (closed for lunch hour). (318) 457-6540.

Liberty Theater Second Street and Park Avenue.

This grand old theater was constructed in 1924. Over the years it has been a vaudeville house, a first-run movie venue, and a dollar cinema before finding new life as home to the Saturday-night broadcast of *Roundez Vous des Cajuns* show (*see* Music listings below). While the Saturday show is not to be missed, the theater is an attraction in itself, donated

Liberty Theater. (Photo by Macon Fry)

to the city and restored by volunteers in the community. The 800-seat auditorium is frescoed with plaster ornaments and painted friezes.

Queen Movie Theater 233 Walnut Ave.

Built in 1939, the Queen is not quite as retro as the venerable Liberty, but at least they are still showing movies (and making their own popcorn). They have split the old auditorium into two screens. During the summer matinees show three days a week. If the weather is hot, this can be the best escape around (a good way to chill out between the Saturday-morning activities in Mamou and the evening show at the Liberty). The Queen is a block north of the Liberty Theater, right beside two other landmarks, Ruby's diner and the Music Machine. (318) 457-3283.

Music Machine 235 Walnut Ave.

The Music Machine has a selection of South Louisiana CDs and cassettes, cold air conditioning, and sno-balls. Its biggest asset is manager Todd Ortego, who is a local DJ and according to his business card: "party starter" and "MAN OF ACTION." Todd knows what is going on. (318) 457-4846.

AREA ATTRACTIONS

Cajun Prairie Restoration Project Martin Luther King, Jr., Drive and Magnolia.

Driving across the Cajun Prairie it is easy to forget that there was ever anything on this flat, moist table of earth but rice and soybean fields. A century ago the Prairie was quite a different place. C. C. Robin visited in 1803 and wrote, "The wide prairie [is] strewn with flowers whose stems raise them to the height of the horse on which the traveler is riding." On a 10-acre site botanists from LSUE have begun to recreate a chunk of "natural" Prairie habitat. Seeds were gathered from scattered strips of virgin Prairie and planted on tilled ground at this site. The result is a chunk of wild Prairie offering a seasonal panoply of colors similar to what Samuel Lockett saw in 1870 when he exclaimed, "I look upon the prairie as naturally the loveliest part of Louisiana." The refuge is located less than a mile north of U.S. 190.

Eunice City Park U.S. 190 W.

This public recreation area on the shores of a large, man-made lake is perfect for fishing, boating, or just picnicking in a sylvan setting. There are seven shelters with smokers and tables, public rest rooms, and a small dock. To get to the park, head west on U.S. 190 two miles from Rte. 13. The park is just past the country club on the north side of the road. The park closes at 10 P.M.

Shrine of Charlene Richard Rte. 1105, Richard.

Charlene Richard has yet to be canonized by the Catholic Church, but if believers around the Prairie have their way, she will soon be recognized as the first Cajun saint. Thousands of South Louisiana Catholics make a pilgrimage each year to the grave of this girl who died of leukemia at age 12 in 1959. Her tomb, in a quiet cemetery in the town of Richard, is festooned with flowers, mementos, and notes to Richard imploring her intercession in all manner of worldly problems. For more information you may contact the Friends of Charlene Association, P.O. Box 91623, Lafayette 70509-1623. To visit the grave, just take Rte. 13 about five miles south from Eunice and turn left (east) on Rte. 370. Go six miles. The cemetery is behind St. Edward Church at the corner of Rte. 370 and Rte. 1105.

SPECIAL EVENTS

★World Championship Etouffée Cook-off Late March.

This is one of the best food festivals in Louisiana. Each year there are about 50 entrants in the cooking competition and spectators can buy samples from each for $1 a cup. There is a Cajun dance pavilion and plenty of other entertainment. The festival usually takes place the next to last weekend in March. (318) 457-2565.

★Mardi Gras

Eunice has the widest array of Mardi Gras activities to be found anywhere in South Louisiana. Unlike the raucous partying of Mamou and New Orleans, Mardi Gras in the Cajun Prairie Capital is a real family event. That isn't to say there is a shortage of beer, spicy food, and Cajun music. It's just that things don't get out of hand here. Many celebrants come from around the state for the three-day celebration, which includes historical and cultural presentations at the Acadian Cultural Center and a traditional Tuesday morning *Courir du Mardi Gras*. For more Mardi Gras information consult the index.

Saturday and Sunday before Mardi Gras: The weekend before Mardi Gras, Eunice is the site of two or three traditional Cajun and Zydeco dances. Held at St. Mathilda's Church and at the Liberty Theater, these events sometimes require that participants mask.

Monday before Mardi Gras: The day before Mardi Gras, the Liberty Theater and Cajun Cultural Center have living history presentations, displays, lectures, and slide shows regarding the Prairie *Courir du Mardi Gras* tradition. These activities begin early in the afternoon and last into the evening.

Fat Tuesday: On Mardi Gras, the revelry begins early. Riders in the *Courir du Mardi Gras* gather on horseback at the National Guard Armory at 8 A.M. The main public celebration takes place in front of the Liberty Theater and courthouse, at the corner of Second and Walnut streets. There is a children's parade shortly after the riders depart, followed by performances by Cajun and Zydeco bands at a half-dozen stages set up around the middle of town. Amidst the hubbub are vendors selling hot boiled crawfish, boudin, gumbo, and homemade sweets. The climax of the day's festivities is around 3 P.M., when a small parade snakes through town followed by the band of triumphant Mardi Gras riders returning from a day of plunder.

FOOD

Allison's Hickory Pit Local Fave, $. 501 W. Laurel (U.S. 190).

Linus Allison and his wife, Wanda, turn out some of the tastiest Ville

Platte-style barbecue on this side of the Prairie. Only a lack of organization and the unavailability of the right meat in New Orleans has kept Linus from the Jazz Fest. Pork steaks and ribs come drenched in an oniony sauce that is not exceedingly sweet or hot, just succulent. BBQ plates cost under $6 and come with very good potato salad and rice dressing. Allison's is about six blocks west of Rte. 13. It is open Thursday through Sunday from 10:30 A.M. to 2 or 3 P.M. (318) 457-9218.

★**Johnson's Grocery** Meat Market/Boudin, $. 700 E. Maple.

This is the high altar of boudin, the home of the golden link! Johnson's has been perfecting their boudin recipe since 1937 and has singlehandedly shattered the rule that states, "The best boudin is always no more than three miles away from home." Folks come all the way from Lake Charles to pick up enough of the spicy links to get them through the week. Back when Johnson's was only making boudin on

High altar of boudin. (Photo by Derick Moore)

Saturday, things got really crazy. In a day Joe Johnson would make, weigh, and sell up to 2,000 pounds. The line for links, or "Rue Boudin," as it was called, would wind through the store and out the door.

There is still a strong Saturday-morning boudin tradition, perhaps because it is the perfect breakfast before spending a morning dancing and imbibing at the Saturday Cajun broadcast at Fred's Lounge. Nothing opens the blinkers like a hot cup of coffee (which you have to get elsewhere) or a cold can of beer and a hot-hot link of boudin. Johnson's boudin is notable for a lack of liver and other by-products, for its even-handed mixture of rice and pork, and for its fiery flavor. Joe Johnson has a wide variety of excellent regional specialties like tasso, garlic sausage, paunce, and fresh meats. The latest addition to his counter is chewy ropes of Cajun beef jerky. Meats can be shipped nationwide.

To get to Johnson's from U.S. 190, take Rte. 13 (called C. C. Duson Drive in town) south to Maple Street. Go east on Maple a few blocks. They are open Monday through Friday from 6 A.M. to 6 P.M. and Saturday from 5 A.M. to 5 P.M. (318) 457-9314.

LeJeune's Sausage Kitchen 108 Tasso Cir. (off the Crowley Road).

I have pals who detour off I-10 just to get smoked garlic sausage from LeJeune's to bring back to New Orleans. The tasso is also very good. To get to LeJeune's travel 3 miles south on Rte. 13 from the intersection of Maple Street in Eunice. Turn right (west) on Rte. 3123 (the airport road), and make an immediate right again on Ardoin Street. LeJeune's is on the left about .5 mile from Rte. 13. It is open Monday through Saturday from 7 A.M. to 5 P.M. (318) 457-8491.

Mama's Fried Chicken Down Home, $. 1640 W. Laurel (U.S. 190).

This is a franchise for the regional Mama's Chicken chain, but it is also a small Cajun restaurant with an independent and creative cook. Lannie Degeyter took over the Mama's in Eunice in the seventies, after picking up cooking while working at Pat's in Henderson. From the beginning he has had an edge in the chicken market because his birds come in fresh every day from the poultry house next door. Lannie's recipe is well seasoned, but tame compared to Popeye's.

It is not chicken, however, on which Lannie has built his reputation. The plaque over the door informs all that Mama's won the Crawfish Etouffée Cook-off in 1987, and it is still the best around. The appetizer size costs under $4 and is quite large. There are daily Cajun plate lunches like fried catfish with potato salad for under $5. The Sunday dinner is a highly seasoned pork roast that begins cooking on Saturday and is served with backbone stew, rice dressing, and potato salad for under $5. My favorite meal is a small etouffée and four chicken wings. Mama's is open Sunday through Wednesday from 10 A.M. to 9 P.M. and Thursday through Saturday until 10. (318) 457-9978.

★Mathilda's Down Home, $. U.S. 190 E.

Mathilda's cooks up delicious plate lunches in a soul-food style with lots of gravy and barbecue sauce, and plenty spicy. About half of Mathilda's business is plate lunches, which sell out by 1 or 2 each day. The other half is Prairie barbecue with traditional oniony barbecue sauce (dinners from $4.50-$6). Both are recommended. The thing that Mathilda does better than anybody (we mean that!) is sweet-dough pies. Often a commercial sweet-dough pie winds up feeling like a wet wad of sweet flour in your mouth. These have the traditional thick crust, but it is light with just a little crispness on the edges and plenty of cinnamon in the dough. The fruit filling tastes like real fruit, not bottled jelly. Somewhere there is a mother or grandmother making better pies, but Mathilda's is the best place to sample this regional specialty. They are open from 11 to 7 Tuesday and Wednesday, until 10 Friday, 8 Saturday, and 3 Sunday. They are located just off U.S. 190 about 1.5 miles east of Rte. 13, beside Perry Pitre Ford. (318) 546-0329.

★Pelican Restaurant Down Home, $. West Laurel (U.S. 190).

The Sunday midday meal at the Pelican is reason enough to spend Saturday night in Eunice or to make the drive from anyplace as close as Lafayette. The key is to either get there early or to arrive between the Catholics, who start pouring into the tiny dining room after Mass at about 11:20, and the Baptists, who arrive closer to 12:30. I would say that this was real home cooking, but few people cook like this at home anymore. For a set price of $5.50, you get either baked duck, pork roast, beef roast, or pit-cooked barbecue (a choice of chicken, ribs, or pork steak) and a choice of three mouthwatering side orders like yams, black-eyed peas, and cornbread or rice dressings. Each dinner comes with complimentary ice tea or coffee, a chilled mustardy potato salad, and dessert. You will simply not find a better home-style meal anywhere! Plate lunches and suppers are offered throughout the week, but after the Sunday dinner, you may not need to eat again for seven days. The Pelican is open Sunday from 6 A.M. to 2 P.M. and Monday through Saturday until 9 P.M. (318) 457-2323.

★Ruby's Cafe Down Home, $. 221 W. Walnut.

Ruby's has been dishing out soul-satisfying plate lunches since the fifties. No midday walk through the shady streets around the Cultural Center and Liberty Theater is complete without a stop here to sample the pork roast, redolent of garlic and covered in a dark gravy. The

Ms. Ruby with a pan of her baked chicken. (Photo by Macon Fry)

facade is worn, but inside Ruby's is a quaint restaurant with fifties-style diner-decor ambiance. From the pink-and-green walls to the formica counter and Mello-Joy clock over the kitchen, there is a distinct impression that Ms. Ruby hasn't changed things much.

There are some things no one wants to see change, and the food here is one of them. The fare is simple. Chicken-fried steak, baked chicken, and the highly recommended pork roast are all served with three or four veggies. The huge "child's plate" costs $2.35 and the truly enormous "large plate" is $4. Don't order the large unless you are mighty hungry! Ruby's is open Monday through Friday from 5 A.M. to 4 P.M. and until 2 P.M. on Saturday, but they often begin to run out of popular items like the pork roast by 1:30. They are located right behind the Liberty Theater and Cultural Center. (318) 457-2583.

MUSIC

Gilton's Lounge Zydeco dance hall. U.S. 190 E. and Rte. 95.

Gilton's is the biggest Zydeco dance hall in the region and possibly in the state, with over 1,500 seats. Proprietor Gilton Lejeune packs the place with the most popular names in Zydeco. Gilton's is located a block off U.S. 190 at the intersection of 190 and Rte. 95 just east of Eunice. Gilton's has Zydeco most Saturdays, but before you make a special trip, call his Zydeco hotline at (318) 457-1241.

★**Roundez Vous des Cajuns** Broadcast/dance. South Second Street and Park Avenue.

This is not only the biggest attraction in Eunice, but one of the premier weekly events in South Louisiana! Every Saturday night at 6, the old Liberty vaudeville theater plays host to the *Roundez Vous des Cajuns*, a two-hour show featuring Cajun and Zydeco bands, humorists, and cooks reciting their favorite recipes. During one show an elderly gentleman explained how to make soap. Many of the directions were in French, but I did make out the main ingredient—"First you need five pounds of fat!"

The show, broadcast live on KBON (101.1 FM), KJJB (105.5 FM), and KEUN (1490 AM) in Eunice and KRVS (88.7 FM) in Lafayette, has been described as a Cajun cross between the Prairie Home Companion and the Grand Ol' Opry. In many ways it harkens back to the days when dances or *fais-do-dos* were held in private homes and halls. It is an event for the whole family and one place where you will hear more people speaking French than English. The emcee is Cajun folklorist Barry Jean Ancelet, who tempers his French patter with enough English to allow the Anglos to follow along. The show starts promptly at 6 P.M. and is over at 8, but it has become so popular that you may want to get there an hour early to get a ticket and a good seat. Admission is $1. Cokes, popcorn, and sweet-dough pies are sold at the concession counter. The Liberty Theater is located downtown at the corner of Second Street and Park Avenue, directly adjacent to the new Cultural Center. There is plenty of street parking and the City Hall lot is open for RV and bus parking during the show.

★**Savoy's Music Center** Cajun jam session. East Laurel (U.S. 190 E.).

This music store on U.S. 190 on the east side of Eunice houses the workshop of Cajun musician and accordion maker Marc Savoy. Savoy is an accomplished accordionist and intense preservationist of Cajun culture. On Saturday mornings he hosts a jam session in the store that often features his wife, Ann Allen Savoy, on guitar and sometimes grows to include three accordions, fiddles, and triangles. This is an

Jam session at Savoy's Music Center. (Photo by Raleigh Powell)

informal but regular gathering that generally gets under way by 10. There is no admission but no one will complain if you bring a six-pack of beer or a couple of pounds of boudin from Johnson's Grocery (*see* Food listings) to pass around. If you get there early, thumb through a copy of Ann Savoy's wonderful book, *Cajun Music: A Reflection of a People,* or ask if Marc is not too busy to show the shop where he produces diatonic accordions under his own "Acadian" brand. (318) 457-9563.

★KBON Radio, 101.1 FM Second Street, downtown.

"Honey, go get some ice and put it in the ice chest; that music is doin' it again!" Those are the words of DJ, Louisiana music-lover, and man with a vision Paul Marx. Marx founded this station in 1997, dedicated to playing Louisiana music throughout the day, seven days a week. Almost from the beginning it was the sound heard coming from every open car window from Basile to Opelousas and Church Point to Ville Platte. On Saturdays it is not unusual to hear announcers fading from French to English and back on many local stations, but on KBON every day is Saturday! KBON is the only station to broadcast the Liberty Theater show uninterrupted. This station is great company for exploring Cajun Country, but as Marx says, keep some ice in the chest. (318) 546-0007.

LODGING

Hotels and Motels:

Best Western 1531 W. Laurel Ave. (U.S. 190).

Finally Eunice has a modern motel suitable for families and business travelers. The motel is located on the western suburban edge of town. Pool, cable TV. $65-$75. (318) 457-2800 or 1-800-528-1234.

Howard's Inn U.S. 190 E.

Howard's Inn is a decent choice for a budget traveler. It is clean and keeps the riffraff out. Some of the beds are quite comfortable. It is a short drive east of downtown attractions. $45. (318) 457-2066.

Stone Country Lodge Old U.S. 190 (three miles east).

The Stone Country Lodge is a motor court dating back to the days when U.S. 190 was the main thoroughfare to Baton Rouge. It is under new management and has been fixed up nicely. The beds are not very comfortable but the place is clean. $40. (318) 457-5211 or 457-4719.

Bed and Breakfasts:

Potier's Prairie Cajun Inn 110 W. Park, downtown.

Potier's offers the anonymity of a hotel with the conveniences of a Bed and Breakfast. They are less than two blocks from the Acadian Cultural Center and Liberty Theater. All the rooms have private outside entrances, private baths, computer modems, kitchens stocked with breakfast supplies, and access to the shady courtyard and Jacuzzi. During the week it is quiet, but anyone who has been in the area on Saturday knows that downtown Eunice can get hopping. You must book several weeks early for Saturday nights and several years early for Mardi Gras! Potier's accepts major credit cards. Rooms are $65. A Cajun cottage just outside of town is also available for $100. (318) 457-5698.

La Petite Maison 530 S. Seventh St., downtown.

La Petite Maison is a traditional Louisiana "double," with an apartment on each side. Each side has a private entrance off the front porch, bedroom with queen bed, living room, kitchen, bath, washer/dryer, cable TV, and phone. The Johnsons did a great job restoring this little house, keeping the original wood walls and ceilings. It is located in a shady downtown residential area, about five blocks from the Liberty Theater and other attractions. $60 a night with continental breakfast. Major credit cards, cash, or checks are accepted. (318) 457-7136, 457-1254, or 457-3851.

★Bob's Frontier Cabins

See Church Point listings.

Camping:

Cajun Campground and Cabins U.S. 190 4.5 miles east of Eunice.

This campground offers everything a tent or RV camper could want, from hot showers and shade to full hookups, a pool, and large pavilion. Rates just went up for the first time in 10 years but are only $13. There is only one cabin (it is right by the entrance road and office) but they also rent a few campers. These are small but can sleep four for $35 a night. (318) 457-5753.

Lakeview Campground Rte. 13, four miles north of Eunice.

This old campground was the choice for Cajun-music lovers when it featured live music every weekend in the campground-dance hall. The hall is closed and the grounds are in some disrepair. Many of the full hookup sites are not operating. It is in a lovely, shaded setting. $12 for full hookups. (318) 457-9263.

Mamou

Mamou, with a population of 3,200, sits near the top and center of the Cajun Prairie, 10 miles north of Eunice on Rte. 13. Nearly a century after C. C. Duson printed handbills exclaiming "Go West, Young Man, Go West and Go to Mamou!", this little town still has the feel of the Old West about it. On Sixth Street, which is the main thoroughfare, businesses (mostly little bars) have the same flat, sun-bleached facades common to little cattle towns in Texas. Actually, the cattle industry long ago made way for cotton and then the rice and soybean fields that now surround the area. Few people come here to view the architecture anyway, unless it is to stay in the totally archaic Cazan Hotel. The main reason folks show up in Mamou is to see the famous Saturday-morning Cajun broadcast from tiny Fred's Lounge and to attend the city's huge *Courir du Mardi Gras* celebration.

ATTRACTIONS

Holiday Lounge Rte. 13 at the Mamou turnoff.

The Holiday may be the most unusual bar in Southwest Louisiana. A couple of questions come to mind. What is a big lounge like this doing in a field 10 miles from the nearest sizable town, and why is there a life-size, full-length portrait of former governor Edwin Edwards over the door? The simple explanation to both questions is that the Holiday was for years the biggest gaming house on the Prairie. The bar and plush booths are wrapped in turquoise vinyl, while the walls are covered in a gaudy tropical-print wallpaper. In one corner is a low stage, backed with mirrors, and in the rear are rooms that once entertained a sporting crowd. Folks around here are mainly proud of aging proprietor Tee-Ed Manual, who made his fortune in the coin-operated machine industry. They will tell you he has the "biggest house in town" and had "the first Cadillac around these parts." This is a great place to stop for a drink. The Holiday is at the Mamou turnoff on the west side of Rte. 13.

Mamou Mardi Gras Late winter.

Mamou was the first town to revive the *Courir du Mardi Gras* tradition, and their celebration is now the biggest in Cajun Country. The festivities begin with a street party on the Monday before Mardi Gras. All of the bars on Sixth Street open their doors and the music, beer, and crowds flow freely. The big event is the Mardi Gras morning *Courir du Mardi Gras* ride. The participants gather on horseback downtown around 7. A noisy throng sees them off and proceeds to party in the street to the sounds of live Cajun bands until the riders return at 3 P.M. For more information on the *Courir du Mardi Gras* and Mardi Gras dates, see the "Special Events in Cajun Country" appendix.

FOOD

Jeff's Cafe at Cazan Hotel Sixth Street.

Jeff's is about the only place to eat in Mamou and it is within staggering distance of Fred's Lounge and crawling distance of the Cazan bar. Breakfasts are cheap and plate lunches on weekdays are $4.50. The rest of the day they serve burgers and sandwiches. The place has a cool fifties design with a curving Formica counter. It is open Monday through Saturday from 5 A.M. to about 9 P.M.

MUSIC

★**Fred's Lounge** Cajun broadcast/dance hall. Sixth Street.

Farmers in jeans and boots, nattily dressed professionals from Eunice and Ville Platte, and Japanese tourists with camera bags can all be found imbibing and dancing at the most famous bar in Cajun Country at 9 o'clock any Saturday morning. You won't find tour buses parked outside Fred's; the place seems scarcely big enough to hold the occupants of a half-dozen minivans. Inside it is decidedly rustic. A piece of twine wrapped around the band area is the only barrier between the musicians and folks hoisting cans of Falstaff. On weekends just before Mardi Gras and just after Lent, the crowd at Fred's is particularly exuberant, but there are signs to remind everyone of the two primary rules of the house: "No substitute musicians" and "No standing on the jukebox"! Fortunately, international fame has done little to change the humble bar or discourage the mostly local clientele

The Saturday-morning show at Fred's. (Photo by Macon Fry)

from beginning their weekend there. Fred is deceased, but his wife, "Tante Sue," is keeping the tradition alive. Fred's is on Sixth Street in the middle of Mamou. Every Saturday the band plays from 8 A.M. to noon. You can tune in to the broadcast on KVPI radio, 1250 AM. (318) 468-5411.

LODGING

Cazan Hotel Sixth Street.

This is not the kind of place where you get a mint on your pillow (you *do* get a pillow!), but it is a remarkable hotel nonetheless. The Cazan was originally built as a bank back in 1912 and became a hotel in 1946. A huge mahogany bar, built by a high-school shop instructor, was installed in the old lobby and a wall of slot machines was placed where the tellers' cages used to be. Upstairs a dozen rooms were remodeled for overnight guests. The slots are gone, but the beautiful thing about this place is that the rooms are basically as they were in 1946. Sure, window air-conditioning units have been added, but the screen doors on interior rooms and transom windows hint at what the climate conditioning used to be like. The heaters are antique gas radiators that work like a charm once you figure out how to light them.

To say that the Cazan is showing its age would be a major understatement. The rooms have become quite shabby. For the highly

Cazan Hotel. (Photo by Raleigh Powell)

adventurous, this is still the ultimate place to spend a Friday night. You can wake up Saturday morning to the strains of Cajun music from Fred's Lounge across the street. After the show at Fred's, be sure to hit the bar at the Cazan, where you can often find proprietor Mr. Burke Perottie (pear-oh-tee) downing beers and telling jokes with his brother, Mayor Warren Perottie. Check out the good selection of South Louisiana faves on the jukebox. A double with one bed is $20. (318) 468-7187.

Ville Platte

Ville Platte, or "Flat Town," as it was aptly named by the early settlers, is located near the northernmost point of today's Cajun Country, about 20 miles northeast of Eunice and 25 miles northwest of Opelousas (I-49 exit #23). This is the last stop for a northbound traveler looking for the sights, sounds, and flavors of real Cajun Country. Ville Platte has an important musical landmark in Floyd's Record Store, as well as the most popular little barbecue stand in South Louisiana. This is the place to stock up and chow down before or after exploring Chicot State Park and the State Arboretum north of town, where the terrain rises into piney-wood hill country and there is plenty of camping, hiking, and fishing to be done.

The area around Ville Platte was first settled in the late 18th century and the town was incorporated in 1858 on what was the main road from Opelousas to Alexandria. With fewer than a thousand residents, Ville Platte became the seat of government for the newly formed Evangeline Parish in 1910, but it was not until the discovery of oil nearby in the thirties that the city really began to grow. Despite its status as a parish seat, the pace of life in this upland Prairie town with a population of 9,000 is decidedly slow. The most exciting event in Ville Platte is the annual Cotton Festival, held the second weekend of October.

Ville Platte Chamber of Commerce 306 W. Main St.

The Chamber has a rack of brochures to local attractions but more importantly the staff here can be very helpful in directing visitors to what they are looking for. When I asked about the best boudin around I was given several choices, including a couple of places way off the beaten path (see Deshotel's). (318) 363-1878.

RECREATION

Louisiana State Arboretum Rte. 3042 N.

The first state arboretum in the nation is located 8 miles north of Ville Platte. There are hiking trails at the Louisiana Arboretum (and in nearby Chicot State Park) that are not only dry, but actually hilly! Some of the hills rise up from Lake Chicot at an incline of 30 percent. Two and a half miles of footpaths wind through the hilly 600-acre arboretum, crossing ravines on wooden bridges and scaling slopes in gentle cutbacks. The place is a majestic and peaceful domain of moss, hollow trees, gullys, and hills, inhabited by woodpeckers and deer. If you are looking for a quiet walk and find the trails at Chicot Park too congested, the Arboretum is a perfect getaway. No pets or picnicking are allowed on the grounds, so exercise your mutt and chow down at Chicot. The Arboretum is located on Rte. 3042 1.5 miles north of the Chicot State Park main entrance.

★Chicot State Park Rte. 3042 N.

Chicot, the largest of Louisiana's state parks, was built in the 1930s on the rolling hills surrounding 2,500-acre cypress-studded Lake Chicot, one of the most popular freshwater fishing spots in the region. It is the only park in Cajun Country where backcountry hiking and camping are available. Nearly 15 miles of trails skirt the lake and climb through the neighboring piney-wood hills. Numerous trailheads with parking areas allow easy access for those wanting to take a short walk or day or overnight trip. Other trails diverge to secluded backwoods camping areas with vistas of the lake. For overnight hikers, maps of the park and its trails, backcountry camping permits (50 cents), and park rules are available at the south entrance.

There are two entrances and main areas in Chicot Park, referred to as North Landing and South Landing. The south entrance, on Rte. 3042, offers access to 27 fully furnished vacation cabins (all you need to bring is soap, towels, and grub). Cabins have screened porches, heat and air conditioning, and equipped kitchens and are located near the boat launch. There are also many campsites with full hookups within walking distance of the lake, several trailheads for hikers, a swimming pool (no swimming is permitted in the lake), and picnic areas with grills. This is by far the busiest section of Chicot.

The North Landing provides access to the best hiking and backcountry camping, over a hundred developed campsites adjacent to Lake Chicot, and a boat launch with fish-cleaning station and boat rentals. Access to the North Landing is possible from a road inside the park from the South Landing or from Rte. 106. This is the quiet end of the park. You can sit by the dock, watch the alligators, and ignore the posted No Fishing sign with impunity.

There are no concessions at Chicot, so you must buy your supplies and bait in Ville Platte. The park is open from 5 A.M. to 10 P.M. on weekends and until 8 P.M. on weekdays. Admission is $2 per vehicle with up to four people. Camping is $12 with hookups. To camp on the trails you must fill out a form and pay a fee of 50 cents per person. Cabins for four are $45; cabins for six are $60. Boat rentals are $8, with a $10 deposit. Chicot is located six miles north of Ville Platte on Rte. 3042. (318) 363-2403.

Crooked Creek Recreation Area Rte. 106 W.

Crooked Creek is a little campground on the shores of a 400-acre lake 12 miles west of Chicot State Park. On weekends the area is frequented by locals who come to swim at the sandy beach, use the picnic shelters (which include smokers as well as grills), and fish. There are two boat ramps (well isolated from the public swimming area) and plenty of spots to fish from the shore or fishing pier. The 100 camping sites, which include full hookups, and the tent camping areas all have views of the lake. The park is open from 7 A.M. to 11 P.M. Day use is $2 per person. Camping is $12 for RVs and $10 for tents. From Ville Platte take Rte. 10 west about 8 miles, then turn north onto Rte. 13. Continue on Rte. 13 for another 7 miles to Rte. 106. Take a left onto Rte. 106 for 5 miles. For information and reservations call (318) 599-2661.

FOOD

B&S Meat Market Lunch/tasso, $. 1914 E. Main St. (Rte. 167).

The tasso here is smoked until it is almost black, as is the local taste, and is well seasoned. Folks from as far away as Washington and Grand

Prairie come for Sunday barbecue dinners. There is no seating; lunches are sold to go. On Sunday you get a half-chicken, grilled to perfection and bathed in Ville Platte-style barbecue sauce (lightly sweet and spiked with onions). This is accompanied by a huge pile of delicious rice dressing. B&S is located on the east end of town, across from the Wal-Mart in a modern gas station. It is open from 7 A.M. to 9 P.M. every day. (318) 363-6868.

★Deshotel ("Dez") Meat Market Boudin, $. 1020 Martin Luther King Dr.

The grocery is named Deshotel for the owner but everybody calls it "Dez." The place makes 150 pounds of boudin fresh every day but do not expect it to last until closing time. Dez is in a predominantly black neighborhood and the taste in boudin runs toward hot. To get to Deshotel head south from Rte. 167 on Soileau Street for about .5 mile. Turn right (west) on Pine Street and go another .5 mile and Deshotel will be on the left. (Pine Street becomes Martin Luther King.) It is open from 7 A.M. to 7 P.M. Monday through Saturday and until 3 on Sunday. (318) 363-2727.

Elmand's Dine & dance, $$. Tate Cove Road.

Elmand's has a selection of fried or boiled seafood, steaks, and stews. Most people choose to eat off the buffet. Buffet food is usually sitting out and warming over, but Elmand's starts with a very good product. If you are there on a busy night and get the gumbos, red beans, delicious crawfish bisque, or etouffée as they come out of the kitchen, you will not be disappointed. Fried food does not hold up under a heat lamp. For $12.95 Elmand's offers the buffet with "all the boiled crawfish you can eat" (in season). The restaurant is open Thursday through Saturday from 6 to 11 P.M. and Cajun bands start at 7:30. To get to Elmand's from Ville Platte head four miles north from Rte. 167 (Main Street) on Tate Cove. Elmand's is on the left. (318) 363-3768.

★Jungle Dinner Club Boiled Seafood/Local Fave, $$. West Main Street (Rte. 167).

The Jungle has a variety of seafood as well as some spectacular steaks, but their specialty is the boiled crawfish. These are some of the most uniquely seasoned and hottest boiled crawfish anywhere. I worked my way up through the Mild, Hot, and Super Hot before attacking the final pinnacle of flame, the Extra Super Hot. These are not even on the menu, podnuh, and for good reason! Unless you have something to prove, or really want the Honorary Cajun Certificate that comes with eating an order of the E.S.H., don't get them. Manager Wendel Manuel simply warned, "Take out your contacts first!"

The real reason you should not get the Extra Super Hot crawfish is so you can better appreciate the other seasonings, which seem to include a little sugar and vinegar. The water running off the crawfish was so tasty, I found myself mopping it up with the tail meat, potatoes, and corn. During the sixties, the Jungle was the most popular bandstand in the area, featuring acts like Fats Domino, Dale and Grace, and country star Ernest Tubb. Take Main Street to the west edge of town. Hours are nightly from 5:30 to 11 P.M. (318) 636-9103.

★Pig Stand Down Home/Barbecue, $. 318 E. Main St. (Rte. 167).

It is fitting that the Pig Stand restaurant sits at the geographic pinnacle of the Cajun cultural heartland, for you will not find a better example of solid and soulful Cajun cooking. Since 1952 this has been the place to find Cajun lunch specials like Turtle or Tasso Sauce Piquante, Smothered Sausage, and Chicken Stew. Of course, most folks come for the Pork Barbecue, either steak or ribs. Northern Cajun Country is well known for its smoked meats, but what sets the Pig Stand apart is the sauce, which is full of onion and garlic. Usually ribs, pork steak, or roast are included on the lunch menu with side orders of black-eyed peas, rice and gravy, rice dressing, and potato salad (enough starches?) for under $6. The T-bone steak with lunch is $6. Often, items from the lunch menu are still available at the same price through dinner. The Pig Stand is the only good late-night spot to eat north of Lafayette. The Stand is a block from Floyd's. Hours are Tuesday through Thursday and Sunday from 6 A.M. to 10 P.M. and Friday and Saturday until midnight. (318) 363-2883.

Good eats on the Cajun Prairie. (Photo by Macon Fry)

Teet's Meat Market Smoked meats/Boudin. 2144 W. Main (Rte. 167).

Teet's is one of the oldest meat markets in Ville Platte. "Teet" De-Ville opened the place in 1955 and moved to his present location in the early seventies. The shop now resides in a new Chevron gas station. Don't be put off by the fuel pumps; this is some of the best smoked meat in Ville Platte. Teet's is located on the western fringe of town beside Snook's Dancehall, just over a mile past the point where Rte. 167 splits. It is open every day from 7 to 7. (318) 363-1839.

MUSIC

Floyd's Record Store 434 E. Main St. (Rte. 167).

Floyd Soileau (pronounced "Swallow") is the biggest distributor of South Louisiana music anywhere. He is also one of the record men responsible for the rebirth of interest in Cajun and Zydeco music in the sixties and seventies. Soileau has released records by most of the important modern Cajun, Swamp Pop, and Zydeco artists, including

Record man Floyd Soileau. (Photo by Julie Posner)

Dewey Balfa and the Balfa Brothers, Clifton Chenier, and Johnny Allan. As many as a third of the records on some jukeboxes in Cajun Country are on Soileau's Jin, Swallow, and Maison de Soul labels. His artists have performed in every place from "American Bandstand" to Carnegie Hall and the Newport Folk Festival.

Floyd's Record Store is a Mecca of sorts for fans of the region's music who know they will find whatever Swamp Pop, Zydeco, or Cajun recordings they are seeking here. Floyd has reprised most of his best-selling regional records on CDs. He also stocks reissue and oldie 45s as well as the latest hits. Want to hear a single before you buy it? Just ask, and they will slap one on the record player at the counter.

While you are in the neighborhood, walk down the street to the Pig Stand for lunch; you will probably see Floyd there. Floyd's is open 8 to 5 Monday through Saturday. (318) 363-2138.

Elmand's Dine & dance, $$. Tate Cove Road.

Elmand's is a big dine & dance establishment that opened to fill the void when nearby Snook's lounge canceled their traditional Cajun dance night in the midnineties. They are now the only place north of Mamou offering regular Cajun dances. The restaurant is open Thursday through Saturday from 6 to 11 P.M. and Cajun bands start at 7:30. Thursday's music is a "jam session" featuring an array of local musicians. To get to Elmand's from Ville Platte head four miles north from Rte. 167 (Main Street) on Tate Cove. Elmand's is on the left. (318) 363-3768.

★Snook's Bar and Dancehall Swamp Pop/Country. Rte. 167 W.

Snook's was one of the oldest Cajun dance halls in the Heartland region. There is no longer Cajun music, but the same old-timers walk through the bar area, pay the $2 admission to enter the adjacent dance hall, and slow dance the evening away. One interesting custom here is the practice of salting beer. There is a shaker on every table. Those who do not wish to dance can listen from the bar and watch the band through a large window between the two areas. (318) 363-0451.

LODGING

Motel:

Platte Motel West Main Street (Rte. 167), $40 double. (318) 363-2148. Adjacent to Jungle Dinner Club.

Bed and Breakfasts:

The Guest Cottage 217 LaSalle (Rte. 167).

This is easily the best place to stay in Ville Platte (there are not many choices). It is a charming two-bedroom cottage with wood floors and painted wood walls. One of the bedrooms has a double canopy bed and the other two single beds. Host Chris Daire has tastefully furnished the place with a wicker sofa, easy chair, and rocker. The bathroom has an old claw-foot bathtub. The kitchen is stocked with breakfast supplies. Modern amenities include a phone and TV. The Guest Cottage is a great deal for budget travelers but, be warned, it is downtown on Rte. 167 and there is a lot of noise from the cars passing. Chris Daire works at the Chamber of Commerce and is able to direct visitors to anyplace they might want. She also hipped me to the great boudin at Deshotel's. (318) 363-7554.

Maison De Ville 513 W. Jackson.

Ethel De Ville operates this Bed and Breakfast in her modern two-story home in downtown Ville Platte. The two guest rooms (upstairs) share a bath. One has a queen-size bed, the other a king. The common areas are downstairs and they include a living room, big kitchen, bar, and beautiful patio. Ethel De Ville was born in nearby Chataignier and has lived in Ville Platte since the sixties. Cajun French was her first language and she speaks it fluently. The house is three blocks north of Rte. 167 at the corner of Reed and Jackson. Double cost $70. (318) 363-1262.

Camping:

Crooked Creek Recreation Area
See description under Recreation section.

Chicot State Park
See description under Recreation section.

Basile

Basile is a community of about 2,500 residents and one fine Prairie dance hall just 11 miles west of Eunice on U.S. 190, at the intersection of Rte. 97. The town was founded in 1905 and named for its first settler, Basile Fontenot. Fontenot is still a common name in the area, with the town's main landmark being Fontenot's Main Street Lounge dance hall (a few blocks north of U.S. 190). A couple of miles west on U.S. 190 is Bayou Nez Pique (French for "tattooed nose"), one of the major streams of the northern Prairie, named for a local tribe of Indians who practiced body art. Today Basile is barely a stop in the road, floating amidst flooded crawfish and rice fields.

FOOD

★**D.I.'s Cajun Restaurant** Boiled Seafood/Dine & dance, $$. Rte. 97 S.

D.I.'s is a place that looks as though God just tossed it out on the Prairie. It stands on a lonely piece of land amidst endless acres of crawfish ponds. Owner and boil chef D. I. Fruge was one of the first big crawfish farmers in the area and started boiling the crustaceans in his barn back in 1979. When folks began to catch on to how good his craw- fish were, he moved the boiling pots from the barn to a lounge down the street and, finally, to the present location. This is a full-service restau- rant with Cajun dances on Tuesdays, Wednesdays, and Fridays, but the main attraction is the uniquely seasoned boiled crawfish. D.I. won't divulge the secret of his seasoning, but in addition to the usual cayenne and salt, his crawfish have an aromatic flavor that might be nutmeg or allspice. A popular side is boiled potatoes, which are quartered, brushed with butter, and dusted with a faintly sweet pepper mixture. Other than these, stick with the crawfish here. D.I.'s is open Tuesday through Satur- day from 5 until 10 P.M. There is a Cajun dance on Tuesday, Wednesday, and Friday nights at 8. From U.S. 190, go 9.5 miles south on Rte. 97. From I-10 go 10 miles north on Rte. 97. (318) 432-5141.

MUSIC

★D.I.'s Restaurant Dine & dance. Rte. 97 S.
  See review in Food section above.

Da Office Lounge Saturday Cajun dance. U.S. 190.
  Great name for a bar! How many times have folks called home from here with the excuse "Honey, I'm staying late at Da Office"? Da Office is a funky little bar/grill/dance hall open every day but Sunday from 10 A.M. to 10 P.M. On Friday and Saturday nights bands play and they stay open until midnight. There is Country and Swamp Pop on Fridays and a Cajun band on Saturdays starting around 8:30. The Cajun show attracts a bunch of old-timers who waltz close. Da Office is impossible to miss, on the north side of U.S. 190 (11 miles west of Rte. 13), in Basile. (318) 432-6697.

Fontenot's Main Street Lounge Thursday Cajun jam. Main Street.
  Fontenot's is one of the oldest dance halls on the Prairie still hold- ing Cajun dances. This creaking whitewashed-wood landmark is worth visiting if you can catch it open. Their schedule is somewhat erratic, but the Thursday jam has been dependable. They are located four blocks north of U.S. 190 at the corner of South Lewis and Main Street (turn off U.S. 190 at the Chunkie Drive Inn). Call before making a special trip out. (318) 432-6697.

Elton

You might miss the town of Elton entirely if it were not for the large rice dryers towering over the horizon. The best reasons to stop

Old Elton Jail. (Photo by Julie Posner)

here are to visit the Coushatta Indian Reservation north of town (where you may purchase lunch or supper) or tour the Estherwood Rice Mill. More people than ever are driving through Elton on their way to the new Coushatta Casino in Kinder (12 miles west). This route takes you out of Cajun Country and into the pine flats of Western Louisiana. It is about 60 miles from Elton to the Texas border on U.S. 190.

The Old Jail U.S. 190, Elton.

This is one of those "tourist attractions" that is hard to understand. The jail is a two-room brick building about five yards off U.S. 190 in Elton. It is grown over with weeds. One side is used as a trash receptacle, while the array of bottles on the floor indicates the town drunks have spent a few nights in the other side (without the nuisance of having the doors locked behind them). To really appreciate the old jail I had to talk to Police Chief Roger LaFleur, whose brother was chief when it was still in use. LaFleur remembered nights when there were "20 men in both cells." According to LaFleur, the new jail is "the most modern in the state. We even got bulletproof glass instead of bars. We just don't have any occasion to use it anymore."

Coushatta Tribe of Louisiana

The Coushatta tribe was recognized by the federal government in 1971. Their reservation and tribal center is located just three miles north of Elton. The Coushatta first entered documented history in the journals of DeSoto in the 16th century. The Coushatta were displaced, their towns were destroyed, and they were exposed to many diseases. The tribe escaped mass removal operations under the leadership of a man named Red Shoes, who led the band to the lower reaches of the Red River in Louisiana.

Today over half the 750 tribal members live in the pine forest above Elton, where they remain close-knit, still speaking their language and carrying on traditional crafts. Regulations requiring a stringent 25 percent bloodline helped maintain tribal integrity and a distinctive Native American appearance. They are the only tribe in Louisiana still speaking their language. Tremendous change visited the tribe in the late nineties with the opening of the Grand Coushatta Casino on tribal land in Kinder. Many of the changes seem to be for the better among a population that suffered some of the worst unemployment in the state. Casino money is being used to build health-care, athletic, and administrative facilities on the reservation. A museum and visitors center are on the horizon. To get to the reservation take U.S. 190 to the west end of town. Turn north on Mayor Stokes Street at the historical

Coushatta baskets. (Photo by Macon Fry)

marker for the Coushatta tribe. Go one block over the railroad tracks and turn left on Martin Luther King. The road immediately curves north for three miles to the reservation center. The tribal chief is Loveland Pancho. (318) 584-2261.

Coushatta Store Coushatta Reservation.

The Coushatta store is the only reliable place to find Coushatta pine baskets for sale. The craft shop has dozens of woven pine-needle baskets for sale by identified tribal craftspeople. They range from under $50 for miniatures to well over $100 for extralarge or fancy baskets with tight-fitting woven lids. There is also a selection of other crafts from beadwork to feathers. See directions to the reservation above. Hours are 6 A.M. to 10 P.M. daily. (318) 584-2260.

Coushatta Restaurant Down home, $. Coushatta Reservation.

This small cafe adjacent to the store sells typical plate lunches, fried seafood, and sandwiches. One Friday evening I had a tasty plate of fried catfish crusted in cornmeal, etouffée, and potato salad for about $6. The store also sells ice cream and sweet-dough pies. Plate lunches Monday through Friday are under $5. See directions to the reservation above. Hours are 6 A.M. to 8 P.M. daily except Monday, when they close at 5. (318) 584-2260.

Estherwood Rice, Inc. U.S. 190, Elton.

There are several rice mills in South Louisiana that advertise tours, but nobody else will invite you into the milling area to watch the process. Estherwood was originally located in the southern Prairie town of the same name. David Bertrand and Tom Lejeune moved the family business to Elton when they took over from their parents in 1984. It is the only mill that processes the much-sought-after popcorn rice (so called because of the rich popcorn aroma that rises when cooking). It is also the only mill that still packs rice in 10- and 20-pound cotton bags. The custom-made bags, printed with South Louisiana scenes and logos, have become a trademark of Estherwood milled rice.

While you are waiting for your tour, check out the wall covered with pictures of old rice-farming scenes and display case of custom-printed bags. Before leaving you can buy one of the 10- or 20-pound cotton bags. Hours are 7 to 4 Monday through Friday, except on holidays. Visit during late summer to midfall, Tuesdays through Thursdays, to see the plant in operation. (318) 584-2218.

15

Western Cajun Country

Western Cajun Country is by far the largest of the six regions defined in this book. It forms a 50-mile-wide band along the Gulf of Mexico and stretches west from Lafayette and Abbeville over a hundred miles to the Texas border. The area is comprised of sparsely settled marsh, prairie, and rice fields, all of which attract huge numbers of migratory and native shorebirds. The most dense settlement is in the towns along U.S. 90 and Interstate 10, which parallel the Southern Pacific Railroad. Along these routes and Rte. 14 to the south, rice fields dominate the landscape, and towns are signaled by rice dryers towering over the flat plain. The railroad arrived in the 1880s, before the first settlers and roads. Anxious to develop the land, the railroad recruited farmers from the Midwest to populate towns along the way. Stations were established approximately every 5 miles, and some of these grew into the succession of communities that exists along U.S. 90 today. Anglo names and Victorian and turn-of-the-century architecture predominate in the charming farm villages.

Most visitors will want to visit the rice and rail communities along U.S. 90, so this chapter is organized in an east-to-west continuum along this route, with recommended side trips to the towns to the south on Rte. 14. For those wishing to get a little farther off the beaten path, Rte. 14 from Abbeville to Lake Charles is a lovely drive with many bird-watching opportunities along the way. Adventurers and wildlife enthusiasts should take the time to drive the lengthy but beautiful Hug the Coast Highway (Rte. 82). Because there are so few opportunities to reach the Hug the Coast Highway (except below Lake Charles and Abbeville) it is described in a separate section at the end of this chapter entitled Scenic Wetlands.

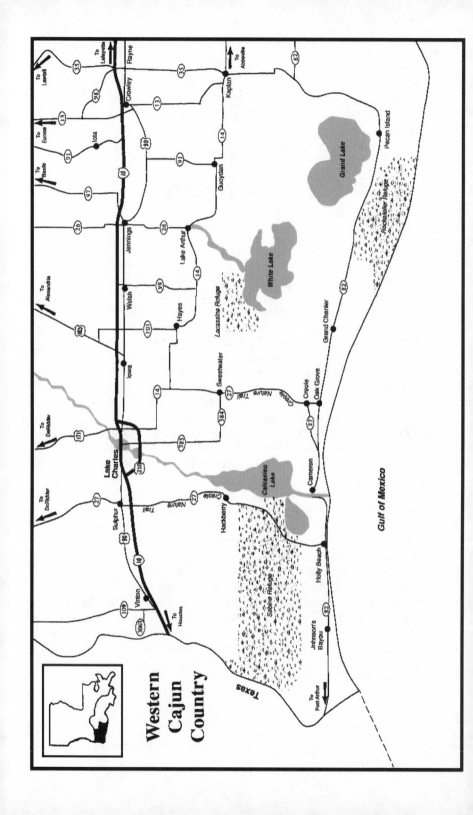

THE RICE BELT
Rayne

This mill and rail town of 10,000 residents, 16 miles west of Lafayette, is known (by legislative decree) as the Frog Capital of the World. Since the many rice-field canals that provided choice habitats for the croaking amphibians have been enclosed, the city has adopted a second title—"The Mural City." The feed stores, warehouses, and stores that greet travelers on U.S. 90 are festooned with a dozen murals depicting frogs fishing, frogs dancing, and frogs playing Cajun music. Rte. 35 crosses U.S. 90 in Rayne and provides access to nearby Kaplan and Church Point (listed in the Cajun Heartland chapter) just 12 miles away. The downtown district is 2 miles south of I-10 where Rte. 35 (Boulevard Street) intersects U.S. 90. The two fine B&B cottages in town are a good base for exploring the Cajun Heartland around Church Point (12 miles north) or the rice country around Kaplan 15 miles south.

Rayne Chamber of Commerce 1023 Boulevard (Rte. 35 S.).

The Chamber has brochures on local attractions. It is on the right at the first light south of I-10 (.3 mile) at exit #87. Hours are weekdays from 9 to 4. (318) 334-2332.

ATTRACTIONS

Jubilee Rouge Collectibles 111 Louisiana Ave.

Jubilee has a tremendous selection of antiques pieces as well as collectibles from the forties and fifties. Their buyer scours estates of the region to come up with a fascinating selection. I found an unused

The Mural City and Frog Capital. (Photo by Ed Neham)

owner's manual and sale brochure for my 1948 Chambers Stove. A friend purchased some hard-to-find Heywood Wakefield Deco-style dining-room furniture. Hours are Thursday through Sunday from 11 to 5. (318) 334-9543.

Comeaux's Antique and Collectibles 113 Louisiana Ave.

Comeaux's is the bargain hunter's delight. The flea market has a half-dozen or so vendors who sell everything from antique furnishings to phonograph records, postcards, and jewelry. Open 9 to 5 weekends. (318) 334-2508.

B.J.'s Dancehall Cajun dance. Polk Street at Edwards.

B.J.'s has a well-attended Cajun dance every Saturday from 9 P.M. to 1 A.M. From U.S. 90 (at Michael's and Sun's restaurant) turn north on Polk Street. B.J.'s is two blocks north of U.S. 90.

Roberts Cove/St. Leo's Shrine Rte. 98 N. (I-10 #exit 87).

I first noticed Roberts Cove while driving to Hawk's restaurant (see review) and were puzzled that there were two signs for the town on the highway, 500 feet apart, with nothing between them but St. Leo's Catholic Church. Roberts Cove is not a ghost town but a rural community united by its church and German heritage. Fr. Peter Leonhard Thevis returned to his native Germany to recruit the 98 friends and family members who settled Roberts Cove in 1882. Elder members of the community speak German and share their culture with the public at an annual Germanfest in October.

St. Leo's Shrine was built in 1890 and for many years was visited by the priest and parishioners on monthly walking pilgrimages. It was recently moved to its present site under St. Leo's live oaks, behind the church. The small shrine is open for personal pilgrimages, meditation, and prayer. Roberts Cove and St. Leo's Church are three miles north of I-10. Take exit #87 (Rte. 35) north one block and turn left on Rte. 98.

★Roberts Cove Germanfest First weekend in October. St. Leo's Church, Rte. 98 N.

Enjoy the international flavors of Octoberfest and Cajun hospitality at this wonderful little festival beside St. Leo's Church. Unless you attend the church, Germanfest is the only time you are likely to find the residents of Roberts Cove together. It is also the one time when their traditional folkways and food are shared with the public. There are bands, folk dancers, and a selection of German beers and food, as well as historical exhibitions and demonstrations of local crafts. Admission is $5. (318) 334-8345 or 783-2180.

Vincent Wildlife Refuge Bird watching. 12 miles south.

See Kaplan.

SPECIAL EVENTS

Frog Festival Labor Day weekend.

The Frog Festival has the best frogleg etouffée and fried froglegs of any festival I've attended. Featured events include Cajun and Zydeco music; frog-eating, -jumping, and -racing contests; and the coronation of a "Frog Queen" (I guess that beats being named the "Boudin Queen" or "Swine Queen"). (318) 334-2332.

FOOD

Michael's and Sun's Local Fave, $ (lunch)-$$ (dinner). U.S. 90.

Michael's and Sun's draws a crowd with their workingman's lunch buffet. Four and a half dollars buys all the down-home grub you could hope to eat. At dinnertime on weekends, folks usually go for Sun's unique Crawfish Fried Rice. This dish is a gigantic pile of rice, stir-fried vegetables, and about half a pound of extralarge crawfish tails. Michael's and Sun's is open Monday through Thursday from 7 A.M. to 3:30 P.M. and Friday and Saturday until 10 P.M. (318) 334-5539.

★Hawk's Boiled Seafood, $$. Rte. 1110 (I-10 exit #87 north).

Hawk Arceneaux serves the largest crawfish ever offered for human consumption. However, it's not the size that most distinguishes the crawfish here; it's the sweet flavor. Hawk describes the secret to his crawfish in one word: "purging." Most restaurants wash the mud off the outside of their crawfish. A few add salt to the wash water, to clean the inside. Only Hawk Arceneaux goes through a 24-hour freshwater purging process. Behind his restaurant are freshwater holding tanks from which his chefs dip and boil up to 1,500 pounds a night. Some people don't like the fact that most of the seasoning here is sprinkled on the outside. Others complain that the craws are actually *too* clean and they miss that "swampy" flavor. To me, these are the ultimate.

Half the fun of going to Hawk's is getting there. Although they are only about seven miles from Rayne, their location is wildly inscrutable. I recommend going there when there is still a little sunlight left, so you can find the place and avoid the crowds that have somehow discovered this great eatery. When it is raining, the road into Hawk's is covered with thousands of frogs, exiting flooded roadside ditches for the perils of life on the road. Hawk's is open Wednesday to Saturday from 5 to 10 P.M. (seasonally—mid-November to mid-June).

From I-10, take the Rayne exit. Go north about 50 yards and make a left on Rte. 98. There are some right-angle turns in Rte. 98. Go 7.8 miles and make a right onto tiny Parish Road 2-7. This is a dirt road marked by a small Hawk's sign. Go .8 mile and Hawk's will be on the left. If you are going to Hawk's from U.S. 190, take Rte. 367 in Eunice and head south 11.7 miles. Turn right on Rte. 1110. Go 1.6 miles and turn left on the small parish road marked with a Hawk's sign. (318) 788-3266.

LODGING

★Maison D'Memoire Bed and Breakfast Cottages Rayne.

Ken and Lyn Guidry have taken two little turn-of-the-century houses and renovated them into very comfortable guest cottages. The inside walls, floors, and ceilings are all tongue-and-groove pine, and both cottages have painted-wood kitchen cabinets. They are furnished with period antiques and comfortable modern features like cozy chairs for reading or watching TV, firm mattresses, central air conditioning, and equipped kitchens. They manage to be charming without being cluttered.

The prairie cottage is a perfect romantic getaway. It is a mile north of I-10, beside Ken and Lyn's house on the Guidry family's 35-acre ranch. Horses graze in the pasture behind a sunny kitchen and at night the air is filled with the sound of frogs. There is a luxurious Jacuzzi where a stained-glass window creates an aura of perpetual sunset. Breakfast is delivered in a picnic basket. Another cottage is available in downtown Rayne, which, though lovingly restored, is across the railroad tracks from U.S. 90. You need to decide if trains passing is romantic or a bummer. The prairie cottage is $85 a night without use of Jacuzzi and $140 with it. The city cottage costs $70. Lodging without the huge breakfast (egg dish, fruit, biscuit, preserves, pastry, and juice) is $10 less. Lyn speaks Cajun French. Cash or Visa are accepted. (318) 334-2477.

★Bob's Frontier Cabins Church Point, 12 miles north of Rayne.

See the review of these cozy cabins under Church Point (Cajun Heartland chapter). Bob and Dot speak French. $55-$65 a night. (318) 684-5431.

Camping:

Acadian Oaks Campground Rte. 98 N. (I-10 exit #87).

This small campground is convenient to I-10 but just far enough off the highway to provide peaceful camping. Tent sites and RV spaces with full hookups and lots of shade cost $10 a night. Exit at Rte. 35 N. Make an immediate left on Rte. 98. The campground is about a mile north of I-10. (318) 334-9955.

Kaplan

Located 17 miles south of Rayne at the intersection of Rte. 35 and Rte. 14 (I-10 exit #87), Kaplan is a tiny rice and cattle town of 5,000 that grew around a rail spur established in 1901. Five years later the town began to celebrate a distinctly non-American festival, Bastille Day. The celebration is still the biggest event in town (aside from the rice harvest) and perhaps the oldest festival in Cajun Country. During most of the year, the only excitement is stirred up by games of bourré at one of the town's several card bars, like Tina's Western Frontier Lounge or Lefty's.

Kaplan Museum 405 N. Cushing St. (Rte. 35).

The Kaplan Museum has an eclectic collection that amounts to a scrapbook of the town. There are hundreds of bits of local history on display. (318) 643-1528.

Vincent Wildlife Refuge Bird watching. Rte. 35, 12 miles south of Rayne.

To anyone but a bird watcher this refuge looks like any other of the open rice fields that predominate the landscape in Southwest Louisiana. It is comprised of 640 acres of startlingly flat land but during spring and fall migrations can fill with over 30 species of shorebirds. Over a hundred species (including a Tropical Parula) were spotted during the 1996 Crowley Bird Count. Prime birding time is when the fields have just been flooded or drained, but anytime from late February to early May or July through October can be good. A single field may attract thousands of birds. There is a dirt and gravel road that winds from the entrance on Rte. 35 for a couple of miles around the fields. The refuge is privately owned but is open to the public and managed cooperatively with the U.S. Fish and Wildlife Service. Vincent is about 6 miles north of Kaplan on Rte. 35. From Rayne drive 12 miles south and look for Rte. 699. The entrance to the refuge is marked with a sign, on the west side, just south of Rte. 699. (318) 643-2763 or 643-6405.

FOOD

Micky's Drive-In Local Fave/Sandwiches, $. 706 First St. (Rte. 14 E.).

When Suire's is not open, this is the place to eat in Kaplan. Owned by State Rep. Micky Frith, Micky's has been a popular Kaplan hangout since it opened as Freezo Drive-In back in 1956. The Cajun Burgers, sandwiches, and ice-cream drinks are popular. Micky's has a clean dining area and can be an oasis for those traveling the sunny stretches of Rte. 14 or Rte. 82 west. It is a couple of blocks east of Rte. 35. Hours are 9:30 A.M. to 9:30 P.M. daily.

★Suire's Store Restaurant Down Home, $. Rte. 35 S.

Suire's is a community gathering place, especially during lunch while Mary Suire is serving up beef brisket in dark gravy with dirty rice, or turtle sauce piquante accompanied by stuffed bread and potato salad. The turtle sauce piquante is always served on Fridays and is the best on the planet. Rich turtle meat cooks down to tasty shreds in a rusty-brown gravy with bits of green pepper and onion. You might talk Mary into serving you some on an off day if she is not too busy. Also excellent are shrimp and egg stew and crawfish etouffée. This is real Cajun cookin'. The customers are mostly farmers and much of the talk is in French. There are four communal tables in the dining area that occupies one side of the store (the other side is general merchandise). Lunch specials are served from 11 until they run out. Turtle sauce piquante is also available to take home, from the freezer case. Go 3.5 miles south from Kaplan on Rte. 35. Hours are Monday through Saturday from 6 A.M. to 8 P.M. (318) 643-8911.

LODGING

Sunnyside Motel Rte. 14, Kaplan (17 miles south of Rayne).

This fifties-style motel with clean rooms, comfortable beds, pine paneling, tile baths, pool, and Jacuzzi is a convenient stopover for birders. Doubles cost $30 to $35. It is seven blocks west of Rte. 35 (Cushing Street). (318) 643-7181.

TRAVEL TIP

Those interested in driving the Hug the Coast Highway (Rte. 82) may learn more about the route by consulting the Gateway to Hug the Coast Highway entry under Abbeville (Central Cajun Country chapter) or by turning to the Scenic Wetlands section at the end of this chapter.

Crowley

Crowley, with 16,000 residents, is the archetypal Cajun Prairie rice and rail town. The seat of Acadia Parish, it is one of the major population centers between Lafayette (24 miles to the east) and Lake Charles. The old historic district, a mile south of I-10 (exit #80), has a distinctly Anglo feel, resembling the kind of town a model-train hobbyist constructs at his favorite rail crossing. It is a city of Victorian homes and shaded streets. The streets emanate out in a neat grid from the railroad, with Parkerson (Rte. 13), the main route, bisecting the town. Crowley is the official Rice Capital of Louisiana and home to a dozen or more rice mills and dryers. The city's best-known attractions are the Crystal Rice Plantation, Rice Museum, and annual Rice Festival. Local businesses joined the boosterism, including Rice City Liquor, Rice City Exxon, Rice Palace Casino, and Rice Hotel. The most notable nonrice business in town is the Modern Music Center,

Downtown Crowley. (Photo by Julie Posner)

where record man Jay Miller opened his pioneering recording studio in 1949. A new suburban Crowley has grown in the swath between U.S. 90 and I-10 at the intersection of Rte. 13. Here you will find such technological advances as fast food, shopping malls, and multiscreen movie theaters.

Acadia Parish Visitors Center I-10 exit #82, Crowley.

The center is in construction at the time of this writing. (318) 783-2108.

ATTRACTIONS

Downtown Walking Tour

Brochures for the walking tour should be available from the new Acadia Parish Visitors Center. The tour runs about six blocks along South Parkerson Avenue (Rte. 13) from the courthouse to the Chamber of Commerce in the train depot. There is plenty of parking. Parkerson is the commercial district, where you can visit the Modern Music Center and get some tamales at Rice City Liquor. The Victorian residential section occupies the three blocks east of Parkerson Avenue.

★Modern Music Center/Master-Trak Studio 413 N. Parkerson.

There is nothing modern about this South Louisiana music Mecca, but it is a pilgrimage site for South Louisiana music lovers from around the world. Vintage instruments hang from the ceiling and racks of 45-RPM records cover one wall. The store was opened in 1949 by Jay Miller, Louisiana's first record man. Until his death on March 23, 1996, Miller could often be found holding forth at the register. The store and the truly modern studios are now managed by his son Mark. Clifton Chenier, Rusty and Doug Kershaw, Jimmy ("C") Newman, Buckwheat Zydeco, Wayne Toups, Sonny Landreth, and country superstar Sammy Kershaw all recorded for Miller. Many of the earliest recordings by these now-famous artists are still available on CDs, vinyl, and cassettes in the store. Hours are Monday through Friday from 9 to 6 and Saturday from 9:30 to 1. (318) 783-1601.

★Crystal Rice Plantation Aquaculture and house tours. South Crowley.

My favorite part of the Crystal Rice tour was a visit to the rice and crawfish production areas of the plantation, where workers were draining and reseeding the fields. At another time of year I might have seen crawfish mechanically sorted or rice harvested. There is always something going on. The tour and very good video provide an overview of the rice and crawfish industry and a firsthand look at the aquaculture in progress.

The plantation was founded by agricultural pioneer Sol Wright in 1890 and is managed by Sol Wright III and sons. The story of four generations of Wright inventors and eccentrics unfolds during the fascinating tours of the Wright Antique Car Museum (12 vehicles) and Blue Rose House (circa 1848). Sol Wright developed crystal-clear rice (trademarked Blue Rose) that could be successfully reseeded. By 1936, 80 percent of domestic production was from his product. Sol Wright II collected Mercedes (rebuilding one with a wood body!) and drove around the plantation in an airplane with the wings removed. He also developed the process for "enriching" rice. Present owner Sol Wright III has created a vitamin supplement used by Kellogg's in breakfast cereals. From I-10 take Rte. 13 S. (exit #80) through downtown Crowley. At U.S. 90 travel four miles farther south on Rte. 13 and turn right on Airport Road. Travel 2.5 miles and turn left. Hours are 8 to 5 Monday through Friday. The $5.50 adult admission includes the car museum, house, and aqua-tour. (318) 783-6417.

Rice Museum U.S. 90 west.

The Rice Museum is west of Crowley on U.S. 90 in a small frame house. The exhibits here were designed when the museum opened in the early sixties and some have become museum pieces in their own right! The Oil Room exhibit is precious, as is the miniature working model of a rice mill. Particularly interesting was a chunk of "climatron," a building material composed of rice hulls, chaff, and cement, which was used to build a couple of local houses in the fifties. If you like your museums with a down-home flair, this one is for you. The

Rice Museum. (Photo by Julie Posner)

museum has opened and closed several times in the last few years. Call the Acadia Parish Visitors Center for information. (318) 783-2108.

Rice Mill Row Mill St.

The biggest concentration of rice mills and dryers in South Louisiana is located on Mill Street at the foot of Parkerson Avenue in Crowley. The tall buildings are the dryers, in which hot air is pumped through the fresh product. In the late summer, this area is enveloped in a cloud of rice dust as trucks are weighed and unload their harvest.

★Le Petit Chateau deLuxe Castle tour. Rte. 92, Mermentau.

See Jennings listings.

SPECIAL EVENTS

The Rice Festival First or second weekend in October.

Inaugurated in 1937, the Rice Festival is Louisiana's oldest harvest festival. The main attraction is a weekend street party in the old downtown district. There are food booths and live Cajun bands. (318) 783-3067.

★Iota Courir du Mardi Gras Exit #72, Egan (five miles west of Crowley).

Iota is a farm community about 14 miles northwest of Crowley that has preserved many aspects of the traditional Courir du Mardi Gras

Iota Mardi Gras. (Photo by Julie Posner)

that have disappeared elsewhere. Most riders wear traditional painted screen masks. Upon reentering town at the end of the ride they are often showered with money. On Mardi Gras day the riders depart about 7 A.M. While they are visiting farms around the countryside, the town holds a folk-craft, food, and music festival downtown. There is dancing and street food. Before the riders return, the children of Iota command the raised dance floor, where they sing the Mardi Gras song and dance. After the performance, they are showered with change from the crowd and a general melee ensues as they chase coins about the stage. This event harkens back to the days when a *"petit Mardi Gras"* was held on Mondays, and children would visit neighbors on foot in a simulation of the adults' *Courir du Mardi Gras.* The riders return to Iota around two o'clock, so it is possible to catch the happenings here and drive over to enjoy the culmination of their Mardi Gras.

FOOD

Frosto Local Fave, $. Third Street at North G Avenue.

The Frosto has been a Crowley institution since the fifties. This vintage burger stand and dairy bar turns out typical fast food. I like their Frosties, which are nothing more than soda pop and ice cream thrown together in a blender (a sure way to cool off from your downtown walking tour and an excellent accompaniment for the tamales from Rice City Liquor). (318) 783-0917.

Rice City Liquor Store Local Fave, $. 630 N. Parkerson.

Folks from out West have been heard to comment that Louisiana tamales are rolls of grits stuffed with meat, but one whiff of the red sauce wafting from the back room here and you will be ordering a dozen instead of six. Pat Istre's family has been running Rice City Liquor since the forties, when liquor was sold only in package stores, but has been surviving since the sixties primarily on the popularity of their homemade tamales. They are open Monday through Friday from 8 to 6 and Saturday from 10 to 4. They make the tamales fresh daily and usually run out by 5. (318) 783-9856.

Super Food Grocery Local Fave/Stuffed bread, $. 222 E. Second St.

Super Food is a grocery store with a lunch counter (no indoor dining) in front. They serve plate lunches, but the hot item (literally and figuratively) is the spicy stuffed bread. Hefty fresh-baked rolls are stuffed with a sauteed sausage, green pepper, and onion. Although this meal in a roll is not recommended for folks with a tendency for heartburn, I love the flavor and portability. (The mild version is not recommended.) They cost under $2 and are often gone by 11:45. Lunch is served from 10:30 to 1:30 weekdays. (318) 783-1078.

LODGING

Hotels and Motels:

★Rice Hotel 125 Third St.

This 1907 hulk is one of the few downtown hotels in South Louisiana that has not yielded to the wrecking ball. The Rice Hotel is far from grand, but it is meticulously clean and infinitely charming, from the antique "Petticoat Junction"-style switchboard to the rooms with their aging but comfortable furnishings, ceiling fans, and window air conditioners. There are no televisions in the rooms, but there is one in the lobby. Doubles are $30 to $40. The hotel is a block west of Parkerson. (318) 783-6471.

Best Western of Crowley 9571 Egan Hwy. (exit #80).

The Best Western is located at I-10 beside the Waffle House. Pool, cable TV. Doubles cost $64. (318) 783-2378 or 1-800-940-0003.

Crowley Inn 2111 N. Cherokee Dr. (exit #80).

This modern motel is located beside I-10 and the Rice Palace video-poker casino. Pool, cable TV. Doubles cost $47. (318) 788-0970 or 1-800-256-4565.

Camping:

Trail's End Campground Exit #72, Egan (eight miles west of Crowley).

Full hookups, pull-through sites, small swimming pool, tennis courts, ice, bathhouse, playground. In season, you can pick your own blackberries, blueberries, and muscadine grapes. Camping is $15 a night. Exit #72, and south 1.5 miles. (318) 783-9810 or 234-2738.

Gueydan

Gueydan (pronounced GAY-don) is a farming community of about 1,600 on Rte. 14, 11 miles south of U.S. 90. From Crowley you will need to drive west on U.S. 90 about 8 miles to Midland and catch Rte. 91 south. The city has been proclaimed the Duck Capital of America for the thousands of ducks that forage in nearby rice fields and winter in the marsh, which stretches south 30 miles to the Gulf of Mexico. For most of a century the Gueydan area has been a prime destination for duck hunters, many of whom own or lease camps in the southern marshes. Each year they celebrate the plentiful waterfowl in the Labor Day weekend Duck Festival. The best reason for a cursory traveler to stop here is to pick up a stock of the locally grown Ellis Stansel's Popcorn Rice at the local feed store.

G&H Seed Company (Popcorn Rice) 300 First St.

G&H is the main outlet for the fabulous Ellis Stansel's Popcorn Rice, as well as feed, seed, fertilizer, garden supplies, and livestock remedies. The popcorn rice, unavailable at major supermarkets, has a rich flavor and firm texture. A 10-pound bag costs about $10, and 5 pounds goes for around $6. The bags are made of cotton and are printed with the Stansel logo. G&H Seed is on Rte. 14 W. at First Street. Hours are Monday through Friday from 7 to 5 and Saturday until noon. (318) 536-6751.

To order Ellis Stansel's Popcorn Rice directly from Mr. Stansel, write: P.O. Box 206, Gueydan, LA 70542.

Jennings

Located about 40 miles from Lafayette and 32 miles east of Lake Charles, Jennings, a quaint railroad town with an interesting historic district, is a gateway to the lovely wetlands around the Mermentau River at Lake Arthur (just 10 minutes south). The town was born when S. L. Cary, a land agent for the Southern Pacific Railway, recruited Anglo and German settlers from the Midwest. Unlike other rice towns, Jennings (which went on to become the seat of Jefferson Davis Parish) experienced a second economic boom in the early 1900s when oil was discovered at the Evangeline field, just north of town. This was the first "bringing in" of an oil well in Louisiana, and it touched off an influx of merchants, speculators, and vice in the formerly conservative

Early oil well. (Courtesy of Lafayette Courthouse Archives)

community. Perhaps sensing that oil was too prosaic to attract tourists, the city changed its motto (by legislative decree!) in 1979 from "The Cradle of Louisiana Oil" to "The Boudin Capital of the Universe." Like Crowley, this city of 12,500 is characterized by a quaint Victorian residential district clustered around a slowly reviving commercial strip. Modern suburbs extend between the historic town center and the interstate to the north.

ATTRACTIONS

Jefferson Davis Parish Tourist Center I-10 exit #64 north.

The Tourist Center is located just north of Interstate 10 in the Oil and Gas Park. Here you will find public rest rooms, city and parish maps, brochures, and a very helpful staff. I recommend that anyone planning on visiting Jennings get a city map here. The town has an unusual street grid (especially confusing when you enter from U.S. 90). Walk next door to view the alligators in the Chateau des Cocodries (description below). The Tourist Center is open Monday through Friday from 8:30 to 5. (318) 821-5521 or 1-800-264-5521.

Chateau des Cocodries I-10 exit #64 north.

Located just north of Interstate 10 in the Oil and Gas Park, the Chateau des Cocodries is one of South Louisiana's more unusual attractions (though not as unusual as the caged tigers at the Tiger Truck Stop at exit #139). The interstate passes through miles of alligator habitat, but the Chateau has the state's only captive gators with easy interstate access (a dubious distinction for the poor reptiles). The Chateau is a small cement and cinder-block cell with viewing area adjacent to the Tourist Center. There is a pay phone in the viewing room so you may call the folks back home and ask them, "Guess what I am looking at right now?" Alligator feeding may be seen on Mondays at 1:30 June through August. The viewing area is open free of charge, Monday through Friday from 8:30 to 5 and Saturday from 10 to 5. 1-800-264-5521.

Oil and Gas Park I-10 exit #64 north.

The Oil and Gas Park was built to commemorate the first producing oil well in the state of Louisiana, which was brought in at the Evangeline field, a few miles north. In 1901, Jules Clement, a rice farmer and rancher, noticed bubbles coming from one of his flooded fields. Inspired by the huge Spindletop gusher struck earlier that year in Texas, he stuck a stovepipe into the ground over the bubbles. When he tossed a match into the pipe, the bubbles ignited and the oil rush was on. With the help of the men who financed Spindletop, the Jules Clement Well #1 was brought in a few months later, producing over 7,000 barrels a day. I haven't noticed any bubbles coming out of the pond at the Oil and Gas Park, but I saw some kids pulling in fish hand over fist. The park is open during daylight hours daily. In addition to the pond, Visitors Center, and alligator, it has a replica of the state's first oil well and picnic tables with a view of the interstate.

DOWNTOWN ATTRACTIONS

A brochure listing downtown attractions is available at the Tourist Center. From I-10 go south on Rte. 26 (Lake Arthur Drive). At Shankland (U.S. 90) go east to Main Street. The historic area stretches a dozen blocks south to the railroad tracks; most of the buildings here were built during the oil boom. Park at either end of Main and you can walk the area in an hour or so.

Jennings Antique Mall 1019 N. Main.

A half-dozen dealers sell everything from collectibles (records, post-cards, and books) to fine furniture. Hours are daily, 10 to 5. (318) 824-3360.

Strand Theater 432 N. Main.

The Strand is an Art-Deco movie palace now featuring live theater. Architectural details are in great condition. Inside, the walls are decorated with two-tone hourglass lamps. Too bad they do not show movies anymore.

W. H. Tupper General Merchandise Museum 311 N. Main.

The W. H. Tupper Store operated from 1910 to 1949 in a rural area north of Jennings. When the store closed, the merchandise remained untouched on the shelves until 1971 when it was put in storage. The housewares, dry goods, patent medicines, clothes, farm implements, and toys are now back on the shelves in this re-creation of the store. Nothing is for sale but there are over 10,000 items to look at (much of it with original packaging and price tags). There is a collection of over 100 Coushatta baskets brought to the store by Indians in trade for supplies. Hours are Monday through Saturday from 10 to 6. Adult admission is $3, students $1.50. (318) 821-5532 or 1-800-264-5521.

Zigler Museum 411 Clara St.

The Zigler Museum houses a small but high-quality collection of work by European masters. Most impressive are the Audubon collection and gallery of works by Louisiana artists. The Central Gallery displays a new exhibit each month. From I-10 take exit #64 south one mile and go left on Clara Street. The museum is four blocks west of Main Street. It is open Tuesday through Saturday from 9 to 5 and Sunday from 1 to 5. (318) 824-0114.

AREA ATTRACTIONS

★Le Petit Chateau deLuxe Rte. 92, Mermentau.

A tour of the "Little Luxury Castle" is a window into the grand dreams of Lovic and Phillip Desormeaux. In 1955 Lovic landscaped nine acres around his small wooden house. Seven years later he started building a 15,000-square-foot Louis IV-style castle inspired by estates he had seen in France. Working without written specifications, Desormeaux's son Phillip built the interior with its grand staircase (which took eight months to construct), four working fireplaces, and basket-weave parquet floor. His father died in 1992 but Phillip continues to work on details, seeking out gilded French furnishings.

Phillip, who traces his ancestors back to Brittany, offers tours in French and English. His dream now includes the construction of an entire village dedicated to the preservation of French culture and heritage. Somehow he farms rice on his 2,000 acres by the Mermentau River, gives tours, continues construction, and imagines building more! The castle is 8 miles southeast of Jennings. From Jennings take U.S. 90 east about 6 miles. Just east of Mermentau go south on Rte. 92 (Mermentau Cove Road) for 2.5 miles. Make a right on Castle Road. Tours are by appointment, Tuesday through Saturday at 10 and 3, at a cost of $4.50.

★**Lake Arthur** Rte. 26, nine miles south.
See Lake Arthur to Hayes/Rte. 14.

★**Lacassine National Wildlife Refuge** Bird watching. 4.5 miles south.
See Lake Arthur to Hayes/Rte. 14.

FOOD

★**Boudin King** Down Home, $. 906 W. Division St.

Although there is a certain novelty to a restaurant whose reputation is built on boudin and that serves the steaming links at a drive-up window, Boudin King has some stuff on the menu that is a heck of a lot better than their sausage. Try the perfectly seasoned fried chicken and crispy homemade onion rings. For a real surprise check out the chicken and sausage gumbo. Never mind the styrofoam bowl; this is some of the best gumbo around! For about $6 you can get a meal to remember—two pieces of chicken, a small gumbo, and small order of onion rings. From I-10, go south on Rte. 26 for two miles to the light at Division Street. Take a right onto Division and the Boudin King is four blocks up on the right. Hours are Monday through Saturday from 8 A.M. to 9 P.M. (318) 824-6593.

LODGING

Best Western Jennings I-10 at exit #65, $55-$60 double. (318) 824-6550.

Holiday Inn Jennings Rte. 26 N. at I-10 exit #64, $55-$65 double. (318) 824-5280, (800) HOL-IDAY.

Thrifty Inn Rte. 26 N. at exit #64, $40-$50 double.

★**Lorraine Retreat Guesthouse** 17 miles west (see Lake Arthur to Hayes/Rte. 14).

TRAVEL TIP

It is 30 miles from Jennings to Lake Charles by way of U.S. 90. or I-10. There are several sleepy towns along the way with small diners and local color. The most interesting attractions are a few minutes south at the Lacassine exit (Rte. 101). See the Lake Arthur to Hayes/Rte. 14 section for reviews of Buckeye Exotic Animal Farm, Lorraine Bridge, and Harris Seafood Restaurant.

LAKE ARTHUR TO HAYES/RTE. 14

Some of the most beautiful wetlands in South Louisiana lie 15 minutes south of I-10 between Jennings and Lake Charles. Anyone interested in getting off the highway for a few minutes should visit Lake Arthur. If you have an extra hour, consider driving along the more scenic Rte. 14 instead of the interstate or U.S. 90. This section covers the towns and attractions along Rte. 14 beginning at Lake Arthur and heading west to Hayes. This is first-class birding territory. If you decide to look for overnight accommodations, there are several tranquil waterside campgrounds and the excellent Lorraine Retreat Guesthouse to choose from (see reviews below).

Lake Arthur

Lake Arthur Park Lakefront, downtown.

A concession stand sells sandwiches and snacks and rents inner tubes and paddle boats. You may pick up a plate lunch or sandwich from the Sausage House restaurant (a few steps away on Arthur Avenue) and enjoy a picnic under the oaks or in one of the picnic shelters. The concession stand and swimming area are open in the summer from 7 A.M. to 9 P.M.; the rest of the park is usable year round.

The Sausage House Down Home/Ice Cream, $. 108 Arthur Ave.

Ice cream is the main attraction; they also sell plate lunches and sandwiches. Try the tasty (though rich) stuffed and fried breads. Hours are Monday through Saturday 11 A.M. to 9 P.M. (318) 774-3703.

Nott's Corner Restaurant Local Fave, $-$$. 639 Arthur Ave.

Nott's is an old country-style restaurant with a super-relaxed atmosphere. Its walls are decorated with historical photographs of the Lake Arthur area. The food is as good as any you will find on Rte. 14 (that is not saying a lot). Try their po' boys or boiled and fried seafood. Nott's is open daily from 7 A.M. to 9 P.M. (318) 774-2332.

★Shady Shores A-Z R.V. Park Bonnie Road.

Shady Shores is a small lakefront campground with stunning

scenery. It opened in 1996 with 15 sites, so this is a good choice for folks who want to escape the hubbub that surrounds many of the big campground franchises. There is a fine dock that extends out over the lake. Two miles west of Lake Arthur on Rte. 14, turn south on Bonnie Road. The campground is about a mile below Rte. 14. RV camping costs $12; tent camping is $10. (318) 774-3211.

West of Lake Arthur

Lacassine National Wildlife Refuge Seven miles west of Lake Arthur.

The Lacassine National Wildlife Refuge encompasses 31,776 acres of freshwater marsh and prime bird-watching territory. It is administered by the United States Fish and Wildlife Service and is designed to protect wetlands wildlife and habitat. Most visitors are bird watchers and fishermen. Over 230 species of birds have been sighted at Lacassine. Winter concentrations of 800,000 ducks and geese have been observed on the Lacassine Pool.

Access to the refuge is limited to a small viewing platform at the refuge headquarters, about 30 miles of levees, and by boat. Hiking the levees (there is a map available at headquarters) is the best way to spot wildlife. Boaters may use one of the two commercial landings or a public launch on the north side of the refuge. Between mid-October and mid-March, access to most of the waterways and a few of the levees is limited. Seven miles west of Lake Arthur (13 miles east of Hayes), turn south on Rte. 3056 (Lowery Road). The offices are 4 miles south of Rte. 14 beside the Mermentau River. Office hours are 7 to 3:30 weekdays. (318) 774-5923.

★Myers' Landing Campground Seven miles west of Lake Arthur.

Myers' is a country campground on the banks of the Mermentau River that appeals to fishermen, bird watchers, and outdoorsmen. The camp store sells bait, fishing supplies, gas, and camping gear. They also stock "essential" groceries like weenies, marshmallows, and beer. Myers' is a special place, from the store, which has a picnic table overlooking the river and sells bait on credit, to the thickly shaded grounds. The rest room is clean, but there are no showers. Full hookups are $11 a night; tent spaces are $6. Visa and Mastercard accepted. The boat launch costs $2. Myers' is a couple of miles above the Lacassine Refuge. Take Rte. 14 for 11 miles west from Lake Arthur. Turn south on Rte. 3056. Myers' Landing is 3 miles south on the left. (318) 774-9992 or 774-2338.

Myers' Landing Cabins Seven miles west of Lake Arthur.

These two cabins by the entrance to Myers' Landing Campground are simple, constructed of salvaged materials and sparsely furnished. Guests will need to bring sheets and towels. Everything else is provided. I love the setting, but the beds are not very comfortable. Ask about this when you call to reserve; they may be upgraded. Cabins rent for $50 a night or $200 a week. Visa and Mastercard are accepted. (318) 774-9992 or 774-2338.

★Harris Seafood Restaurant Dine & dance, $-$$. Rte. 14, Hayes.

I don't know where they come from, but huge crowds rendezvous at this restaurant/dance hall every Wednesday, Friday, and Saturday night. In fact, you can forget getting a seat in the dance-hall area unless you call in advance for reservations or get there before 6. Harris has the formula for success pared down to the Cajun essentials: fresh boiled and fried seafood served in a no-frills (cement floor) dining room, and a great big dance floor. By far the most popular items on the menu are the fried seafood platter, boiled crawfish, and crabs. These are washed down with "buckets of beer," six longnecks served in a bucket of ice. Cajun and Country bands play on Wednesday, Friday, and Saturday, from 7:30 to 11 P.M. Harris is west of Rte. 101 in Hayes, 20 miles west of Lake Arthur and 8 miles south of I-10 in Lacassine. Hours are Tuesday through Saturday, from 11 A.M. to 11 P.M., and Sunday from 5 to 10 P.M. Closed Monday. (318) 622-3582.

★Lorraine Bridge Lorraine Road (north of Hayes).

A two-mile detour east from Rte. 101 takes travelers to an enchanted corner of Cajun Country. In the late 1800s, the community of Lorraine flourished at the juncture of Bayou Lacassine and Bayou

Lorraine Bridge. (Photo by Julie Posner)

Chene, streams that carried schooners laden with lumber and rice through the marshes and into the Gulf. A small buggy bridge was built over the bayous just below their convergence. That bridge was destroyed and a new, all-wooden one built in 1920. This is the bridge that is still standing (barely!). With the arrival of the railroad, bayous lost much of their importance as commercial thoroughfares, and Lorraine became a virtual ghost town. There is little left of the town today except a cemetery. The once-busy Bayou Lacassine crossing is silently reflected in the murky waters of the forking streams. A rare pickup rattles by, shaking the old wooden bridge for all it's worth before disappearing in the cypress-and-oak forest.

★Lorraine Retreat Guesthouse Lorraine Road, 10 minutes from I-10.

Whether one wants a night in one of the most beautiful spots in South Louisiana, access to excellent bird watching, or a chance to enjoy Cajun-French language and culture, the Retreat Lorraine has it all. Judy and Tony Zaunbrecher operate this Bed and Breakfast in a recently constructed cottage behind their modern estate. It contains one large room with private bath, kitchenette, queen bed, and fold-out sofa. In this lovely corner of Cajun Country it is unlikely you will want to spend much time inside. The residence is a short walk from the Lorraine Bridge, 10 minutes from the interesting Buckeye Exotic Animal Farm, 20 minutes from the Lacassine Wildlife Refuge and Lake Charles, and 30 minutes from the Cameron Prairie Wildlife Refuge (see reviews of these attractions). Judy Zaunbrecher is a direct descendant of the Lorraine family for whom the settlement is named. Her husband, Tony, was a French major and works in the Elderhostel Program at McNeese State University. Both speak French fluently and are familiar with regional folkways and culture. The retreat is 5 minutes north of Rte. 14 and 10 south of I-10. Cost, $55-$65. (318) 622-3412.

★Buckeye Exotic Animal Farm and Garden Lacassine (five minutes south of I-10).

Lou Fontenot has created a backyard zoo and native-plant garden that is one of the most interesting attractions in Western Cajun Country. She has hundreds of animals on five shaded acres as well as a barn housing Angora Bunnies, Dancing Mice, Zebra Mice, Jerboas, Micro Squirrels, and "Sonic" the hedgehog. Her penned animals such as pygmy goats, prairie dogs, miniature horses, and "Skippy" the Wallaby seem happy in the wooded environs and readily approach visitors. It is hard to believe the scale of Ms. Fontenot's creation, but she has a feed bill of over $8,000 a year! She gives an excellent tour, introducing animals and providing trivia. (It takes 300 chinchillas to make a

Lou Fontenot and "Sonic" the hedgehog at Buckeye Farm.
(Photo by Macon Fry)

jacket.) Pine trees tower over the farm and gardens and keep the air about 10 degrees cooler than anyplace else in South Louisiana. In the fall and early spring these trees and bushes fill with birds looking to steal scattered animal feed. From I-10 take the Lacassine exit (Rte. 101) south about three miles and turn left on Ardoin Cove Road. Go one mile and turn right on McGee Road. Ardoin Cove Road is about five miles north from Rte. 14. Admission is a bargain at $3. Hours are 10 to 4 daily, but call first to make sure Ms. Fontenot is there and also to avoid any school groups. (318) 588-4346.

Lake Charles

Lake Charles rests on the east bank of the Calcasieu River, 70 miles west of Lafayette. The seat of Calcasieu (Indian for "crying eagle") Parish, it is one of the two major population centers in Cajun Country, with 75,000 residents. In this western outpost, the people, scenery, and way of life have more in common with Texas (30 miles to the west)

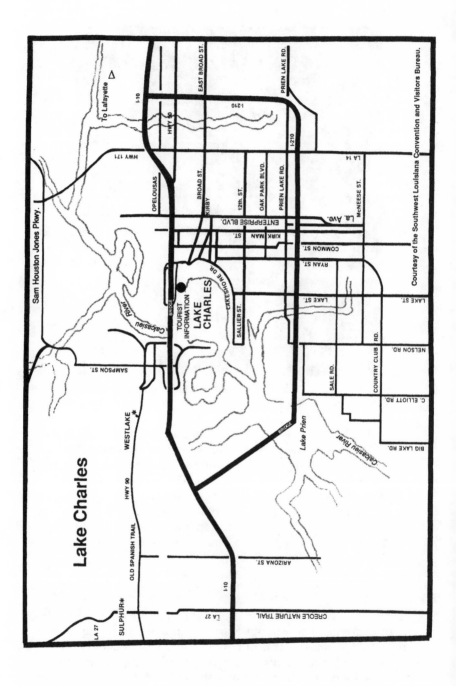

Lake Charles

Courtesy of the Southwest Louisiana Convention and Visitors Bureau.

than with the rest of South Louisiana. Cowboy attire is common, and most residents find employment in the Port of Lake Charles, at nearby chemical plants, or in the oil industry. Restaurants are more likely to serve a plate of barbecued ribs than etouffée, and the music of choice is Country, not Cajun. Visitors can make a quick tour of the city, visit the legendary Eddie Shuler's Goldband Record Store and Recording Studio, and spend a day exploring the wetlands to the south, which are the biggest attraction in the area (see the Scenic Wetlands section at the end of this chapter).

Until 1821, Lake Charles was the last secure settlement in Southwest Louisiana, as the lands to the west of the Calcasieu River were alternately claimed by Spain and Mexico. The city and adjacent lake (which is actually a basin in the Calcasieu River) were named for early settler Charles Sallier, who arrived in the 1780s. The town began as a stop on the Old Spanish Trail and grew as a schooner port with access to the Gulf of Mexico, 34 miles to the south. At the end of the War Between the States, Lake Charles had only 400 residents. With the arrival of the Southern Pacific Railway and deepening of Calcasieu Pass (the main Gulf outlet for the Port of Lake Charles), the population grew to 3,000 by 1890. Like in most of Cajun Country, lumbering was the main industry at the turn of the century, but it was replaced by oil and petrochemicals in the 1930s. Unlike other cities, however, Lake Charles held closer ties with its western neighbors than with Cajun Country and most goods were shipped to Galveston.

Lake Charles spent more than a decade recovering from the collapse of oil prices in the eighties. The oil debacle virtually closed the downtown commercial district and brought double-digit unemployment. Riverboat gambling was introduced in the midnineties but not too many gamblers are getting rich. The business district near the boat terminal remains quiet.

Southwest Louisiana Visitors Center 1211 N. Lakeshore Dr.

In Lake Charles, the interstate is an elevated highway, so it is hard to decide where to jump off to look around. Some of the exits are staggered so the exit numbers are different eastbound and westbound. If you need orienting beyond the suggestions here, the Visitors Center has a helpful staff, parish and city maps, and a ton of brochures. Among the more interesting maps is one locating and listing the hundreds of chemical plants that adorn the banks of the Calcasieu River. I recommend that you pick up brochures to the Historic Charpentier District and the Creole Nature Trail (a must see!). The center is open Monday through Friday from 8 to 5 and Saturday and Sunday from 10:30 to 3:30. From I-10, exit at Lakeshore Drive (the last exit on the east side of the Calcasieu River Bridge). Lakeshore Drive will curve beneath the interstate. The Visitors Center is on the south side of I-10. (318) 436-9588 or 1-800-456-SWLA.

ATTRACTIONS

Casino Gambling in Lake Charles

There are two riverboat-casino terminals on Lake Prien: the Players Casino on Lakeshore Drive downtown and the Isle of Capri Casino across the bridge in Westlake. These casinos came up with a legal way around Louisiana's law requiring gambling boats to sail. Instead of the common practice of simply claiming the weather was too windy or rainy or foggy (or whatever!), they got another boat and then alternate the boats on 1½-hour cruises. There is always a boat at each dock. If you are a nongambler looking to enjoy a free cruise, these boats are especially nice at night when the city lights and chemical plants brighten the sky. Otherwise I have not found a significant difference among casino-gambling establishments. They all have a multitude of ways to lose your money. Most serve decent food at a reasonable price but nothing to go out of your way for. Call the casinos and Southwest Louisiana Visitors Center to check on hotel/gambling/dining packages as low as $50 per person a night.

Players Island Riverboat Casinos I-10 at Lakefront.

Players has an adjacent hotel. It is open seven days a week with no admission charge. There is valet parking and free, secure satellite parking (open air). The Players terminal is at 507 N. Lakeshore Dr., close by downtown Lake Charles. From the west, take I-10 exit #29. From the east take exit #30 A. For information call 1-800-977-7529, group information 1-800-625-2628, or hotel information 1-800-871-7666.

Isle of Capri Riverboat Casinos I-10 at Westlake (exit #27).

Isle of Capri is now marketing itself as the closest casino to Texas (never mind that it is only about ½ mile closer than the others). The Isle has a huge parking garage as well as valet parking. There is no hotel at the complex but plenty of lodging nearby. 1-800-843-4753.

Charpentier District Walking/Driving Tour

Much of the downtown area in Lake Charles burned in the great fire of 1910, so homes and businesses vary from Victorian to modern. The Charpentier (carpenter) District is a roughly six square block area just south of the interstate where one can view dozens of homes constructed between 1885 and 1920 (a tour map and brochure is available from the Visitors Center). At the time when most of these houses were built, there was no architect living in Lake Charles. Thus they bear unique touches scribed by the carpenters who created them. Spires, galleries, and oddly ballustraded porches abound. The area is bounded by Hodges Street on the west, Kirby on the south, Louisiana Avenue on the east, and Beldon on the north. From I-10 westbound, exit at Enterprise Boulevard. Travel south about eight blocks and turn right onto First Street. This will intersect Louisiana Avenue at the southeast edge of the district.

Fire and Water Driving Tour Industrial loop.

For a startling look at the churning and burning petrochemical plants that glower across the lake at Lake Charles, cross Prien Lake on the swooping Interstate 210 bridge and descend into the chemical corridor of Westlake industries. Upon intersecting I-10 on the west side, you may return to Lake Charles via the I-10 bridge over the Calcasieu River. I recommend that you take this drive at night, when the natural-gas flares, thousands of plant lights, and smoking stacks set the Calcasieu aglow like the river Styx. Hold your nose.

Lakeshore Drive

The five-mile course of Lakeshore Drive, along the edge of Lake Charles and Lake Prien to the south, offers a view of some of the grandest homes in the city and a broad vista of the smoking stacks of Westlake industries. Catch Lakeshore Drive at the Visitors Center

North Beach, Lake Charles. (Courtesy of Louisiana Office of Tourism)

beside the Calcasieu Bridge. Just south of the North Beach recreation area and casino terminal the road passes the Lake Charles Civic Center. The rest of the drive is mainly past lakefront residences.

Imperial Calcasieu Museum 204 W. Sallier.

The Imperial Calcasieu Museum houses an extensive collection of books, documents, and artifacts relating to the history of the parish and Lake Charles. There is a library and reading room packed with documents and texts, a pharmacy exhibit, Victorian bedroom suite, and art gallery. Most interesting is the collection of materials on the War Between the States. I lost myself for an hour, reading letters and firsthand accounts sent home from the front by local soldiers. The museum is located on property that belonged to the early settler Charles Sallier. Behind the building stands the 300-year-old Sallier Oak. From I-10, exit on Enterprise Boulevard south to 12th Street. The museum is located 12 blocks west, at the corner of Ethel Street. Hours are Tuesday through Friday from 10 to 5 and Saturday and Sunday from 1. Admission is $1. (318) 439-3797.

Children's Museum 809 Kirby St.

The Children's Museum of Lake Charles is a place where kids can learn from participatory exhibits. There is an airplane simulation, mock dentist's office, and several other vocational exploration booths. From I-10, go south on Enterprise Boulevard to Kirby Street. Turn right onto Kirby and look for the Children's Museum a few blocks down on the right. The museum is open Tuesday through Sunday from 2 to 5 and Saturday from 10 to 4. It is closed on major holidays, the last week of August, and first two weeks of September. Admission is $1. (318) 433-9420 or 433-9421.

McNeese State University Ryan Street and McNeese Street.

McNeese was founded as a two-year junior college in 1939. In 1940 it was named for John McNeese, who became the first state superintendent of schools in 1888. In 1950 it became a four-year state college. The nickname of the school's athletic teams is the Cowboys. McNeese hosts annual rodeo competitions.

Elderhostel Program at McNeese State University

Elderhostel is a program operating at universities throughout the world offering senior citizens an opportunity to expand their horizons through intellectual, recreational, and social activity as well as travel. The program, which was initiated in 1975, offers a week of activities, classes, room and board, and local transportation for the incredible price of around $350. The program at McNeese is usually held the last week in September and the first week of October. It includes courses in Louisiana's political heritage, Cajun cuisine, and Cajun culture (attendance is required at one of the three courses). Housing is provided in a campus dormitory. Hostelers must be 60 years or older (but may bring a companion 50 or over). For more information on the Elderhostel Program, contact the national office at ELDERHOSTEL, P.O. Box 1959, Dept. TN, Wakefield, MA 01880-5959.

Louisiana Peace Memorial North Lakeshore Drive.

The 120-foot-tall structure on the lakefront in downtown Lake Charles is a birdhouse (said to be the largest in the world), constructed as a memorial to veterans who served in Vietnam.

Mass Grave for Hurricane Victims 2700 E. Opelousas St.

Hurricane Audrey, which slammed the Gulf coast of Louisiana due south of Lake Charles on June 28, 1957, was the kind of event that people who experienced it tend to measure all others by. A 10-foot storm surge ripped across the coastal *cheniers* and wiped out homes and livestock 20 miles inland. There were estimated to be over 500 fatalities. Two hundred of these victims are buried in a mass grave at Combre Memorial Park Cemetery in Lake Charles (where relief efforts were based). From I-10, go one block south on Rte. 14 and take a left onto Opelousas Street. The cemetery is on the left. (318) 436-3341.

RECREATION

★Sam Houston State Park, Campground, & Cabins

Sam Houston Park is named for the Texas folk hero of the Alamo, who traveled extensively in Southwest Louisiana. The 1,068-acre park

Mass grave of Hurricane Audrey victims. (Photo by Julie Posner)

is situated on the west fork of the Calcasieu River, a wooded area north of Lake Charles. Sam Houston offers the loveliest camping in the Lake Charles area and some great day-use facilities. There are two nature trails (about three-quarters of a mile long), which wind through the woods at the river's edge, and boat rentals ($8 for jonboat, paddles, and life jackets). Many visitors come for the day to picnic along the water and fish from the bank. The day-use area is equipped with a bathhouse, barbecue pits, and picnic tables.

The park offers 12 vacation cabins (sleep six) at $60 a night. They have screened porches overlooking the river and are completely furnished except for kitchen and bath towels. They have central air conditioning and heat. There are also 73 camp sites ($12 a night) with water and electrical hookups. Many have views of the water. The park is eight miles north of Lake Charles. From I-10 take Rte. 171 north and turn left on Rte. 378. Go three miles and turn right at the park sign. From there it is a little over a mile to the park and the route is well marked. (318) 855-2665.

★Creole Nature Trail/Hug the Coast Highway

The marshland south of Lake Charles offers wetlands vistas, fishing, and the best birdwatching on the Gulf coast. This area is the primary tourist attraction in Western Cajun Country and is covered at the end of this chapter in the section Scenic Wetlands.

SPECIAL EVENTS

★Boozoo's Dog Hill Day Zydeco Festival Labor Day. 115 Petah St.

Boozoo Chavis hosts this Zydeco blowout in a large pavilion beside his house in suburban Lake Charles. It attracts a big crowd of locals and plenty of people who come over after attending the Zydeco Festival in Plaisance (Saturday). Admission is $10 and you can park in the field next to his house. There are barbecue, red beans, sweet-dough pies, and beer for sale. The party starts at 10 A.M. and big-name Zydeco artists perform in the afternoon. Boozoo closes the show with a performance that ends at 10. Take I-210 and get off on Ryan Street south. Go 1.5 miles and turn left on McNeese, then make a right at Common Street. (From here you should be able to follow the signs.) Go one mile south on Common and turn right on Legur Street; one-half mile farther make a right on Petah Street. (318) 478-5855.

Contraband Days First two weeks in May.

This festival celebrates Lake Charles' pirate legacy with outdoor concerts, food booths, and a carnival. The celebration begins with an enactment of buccaneers storming the lakefront area near the Civic

Center and throwing city officials into the lake. There are plenty of other cities that would like to try this with their own politicians. (318) 436-5508.

FOOD

Lake Charles has the full range of fast-food restaurants but very few really great regional eateries. The best food around town is the seafood, barbecue, and boudin.

Alladin Mediterranean Restaurant Local Fave, $-$$. 2009 Enterprise Blvd.

It is a sign of the times in Lake Charles that not only is the city's ethnic base expanding but so is its tastes. Even if it were not a very popular local eatery, this new arrival on the restaurant scene would rate a mention as one of the only places in the city to get something light. (318) 494-0062.

Cajun Cafe Down Home, $. 1317 Broad St.

The Cajun Cafe is one of the best lunch spots in Lake Charles. Octogenarian owner and cook "Ms. Lilly" has been serving plate lunches since the seventies. If you follow police, hard hats, or blue collars in your search for good food, you are likely to end up here! Pick from a half-dozen stewed or baked meats and twice as many veggies. The jambalaya and beef stew are first rate. You get homemade yeast rolls and cornbread sticks flavored with bits of ham to mop up the plate. Order the bread pudding, which has a light caramel flavor. Get here early. Towards closing time things seem a bit overcooked. You have to dodge some pond-size puddles in the parking lot to get into this cinder-block restaurant, but everything is bright, clean, and bustling in the small dining room. From I-10 take exit #33 (Rte. 14) south and turn right on Broad. Lunch costs under $5. Hours are 10:30 A.M. to 2 P.M. weekdays. (318) 439-3722.

★Crab Palace Boiled Seafood, $-$$. 2218 Enterprise Blvd.

The Crab Palace serves gumbos, stews, and fried seafood, but the minimalist decor, plastic tablecloths, and line out the door mark it as a classic boiling point. Their boiled crabs are the best west of New Iberia. Fried hard-shell crabs are also popular. The hard crab is actually battered and dropped into boiling grease. Barbecued hard-shells are the same as the fried ones, only drenched in barbecue sauce. These are superbly messy. The Palace is open Tuesday through Saturday from 10:30 A.M. to 9 P.M. (318) 433-4660.

Geyen's Barbecue Local Fave, $. Broad Street at Third Avenue.

Geyen has moved his soul-food and rib shack a couple of times since the seventies, but this has remained one of the most unusual and fun places to eat. His new location looks more than a little down at the heels, but it is a friendly place with all the soul in the world. Play some Zydeco on the jukebox, split a slab of ribs and rice dressing with a pal, and you will each walk away having spent under $8. Or try one of the other specialties like tamales ($6 a dozen), cracklins, or huge fried pork chops. On Fridays you will find fried seafood and stews on the menu. Orders are taken at the counter and dinner delivered to one of the three or four booths that line the walls. Geyen's is open Monday through Saturday from 9 A.M. to 11 P.M. (318) 433-1741.

★Granger's Seafood, $-$$. Old Town Road (Rte. 3059 E.).

Granger's is my favorite restaurant in Lake Charles. It is a wild joint serving the best boiled crawfish around, fresh-ground hamburgers, fried seafood, and plate lunches in a tavernlike atmosphere. One room houses a bar while another has a pool table and jukebox. Naturally there is quite a hubbub in the dining area between these two rooms! Granger's also has a drive-through lane where folks can get hot crawfish and cold beer without leaving their car. I eat here whenever I am in Lake Charles, but the best time to visit is during crawfish season. When mudbugs are plentiful, Granger's often runs $2-a-pound specials. Eat them at the bar to get into the spirit of the place. Granger's is two miles north of I-10. Take exit #33 north (Rte. 14/171) to the traffic light at Rte. 3059 (Old Town Road). It is a half-mile east on the left-hand side. (318) 433-9130.

★Hackett's Cajun Kitchen Down Home Lunch/Boudin, $. 5614 Rte. 14.

Charles Hackett grew up making boudin at his daddy's grocery down in Sweetlake. He now offers the traditional family recipe, along with four flavors of his own creation. Try the smoked, shrimp, or catfish varieties. All have a spiciness that comes on slow but has a powerful afterburn. You can also purchase tasso crusted in red pepper, and chewy strands of beef jerky (popular among hunters). Plate lunches are dished up on Monday through Friday and may be eaten in a small dining area. A plate of pork chops, rice with gravy, corn, and fried okra costs $4.50. Fried catfish is usually served on Monday and shrimp Creole on Friday. Lunch is served Monday through Saturday from 10 to 2. The market is open until 6 weekdays and 3 P.M. weekends. (318) 474-3731.

★Miller's Cafe Local Fave/Down Home, $. 138 Louisiana Ave.

Miller's Cafe has been serving Lake Charles mountainous plates of soul food and homemade sweet-dough pies since the fifties. It is located in a decaying, predominantly black neighborhood one block north of I-10. Folks from all over cut a path to this venerable old cafe

Miller's. (Photo by Julie Posner)

for the best lunches and dinners in town. Their business card boasts, "Everything good to eat," and it is a promise fulfilled. I go for the smothered chicken and chops, and steaming crawfish stew. These are heaped beside rice and a choice of two vegetables (three without the rice) for under $5. The vegetables are mostly fixed from scratch and include okra, mustard greens, yams, and highly seasoned black-eyed peas. You can dine at the counter or one of a dozen wooden tables or get a plate to go. In cool weather, I usually snag a go-plate and eat by the lakefront on Lakeshore Drive. From I-10 take the Enterprise Boulevard exit north and turn left on Louisiana. Hours are Monday through Friday from 7 A.M. to 8 P.M. and Saturday until 7. (318) 433-9184.

Mr. D's on the Bayou Seafood, $$. 3205 Common St.

Mr. D's serves all manner of seafood preparations, but they really excel with fried food. One out of every three plates is piled high with crisp catfish filets, crusted in a thin cornmeal batter. Seafood dinners range from $9 to $12 and come with baked potato, cole slaw, and cornbread. I recommend substituting a small order of greens for the cole slaw. If you just want fish, Mr. D's accommodates with a one-pound pile of catfish filets for $9. Mr. D's is situated in a building that was formerly a fried-fish franchise, but don't be put off by the decor. From the ice tea to the greens and fried shrimp, everything is freshly prepared.

Owner John Madison roams the floor, where he greets and is greeted by virtually every patron. Hours are Monday through Saturday from 10 to 10. (318) 433-9652.

Smokey Joe's Bar-B-Que 406 W. McNeese St. Local fave, $.

Smokey Joe's won readers' choice honors in *Louisiana Life* magazine for "best barbeque in south Louisiana." Joe explains, "I just fix barbecue the way I like to eat it." He does all the work himself, cutting the meat into strips and marinating it overnight. The ribs and chopped-beef sandwiches here are served in a red sauce. It gets my vote for best in Lake Charles. A lot of people go for the cardboard boxes of fried catfish, while kids will enjoy the sno-balls. Smokey Joe's is housed in an old hamburger stand, and the smokehouse out back is almost as big as the kitchen. Dining is on outdoor picnic tables. Hours are daily from 10 to 8. (318) 478-3352.

MUSIC

Boozoo's Dog Hill Day Zydeco Festival Labor Day.

See Special Events section.

★Goldband Records 313 Church St.

Goldband Record Store and Recording Studio shares space with Quick Service TV Repair in an old wood-frame house on the run-down north side of I-10. The Goldband shop looks much the same as it did when record-producer Eddie Shuler opened it in the early fifties. At that time he was recording such well-known artists as Iry Lejeune, Boozoo Chavis, "Little" Dolly Parton, and Jimmy C. Newman. Shuler released the first Zydeco record with "Paper in My Shoe" by Boozoo Chavis and cracked the national Hot 100 charts with the pounding "Sugar Bee" by Cleveland Crochet in 1961.

Shuler has had triple-bypass heart surgery and no longer answers the phone with a disturbing "Hello, quick!" However, his energy is boundless and, against all odds, he always has a new recording to play that "is my next hit!" Shuler has kept hundreds of his old recordings in print, including 45s and albums, which he sells briskly to overseas collectors. There is no telling what you might uncover in the dusty racks of records in his shop, which are remnants from his decades in business. From I-10 take Ryan Street north and make a right on Church Street. (318) 439-8839 or 439-4295.

★The Triangle Club Swamp Pop dance hall. Rte. 171 N. (exits #32 or #33).

I had no idea the Triangle Club existed until one night in '96 when I drove by on my way to Sam Houston State Park and heard the strains

Record man Eddie Shuler. (Photo by Julie Posner)

of Warren Storm's Swamp Pop combo. How could I have missed it before? The Triangle is a classic wood-frame, low-ceilinged honky-tonk with a big dance floor. Owner and Swamp Pop fanatic Roscoe Broussard keeps the jukebox jammed with South Louisiana favorites. On Wednesdays and Fridays Broussard often caters to a younger crowd with rock and roll bands, but call ahead and see if he is reserving Saturday night for Mel ("Love Bug") Pellerin, Warren Storm, or Johnny Allan. On those nights the dance floor gets so thick, as Broussard would put it, "those folks look like skeeters on a pond." The club is about a mile north of I-10 on Rte. 171. It sits about 30 yards off Rte. 171 on the west side. (318) 439-8068.

★Gee Gee's Club 2730 Broad St. (exits #32 or #33).

Gee Gee Shinn is Lake Charles' most popular lounge performer (now that Charles Mann has faded from the scene). He is a local hero of sorts, having played a lengthy tour of duty with the original Boogie Kings and done a long solo stint in Vegas. He now runs this nightclub at the Belmont Motel and performs a show of Vegas-style Swamp Pop and lounge music every Friday and Saturday. Best of all he brings in big-name artists like Johnny Allan during the week. The club is a couple blocks east of Rte. 14 on Broad. Music starts about 9:30. Admission is usually $5 on weekends and $3 during the week. (318) 491-9944.

★VFW Post Cajun dance hall. 2130 Country Club Rd.

This VFW in southern Lake Charles claims to have the longest continually running Cajun dance in Southwest Louisiana, held each Saturday night since the sixties. The hall featured legendary accordionist Joe Bonsal as a regular for years. Jesse Leger's is now the house band. The hall has a huge dance floor and its walls are festooned with photos of the Cajun Music Hall of Fame musicians. Cajun bands play from 8 P.M. to midnight every Saturday. The VFW has a list of rules to keep the peace: "no shorts (men or women), no halters or tank tops or mini skirts (shorter than 3" above the knee), no dancing without shoes or with lit cigarettes or drinks in hand, Western attire permissible (but must be clean), and no rubber boots or shower thongs." Take Ryan Street south from I-210. Ryan becomes University Drive before bending and becoming Country Club Road. (318) 477-9176.

★Thibodeaux's Hall 626 Enterprise Blvd.

For 25 years Thibodeaux's was known as Walker's Hall. The odd two-story dance hall still features the best in Zydeco entertainment a couple of weekends each month. The old hall has an Enterprise Boulevard address but is actually located a block east of the boulevard in the shadow of I-10. Exit I-10 at Enterprise Boulevard south. Turn left on the south side of I-10 and the hall will be one block down, at the corner of Franklin Street. (318) 439-4255.

LODGING

Hotels and Motels:

Best Western Richmond Suites Hotel 2600 Moeling (exit #32), I-10 and Rte. 171, three miles from downtown. $95 to $115 double. (318) 433-5213, (800) 643-2582.

Chateau Charles Hotel & Suites 2900 U.S. 90, Westlake (exit #26), 10 minutes west near Isle of Capri Casino. $80 to $90 double. (318) 882-6130, (800) 324-7647.

Days Inn 1010 N. Martin Luther King (exit #32), at I-10 and Rte. 171, three miles from downtown. $55 to $65 double. (318) 433-1711.

Holiday Inn 505 N. Lakeshore Dr. (exit #30 A), lakefront downtown, near casino. $90 to $130 double. (318) 433-7121, (800) 433-8809, (800) 367-1814.

Imperial Inn 825 Broad St. (Enterprise Boulevard exit), eight blocks west of downtown. $50 double. (318) 436-4311.

Inn on the Bayou 1101 W. Prien Lake Rd. (I-210), at Prien Lake exit. $75 double. (318) 474-5151, (800) 642-2968.

Motel 6 335 Rte. 171 (exit #32), north of I-10, three miles from downtown. $45 to $50 double. (318) 527-8303, (800) 440-6000.

Players Island Hotel 507 N. Lakeshore Dr. (exit #30 A), casino complex, downtown lakefront. $70 to $80 double. (318) 433-0541, (800) 871-7666.

Travel Inn 1212 N. Lakeshore Dr. (exits #29 or #30 A), lakefront, across I-10 from Players Casino. $65 double. (318) 433-9461.

Bed and Breakfasts:

★**Ramsay Curtis Mansion** 626 Broad St., Downtown.

This is the grandest and most comfortable of Lake Charles' several B&Bs. The mansion was built in the 1880s by lumber baron William E. Ramsay. As you might expect in the home of a lumber magnate, the place has lavish hardwood and cypress detailing. There is a shaded veranda and formal dining room for guest use. The second floor houses two guest suites and two conventional rooms, all with private baths, direct-dial phones (with data ports), and color televisions. The Master Suite is suitable for a luxury (expensive) romantic getaway. It has a king bed and sole access to the second-floor balcony, which overlooks Broad Street. Owners Michael and Judy Curtis live on the third floor and are relatively invisible. An expanded continental breakfast is served downstairs with an emphasis on healthy foods. The mansion is walking distance from the lakefront, convention center, and casinos. Double occupancy is $90 to $165 (for the Master Suite). Major credit cards are accepted. (318) 439-3859 or 1-800-52-CHARM.

Walter's Attic 618 Ford St., Downtown.

The guest room is located on the second floor of this turn-of-the-century home. It has a private side entrance with access to an outdoor hot tub and bicycles. The bikes are especially nice for sight-seeing homes in the Charpentier District (see listing above) or cruising the lakefront in the evening. The room has a private bath, telephone, cable television, microwave, refrigerator, and coffee fixin's. Double rates are $75 to $100. American Express, Mastercard, and Visa are accepted. (318) 439-3210.

Aunt Ruby's Bed and Breakfast 504 Pujo St., Downtown.

Aunt Ruby's is great for folks who do not like to feel as though they are in someone else's home. It was originally constructed and functioned as a guesthouse for 40 years. It is freshly renovated and simple in its decoration. Constructed in 1911, the house has six guest rooms with private baths and period furnishings. A gourmet breakfast is placed in the sitting room downstairs and may be enjoyed on the veranda or in your room. Doubles are $85-$100. American Express, Mastercard, Visa, and Discover are accepted. (318) 430-0603.

Camping:

Duplantis Campground U.S. 171 and Phil Lane (10 miles north of Lake Charles). Full hookups and showers. 170 spaces, pull-throughs, pavilion, and store. (318) 885-3985.

★Sam Houston State Park Cabins and camping. Eight miles north. See the Recreation section.

VFW R.V. Park 1900 Country Club Rd. (I-210 exits #3 or #4).

Full hookup RV park with laundry, propane, and supplies on the grounds of VFW Post 2130. From the east take I-210 exit #4 (Lake Street) south to Country Club Road. From the west take exit #3 (Ihles Road) south. Every Saturday evening the VFW hosts the longest-running Cajun dance in the whole region. Pads are gravel with little shade. Full hookup camping costs $15 a night. (318) 477-9176.

WEST FROM LAKE CHARLES: THE RIO HONDO TERRITORY

During most of the first 50 years of settlement in the Lake Charles area, the territory between the Calcasieu and Sabine rivers was the province of pirates, outlaws, and quarreling squatters. This area came to be known as the Rio Hondo, after the Sabine River, which was called *Arroyo Hondo*. Much of the lawlessness in the region owed to a border dispute that put sovereignty over the land in question. It was alternately claimed by the Spanish, French, Americans, and Mexicans. In 1821, the Sabine River was made the western boundary of Louisiana and the United States. Brazen lawlessness subsided, but the threat of conflict remained throughout the War Between the States, when the Sabine was traveled by blockade runners.

Pistols on the Calcasieu River Bridge. (Photo by Julie Posner)

Today the Calcasieu River Bridge on I-10 (built in 1952) bears a striking symbol of the conflict that characterized the region; 10,000 cast-iron buccaneer pistols adorn its guard rails in a criss-cross pattern. An air of the Wild West pervades the roughly 30-mile-wide strip of Louisiana between Lake Charles and the Texas border. There are rough-and-tumble Country music bars along U.S. 90, a horsetrack, and a huge cockpit attracting characters from both sides of the Texas-Louisiana border.

Sulphur

The city of Sulphur was laid out in 1878, shortly after the arrival of the Southern Pacific Railroad. It was named Sulphur City for the huge mineral deposits discovered in a salt dome on the west end of town. After scientist Hermann Frasch pioneered a new technique for mining sulphur, the dome became the most productive sulphur mine in the United States. It closed in the 1920s and is now used as a storage facility by the National Petroleum Reserve. The big employers in the area are oil and petrochemical companies. Visitors to Sulphur, which lies just north of I-10, seven miles west of Lake Charles, can view artifacts of the mining days at the Brimstone Museum. Sulphur is at the western end of the Creole Nature Trail (Rte. 27), which wends through the marshes and prime bird-watching areas to the south (*see* section on tour of scenic wetlands below).

Visitors Center and Brimstone Museum 800 Picard Rd.

The Brimstone Museum and Sulphur Visitors Center are housed in the Sulphur depot of the Southern Pacific Railroad, which was moved to Frasch Park in 1976. A one-ton obelisk of sulphur marks the museum entrance. The museum commemorates the development of the Frasch process of mining sulphur. This process involved pumping superheated water into a well, then pumping liquified sulphur to the surface. There is a display detailing the process and a number of photographs of the mining operations. Employing the Frasch Process, the Union Sulphur Company began operations here in 1905. The mine produced over 10 million tons of sulphur before it was closed in 1926. Most of the artifacts in the museum are either directly related to the industry or are representative of life in Sulphur during the heyday of the mining. From I-10 (exit #20) take Rte. 27 north a quarter of a mile and turn left on Parish Road. Travel a quarter of a mile and take a right onto Picard Road. The museum is a half-mile down on the left. Hours are Monday through Friday from 9:30 to 5. (318) 527-7142.

FOOD

Richard's Cajun Restaurant Local Fave, $. 2250 E. Napoleon (U.S. 90).

Richard's is the best place to eat west of Lake Charles. They have a seafood market and meat counter in the front of the restaurant, so you can be sure everything is fresh. The seafood and plate-lunch specials are tasty. Thursday is barbecue day. For $5 you get potato salad, baked beans, rice dressing, sausage, a quarter-chicken, and two ribs. Fried-seafood dinners are under $10. Hours are Monday through Wednesday from 8 A.M. to 8:30 P.M. and Thursday through Saturday until 9 P.M. (318) 625-8474.

LODGING

Motels:

Holiday Inn 2033 Ruth St. (I-10 exit #20), $70 to $80 double. (318) 528-2061, (800) 645-2425.

La Quinta 2600 S. Ruth St. (I-10 exit #20), $75 to $85 double. (318) 527-8303, (800) 531-5900.

Camping:

Hidden Ponds R.V. Park I-10 exit #21 south.

Level concrete pads, full hookups, pavilion, washateria, showers, rest rooms, lovely setting. Convenient to Creole Nature Trail. $17 a night. (318) 583-4709 or 1-800-440-4709.

WEST OF SULPHUR

Oak Archway on Old Spanish Trail U.S. 90 between Vinton and Sulphur.

The 14 miles between Sulphur and Vinton may be the single most beautiful stretch of the Old Spanish Trail (U.S. 90). In the 1930s, the WPA planted uniform rows of live oaks on either side of the road. Today these trees have grown to form a long, cool, green tunnel.

Delta Downs Racetrack Rte. 3060, Vinton (I-10 exit #4).

Delta Downs is a small racetrack with all the good-time atmosphere of a country "bush track." There is ample seating in the air-conditioned clubhouse ($2.50), but many folks bring lawn chairs to set up by the track. Quarterhorse races are held April through August, and Thoroughbreds are run September through March.

The track entered the annals of horse-racing infamy on January 11, 1990. In the great "Race in the Fog," also known as the "Disappearing Horse Race," jockey Sylvester Carmouche and his mount disappeared after falling badly behind on a fog-shrouded track. As the two-lap race came to a close, Carmouche emerged from the fog and crossed the wire with a 24-length lead! The fog was so thick that even after cameras were consulted, it was unclear whether he had ever completed the first lap! Carmouche was suspended, but there are still some wonderfully foggy races here, and there is no telling what you might (or might not) see. General admission is $1.25 (minimum age 18). Thursday through Saturday, races begin at 6:30 P.M. Sunday races start at 1 P.M.

From I-10, take exit #4 (Toomey/Starks). Go three miles north on Rte. 109 and take a right onto Rte. 3060. The racetrack is one mile down on the right. (318) 433-3206 or 1-800-589-7441.

★Niblett's Bluff Park Campground and Cabins Rte. 3063 (I-10 exit #4).

Niblett's Bluff is three miles north of I-10 on the bank of the Sabine River. Although they have been called "bluffs" for a century and a half, the shores of the Sabine actually rise only two to three feet above the water. Niblett's Bluff is free for day-use activities such as swimming, boating, fishing, and picnicking. For $21 one can rent a very simple air-conditioned one-room cabin. Cabins have a sink and barbecue pit on the porch but no kitchen. They are furnished with a double bed and bunk beds. Bathhouses are located nearby. The park is a good swimming hole and gets very crowded on weekends in the summer. Jet skis and air boats roar up and down the river.

During the week and in the cooler months, Niblett's Bluff is a fantastic day-use or overnight facility. You can walk the wooded grounds and see the breastworks of a fort constructed during the War Between the States, or take a dip in the quiet river. At night, make the short drive over to Delta Downs Racetrack. The park is open for free from 6 A.M. to 10 P.M. Camping with hookups is $10.50. Tent camping is $5.15. From I-10, take exit #4 and head north on Rte. 109 for 3 miles. Turn left on Rte. 3063 and Niblett's Bluff is 2.6 miles east. (318) 589-7117.

★Circle Club Cockpit Rte. 109 S. (I-10 exit #4).

The Circle Club is everything you would expect of a big border-town tavern, attracting a wagering and cockfighting crowd from East Texas and the wild Rio Hondo territory. Actually, folks come from around the South to the big derby weekends. You know this is cockfighting territory by the training grounds and 75 cock tepees in the yard between the club and the interstate. You enter through the bar, a big room where steaks and burgers are grilling and cock handlers and spectators are noisily sharing beers. In one corner, there is a spur concession where handlers can purchase sharpened gaffs to arm their fowl. There is a fee ranging from $8 to $15 to enter the pit area in back, which is a circular arena with tiered grandstand seating for several hundred. In the rear of the pit, there is an area called the "drags" where fights that are not quickly decided in the main arena may continue to a decision. During big tournaments, there are often two or

Circle Club Cockpit. (Photo by Julie Posner)

three fights occurring in the crude dirt-floor drags, while a new match is being consummated in the arena.

If you have never been to a cockfight, you should be warned that the spectacle of two animals engaged in sometimes mortal combat is not for everyone. However, owner Delane Navarre (president of the Louisiana Cockers Association) runs an orderly establishment. The Circle Club is open to anyone who pays the admission and refrains from troublemaking. No cameras are permitted. The cockfighting season runs from the second weekend in October to the first weekend in August. The big derbys can run for 12 hours. Navarre gets the outdoor barbecue pit (which is the size of your typical small-town water reservoir!) smoking and serves free barbecue and fried fish. Most Saturdays fights begin at noon. Friday fights begin at about 10 P.M. The Circle Club is located immediately south of I-10 on Rte. 109 (exit #4 at Toomey/Starks). (318) 589-2921.

Louisiana Welcome and Tourist Information Center I-10 Eastbound.

This center, located two miles from the state line, has the biggest collection of brochures and maps for South Louisiana attractions. In addition to maps of the parish and Lake Charles, I recommend picking up pamphlets for the Lake Charles Charpentier District and the Creole Nature Trail. The center is located on the edge of Lake Bienvenu, which is bordered by a beautiful cypress swamp. There are picnic tables and barbecue pits by the water and a short elevated walking path through the swamp.

LODGING

Best Western Delta Downs Motor Inn I-10 exit #4. $65 double. (318) 589-7492, (800) 282-8081.

KOA Vinton (Cabins) 1514 Azema St. (I-10 exit #8).

Typical KOA playground, pool, store, and laundry. An RV space is $21.50 for two people. Cabins are $27.50. The campground is right beside I-10. (318) 589-2300, (800) 562-1899.

Niblett's Bluff Campground I-10 exit #4.

Cabins, RV, and tent camping. See description above.

SCENIC WETLANDS

The coastal wetlands, Prairie marsh, and beaches of Cameron Parish are the primary attraction in Western Cajun Country, and one of the most remarkably wild areas in all of Louisiana. Until the 20th century, the area was virtually inaccessible except by boat. Now it is reached by the Creole Nature Trail, which forms a scenic 100-mile loop south of Lake Charles, and the Hug the Coast Highway (Rte. 82), which parallels the Gulf Coast for 135 miles from the Texas border to the Central Cajun Country village of Abbeville. The area is home to three national wildlife refuges, a coastal bird sanctuary, and miles of sandy Gulf coast beach. It is a prime area for bird and alligator watching, as well as fishing and hunting. Brochures to the area are available from the Lake Charles Tourist Center and the Louisiana Welcome Center.

Most of the scenic wetlands of Western Cajun Country lie within Cameron Parish. Cameron is Louisiana's largest and least densely populated parish. Its six residents per square mile is less than half the number of the next most densely populated area. Few places in Cameron are over two feet above sea level, with permanently flooded marsh the predominant feature. It was originally inhabited by Attakapas Indians, who named the Mermentau and Calcasieu rivers after tribal chieftains. The first white settlers, people of Scots-Irish descent, arrived in the mid-1800s and built homes on the coastal *cheniers*. These slightly elevated oak-covered ridges along the coast comprise the only significant high ground in Cameron and include the present ranching and trapping communities of Grand Chenier and Pecan Island.

Creole Nature Trail

The Creole Nature Trail (Rte. 27) plunges south from the city of Sulphur, about 10 miles west of Lake Charles. It may be traveled as a full loop (returning to I-10 east of Lake Charles) or as a means of reaching the Hug the Coast Highway between Holly Beach and Abbeville. The loop is a hundred miles, and with stops, the drive will occupy most of a day. The best accommodations are guesthouses in Cameron or Constance Beach. Stock up on sun screen and bug spray before leaving, and consider packing a picnic. There are several markets and a few cafes but no good eateries along the way.

Hackberry About 17 miles south of I-10.

The town of Hackberry claims to be the "Crab Capital of the South." This is the site of a large storage facility of the National Strategic Petroleum Reserve and home to a couple of popular "gun and rod" clubs. You will find bait and tackle shops here where you can get fishing or crabbing supplies and tips on where they are biting.

★Sabine Wildlife Refuge

The Sabine National Wildlife Refuge, established in 1937, contains

142,000 acres of salt- and freshwater marsh. There are over 150 miles of waterways in the refuge open to boat travel, but most visitors will spend time at the Sabine visitors interpretive center, hiking the elevated Sabine Nature Trail, or fishing and crabbing at roadside access points. The refuge was established with the primary goal of protecting the wetlands habitat of the millions of migratory waterfowl that visit the area as they traverse the Central and Mississippi flyways. Bird watchers toting binoculars flock to this area, but many eyes are also turned towards the alligators, nutria, and snakes that abound in its muddy sloughs.

Recreational fishing is permitted from the banks or by boat. Where the Creole Nature Trail cuts through the refuge, there are several small bridges and easements where you can throw a castnet for shrimp or crab, or cast for speckled trout and redfish. There is no camping allowed within the refuge, but sites are available to the north at the Intracoastal Waterway and to the south at Holly Beach.

★Sabine Visitors Center and Headquarters

The Sabine Visitors Center, 25 miles south of I-10 (at Sulphur), is home to one of the only two Cajun robots in the world! (See his female counterpart at the Cameron Wildlife Refuge on the eastern leg of the Creole Nature Trail.) Speaking in a thick Cajun dialect, this figure of an old fisherman tells about life in the marsh as his fishing pole jerks with a strike and an alligator snaps its jaws. Over 50,000 dollars were spent on this lifelike diorama.

The Visitors Center also has exhibits describing the flora and fauna of the region, what months are best for fishing and crabbing, which birds to look for, and where to watch for alligators nesting. There are also several brochures describing seasonal wildlife activity. There is staff on duty and public rest rooms. It is open year round, Monday through Friday from 7 to 4 and weekends from noon to 4. (318) 762-3816.

★Sabine Nature Trail Rte. 27, four miles south of refuge headquarters.

Whether you are looking for alligators, roseate spoonbills, or just a scenic walk in the salt air, the Sabine Nature Trail is a fascinating stop. The Nature Trail is a 1.5-mile-long boardwalk through the marsh, leading to a wooden observation tower. I have never seen as many alligators in such a small area as I did one hot August morning on the Nature Trail. A brochure is available at the rest station (public bathrooms) at the trail head. This pamphlet has numbers corresponding to different wetlands features along the trail. The trail begins at a parking area on Rte. 27, 4 miles south of the Refuge Visitors Center and Headquarters (about 6 miles north of Holly Beach).

Sabine Nature Trail. (Photo by Julie Posner)

Hug the Coast Highway

Thirty-six miles south of I-10 (at Sulphur), the Creole Nature Trail intersects the Hug the Coast Highway at the town of Holly Beach. At this point travelers may want to head west to Constance Beach (4 miles) or the Peveto Woods Bird Sanctuary (9.5 miles). To complete the Creole Nature Trail loop or travel the Hug the Coast Highway to Abbeville, turn east on Rte. 82. Until the construction of the Hug the Coast Highway in 1953, most of the Gulf settlements of Cameron and Vermilion Parish were accessible only by boat. Mail was delivered by water. Electrical and phone services were not established in most areas until around 1960. Along this route you will pass the coastal *chenier* communities with their gnarled oak trees, fields of unfenced cattle, and miles of open marsh.

Constance Beach

Constance Beach, just four miles west of Holly Beach, would not merit notice except for Mickey's Shell Art and several guesthouses. Not only is there no beach left here at high tide, but the Gulf has actually swallowed an entire street and three rows of camps. When the water is down, Constance Beach has the best shelling on the coast. Since most folks just make the eastern loop on Rte. 27 they never see this quiet community.

★**Mickey's Shell Art** Constance Beach (four miles west of Holly Beach).

Mickey Guilbeau has been practicing shell art since 1975 when she saw a friend's shell mirror and had to have one. Her best sellers are not such functional items but include the Cajun Couple (he fishing, she sweeping) and the Texas Armadillo, which reclines on its back apparently guzzling a can of Lone Star beer. These and many other scenes and figures are made from shells Mickey and her husband, Rodney, find on nearby beaches. She never paints the shells but relies on their natural color and texture to create her designs and figures. One year Rodney collected and sold 108 milk crates (1.5 tons) of whelk shells to a buyer in India (where they are used in religious rituals). My favorite item is the Hamburger Bean, which looks like a tiny petrified hamburger but is actually the seed of a Central American tree that washes up here.

Mickey's shop is the informal tourist-information office for the region and Rodney, who is on the Governor's Commission on Coastal Erosion, can provide insight into the land-loss debacle playing itself out here. You may recognize Rodney's voice if he slips into a Cajun accent; he is the humorist who did the voice of the Cajun robot at the Sabine Visitors Center! The shop is usually open daily from 8 until dark. (318) 569-2159.

Peveto Woods Bird Sanctuary Rte. 82 W.

Formerly known as Holleyman-Sheely, this bird sanctuary is located on a quiet, 12-acre *chenier,* just east of the community of Johnson's Bayou. During cool spring months, millions of birds drop into the canopy of oaks. On particularly cool days a phenomenon known as "fall-out" occurs, and the sanctuary is filled with the cries of exhausted migratory birds seeking refuge. Record bird sightings of several types have been registered here. Among the most commonly sought species are warblers, scarlet tanagers, orioles, and rose-breasted grosbeaks. There is plenty of other wildlife to look out for in the area (especially mosquitoes). The sanctuary is open daily, free of charge. Eight and a half miles west of Holly Beach (across from the Stingray Plant), turn left on Parish Road 528. Take the second street to the left (unpaved) and continue to the end. Bring boots and bug spray. There are no developed paths.

LODGING

Unlike the accommodations in Holly Beach, any of these can be recommended as clean, quiet, and fairly comfortable even if the beds are not brand new. They are not right on the water, but when you see the condition of the beach here you may feel safer a block back!

Allen Broussard Guesthouse 245 Kathy Dr., Constance Beach.

Several apartments with outside entrances, 20 feet from the shore. Most have two rooms with two queen beds and furnished kitchen. Bring sheets and towels. Mr. Broussard also rents a large house (sleeps 10) on the water. Apartments are $50 a night. Mr. Broussard speaks French. (318) 569-2375.

Judy Miller Guesthouse 317 Kathy Dr., Constance Beach.

This house one block off the beach sleeps four. Sheets, towels, pots, and pans are provided. Four people cost $50 a night. Ms. Miller speaks French. (318) 569-2498.

Nancy Prioux Guesthouse 321 Richard Ln., Constance Beach.

Ms. Prioux speaks French. (318) 569-2368.

Holly Beach

Holly Beach is known to denizens of South Louisiana by the hyperbolic nickname "the Cajun Riviera." Don't expect any glamorous resorts or a white-sand beach. It is actually nothing more than a collection of ramshackle camps, fishermen's motels, and a couple of shops tumbling into the warm waters of the Gulf of Mexico. The beach itself is broad and open to the public, but it is better known for its collection of flotsam tossed up by the Gulf than for its sand or water. It seems as though everyone who has frequented the area has a story

Holly Beach. (Photo by Julie Posner)

(probably untrue) about relaxing on the beach, sticking their hand into the sand, and finding a dead dog or wild pig! During the summer (the absolute worst time to visit this shadeless strand), the 525 campsites and dozens of rentals fill up with college students and Cajun families hell-bent on enjoying the only beach around. The popularity of the place as a summer destination was obvious from a sign we saw on a restaurant a hundred miles away in Kaplan, which read, "We are NOT going to Holly Beach for the 4th of July!" When the summer crowd departs, Holly Beach returns to its "permanent population level" of 150 residents. This is the best time to visit and roam over six miles of public beach, fish for reds and trout in the surf, and comb the shore for shells and waterborne debris.

LODGING

There are a hundred rooms or cabins for rent in Holly Beach and if you go during the week or off season you will find something. I visited dozens of places and could not find any that were not dingy. The campgrounds are just as bad. If you do not need hookups you can camp for free on the stretches of public beach to the west. Try the guesthouses at Constance Beach.

Gulfview Cabins On the beach, $45-$75. (318) 569-2385.

Sea Breeze Apartments On the beach, $45-$65. (318) 569-2385.

★**Cameron Bed and Breakfast Guesthouse** Off Rte. 82, Cameron. Best accommodations on the coast. See Cameron listings.

Cameron

Free Ferry across Calcasieu Ship Channel

A 50-car ferry across the Calcasieu Pass is the only link between the town of Cameron and the western reaches of Rte. 82 and the Creole Nature Trail. The ferry runs 24 hours, crossing approximately every 20 minutes.

A sign greets visitors to Cameron, proclaiming its attractions: "No pollution, no traffic light, no big-city life, no city police, no trains (just boats)." That is life as it should be in a city that was isolated to all but waterborne commerce until the 1950s. Cameron is the only deepwater port between the Mississippi and Galveston and is the seat of Cameron Parish government. Its 3,200 residents work mainly in the fishing and petroleum industries. The isolated existence of the coastal cities in Cameron Parish has made them veritable death chambers when tropical storms have directed themselves at the Gulf coast. Folks around Cameron quit taking chances with "riding out" storms when

Welcome to Cameron. (Photo by Julie Posner)

Hurricane Audrey rolled a tidal wave 13 feet up the courthouse wall on the morning of June 27, 1957. The storm scattered smashed houses through the marsh, left tangled debris around the tops of telephone poles, and destroyed homes 20 miles inland on the north side of the Intracoastal Waterway. Audrey left 525 dead in Cameron Parish, including 35 in one family, and left its imprint on the memories and lifestyles of those who survived.

Cameron Chamber of Commerce

Open Monday through Friday 8 to 4, closed noon to 1. (318) 775-5222.

★Louisiana Fur and Wildlife Festival Second weekend in January.

This has the distinction of being Louisiana's "coolest festival." Celebrants have a great time trying to keep warm and watching such events as the men's and women's nutria-skinning, trap-setting, and duck-calling contests. (318) 772-5222.

Hurricane Audrey Shrine and Monument Three miles east of Cameron.

Located in front of the Our Lady Star of the Sea Church is a shrine and monument dedicated to the 525 victims of Hurricane Audrey. The shrine was built in 1963 and stood alone on the marsh road until the church was built in 1971. The actual burial location of most of the victims is a mass grave at Lake Charles. The Hurricane Audrey Shrine is located three miles east of Cameron and four miles west of the Rte. 27 and Rte. 82 fork.

★Cameron Bed and Breakfast Guesthouse

This is the best place to stay on the Hug the Coast Highway, offering privacy, charm, and comfort. Host Marianna Tanner, who lives next door, is a member of the Gulf Coast Bird Club and active in the Louisiana Ornithological Society. She can direct people to prime birding sites all over the coast, including a few just minutes away. Plenty of birds can be seen from the rocking chairs on the back porch, which looks out over a hummingbird garden. The guesthouse, which sits on a quiet tree-lined street in downtown Cameron, was built after Hurricane Audrey hit in 1957. A 10-foot storm surge carried her mother's house several blocks from the site and deposited it behind the courthouse. Marianna's family has been in Cameron for generations so she can share a few hurricane stories. A bedroom with queen bed and connected bath rents for $65. A second bedroom with two twin beds and bath in the hall costs $55. Usually there is only one room rented. If the fold-out sofas are used and baths shared, the house can sleep a group of eight. (318) 775-5347.

TRAVEL TIP

From Cameron, Rte. 82 and Rte. 27 east run concurrently for seven miles and then split into a Y. Rte. 27 (the Creole Nature Trail) heads north through the city of Creole and Rte. 82 continues east through Oak Grove. Those interested in following the Hug the Coast Highway may want to skip the following section, detailing the eastern leg of the Creole Nature Trail loop to Lake Charles.

Creole Nature Trail (Rte. 27 N.)

At the town of Creole about 14 miles east of Cameron, Rte. 27 veers north for 40 miles to intersect I-10 in eastern Lake Charles. The highlight of this stretch is the Cameron Wildlife Refuge and Interpretive Center. Folks who want to stay overnight should consider the Lorraine Retreat. There is also food and dancing at Harris Seafood in nearby Hayes (see Lake Arthur to Hayes/Rte. 14 section).

★Cameron Prairie Wildlife Refuge Rte. 27 above Creole.

The Cameron National Wildlife Refuge (Gibbstown Unit) contains about 9,600 acres of freshwater marsh and prairie, stretching north from the Intracoastal Waterway. The refuge was first established under the North American Waterfowl Management Plan to protect wintering waterfowl and their habitat. It is one of the premier birdwatching spots along the Gulf coast. Most of the area is accessible only by boat, but the new Pintail Wildlife Drive and Interpretive Center are both recommended.

★Cameron Wildlife Refuge Interpretive Center Rte. 27.

The Cameron Refuge Interpretive Center is 15 miles north of Creole (22 miles south of I-10) on Rte. 27. The center is home to Tante Marie, one of two Cajun robots exhibited on the Creole Nature Trail (see the Sabine Visitors Center in this chapter for information on Marie's male counterpart). Tante Marie is an amazingly lifelike robotic rendering of an elderly Cajun woman who delivers a spiel on the changing prairie while fishing from a pirogue laden with blue crabs. There are several interesting displays on the prairie habitat. Behind the center a boardwalk and observation platform stretch into the marsh. A telescopic viewer is mounted at the end for bird or alligator watching. I got there late one day and jumped the railing to go around back to the viewing area. At least three alligators lunged into a pond nearby. I recommend staying on the walkways. There are brochures and bird lists available inside, as well as a helpful staff. Serious birders will want to head 2 miles south to walk or slowly cruise Pintail Drive. Inquire about two walking trails that are in the planning phase at the time of this writing. The Interpretive Center is open Monday through Friday from 8 to 4:30 and Saturday from 10 to 4. (318) 598-2216.

Pintail Wildlife Drive Two miles south of Interpretive Center.

Pintail Drive is a three-mile loop through the prairie on the east side of Rte. 27, two miles south of the Interpretive Center. There is no shade on this patch of prairie but if the weather is very cool or the sun is low, I recommend walking the loop. The grasses and shrubs here are spilling over with birds and other wildlife. I drove through at 10:30 one morning and the road was still dotted with snakes and turtles. If you must drive, go slowly. The drive is open Monday through Friday from 7 A.M. to 3 P.M. and Saturday from 10 A.M. to 4 P.M.

Rte. 82 East of Creole

Rutherford Beach

This beach is located immediately south of Oak Grove, the first community east of the Rte. 27 and Rte. 82 split. The swimming and beach at Rutherford are much the same as at Holly Beach to the west (debris-strewn sand and warm water), but it is undeveloped. You may drive onto the sand and camp on the beach for free.

Grand Chenier Rte. 82, nine miles east of Creole.

Grand Chenier is the most heavily populated "oak island" on

Louisiana's Gulf coast, with over 1,000 residents. One of two *cheniers* accessible by car, it stretches almost 15 miles from southeastern Cameron Parish into Vermilion Parish. The ridge is about 6 miles inland from the Gulf coast.

In the early 1800s, the isolated ridge of oaks was a refuge for outlaws. Legitimate settlement began with the arrival of homesteaders of Scots-Irish descent around 1850. These settlers lived in cane and palmetto shacks and raised citrus fruits and subsistence crops on the two-mile-wide swath of slightly arable ground. Hurricanes wiped out the citrus crop, and residents turned to trapping, hunting, and ranching. Since the *cheniers* were connected to the outside world by road in the early 1950s, some residents have found part-time work as hunting guides, or dressing wild game, but for the most part their daily pursuits have changed little in the last century. Cattle may still be seen grazing on unfenced patches of grass floating in a sea of marsh.

★**Rockefeller Wildlife Refuge** Rte. 82, Grand Chenier.

Rockefeller has the best land access of all Louisiana's coastal wildlife refuges. Visitors can enter the heart of the marsh by way of Price Lake Road to crab, fish, and scout for wildlife. The refuge sprawls along 26 miles of coastal marsh in Cameron and Vermilion parishes. Its 84,000 acres are sandwiched in the 4- to 6-mile-wide strip between Rte. 82 and the Gulf. The area was purchased by naturalist E. A. McIlhenny in 1912. McIlhenny sold the land to the Rockefeller Foundation and convinced the foundation to establish a wildlife sanctuary. Today, water-management and conservation projects are under way to protect the wetlands, which are a landing strip for millions of migratory birds each year. Over 400,000 ducks winter at the refuge, alongside a growing population of Canadian geese and a huge number of other temporary avi-residents. The best place to enjoy the refuge is at the Price Lake Road access point (see review below). (318) 538-2276.

Rockefeller Refuge Headquarters Rte. 82, 5.5 miles east of Grand Chenier.

The Rockefeller headquarters is mainly offices; however, they have several brochures and a friendly staff. There is an exhibit of artifacts from the Spanish merchant vessel *El Nuevo Constante*, which wrecked off the coast in 1766. The wreck was discovered when a Texas shrimper pulled in a net of copper ingots. Two boxes on the ship manifest were listed as containing "gift items and nick-nacks." Several of these ceramic items are displayed in a case with photographs of more valuable artifacts. The refuge headquarters has a public rest room. Hours are Monday through Friday 7 to 4. (318) 538-2276.

★Price Lake Road Rockefeller Refuge.

Price Lake Road (a half-mile west of refuge headquarters) is the primary public-access area and bird-watching site in the refuge. As you enter Price Lake Road a sign instructs recreational crabbers, "Limit 12 dozen crabs and 25 lbs. shrimp per day"! They are not kidding. A mile down, the shell road opens on either side to wide shallow lakes and continues another two miles before dead-ending in the marsh. Crabbers using nothing more than a dip net, rotten chicken necks, and weighted string may be seen filling 50-gallon garbage cans with crustaceans! Recreational fishermen share the harvest with waterbirds that wade among their lines, while alligators sun in the mud 10 feet away. From a three-story observation tower, bird watchers can see clear to the coastal fringe. The Price Lake Road area is closed between December 1 and March 1.

Pecan Island Rte. 82, 40 miles southwest of Abbeville.

Pecan Island is one of two (the other is Grand Chenier) populated *cheniers* accessible by car. It is a 16-mile-long and 2-mile-wide ridge (6 miles inland from the coast) discovered by Texas cattleman Jake Cole in the mid-1800s. Cole stumbled on the raised earth while looking for a place to graze his cattle. He reportedly found the island covered with bleached bones and Indian burial mounds 20 feet high. Many of the island's mounds were desecrated by treasure hunters (looking for pirate Jean Lafitte's loot) in the 1920s, but a few still remain within sight of the road. From Pecan Island, Rte. 82 turns north and crosses the Intracoastal Waterway. From this point travelers may head due north on Rte. 35 to Kaplan or wind northeast 21 miles to Abbeville.

TRAVEL TIP

Those interested in the eastern terminus of the Hug the Coast Highway should consult Gateway to Hug the Coast Highway under Abbeville (Central Cajun Country chapter).

Appendix A

SPECIAL EVENTS IN CAJUN COUNTRY

South Louisiana is the site of at least one festival every weekend of the year. The biggest event is Mardi Gras, which is described in detail following this list. Other events tend to be harvest celebrations, like the Yambilee Festival in Opelousas. Many have a religious component, such as the Shrimp Festival in Morgan City, during which a priest conducts a ceremonial "Blessing of the Fleet." More recently ethnic festivals have sprung up, celebrating Cajun or French culture. The biggest of these are the Festivals Acadiens and Festival International in Lafayette. Some ethnic festivals have a particular food item as their object, including the Cracklin' Festival in Port Barre and the Crawfish Festival in Breaux Bridge. Nearly all of the festivals feature live Cajun or Zydeco music and good regional eats. This is a list of the best festivals in Cajun Country, those worth planning a vacation around. Full-length reviews are provided in the text. For complete listings and information on festivals and events check out *Huli's Calendar of Festivals and Events,* available in bookstores throughout Louisiana or by mail (see appendix D).

Major Festivals

Louisiana Fur and Wildlife Festival, Cameron. 2nd weekend in January.

Mardi Gras (*see* Mardi Gras section following this list).

"Here's the Beef" Cook-Off, Opelousas. 3rd weekend in March.

World Championship Etouffée Cook-off, Eunice. Late March.

Festival International de la Louisiane, Lafayette. Late April.

Breaux Bridge Crawfish Festival, Breaux Bridge. 1st weekend in May.

Zydeco Festival, Plaisance. Saturday before Labor Day.

Boozoo's Dog Hill Day Zydeco Festival, Lake Charles. Labor Day.

Festivals Acadiens, Lafayette. 3rd week in September.

Roberts Cove Germanfest, Roberts Cove. 1st weekend in October.

French Food Festival, Larose. Last weekend in October.

Celebration of the Giant Omelette, Abbeville. 1st weekend in November.

Festival of the Bonfires, Reserve. Weekend before winter solstice.

Mardi Gras Riders in Mamou. (Courtesy of Louisiana Office of Tourism)

Mardi Gras

Mardi Gras, or "Fat Tuesday," is the day before Ash Wednesday. In this predominantly Catholic area, it is a time of determined abandon as many residents enjoy their last dances, last beers, and last cigarettes before Lenten fasting begins. This is a great time to visit Cajun Country. Crawfish are in season at local restaurants, and bars, dance halls, and nightclubs reverberate with Cajun and Zydeco music.

Many cities in South Louisiana have New Orleans-style Mardi Gras parades, with masked riders tossing trinkets from floats. The *Courir du Mardi Gras,* which takes place in perhaps a dozen communities in rural Cajun Country, is a very different type of celebration, with roots in ancient Roman and Medieval festivals. Masked riders gather on horseback on Mardi Gras morning. They usually meet in the town hall around 7, where the *capitaine* (who holds the office for life) reads the rules of the ride. Typically participants must be men at least 18 years old. For the youngsters, the ride acts as a rite of passage into manhood. The riders form a rowdy procession of horses, flatbed trucks, and beer and band wagons as they ride out of town.

Upon reaching the designated stops, the *capitaine* receives clearance from the homeowners before allowing his band to charge into the yard. There, the riders dismount to seek their booty, singing, dancing, and otherwise cutting up. Contributions range from rice and money to live chickens, which are thrown into the air and pursued with drunken abandon by the riders.

During the rides, communities (listed below) have daytime dances, food, and beer to entertain those waiting for the riders' return. Excitement builds as the time for the processional return nears (usually about 3). Crowds line the streets to watch the inebriated ensemble enter town, often riding backwards on, standing on top of, or falling off of their mounts! The accumulated booty is gathered and a gumbo is prepared for consumption at an evening dance (open to the public). Mamou was the first town to revive the century-old *Courir du Mardi Gras* tradition in the midfifties. It is now possible to travel between nearby towns and enjoy several different Mardi Gras celebrations. Those listed below are most recommended. Note that Church Point holds its *Courir du Mardi Gras* (highly recommended) on Sunday before Fat Tuesday.

Mardi Gras Dates:

1999—February 16	2004—February 24
2000—March 7	2005—February 8
2001—February 26	2006—February 28
2002—February 12	2007—February 20
2003—March 4	2008—February 5

Mardi Gras Mamou: Monday night there is a street party. Tuesday, *Courir du Mardi Gras* riders depart around 7 and return around 3.

Mardi Gras Church Point: Sunday, *Courir du Mardi Gras* riders depart around 7, returning around 3. A Cajun dance and gumbo take place during the day at the Saddle Tramp Club.

Mardi Gras Iota: Tuesday, *Courir du Mardi Gras* riders depart around 7, returning around 2. Food and craft booths and a Cajun/Zydeco bandstand operate throughout the day.

Mardi Gras Eunice: Monday, the Cajun Cultural Center and Liberty Theater host interpretive presentations and performances during the afternoon and evening. Tuesday, *Courir du Mardi Gras* riders depart around 8, returning around 3. Daytime activities include a children's parade, band performances, and plenty of good eating.

Appendix B

RECOMMENDED BOOKS

Cajun History and Culture

Ancelet, Barry Jean, Jay D. Edwards, and Glen Pitre. *Cajun Country*. Jackson, Miss.: University Press of Mississippi, 1991.

Conrad, Glenn R. *Cajuns*. Lafayette, La.: USL-Center for Louisiana Studies, 1978.

South Louisiana Music

Ancelet, Barry Jean. *The Makers of Cajun Music*. University of Texas, 1984.

Bernard, Shane K. *Swamp Pop: Cajun and Creole Rhythm and Blues*. Jackson, Miss.: University Press of Mississippi, 1996.

Broven, John. *South to Louisiana*. Gretna, La.: Pelican Publishing, 1983.

Savoy, Anne Allen. *Cajun Music: A Reflection of a People*. Eunice, La.: Bluebird, 1984.

Cajun Food

Prudhomme, Paul. *The Prudhomme Family Cookbook*. New York: William Morrow, 1987.

Louisiana Travel

Hansen, Harry, ed. *Louisiana: A Guide to the State*. New York: Hastings House, 1971.

Posner, Julie. *Huli's Calendar of Festivals and Events*. Metairie, La.: Huli Publishing, annual.

Bayou Country and Teche Country

Caffery, Debbie Fleming. *Carry Me Home*. Washington, D.C.: Smithsonian, 1990.

Kane, Harnett T. *Bayous of Louisiana.* New York: William Morrow, 1943.

Uzee, Philip D. *The Lafourche Country.* Lafayette, La.: USL-Center for Louisiana Studies, 1985.

Atchafalaya Basin

Delcambre, Kenneth P. *Lords of the Basin.* Breaux Bridge, La.: Privately printed, 1988.

Guirard, Greg. *Atchafalaya Autumn.* St. Martinville, La.: Privately printed, 1995.

——. *Cajun Families of the Atchafalaya.* St. Martinville, La.: Privately printed, 1989.

McPhee, John. *The Control of Nature.* New York: Farrar, Straus & Giroux, 1989.

Coastal Wetlands

Hanks, Amanda Segrera. *Louisiana Paradise: The Cheniers and Wetlands of Southwest Louisiana.* Lafayette, La.: USL-Center for Louisiana Studies, 1988.

Plantation Homes

Arrigo, Joseph, and Dick Dietrich. *Louisiana's Plantation Homes: The Grace and the Grandeur.* Stillwater, Minn.: Voyageur Press, 1991.

RECOMMENDED VIDEOS

Spend It All Cajun Culture documentary.

J'ai Eté au Bal Cajun and Zydeco music documentary.

Yum Yum Yum Cajun food documentary.

Marc and Ann Marc and Ann Savoy's Cajun love story documentary.

Hot Pepper Clifton Chenier/Zydeco documentary.

Dry Wood Bois Sec Ardoin/Zydeco documentary.

Belizaire the Cajun Fictional account of a faith healer during vigilante days.

Anything I Catch Remarkable handfishing documentary.

Crawfish Crawfish industry documentary.

Appendix C

RECOMMENDED RECORDINGS

Cajun Recordings

Nathan Abshire *The Best of Nathan Abshire* Swallow CD 6061

The Balfa Brothers *Play Traditional Cajun Music, Vols. 1 & 2* Swallow CD 6001

Cleveland Crochet *Cleveland Crochet and the Sugar Bees* Goldband CD 7749

D. L. Menard *The Back Door* Swallow Casette 6038

D. L. Menard *Cajun Saturday Night* Rounder CD 0198

Cajun Anthologies

Cajun Saturday Night Swallow CD 102

Le Gran Mamou Country Music Foundation CMF 013D

Louisiana Cajun Music Special Swallow CD 103

Zydeco Recordings

Clifton Chenier *Bogalusa Boogie* Arhoolie CD 347

Clifton Chenier *60 Minutes with the King of Zydeco* Arhoolie CD 301

Boozoo Chavis *The Lake Charles Atom Bomb* Rounder CD 2097

Zydeco Anthologies

Zydeco Blues Flyright Fly CD 36

Zydeco Festival Maison de Soul MdS CD 101

Zydeco Volume 1 Arhoolie CD 307

Swamp Pop Recordings

Johnny Allan *Swamp Pop Legend* Jin CD 9044-2

Bobby Charles *Chess Masters* Chess CH 9175

Cookie and the Cupcakes *By Request* Jin CD 9037-2

Jimmy Donley *Give Me My Freedom* Charly LP CR 30265

Tommy McLain *Essential Collection* Jin CD 9054

Charles Mann *Walk of Life* Gumbo CD002

Warren Storm *Night After Night* Jin CD 9036-2

Various Artists *Swamp Gold, Vols. 1 & 2* Jin CD 106, 107

Cajun and Zydeco Compilations

Alligator Stomp Rhino CD R270946

Jai Eté au Bal Vol. 1 Arhoolie CD 331

Jai Eté au Bal Vol. 2 Arhoolie CD 332

Appendix D

SOURCES FOR RECORDED AND PRINTED MATERIAL ON CAJUN COUNTRY

State Agencies

Louisiana Department of
Culture, Recreation and
Tourism
Office of Tourism
P.O. Box 94291
Baton Rouge, La. 70804-9291
1-800-633-6970

Louisiana Department of
Wildlife and Fisheries
P.O. Box 9800
Baton Rouge, La. 70898-9000
504-765-2496 or 765-2800

Louisiana Office of State Parks
P.O. Box 44426
Baton Rouge, La. 70804-4426
1-888-677-1400

Lafayette Visitors Commission
P.O. Box 52066
Lafayette, La. 70505
1-800-346-1958 (1-800-543-5340
in Canada)

Louisiana Visitors Commission
1-800-33-GUMBO

Southwest Louisiana Visitors
Commission
P.O. Box 1912
1211 Lakeshore Dr.
Lake Charles, La. 70602
1-800-456-SWLA

Houma-Terrebonne Visitors
Commission
P.O. Box 2792
Houma, La. 70361
1-800-688-2732

Iberia Parish Tourist Commission
2690 Center St.
New Iberia, La. 70560
318-365-1540

Music Sources in Cajun Country

Modern Music (Master Trak
    Enterprises)
P.O. Box 856
413 N. Parkerson
Crowley, La. 70526
318-783-1601
(Retail and mail order.)

Goldband Records
P.O. Box 1485
313 Church St.
Lake Charles, La. 70601
318-439-4295
(Retail and mail order.)

Floyd's Records (Flat Town
    Music)
P.O. Drawer 10
434 E. Main St.
Ville Platte, La. 70586
318-363-2184
(Retail and mail order.)

Music Sources outside Cajun Country

Arhoolie & Old Timey Records
10341 San Pablo Ave.
El Cerrito, Ca. 94530
510-525-7471
(Mail order.)

Louisiana Music Factory
210 Decatur St.
New Orleans, La. 70130
504-586-1094
(Retail and mail order.)

Roundup Records
P.O. Box 154
N. Cambridge, Ma. 02140
617-661-6308
(Mail order.)

Tower Records
408 N. Peters
New Orleans, La. 70130
504-529-4411
(Retail.)

Printed Material Sources

USL
Center for Louisiana Studies
P.O. Box 40831, USL
Lafayette, La. 70504-0831
318-231-6039
(Retail or mail order.)

Louisiana Catalog Store
P.O. Box 1610
Larose, La. 70373
1-800-375-4100
(Retail or mail order.)

Bluebird Press (*Cajun Music: A Reflection of a People*)
P.O. Box 941
Eunice, La. 70535
(Mail order.)

Greg Guirard (*Cajun Families of the Atchafalaya*)
Rte. 2, Box 2388
St. Martinville, La. 70582
(Mail order.)

Huli Publishing (*Calendar of Louisiana Festivals and Events*)
P.O. Box 851
Metairie, La. 70004
504-733-5923
JuliePosner@aol.com

Bibliography

Acadiana Profile magazine. Vol. 13, No. 2, 1987.

Acadiana Profile magazine. Vol. 13, No. 4, 1988.

Ancelet, Barry Jean. *Cajun Music: Its Origins and Development.* Lafayette, La.: USL-Center for Louisiana Studies, 1989.

Ancelet, Barry Jean. *Capitaine Voyage ton Flag.* Lafayette, La.: USL-Center for Louisiana Studies.

——. *The Makers of Cajun Music.* University of Texas, 1984.

——, Jay D. Edwards, and Glen Pitre. *Cajun Country.* Jackson, Miss.: University Press of Mississippi, 1991.

Andrepont, Carola Ann. "History of Opelousas." Opelousas, La.: Privately printed brochure.

Broven, John. *South to Louisiana.* Gretna, La.: Pelican Publishing, 1983.

Butler, W. E. *Down Among the Sugar Cane.* Baton Rouge, La.: Moran Publishing, 1980.

Caffery, Debbie Fleming. *Carry Me Home.* Washington, D.C.: Smithsonian, 1990.

Calhoun, Milburn, and Susan Cole Doré, eds. *Louisiana Almanac 1997-98.* Gretna, La.: Pelican Publishing, 1997.

Center for Louisiana Studies. *Louisiana Sugar.* Lafayette, La.: USL-Center for Louisiana Studies, 1980.

Conrad, Glenn R. *Cajuns.* Lafayette, La.: USL-Center for Louisiana Studies, 1978.

——, ed. *The Cajuns.* Lafayette, La.: USL-Center for Louisiana Studies, 1983.

——. *New Iberia.* Lafayette, La.: USL-Center for Louisiana Studies, 1986.

De Hart, Jess. *Louisiana's Historic Towns.* New Orleans, La.: Hamlet House, 1983.

Delcambre, Kenneth P. *First Facts About Breaux Bridge.* Breaux Bridge, La.: Privately printed, 1988.

——. *Lords of the Basin.* Breaux Bridge, La.: Privately printed, 1988.

Feibleman, Peter S. *The Bayous.* New York: Time-Life Books, 1973.

Gahn, Robert, Sr. *A History of Evangeline Parish.* Claitor Publishing, 1972.

Guirard, Greg. *Cajun Families of the Atchafalaya.* St. Martinville, La.: Privately printed, 1988.

Hanks, Amanda Segrera. *Louisiana Paradise: The Cheniers and Wetlands of Southwest Louisiana*. Lafayette, La.: USL-Center for Louisiana Studies, 1988.

Hansen, Harry, ed. *Louisiana: A Guide to the State*. New York: Hastings House, 1971.

Hildebrand, Franklin. *As I Remember*. Jennings, La.: Creative Printing, 1977.

Kane, Harnett T. *Bayous of Louisiana*. New York: William Morrow, 1943.

Kniffen, Fred B., Hiram F. Gregory, and George A. Stokes. *Historic Indian Tribes of Louisiana*. Baton Rouge, La.: Louisiana State University Press, 1987.

Leeper, Clare D'Artoir. *Louisiana Places*. Baton Rouge, La.: Legacy Publishing, 1976.

Lewis, Peirce F. *New Orleans: The Making of an Urban Landscape*. Cambridge, Mass.: Ballinger, 1976.

Looney, Ben Earl. *Cajun Country*. Lafayette, La.: USL-Center for Louisiana Studies, 1985.

McPhee, John. *The Control of Nature*. New York: Farrar, Straus & Giroux, 1989.

Prudhomme, Paul. *Chef Paul Prudhomme's Louisiana Kitchen*. New York: William Morrow, 1984.

Savoy, Anne Allen. *Cajun Music: A Reflection of a People*. Eunice, La.: Bluebird, 1984.

Sonnier, Austin, Jr. *Second Linin': Jazzmen of Southwest Louisiana 1900-1950*. Lafayette, La.: USL-Center for Louisiana Studies, 1989.

Stahls, Paul F., Jr. *Plantation Homes of the Teche Country*. Gretna, La.: Pelican Publishing, 1979.

Uzee, Philip D. *The Lafourche Country*. Lafayette, La.: USL-Center for Louisiana Studies, 1985.

Vermilion Historical Society. *History of Vermilion Parish, Louisiana*. Abbeville, La.: The Society, 1983.

Index

A. B. Henderson Gator Cove, 300
Abbeville, 324-33
   attractions, 325-28
   food, 328-31
   lodging, 332-33
   music, 331-32
   tourist information center, 325
A-Bear's Restaurant, 158, 161
Academy of the Sacred Heart, 318
Acadian Connection, 358
Acadian Cultural Centers
   Eunice, 368
   Lafayette, 284
   Thibodaux, 147
Acadian Memorial, 241
Acadian Village, 285
Acadiana Mall, 290
Acadiana Park Nature Station, 288
Acadians. *See* Cajun culture
Adam's Fruit Market, 127
African-American historical sites
   African American Museum, 99
   Laura Plantation, 106
   Old Dorsey School, 112
African American Museum, 99
Air connections, 81
Airboats, Inc., 236
Airline Motors Restaurant, 90
Alladin Mediterranean Restaurant,
   425
Alligators, 33, 42-43, 410, 439
Allison's Hickory Pit, 372
Andouille, 55-56, 89-91
   Cox's Meat Market, 90
Angelle's Atchafalaya Swamp
   Tours, 263
Annie Miller's Swamp Tours, 173

Antique stores and flea markets
   Jennings, 411
   Lafayette, 291
   Rayne, 397-98
   Washington, 358
Arlington Plantation, 202, 356
Artists' Alliance, 278
Atchafalaya Basin, 18-20, 41, 42, 193,
   260-64, 268, 269, 339, 340
Atchafalaya Basin Airboat Tours,
   182
Atchafalaya Basin Backwater
   Adventure, 176
Atchafalaya Experience Swamp
   Tours, 251
Atchafalaya River, 18-20, 181, 186,
   337, 339, 340
Avery Island, 228-32
   Bird City, 231
   Jungle Garden, 230-32
   Salt Mine, 229
   Tabasco Factory, 229

Back in Time Sandwich Shop, 348
Back to Back, 311
Bald cypress, 37, 92, 93
B&C Cajun Deli, 106
B&S Meat Market, 385
Barbecue
   Eunice, 372, 375
   Lafayette, 298
   Lake Charles, 425, 428
   Raceland, 125
   Ville Platte, 387
Basile, 390-91
Baton Rouge, 337, 338
Bayou Boudin and Cracklin, 254

Bayou Cabins Bed and Breakfast,
    259
Bayou Country map, 120
Bayou Lafourche, 24, 121, 122,
    125-53
Bayou Lafourche Folklife Museum,
    128
Bayou Teche, 179-80, 213-14, 341
Bayou Terrebonne, 24
Bayou Vista, 196, 197
Bed and Breakfasts
    Abbeville, 332-33
    Breaux Bridge, 259
    Cameron, 445
    Carencro, 316-18
    Church Point, 367
    Constance Beach, 442
    Convent, 99
    Cut Off, 132
    Eunice, 379
    Franklin, 204
    Houma area, 162-64
    Jefferson Island, 234
    Krotz Springs, 340
    Lacassine, 416
    Lafayette, 312-15
    Lake Arthur, 414
    Lake Charles, 431-32
    Larose, 130
    Lockport, 129-30
    Napoleonville, 152
    New Iberia, 225-27
    Opelousas, 352-53
    Rayne, 400
    St. Martinville, 247-48
    Sunset, 322
    Thibodaux, 150-51
    Vacherie, 108
    Ville Platte, 389-90
    Washington, 360, 362
    White Castle, 114
Bertrand's, 330
Best Stop, 305
Bicycling, 78, 79
    Pack & Paddle, 290

Big John's Seafood Patio, 334
Bird City, 231
Bird watching, 38-39, 79-80, 137
    Avery Island Rookery, 231
    Breaux Bridge, 251
    Cameron, 445
    Cameron Prairie Refuge, 445
    Grand Isle, 136, 137
    Houma, 163
    Hug the Coast Highway, 327
    Kaplan, 401
    Krotz Springs, 340
    Lacassine National Wildlife
        Refuge, 414
    Lafayette, 290
    Peveto Woods Bird Sanctary,
        440, 441
    Rockefeller Wildlife Refuge,
        447, 448
    Sabine Wildlife Refuge, 438
Birds, 38-39
B.J.'s Dancehall, 398
Black's Oyster Bar, 329
Boat Building Museum, 147
Boat/canoe rentals
    Atchafalaya Backwater
        Adventure, 76, 177
    Chicot State Park, 385
    Henderson, 262
    Lake Fausse State Park, 240
    LaPlace, 90
    Sam Houston State Park, 424
Bob's Frontier Cabins, 367
Boiling Point, 219
Bonfires on the levee, 96
Bonin's Boudin and Cracklin's, 220
Bonnet Carre Spillway, 88
Bonnet Carre Spillway Recreation
    and Camping Area, 89
Borden's Ice Cream, 295
Borque's, 366
Boudin, 55
    Best Stop, 305
    Bonin's Boudin and Cracklin's,
        220

Boudin King, 412
Deshotel ("Dez") Meat Market, 386
Hackett's Cajun Kitchen, 426
Joe's "Dreyfus Store" Restaurant, 338
Johnson's Grocery, 373
Ray's Boudin, 349, 351
Rowena's, 321
Boudin King, 412
Boudreaux's Restaurant, 124
Bourgeois Meat Market, 148
Bowie Junction Barbecue, 125
Breaux Bridge, 245, 249-60
attractions, 252-53
Crawfish Festival, 41, 250
food, 254-56
lodging, 259-60
music, 256-59
recreation, 251-52
tourist information center, 250
Brenda's Restaurant, 221
Brimstone Museum, 434
Bruce's U-Need-A-Butcher, 306
Bubba's II Restaurant & Sports Lounge, 149
Buckeye Exotic Animal Farm and Garden, 416
Bunk Johnson's Grave, 218
Burns Point, 199-200

Café Des Amis, 254
Cafe Jefferson, 234
Cafe Vermilionville, 298
Caffery's Alexander Ranch, 256
Cajun Antique Flea Market, 358
Cajun Cafe, 425
Cajun Country Store, 291
Cajun culture
history, 25-29
language, 28-29
Cajun dance halls, 68
chart, 71
map, 70
Cajun food. *See* Food

Cajun French Music Association Hall of Fame, 369
Cajun Heartland map, 336
Cajun history, 25-29
Cajun House Boat Rentals, 191
Cajun Jack Swamp Tours, 198
Cajun Man Swamp Tour, 174
Cajun music, 63-64
chart, 71
dance halls, 70, 71
map, 70
sources, 454-55
Cajun Prairie, 37-38, 371
Cajun Prairie Restoration Project, 371
Cameron, 32, 443-45
Cameron Prairie Wildlife Refuge, 445
Camping
Bayou Vista, 199
Bonnet Carre Recreation and Camping Area, 89
Burns Point, 200
Butte La Rose, 269
Crowley, 407-8
Eunice, 380
Grand Isle State Park, 138
Houma, 154, 165
Lafayette, 315
Lake Arthur, 413-15
Lake Charles, 423-24, 432
Morgan City, 192
New Iberia, 227-28
Opelousas, 353
Patterson, 199
Rayne, 400
St. Martinville, 248
Starks, 435
Sulphur, 434
Ville Platte, 384-85
Washington, 362
Canoeing. *See* Boat/canoe rentals
Carencro, 316-18
Casino gambling
Charenton, 208

Coushatta, 24
Grand Coushatta Casino, 393
Lake Charles, 420
Catahoula's, 320
Cattle industry, 48-49
Cazan Hotel, 382
Cedar Deli, 296
Chackbay, 124-25
Charenton, 23
Charlene Richard Shrine, 371
Charlie G's Seafood Grill, 301
Charlieville, 193
Charpentier District, 420
Chateau des Cocodries, 410
Chauvin, 167-69
Chemical industry, 46
Chenier, Clifton, 235-36, 350
Chenier Caminada, 126, 135-36
Cheniers, 15, 17, 34, 126, 135-36,
440, 441, 446-48
Chester's Cypress Inn, 175
Chicot State Park, 384
Children's Museum (Lake Charles),
422
Children's Museum of Acadiana,
281
Chilly's Dance Hall, 190, 195
Chitimacha Indians, 23
crafts, 24
Cypress Bayou Casino, 208
reservation, 23, 207
Chrétien Point Plantation, 320
Church Point, 363-65
Cigar's Store & Restaurant, 136,
139, 141
Circle Club Cockpit, 436
City Cafe, 117
Clem's "Bush Track" Horse Racing,
327
Clifton's Club, 236
Climate, 31-32, 33
Cockfighting, 76-78
Cockpits
Circle Club Cockpit, 436
Hebert's Cockpit, 327

Sunset Game Club, 321
Cocodrie, 169-70
CODOFIL, 279
Constance Beach, 440-42
Country Cuisine, 298
Courir du Mardi Gras. See Mardi
Gras
Coushatta Indians, 24, 393
reservation, 393
store, 394
Cowboy's, 311
Cox's Meat Market, 90
Crab Palace, 425
Cracklins
Bayou Boudin and Cracklin',
254
Bonin's Boudin and Cracklin's,
220
Bruce's U-Need-A-Butcher, 306
Craftsmen
Coushatta Store, 394
D. L. Menard's Chair Factory,
333
Harris Split Oak Baskets, 357
Louisiana Native Crafts Festival,
294
Mickey's Shell Art, 441
Runyon Products, Inc., 346
Soileau's Cowhair Chairs, 358
Swamp Ivory Creations, 326
Terrace Woodworks, 244
Crawfish, 41-42
Crawfish etouffée, 57
Crawfish Festival, 41
Crawfish restaurants
A. B. Henderson Gator Cove,
300
Boiling Point, 219
Crawfish Town USA, 265
D.I.'s Cajun Restaurant, 390
Granger's, 426
Guiding Star, 222
Harris Seafood Restaurant, 415
Hawk's, 399
Jungle Dinner Club, 386

Richard's Seafood Patio, 331
Crawfish Town USA, 265
Creole Lunch House, 301
Creole Nature Trail, 34, 424, 438-46
Creoles, 27-28
Crepe Myrtle/Wilderness Trail, 289
Crooked Creek Recreation Area, 385
Crowley, 402-8
Crystal Rice Plantation, 404
Cut Off, 131-32

D. L. Menard's Chair Factory, 333
Da Office Lounge, 391
Danna's Bakery, 221, 245
Davis Lounge, 256
De la Houssaye's Swamp Tours, 251
De la Morandiere, 355
Dean-O's Pizza, 298
Delcambre, 335
Delta Downs Racetrack, 435
Des Allemands, 122
Deshotel ("Dez") Meat Market, 386
Destrehan Plantation, 87
D.I.'s Cajun Restaurant, 390
Donaldsonville, 109-11
Double D Cotton Club, 257
Doug's Restaurant, 149
Dow Chemicals Plant Tour, 117
Downtown Alive!, 277, 292
Duet's Bakery, 131, 133
Dugas Cafe, 321
Dulac, 24
Dupuy's, 329
Dwyer's Cafe, 297

Edie's, 303
El Sido's, 306
Elderhostel Program at McNesse State University, 422
Elderhostel Program at USL, 281

Elmand's, 386, 389
Elmer's Island, 139
Elton, 391-94
Environmental issues, 49-50
Erath, 333-35
Estherwood Rice, Inc., 394
Estorge-Norton House Bed and Breakfast, 226
Eunice, 368-80
    attractions, 368-71
    food, 373-76
    lodging/camping, 379-80
    music, 377-78
    tourist information center, 368
Eunice Museum, 369
Evangeline, 238, 240-43
Evangeline Downs, 289
Evangeline Oak, 241-42

Ferries
    Avoca Island, 185
    Cameron, 443
    Carville/White Castle, 101
    Plaquemine, 103, 114
    Reserve/Edgard, 91, 105
Festival International de la Louisiane, 292
Festivals, 449-51
    Acadiens, 293
    Bonfire Festival, 96
    Boozoo's Dog Hill Day Zydeco Festival, 424
    Celebration of the Giant Omelette, 326
    Contraband Days, 424
    Crawfish Festival, 41, 253
    Etouffée Cookoff, 372
    Festival International de la Louisiane, 292
    French Food Festival, 130
    Frog Festival, 399
    "Here's the Beef" Cook-Off, 347
    Louisiana Fur and Wildlife Festival, 444
    Rice Festival, 405

Roberts Cove Germanfest, 398
Shrimp and Petroleum Festival, 188
Yambilee, 347
Zydeco Extravaganza, 294
Zydeco Festival, 347
Fish, 41-42
Fishing, 74-76
  Grand Isle, 136-40
Flood of 1927, 20, 261
Flora, 33-38
Floyd Sonnier's Beau Cajun Art Gallery, 286
Floyd's Record Store, 388
Fontenot's Main Street Lounge, 391
Food, 51-61
  Cajun/Creole, 52-53
  glossary, 56-58
  map, 59
  meat markets, 55-56
  restaurant chart, 60-61
  restaurant guide, 53-56
  seafood, 54-55
Forest Inn Restaurant, 203
Four Seasons Lodge, 311
Fourchon, 134-35
Franklin, 199-205
  attractions, 202-3
  food, 203-4
  lodging, 204-5
  tourist information center, 202
Fred's Lounge, 381
Friendly Inn, 308
Friendly Lounge, 258

Garyville, 92-93
Garyville Timbermill Museum, 93
Gateway Antiques, 291
Gee Gee's Club, 430
Geyen's Barbecue, 425
Gilton's Lounge, 377
Girard Park, 283
Goldband Records, 428
Golden Meadow, 132-34

Golden Ranch Plantation, 128
Gramercy, 94-95
Grand Chenier, 446-48
Grand Coteau, 318-20
Grand Coushatta Casino, 393
Grand Isle, 121, 136-42
  fishing, 137-39
  food, 140-41
  lodging/camping, 141-42
Grand Isle State Park, 138
Granger's, 426
Grant Street Dance Hall, 309
Grevemberg House, 202
Gueydan, 408
Guiding Star, 222
Guidry's Friendly Lounge, 366
Gumbo, 57

Hackberry, 438
Hackett's Cajun Kitchen, 426
Hamilton's Place, 307
Harris Seafood Restaurant, 415
Harris Split Oak Baskets, 357
Harry's Cajun Dance Hall, 258
Hawk's, 399
Hebert's Cockpit, 327
Hebert's Meat Market, 330
Hebert's Specialty Meats, 323
Henderson, 260-69
  attractions, 264-65
  food, 265-67
  lodging/camping, 268-69
  music, 267
  recreation, 262-64
Heymann Oil Center, 284
Hiking, 79
  Chicot State Park, 384
  Lake Fausse Pointe State Park, 239, 240
  Lake Martin/Cypress Island Swamp, 251
  Louisiana State Arboretum, 384
  Magnolia Ridge Plantation Trails, 356
  Pack & Paddle, 290

Hinckley House, 355
Holiday Lounge, 380
Holly Beach, 442-43
Horse racing, 77
    Clem's "Bush Track" Horse
        Racing, 327
    Delta Downs Racetrack, 435
    Evangeline Downs, 289
Houma, 24, 154-65
    attractions, 156-58
    food, 158-60
    history, 154-56
    lodging, 162-65
    music, 161
    recreation, 156
    tourist information center, 156
Houma Indians, 24
    Dulac, 171
Houmas House Plantation, 100
House Boat Adventures, 268
Houseboat rentals
    Henderson, 268
    Morgan City, 191
Hub City Diner, 299
Hug the Coast Highway, 34, 327,
    402, 424, 438, 440-48
Hurricane Audrey, 32, 423, 444
Hurricanes, 32

Imperial Calcasieu Museum, 422
Indian tribes, 22-24
    Chitimacha, 22-24, 207, 208
    Coushatta, 24, 393
    Houma, 24, 171, 172
Intracoastal City/Leland Bowman
    Locks, 327
Isle of Capri Riverboat Casinos, 420

J. B. Sandoz Store, 345
Jeanerette, 209-13
    attractions, 209-10
    food, 211-12
    lodging, 212-13
Jefferson Davis Parish Tourist
    Center, 409

Jefferson Island, 232-35
Jefferson Street Market, 280
Jennings, 408-13
Jim Bowie Museum and Visitor
    Center, 343
Joe's "Dreyfus Store" Restaurant,
    338
Johnny's Time in a Bottle, 196
Johnson, William Geary ("Bunk"),
    218
Johnson's Grocery, 373
Judice Inn, 299
Jungle Dinner Club, 386
Jungle Gardens, 230-32
Justine Antebellum Home, 219
Justin's Observatory, 210

Kaplan, 400-402
Kaplan Museum, 401
Kelly's Country Diner, 349
Kelly's Country Meat Block, 348
Kissinoaks Bed and Breakfast
    Cottage, 332
Kitchen Shop and Tea Room, 319
Knot's Corner Restaurant, 414
Konriko Rice Mill, 217
Kraemer, 106, 122-24
Krotz Springs, 340-41

La Caboose Bed and Breakfast, 322
La Chaumiere Bed and Breakfast,
    360
La Maison Bed and Breakfast, 226
La Maison de Compagne Bed and
    Breakfast, 317
La Place d' deVille Guest House,
    362
La Poussiere Cajun Dance Hall,
    258
La Trouvaille Restaurant, 168
Labadieville, 151
Lacassine National Wildlife
    Refuge, 414
Lafayette, 271-315
    attractions, downtown, 277-81

attractions, metro area, 284-88
attractions, university area, 281-84
events/festivals, 292-95
food, 295-306
getting there and getting around, 275-77
history, 273-75
lodging/camping, 312-15
map, 272
music, 306-11
professional sports, 312
recreation, 288-90
shopping, 290-92
tourist information center, 276
Lafayette Antique Market, 291
Lafayette *Daily Advertiser,* 280
Lafayette Museum, 277
Lafayette Natural History Museum and Planetarium, 284
Lafayette Swampcats, 312
Lafourche Parish Tourist Commission, 127, 143
Lagniappe Too, 223
Lake Arthur, 413
Lake Charles, 32, 417-33
attractions, 420-24
food, 425-28
history, 417-19
lodging/camping, 430-32
map, 418
music, 428-30
recreation, 423-24
tourist information center, 419
Lake End Park, 182
Lake Fausse Pointe State Park, 239, 240
Lake Martin, 43, 79, 251, 252
Lake Palourde, 182, 193
Lake Peignur Disaster, 233
LaPlace, 89-90
Larose, 130-31
Laura Plantation, 106
Laurel Valley Village, 146
Le Beau Petit Musée, 209

Le Centre International de Lafayette/Old City Hall, 279
Le Petit Chateau deLuxe, 411
Le Rosier Restaurant, 223
Leeville, 135
LeJeune's Bakery, 211
LeJeune's Sausage Kitchen, 374
Levy's Place, 331
Liberty Theater, 369
Lil's Kitchen, 212
Live oaks, 34,
Livonia, 338-40
Lockport, 128-30
Longfellow, Henry Wadsworth, 180
Longfellow Evangeline State Commemorative Area, 243
Loreauville, 235-37
Lorraine Bridge, 415
Lorraine Retreat Guesthouse, 416
Louisiana Catalog Store, 131
Louisiana Ice Gators, 312
Louisiana Museum of Military History, 287
Louisiana State Arboretum, 384
Lourdes Grotto/St. Michael's Church, 98
Lumber industry, 37, 92-94, 196
LUMCON, 169
Lutcher, 94-96

McGee's Atchafalaya Basin Swamp Tours, 264
McNeese State University, 422
Madewood Plantation, 151
Magnolia Ridge Plantation, 356
Maison Des Amis, 259
Maison D'Memoire Bed and Breakfast Cottages, 400
Maison du CODOFIL, 279
Mama's Fried Chicken, 374
Mamou, 380-83
Manresa House of Retreats, 97
Maps
Bayou Country, 120
Cajun Country Highway, 14

Cajun Country Regions, 83
Cajun Heartland, 336
Central Cajun Country, 270
    food map, 59
    Houma, 155
    Lafayette, 272
    Lake Charles, 418
    Mississippi River Region, 84
    music, 70
    Opelousas, 342
    state highway, 10
    Teche Country, 178
    Western Cajun Country, 396
Mardi Gras, 450-51
    Church Point Courir du
        Mardi Gras, 365
    Eunice Courir du Mardi Gras,
        372
    Iota Courir du Mardi Gras, 405
    Lafayette, 295
    Mamou Courir du Mardi Gras,
        381
Master-Trak Studio, 403
Mathilda's, 375
Maurice, 323-24
Menard, D. L., 333
Michael's and Sun's, 399
Mickey's Shell Art, 441
Miller, Jay, 404
Miller's Cafe, 426
Miss Garret's Pie Kitchen, 246
Mississippi Alluvial Plain, 17
Mississippi River, 17, 19, 20, 85, 86
Mr. Charlie Oil Rig Tour, 184
Mr. D's on the Bayou, 427
Modern Music Center, 403
Montegut, 166
Morgan City, 153, 154, 172, 175,
        180-92
    attractions, 183-88
    food, 189-90
    lodging/camping, 191-92
    music, 190-91
    recreation, 182-83
    tourist information center, 182

Morganza Spillway, 337, 339
Mulate's, 255, 258
Munson's Swamp Tours, 158
Music, 63-71. *See also* "music"
        under town names
    Cajun. *See* Cajun music
    chart of dance halls and clubs,
        71
    family entertainment, 68, 69
    map, 70
    radio shows, 67
    record stores. *See* Record stores
    Swamp Pop. *See* Swamp Pop
        music
    Zydeco. *See* Zydeco dance halls,
        Zydeco music
Music Machine, 370

Napoleonville, 151-53
National Hansen's Disease Center,
        101
New Iberia, 213-28
    attractions, 215-19
    food, 219-25
    lodging/camping, 225-28
    music, 225
    recreation, 215
    tourist information center, 215
Niblett's Bluff Park Campground
        and Cabins, 435
Nicholls State University, 147
Nicholson House of History, 355
Norbert's, 303
Nottoway Plantation, 112-14
Nubby's Country Kitchen, 151
Nutria, 39-41

Oak Alley Plantation, 108
Oak and Pine Alley, 245
Oaklawn Manor Plantation, 205
Offshore Lounge, 352
Oil and Gas Park, 410
Oil industry, 44-46
    Jennings, 408-10
    Lafayette, 274, 284

Old Castillo Hotel Bed and
    Breakfast, 248
Old Tyme Grocery, 300
Old Washington Antique School
    Mall Flea Market, 358
Opelousas, 337, 341-53
    attractions, 343-47
    food, 348-50
    lodging/camping, 352-53
    map, 342
    music, 350-52
    tourist information center, 343
Opelousas Museum and
    Interpretive Center, 346
Ormond Plantation, 87
Oysters (Abbeville), 328-30

Pack & Paddle, 290
Paincourtville, 153-54
Palace Cafe, 349
Patio Restaurant, 235
Pat's Fisherman's Wharf
    Restaurant, 266
Patterson, 196-99
Paul's Pirogue, 316
Pecan Island, 448
Pelican Restaurant, 375
Petroleum Museum, 187
Pierre Part, 154, 192, 194-96
Pig Stand, 387
Plaquemine, 114-18
Plaquemine Ferry, 114
Plaquemine Locks, 115-17
Plattenville, 153
Players Island Riverboat Casinos, 420
Poche's Meat Market and
    Restaurant, 256
Pointe Salé, 200
Polito's Cafe/Bar and Grill, 204
Ponderosa Lounge, 332
Popcorn rice, 408
Port Barre, 341
Poupart's Bakery, 305
Prairie, 17
Prejean's, 304, 308

Prudhomme's Cajun Cafe, 304

Raceland, 143-44
Radio KBON, 378
Rainbeaux Club, 225
Rainbow Inn, 191, 195
Ramsay Curtis Mansion Bed and
    Breakfast, 431
R&K's Oyster Place, 139
Randol's Seafood Restaurant, 305,
    308
Randolph's, 133
Rayne, 397-400
Ray's Boudin, 349
Record stores, 66-67
    Floyd's, 388
    Goldband Records, 428
    Modern Music Center, 403
    Music Machine, 370
    Sound Center, 364
Recreation, 72-80
Religious shrines
    Convent, 98
    Eunice, 371
    Grand Coteau, 318, 319
    Lafourche Shrine, 133
    Leeville, 134
    Plattenville, 153
    Rayne, 398
    Thibodaux, 145
    White Castle, 114
Rice Hotel, 407
Rice industry, 48, 404-5
Rice Museum, 404
Richard's Cajun Restaurant, 434
Richard's Club, 351
Richard's Seafood Patio, 331
Rip Van Winkle Gardens Bed and
    Breakfast Cottage, 234
Rita Mae's Kitchen, 190
River Road, 85-119
    travel tips, 86
River Road east bank, 86-104
    food, 103-4
    lodging, 103

River Road west bank, 85, 86, 104-
19
food, 119
lodging, 119
Roberts Cove, 398
Robin's Restaurant, 266
Rockefeller Wildlife Refuge, 327,
447, 448
Roundez Vous des Cajuns, 377
Rouse's Supermarket Bakery, 143,
150, 160
Rowena's Meat Market, 321
Ruby's Cafe, 375
Runyon Products, Inc., 346
Rutherford Beach, 446

Sabine National Wildlife Refuge,
438-40
St. James Parish Historical Society
Bonfire Museum, 95
St. John's Cathedral, Oak Tree,
and Cemetery, 278
St. Leo's Shrine, 398
St. Martin de Tours Catholic
Church, 240
St. Martinville, 23, 213, 214, 237-48
attractions, 240-45
food, 245-47
lodging/camping, 247-48
recreation, 239-40
Sam Houston State Park, 423
San Francisco Plantation, 91
Savoy's Music Center, 377
Savoy's Sausage and Food
Products, Inc., 346
Scully's Swamp Tours, 183
Seafood industry, 46-47
Shadows on the Teche, 215
Sherburne Wildlife Area, 340
Shucks!, 330
Shuler, Eddie, 428
Slim's Y-Ki-Ki, 350
Smiley's Bon Ami, 335
Smokey Joe's Bar-B-Que, 428
Snook's Bar and Dancehall, 389

Soileau, Floyd, 388, 389
Soileau's Cowhair Chairs, 358
Soileau's Dinner Club, 350
Soop's Restaurant, 323
Sound Center, 364
Southdown Plantation/
Terrebonne Museum, 157
Southwest Louisiana Visitors
Center, 419
Spahr's Catfish Pond, 122
Spanish moss, 35
State agencies, 456
State parks
Chicot State Park, 384
Cypremort Point, 208
Lake Fausse, 239, 240
Sam Houston State Park, 423
Steamboat Warehouse Restaurant,
356, 359
Steen's Syrup Mill, 325
Stephensville, 192-93
Storm, Warren, 311
Sugarcane industry, 47-48, 210
Suire's Store Restaurant, 401
Sulphur, 433-34
Sulphur Visitors Center, 434
Sunset, 320-22
Sunset Game Club, 321
Swamp Gardens and Wildlife Zoo,
183
Swamp Ivory Creations, 326
Swamp Pop music, 66, 455
Swamp tours, 73-74
Swamp Water Saloon, 309
Swamp's Tavern, 267

Tabasco Factory, 229
Tarzan, 187
Tasso, 58
B&S Meat Market, 385
Bourgeois Meat Market, 148
Johnson's Grocery, 373
T-Coons, 297
Terrace Woodworks, 244
Tezcuco Plantation/Village, 98-100

African American Museum, 99
Tezcuco Bed and Breakfast, 99
Thibodaux, 144-51
    attractions, 144-48
    food, 148-50
    lodging, 150-51
    music, 150
Thibodeaux's Hall, 430
Times of Acadiana, 280
T-Man Bailey's Bar and Grocery, 193
Tony Chachere's Creole Foods, 346
Torres' Cajun Swamp Tour, 123
Train Depot Cajun Jam, 367
Train service, 82
Triangle Club, 428
Turn-of-the-Century House, 187

University of Southwestern
        Louisiana, 281-84

Vautrot's Meat Market, 365
Vermilionville, 285
Vern's Barbecue, 224
VFW Post Dancehall, 430
Victor's Cafeteria, 224
Ville Platte, 383, 390
    chamber of commerce/tourist
        information, 384
    food, 385-88
    lodging/camping, 389-90
    music, 388-89
    recreation, 384-85

Vincent Wildlife Refuge, 401
Vinton, 435

W. H. Tupper General
        Merchandise Museum, 411
Warehouse Restaurant, 301
Washington, 353-62
    attractions, 354-56
    food, 359-60
    lodging/camping, 360-62
    shopping, 358-59
    tourist information center, 354
Water hyacinth, 35-36
Waterford Nuclear Plant Visitor
        Center, 105
Way of the Cross, 245
Wedell-Williams Memorial Aviation
        Museum, 197
Whiskey River Landing, 267
Wild Birds Unlimited, 290
Wildlife Gardens, 172

Zam's Bayou Swamp Tours, 123
Zigler Museum, 411
Zoo of Acadiana, 287
Zydeco dance halls, 63-65
    chart, 71
    map, 70
Zydeco music, 64-65, 350, 454, 455
    chart, 71
    map, 70